# Constitutional Democracy

# Constitutional Democracy

*Second Edition*

## Peter Woll
*Brandeis University*

## Little, Brown and Company
*Boston     Toronto*

Library of Congress Cataloging-in-Publication Data

Woll, Peter, 1933–
    Constitutional democracy.

    Includes bibliographies and index.
    1. United States — Politics and government.    I. Title.
JK274.W734    1986        320.973        85-19814
ISBN 0-316-95173-0

*Library of Congress Catalog Card No. 85-19814*

ISBN 0-316-95173-0

*9 8 7 6 5 4 3 2 1*

HAL

*Published simultaneously in Canada by Little, Brown & Company (Canada) Limited*

*Printed in the United States of America*

*For Ellen*

# Preface

As the bicentennial celebration of the Constitution approaches, this text for students of American government develops the theme of constitutional democracy throughout and relates it to political institutions and processes. It examines not only how government works, but also the ways in which it enhances, or in some instances impedes, our system of constitutional democracy.

The first three chapters of Part I cover the Constitutional Convention of 1787, federalism, and civil liberties and civil rights respectively. Conveyed to students in chapter one is the excitement of the politics of the Constitutional Convention as the state delegations and their often brilliant and colorful leaders met in the sweltering Philadelphia summer heat. They hammered out a Constitution that was to become the wonder of the world. James Madison, Alexander Hamilton, and other delegates speak for themselves in chapter one as they debate what form the new government should take. The delegates were not, as John Roche has pointed out, Platonic Guardians, but practical politicians who not only had the national interest at heart but also were concerned with advancing the interests of their home states.

Federalism, an issue that seems remote to most students today, is discussed in chapter two, which stresses the primacy of state sovereignty at the time the Constitution was framed. That the states would relinquish so much of their sovereignty to the new national government was, by any measure, a political miracle that came far closer to failing than is commonly thought. Contemporary issues of federalism are discussed in the context of the Constitution and the ebb and flow of decentralizing and centralizing political forces that have so importantly shaped intergovernmental relations.

Constitutional issues and concerns of federalism merge in the Bill of

Rights and its evolution. Chapter three notes the irony that the Bill of Rights, which was not even part of the original Constitution, has become one of the most important components of constitutional democracy, protecting the freedom of expression and the civil rights that are an integral part of its foundation. Relatively new constitutional trends, such as the expanded definition of equal protection of the laws, are covered as each part of the Bill of Rights is presented and discussed in detail.

The text turns to the political process in Part II and discusses political parties and interest groups in chapters four and five. Covered is the 1984 presidential election and its possible future implications in terms of party realignments, third parties, and internal party changes. Included also is new research relating to the commonly presented theme of party decline. A skeptical public image of parties, and the political elite's focus upon personalities and images more than issues, may contribute to growing instability, particularly in presidential politics.

Included in chapter five is new material on political action committees (PACs) which were so important in the congressional campaigns of 1982 and 1984. Of growing concern is the influence of special interests in government, particularly on Capitol Hill, and some cynics proclaim that Congress is "the best that money can buy." While presenting both sides of the issue, the theme of the chapter is that interest groups fit nicely into the system of constitutional democracy. The pluralistic political environment in which they function limits them at the same time that they contribute to broadened democratic participation.

The remaining chapters cover government institutions, and chapter six begins with an examination of the presidency. Discussed are the president's powers and responsibilities and the important role the Executive Office of the President always plays in helping to carry them out. The chapter investigates the ebb and flow of power between the president and Congress, presenting both the imperial presidency and resurgent Congress themes that have received such wide currency. Analyzed in the new edition is how these trends relate to the presidency of the 1980s.

Regardless of how powerful the president may be it is Congress, the subject of chapter seven, that has been called the keystone of the Washington establishment. Through vignettes tied to contemporary research, the text introduces students to the excitement of Capitol Hill — a bastion of political free enterprise and entrepreneurship. Described are the many committees, the little legislatures of Capitol Hill, and the attempts that have been made to "reform" and reorganize them. Analyzed also are congressional parties, caucuses, and special groups including state delegations — all of which have an important influence on congressional behavior. Within the framework of the tug-of-war between the pressures for centralization and decentralization, new material on the ever-changing Capitol Hill budget process is given.

Some congressional scholars, such as David Mayhew, have concluded that the primary purpose of Congress is to get its members reelected. Chapter seven examines the lively world of congressional elections, pointing out that while many activities of members advance their reelection, Washington careers and reelection pursuits may be quite different.

Both Congress and the president are closely linked with the bureaucracy — the topic of chapter eight. Analyzed are the structure and functions of the bureaucracy with a particular emphasis upon its political character. Twentieth century presidents from Theodore Roosevelt to Ronald Reagan have attempted to rein in the administrative branch by bringing it under White House control, but the bureaucracy remains a semi-autonomous branch that is not easily influenced by the president or Congress as it plays one off against the other in an extension of the intricate game of checks and balances invented by the Founding Fathers.

Finally, chapter nine discusses the courts, highlighting their important political role in a system of constitutional democracy that stresses the rule of law. Themes that are developed are judicial independence, activism, and self-restraint. Covered also is the controversy between conservatives in the 1980s and the Supreme Court they attack as a supra-legislature, reminding observers with a sense of history of the liberal assault on the Court during Franklin D. Roosevelt's New Deal.

I would like to thank my editor John Covell who launched the second edition of this book and provided support and assistance throughout the long revision process. Special thanks are also due Billie Ingram and the entire Little, Brown crew who oversaw the book's production, and to Rachel Parks whose keen eye and original perspective selected outstanding photographs that convey the political flavor of American government.

Consultations with Rochelle Jones have as always helped to give the book the insights of a Washington insider. Barbara Nagy's typing skills and professionalism once again helped to give me the intrastructure I needed to complete the project. Thanks are also owed to Lisa Carisella and Elaine Herrmann who helped prepare the manuscript in its final stages.

# Contents

**Part I   The Constitutional Context**                                    **1**

*1. Constitutional Government*                                              *3*

Framing the Constitution      3
Major Features of the Constitution      4
    Federalism      4
    The Separation of Powers and Checks and Balances      5
    Judicial Review      7
How the Government Works Under the Constitution      8
    Article I: Legislative Power      8
    Article II: Executive Power      13
    Article III: Judicial Power      14
    Article IV: Interstate Relations      15
    Article V: Amending the Constitution      16
    Article VI: The Supremacy Clause      16
    Article VII: Ratification of the Constitution      16
    The Bill of Rights      17
Perspectives on the Constitution      17
    The Madisonian Model of Constitutional Government      18
    The Hamiltonian Model of the Constitution      19
    The Supremacy and Scope of National Power      20
Conclusion      23
Suggestions for Further Reading      24


*2. Civil Liberties and Civil Rights Under the Constitution*               *27*

Civil Rights in the Original Constitution      27

The Debate over the Bill of Rights    28
Drafting the Bill of Rights    29
An Overview of the Bill of Rights    29
    The First Amendment: Freedoms of Speech, the Press, Religion, and
        the Rights of Assembly and Petition    29
    The Second Amendment: The Right to Bear Arms    30
    The Third Amendment: Limits on Quartering of Soldiers    31
    The Fourth Amendment: Protection Against Unreasonable Searches
        and Seizures    32
    The Fifth Amendment: Grand Juries, Double Jeopardy, Self-
        Incrimination, Due Process, and Eminent Domain    35
    The Sixth Amendment: The Rights of the Accused in Federal
        Criminal Trials    42
    The Seventh Amendment: Trial by Jury in Common Law
        Cases    50
    The Eighth Amendment: Prohibition of Excessive Bail, Fines, and
        Cruel and Unusual Punishments    50
    The Ninth Amendment: Rights Retained by the People    53
    The Tenth Amendment: The Reserved Powers of the States    56
The Process of Nationalization of the Bill of Rights    58
    Applying the Bill of Rights Under the Due Process Clause    58
A Note on Equal Protection of the Laws    62
    How the Problem of Equal Protection Arises    64
The Role of the Bill of Rights in Constitutional Democracy    66
Suggestions for Further Reading    67


3. *The Dynamics of the Federal System*    69

Original State Sovereignty    69
    The Articles of Confederation    70
    The Emergence of the Union    71
The Constitutional Background of Federalism    71
    Definition of Federalism    71
    Establishing Federalism    73
    Federalism in the Constitution    73
How the Constitution Shapes the Federal System    74
    Early Constitutional Interpretation of Federalism    74
The Development of Constitutional Standards Governing
    Federalism    78
    Restricting National Power    78

The End of the *Lochner* Era: Resurgence of National Power     80
Constitutional Doctrines Affecting Federalism After the New
   Deal     81
Judicial Activism in Defining National Standards for Civil Liberties
   and Civil Rights     83
The Politics of Federalism     84
   A Historical Perspective     84
   Changing Patterns of Federalism: The New Deal and Centralization
     of Power     87
   The Changing Federal System of the 1960s     88
   The "New Federalism" of the 1970s     90
   Washington Politics and Federalism     91
   Federalism in the 1980s     91
Federalism and Constitutional Democracy     92
Suggestions for Further Reading     93


**Part II   The Political Process**     **95**

*4. Political Parties, Elections, and the Electorate*     **97**

The Problem of Faction     97
   Madison's View     97
The Liberal–Democratic Model of Party Government     99
   The Role of Parties     100
   Stages of Discussion     100
   Parties as Policy Instruments     101
Parties and the Electoral Process     103
   Presidential Parties     105
   Congressional Parties     105
Reforming the Party System     106
   The Dispute over Reform of the Presidential Nominating
     Process     106
   The McGovern Revolution     108
   Selection of Presidential Candidates at the Grass-Roots
     Level     109
   1984 and Beyond     110
   Effects of Grass-Roots Participation on the Presidential
     Parties     111
Electoral Choice, Parties, and Public Policy     114
   Parties and Issue Identification     115

The Background and Basis of Party Policy Differences     115
Parties and Policy, 1960–1980     119
Parties and Policies in the 1980s     120
Party Trends in the Wake of the 1984 Elections     120
The Meaning of Party Platforms     122
Parties and Voters     123
Changing Voter Attitudes Toward Parties     123
Conclusion: Parties and Constitutional Democracy     124
Suggestions for Further Reading     125

5. *Interest Groups and Political Participation*     *129*

The Group Theory Model of Government     130
The Origins of Group Theory: John C. Calhoun's Concept of
    "Concurrent Majorities"     131
Modern Group Theory     133
"Potential" Groups     134
Defining the National Interest     135
Imperfect Mobilization of Political Interests     136
Countervailing Power     138
Constitutional Checks     138
The Formal Context of Group Action     140
The Effects of Federalism     141
Constitutional Protection of Interest Groups     141
The Informal Context of Group Action     145
The Lack of Disciplined Parties     145
Laissez-faire Capitalism     145
Rise of Voluntary Associations     146
Government Decision Making as a Group Process     147
Group Influence on Congress     147
Group Influence on the Executive Branch     150
Use of the Judiciary by Interest Groups     153
Judicial Response to Group Influence     154
Group Influence on Public Policies     155
Group Power in Contrasting Policy Arenas     156
Redistributive Policies     156
Distributive Policies     157
Regulatory Policies   158
Other Policy Arenas   159
Governmental Interest Groups     160
Executive Branch Assistance to Congress     160
Executive Branch Lobbying and Public Relations     160

Presidential Control of Executive Branch Lobbying      161
Controlling Interest Group Activity      162
   The Ineffectiveness of Legislative Controls      162
   Public Interest Groups      164
Evaluation of Group Politics      165
   The Failure to Uphold Statutory Standards      166
   The Limits of Judicial Review      166
   The Drawbacks of Brokered Politics      166
   Defining the National Interest      167
Conclusion: Constitutional Democracy and Faction      167
Suggestions for Further Reading      168


**Part III    The Governmental Process**                                     **169**

 6. *The Presidency*                                                      *171*

The Context of the Presidency      172
   Effects of the Separation of Powers      172
   Clerk or King?      172
   Need for Presidential Leadership      173
The President's Powers and Responsibilities      174
   Chief of State      174
   Chief Executive      175
   Commander in Chief      176
   Chief Diplomat      180
   Chief Legislator      182
   Other Presidential Responsibilities      182
The Institutional Presidency      188
   The Office of Management and Budget (OMB)      188
   The White House Staff      191
   The National Security Council      192
   The Council of Economic Advisors      192
   Other Executive Office Components      193
The Presidency as an Instrument of Policy Innovation      196
   Franklin D. Roosevelt and the New Deal      196
   Post–New Deal Initiatives: John F. Kennedy and Lyndon B.
      Johnson      197
   The Conservative Tide: Richard M. Nixon and Ronald
      Reagan      197
Presidential Prerogative Powers      198
   The Korean Decision      199

The Vietnam Decision     199
The War Powers Resolution     199
The Role of the President in Constitutional Democracy     201
Suggestions for Further Reading     202


7. *Congress*                                                                *205*

The Constitutional Context of Congress     205
   The Formal Structure of Congress     205
   Constitutional Division of Power     207
   Judicial Interpretation of Policy-Making Authority Under
      Article I     208
Committees: The "Little Legislatures" of Capitol Hill     212
   A Map of Committees     214
   The Role of Committees     215
   Basic Types of Committees     217
Reform of the Congressional Committee System     218
   The Trend Toward Decentralization in the House     218
   Senate Committee System Reform     220
Congressional Parties, Caucuses, and Special Groups     221
   The Speaker of the House     224
   Party Floor Leaders     226
   Party Whips     227
   Party Committees, Caucuses, and Conferences     228
   The Caucuses and Special Groups of Congress     229
   The Growing Role of Staff     230
The Congressional Budget-Making Process     231
   The Budget and Impoundment Control Act of 1974     233
   The Budget Committees and Budget-Making Process     234
   Reconciliation     237
Congress and the Washington Political Establishment     238
   The President and Congress     238
   Congress and the Bureaucracy     239
   Interest Groups and Congress     241
Congressmen and Constituents: The Pursuit of Reelection     242
   Reelection Activities     242
   Reelection Goals and Washington Careers     244
   Home Style Versus Washington Style     244
   Interest Representation     245
The Role of Congress in Constitutional Democracy     246
Suggestions for Further Reading     247

8. *The Bureaucracy*    *249*

   The Constitutional Context of the Bureaucracy    250
     Presidential Versus Congressional Control of the
       Bureaucracy    251
     Quasi-legislative and Quasi-judicial Functions    252
   The Political Context of the Bureaucracy    255
     Agency Response to Political Support    255
     The President Versus the Bureaucracy    255
   Constitutional Democracy and Administrative Responsibility    258
     Controlling Administrative Discretion    258
     The Definition of Responsibility    259
     Accountability to Congress    260
     Accountability to the President    262
     Administrative Independence    264
   Suggestions for Further Reading    265


9. *The Courts*    *267*

   The Constitutional Context of the Judiciary    267
     Judicial Review    267
     Judicial Procedures and Behavior    270
     Judicial Independence    274
     Judicial Activism and Self-Restraint    276
     The Procedural Boundaries of Judicial Decision Making    277
   Examples of Judicial Policymaking    278
     Economic Policy    278
     The Court in the New Deal Period    281
   The Post–New Deal Period    282
     From Judicial Restraint to Activism    282
     The Warren Court    283
   Contemporary Judicial Policymaking    283
     The Abortion Decision    284
     Reagan's Impact on the Court    284
   The Courts and Constitutional Democracy    286
   Suggestions for Further Reading    287


*Appendix A: The Constitution of the United States of America*    *289*

*Index*    *313*

*part* I

# *The Constitutional Context*

# chapter 1

# Constitutional Government

The Constitution provides the formal framework of American government. The Founding Fathers, although wary of potential governmental abuse of power, nevertheless recognized the need for a strong national government. While providing for the separation of powers and checks and balances system to prevent the hasty, irrational, and arbitrary exercise of power, they at the same time provided the framework for a strong national government capable of acting directly upon citizens in a wide range of areas without first having to secure the approval of state governments.

The Constitution can be viewed from the contrasting perspectives of James Madison and Alexander Hamilton. Although both supported a powerful national government, Madison viewed the separation of powers as a major constraint, while Hamilton viewed it as giving to the presidency both the independence and the prerogative powers that are essential to proper governmental performance. The Supreme Court, the president, and Congress have drawn upon each interpretation of the Constitution to support their positions and powers.

## Framing the Constitution

The Constitution has been a beacon that has guided Americans in their quest for self-government from the beginning of the Republic to the present. It is an unusually frugal document, embodying the visions and hopes of the remarkable men who drafted, redrafted, debated, compromised, and finally agreed upon its major principles.

Benjamin Franklin, at the close of the Constitutional Convention in Philadelphia in 1787, expressed the views of many of his fellow delegates when he declared, "I confess that there are several parts of this Constitution which

I do not at present approve, but I am not sure I shall never approve them." Franklin continued, "I agreed to this Constitution with all its faults, if they are such; because I think a general government necessary for us, and there is no form of government but what may be a blessing to the people if well administered, and believe further that this is likely to be well administered for a course of years, and can only end in despotism as other forms have done before it, when the people shall become so corrupted as to need despotic government, being incapable of any other."[1]

While the Constitution was, as John Roche has pointed out, a practical political document that embraced compromises often reluctantly made between the sharply contrasting viewpoints of the state delegations, the final document embodied overarching principles and practices that have profoundly affected the way in which government functions.[2]

## Major Features of the Constitution

The Constitution is the most spare document that has ever been devised to govern successfully the affairs of a great nation. Its apparent simplicity belies its true character, which is a skillful blending of theoretical and practical considerations to forge a new government that would be powerful enough to deal with national concerns but sufficiently limited to protect state sovereignty and the liberties and rights of all citizens.

Federalism, the separation of powers and checks and balances, and judicial review are the central principles of the Constitution. Nowhere does the Constitution explicitly declare that the new system of government was to be federal, or that the three branches of the government were to check and balance each other. Moreover, the important principle of judicial review of congressional, executive, and state actions can only be inferred from the debates of the Constitutional Convention and the explanations of the Constitution written by Alexander Hamilton, James Madison, and John Jay that appeared in *The Federalist*.

### Federalism

A federal government is one in which there is a constitutional division of governmental authority between a central government, on the one hand, and constituent or state units on the other. Under the federal form the na-

---

[1]Max Farrand, ed., *The Records of the Federal Convention of 1787*, 4 vols. (New Haven: Yale University Press, 1911), 2:641–42.
[2]John P. Roche, "The Founding Fathers: A Reform Caucus in Action," *American Political Science Review* 55 (December 1961): 799–816.

tional government may exercise only those powers explicitly or implicitly granted to it, while the constituent units or states retain all other governmental authority.

The federal character of the Constitution lies in its explicit granting of authority to the national government, most particularly to Congress. The national government is limited to the exercise of the enumerated powers of Congress under Article I, as well as those means that are "necessary and proper" to carry out the expressly stated powers. Specific grants of authority are also made to the president, who, for example, makes treaties by and with the advice and consent of the Senate. Finally, only the Supreme Court is to decide cases and controversies arising under the Constitution, treaties, and the laws of the land. The combined constitutional powers of the three branches of the national government constitute the boundaries beyond which the national government may not go.

Within its sphere of power the national government is supreme under the terms of Article VI, which binds state judges to respect the Constitution, laws of the United States made in pursuance thereof, and all treaties made under the authority of the United States. Moreover, Article VI provides that no state constitution or law may supersede the federal Constitution or laws.

The federal character of the Constitution is further defined by denying certain powers, such as the authority to pass bills of attainder or ex post facto laws, to both the national and state governments. Some denials of power apply only to the national government (Art. I, sec. 9), while others apply only to states (Art. I, sec. 10).

Finally, the Tenth Amendment adopted in 1791 unequivocally restated the federal character of the new government by providing that the states were to retain all powers that the Constitution neither delegated to the United States nor prohibited to the individual states.

### The Separation of Powers and Checks and Balances

The separation of powers refers to the separation of the three branches of the national government from each other in their exercise of *primary* legislative, executive, and judicial authority. The separation of powers does not mean, however, that the three branches are to be totally separate and distinct. The separation of the three branches can be maintained only by the sharing of *secondary* powers as far as is necessary to bring about adequate checks and balances (see Figure 1.1).

The separation of the three branches of the government is accomplished not only through separation of powers and checks and balances, but also by giving each branch a separate political constituency. Moreover, Congress itself is divided so that — in the view of the framers — the Senate would

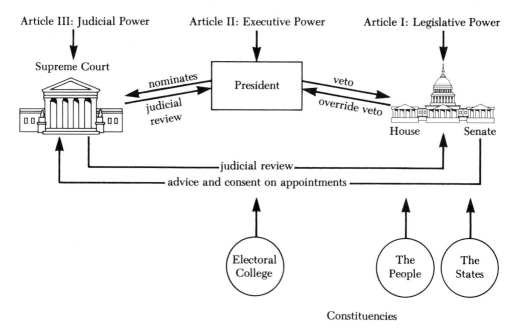

Article III: Judicial Power    Article II: Executive Power    Article I: Legislative Power

**Figure 1.1.** *The Separation of Powers: Checks and Balances. Separate and shared powers and separate constituencies were designed to guarantee checks and balances among the three branches of the government.*

act as a check upon the House. The authors of the Constitution hoped to supply the necessary political incentives to maintain the separation of powers: each department would have not only the *means* to resist encroachments from coordinate branches, but also the *motives* to remain independent.

Important components of the separation of powers and checks and balances system include the presidential veto of congressional laws, the requirement that the president sign all legislation, and the sharing of the treaty-making and appointment powers between the president and the Senate. By implication, the authority of the Supreme Court to overturn executive actions and congressional laws is also an important part of the system.

The separation of powers doctrine prevents the three branches of the government from going beyond constitutional prescriptions in the exercise of their coordinate functions. Moreover, no branch can exercise the "whole" power of another branch, or its primary authority under the Constitution. The president, for example, cannot legislate on his own. Congress cannot take over the function of appointing executive officers. Neither the Supreme

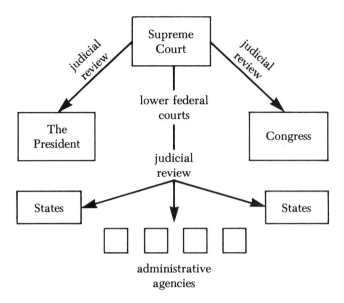

**Figure 1.2.** *Judicial Review. The Supreme Court and lower federal courts may review presidential, congressional, administrative, and state actions where proper cases and controversies exist.*

Court nor constitutional courts — lower courts created by Congress — can become executive agencies or legislative bodies.

While the theory of the separation of powers seems clear, it is not always easy to interpret in practice. For example, when Congress creates an administrative agency, how far can it go in delegating legislative responsibilities to the agency? At what point does the agency become a legislative body on its own independent of congressional control? Generally the courts have required, in theory at least, that Congress clearly state its purpose in delegating legislative authority to the bureaucracy to ensure that the intent of Congress will be carried out.

*Judicial Review*

Judicial review refers to the power of the Supreme Court and lower federal courts to declare congressional or presidential acts unconstitutional, or presidential, administrative, or state actions to be beyond the authority of the Constitution or statutory law (see Figure 1.2). This authority is a critical part of the checks and balances system at the national level, and it is vital to the preservation of the supremacy of federal law.

Judicial review was not discussed at the Constitutional Convention because the delegates assumed that, once they gave the federal courts jurisdiction to hear cases and controversies arising under the Constitution, treaties, and federal law, they would necessarily have the authority to declare unconstitutional and unlawful legislation and actions that went beyond constitutional or lawful authority. At the time the convention met it had been the practice in many states for courts to overturn laws contrary to state constitutions. Several times during the convention delegates made statements that assumed that the power of judicial review would reside with the federal courts, and no objections were heard. Arguing for the adoption of the Constitution, Alexander Hamilton explicitly stated in *The Federalist* (No. 78) that the Supreme Court would have the power to declare acts of Congress unconstitutional. With respect to declaring state actions unconstitutional, it seems clear that the supremacy clause combined with the grant of jurisdiction to the Supreme Court to hear cases arising under the Constitution and federal law implied federal judicial power over the states.

## How the Government Works Under the Constitution

The Constitution defines the extent and limits of governmental power. The first three articles of the Constitution are the "distributing clauses," which define the basic legislative, executive, and judicial powers that are to be exercised by Congress, the president, and the judiciary, respectively.

### Article I: Legislative Power

Article I provides first that

All legislative Powers herein granted shall be vested in a Congress of the United States, which shall consist of a Senate and House of Representatives.

This clause ensures that the *primary* legislative authority of the government will reside in a bicameral legislature. The framers of the Constitution recognized that Congress would be the lawmaking body for the nation, although they did delegate to the president veto power over congressional legislation as well as the responsibility for recommending laws to Congress. Moreover, the president was given extensive explicit and implicit authority to make foreign policy. But there was no doubt that Congress was to be the supreme legislative body in the domestic sphere. Under constitutional theory as developed by the courts, Congress can delegate its legislative authority to the executive and administrative branch only if it clearly states its legislative intent.

The bicameral structure was designed to provide checks and balances within the legislative body itself. The Senate was to act as a check upon the House, which was conceived to be more subject to the ill-considered whims of popular majorities. The representatives of small states also viewed the Senate as an important federal body in which all states would have equal representation.

*Term of Office and Method of Election.* Members of the House were to be elected by the people for a term of two years, and those of the Senate were to be chosen by state legislatures for staggered six-year terms — one-third of the Senate is elected every two years.

The two-year term of office was designated to keep members of the House close to the electorate, while the six-year term of the Senate combined with the indirect election of its members was to give the upper body a more conservative and deliberative cast than the popularly elected House. The adoption of the Seventeenth Amendment in 1913 established the popular election of the Senate, but the longer term of office that gives senators a certain degree of protection from direct and constant popular pressures was not changed.

*Apportionment of the House.* The Constitution provides that "the number of representatives shall not exceed one for every 30,000, but each state shall have at least one representative." Within this limitation the size of the House is determined by Congress itself, and it is now set by law at 435 members. From the beginning, the House was to be apportioned according to the populations of the individual states. Article I, sec. 2 requires a census to be taken every ten years and House apportionment changed accordingly as population shifted from one state to another. Nothing in the Constitution explicitly requires congressional electoral districts to be equal in population, although the framers clearly supported the "one-person-one-vote" principle in general terms. The Three-fifths Compromise diluted voting equality among the states by giving the free inhabitants of slave states a proportionately greater voting strength than their compatriots in the free states, but it was reluctantly adopted by the delegates to the convention only as a political necessity to save the Constitution.[3]

*Qualifications of Members of Congress.* Members of both the House and the Senate must be citizens and residents of the states they represent. Representatives must be at least twenty-five years of age, while senators are

[3]The Three-fifths Compromise counted slaves as three-fifths of a person in the determination of a state's population, upon which its congressional representation was based.

required to be at least thirty. The higher age requirement for the Senate was based in part upon the belief of many framers that age begets wisdom. The framers seriously discussed imposing property qualifications for members of Congress but rejected the idea after extensive debate.

Article I, sec. 5 provides that "each house shall be the judge of the elections, returns and qualifications of its own members." Congress cannot extend qualifications for membership beyond those already specified in the Constitution; it may only judge whether or not its members meet the constitutional standards of citizenship, residency, and age.

*The Power of Expulsion.* Either branch of the national legislature may, under the terms of Article I, sec. 5, "punish its members for disorderly behavior, and, with the concurrence of two-thirds, expel a member." Expulsion may be for failure to meet constitutional qualifications, or for other reasons such as unethical behavior or criminal indictment and conviction. At the outset of the Civil War several Confederate members were expelled for treason, but Congress has otherwise seldom used this power. Most members faced with the prospect of expulsion have resigned before such action was taken.

*Congressional Organization and Procedures.* Bicameralism is the major organizational feature created by the Constitution. It was established by providing different constituencies for the House and the Senate, the House to be the popular body and the Senate to represent the states. Moreover, the two branches of the legislature exercise different powers in some spheres. For example, the Senate has exclusive authority to advise and consent on treaties by the president with foreign governments, as well as on presidential appointments of "public ministers" and other officials designated by Congress. The House has exclusive authority to originate legislation to raise revenue. The House may impeach civil officers, while the Senate has the ultimate power to convict impeached officials of "high crimes and misdemeanors."

Apart from bicameralism, the Constitution offers few details for congressional organization and procedures. Article I, sec. 2 provides that the members of the House "shall choose their Speaker and other officers," making the Speaker a constitutional officer. In the upper body, the vice-president "shall be president of the Senate, but shall have no vote, unless they be equally divided" (Art. I, sec. 3). Members of the Senate "shall choose their other officers, and also a President Pro Tempore in the absence of the Vice President, or when he shall exercise the office of President of the United States" (Art. I, sec. 3).

Other constitutional provisions require Congress to assemble each year, provide that a majority of each house shall constitute a quorum to do business, and prohibit either branch of the legislature from adjourning for more than three days during a session of Congress without the consent of the other, nor may either house adjourn "to any other place than that in which the two houses shall be sitting" (Art. I, sec. 5).

Finally, Congress is required to keep an official journal of its proceedings. The journal is a record of bills and resolutions that have been introduced and votes that are taken. The yeas and nays of members must be recorded on any question at the request of one-fifth of the members present. The journal is separate from the Congressional Record, which includes what is said on the floor of the House and the Senate as well as anything else members choose to put in it. The Record, which began in 1873, contains much of what is in the journal, but also a great deal of extraneous material from newspaper articles to birthday and anniversary congratulations to constituents.

*Support and Protection of Congress.* The framers of the Constitution provided that senators and representatives would be paid out of the federal treasury. The level of pay is to be determined by Congress itself. Many delegates argued against giving the legislature the authority to determine its own pay, but the only alternative proposed at the convention was to allow the states to determine the pay of their representatives. The nationalists, many of them reluctantly, supported the compensation provision of the Constitution because they recognized that state control over congressional pay would give state legislatures too much direct influence over their representatives.

In addition to supporting Congress by giving it the authority to determine its own compensation, the Constitution protects members by providing in Article I, sec. 6 that members of Congress

shall in all Cases, except Treason, Felony and Breach of the Peace, be privileged from Arrest during their Attendance at the Session of their respective Houses, and in going to and returning from the same; and for any Speech or Debate in either House, they shall not be questioned in any other Place.

The Constitution does not exempt congressmen from the legal obligations that pertain to other citizens, but merely protects them from arrest while they are attending congressional sessions, and from actions such as libel against them for what they say during the course of congressional proceedings or what they write in committee reports and other documents.

*The Powers of Congress.* Article I, sec. 8 enumerates the powers of Congress, the most important of which are those to lay and collect taxes, to provide for the common defense and general welfare, and to regulate commerce with foreign nations and among the states. Authors of the Constitution considered each of these powers critical to effective national government, and over the years Congress has relied upon these provisions to expand vastly the power of the national government over that of the states.

After listing seventeen separate congressional powers, the Constitution gives the legislature the authority to make all laws "which shall be necessary and proper for carrying into execution the foregoing powers, and all other powers vested by this Constitution in the government of the United States, or in any department or officer thereof." The "necessary and proper" or "implied powers" clause, as this section of the Constitution is called, has been interpreted from the very beginning of the Republic to broaden the constitutional authority of Congress. The legislature is not limited to the *explicit* powers specified by Article I, but rather can exercise authority that derives from the enumerated powers to include whatever reasonable means Congress considers necessary to implement its powers.

*Limitations on Congressional Powers.* Article I, sec. 9 provides that Congress cannot suspend the writ of habeas corpus "unless when in cases of rebellion or invasion the public safety may require it." Moreover, the legislature cannot pass a bill of attainder or ex post facto law.[4]

Other limits on Congress include the prohibition upon levying a capitation or other direct tax on individuals or property unless it is proportionately divided among the states in accordance with their populations or respective number of articles to be taxed. Congress is prohibited from taxing articles exported from any state, and the legislature cannot discriminate against particular states in the regulation of foreign and domestic commerce.

*Limitations on the States.* In order to facilitate the development of national power, the Constitution places both implicit and explicit limitations on the powers of the individual states. Implicitly, the states cannot pass laws that interfere with the exercise of national power under Article I; they may exercise concurrent legislative authority only insofar as their laws do not conflict with national law. Explicitly, the Constitution in Article I, sec. 10

---

[4]A bill of attainder is a legislative act that convicts and punishes a person for committing a crime. An ex post facto law retroactively makes criminal an act which was not a crime when the act was committed, or which increases the punishment for a crime committed in the past beyond the punishment that existed at the time the act was committed.

prohibits the states from engaging in foreign relations, coining or printing money, and passing bills of attainder, ex post facto laws, or laws impairing the obligation of contracts. No state may lay duties or imposts on the imports or exports of another state "except what may be absolutely necessary for executing its inspection laws." States cannot keep troops, engage in war, or negotiate agreements or compacts with other states.

### Article II: Executive Power

As James Madison pointed out in *The Federalist* (No. 48), under the Constitution the executive power is restrained within a narrower compass and is simpler in its nature than congressional power. Taken at face value, Article II is far more economical than Article I: it simply vests the executive power in *one* president, who must be a natural-born citizen chosen by the electoral college in which each state is represented in proportion to its congressional delegation.

The office of vice-president was created to provide someone who could assume the duties of the presidency in the event of the removal of the president from office or his death, resignation, or inability to discharge the powers and duties of office.

*Powers of the President.* Article II says very little about the powers of the president, which seems especially surprising now that the presidency has become one of the most powerful and important institutions of the federal government. While they are few in number, the powers conferred by Article II are in critical domestic and foreign policy areas.

First, all executive power is delegated to the president, who is to "take care that the laws be faithfully executed." This provision makes the president the chief executive, a responsibility that is further confirmed by his constitutional authority to nominate public ministers and executive officers — by and with the advice and consent of the Senate — and, if necessary, remove executive officials. The Senate may vest in the president sole authority to appoint temporary public officials. The authority of chief executive is an important prerogative power of the office that gives the president wide latitude to choose appropriate means to carry out the law.

Second, the principle of civilian control over the military was established by making the president commander in chief of the armed forces. This authority too has been broadly interpreted as a prerogative power of the president, who not only directs the armed forces but also may engage them in wars, or what are euphemistically termed "conflicts" or "police actions."

Third, the role of the president in foreign policymaking is derived from his authority to make treaties by and with the advice and consent of two-thirds of the Senate. In addition, the president appoints ambassadors and consuls subject to Senate confirmation. The president also receives foreign ambassadors. By implication, Article II makes the president chief of state, the representative of the nation abroad and at home in the performance of the ceremonial functions of government.

Finally, the Constitution delegates important legislative responsibilities to the president, not only by giving him the veto power over congressional laws, but also by directing him to recommend legislation to Congress and to give the legislature information on the state of the Union from time to time. Moreover, he may convene Congress on extraordinary occasions, and even adjourn the legislature in cases where the two houses do not agree on a time of adjournment (Art. II, sec. 3).

In summary, Article II establishes a uniquely American institution, an constitutional presidency with an independent constituency and potentially vast powers, but at the same time limited within the framework of the checks and balances system.

### Article III: Judicial Power

At the outset, Article III provides that

The judicial Power of the United States, shall be vested in one supreme Court, and in such inferior Courts as the Congress may from time to time ordain and establish.

Judicial power is exercised under Article III by constitutional courts — that is, courts created under the terms of Article III and subject to its conditions. The Supreme Court is the only constitutional court required by Article III, although the framers definitely foresaw the creation of additional federal courts by Congress.

The prescribed conditions for federal courts under Article III limit judicial power to cases and controversies arising under the Constitution, laws, and treaties. The federal courts cannot initiate cases.

Another important condition of Article II guarantees judges' tenure during good behavior as well as compensation that cannot be reduced during their continuance in office.

Article III states the original jurisdiction of the Supreme Court — that is, cases that go immediately to the Supreme Court for a decision. This original jurisdiction extends to cases affecting ambassadors and other public (foreign) ministers and consuls, as well as to cases in which a state is a party. In all other cases the Supreme Court is given appellate jurisdiction under regulations established by Congress.

*Article IV: Interstate Relations*

Article IV governs various aspects of interstate relations.

*Full Faith and Credit.* Each state must honor, or give full faith and credit, "to the public acts, records, and judicial proceedings of every other state." This provision requires states, for example, to honor divorce decrees, drivers' licenses, and court judgments of all kinds awarded or given by other states.

*Privileges and Immunities.* In addition to providing for full faith and credit among the states, the Constitution requires that the citizens "of each state shall be entitled to all privileges and immunities of citizens in the several states." States cannot grant their own citizens fundamental rights different from those granted to out-of-state citizens. For example, out-of-state citizens cannot be discriminatorily taxed or denied access to state courts. Where fundamental rights are not jeopardized, however, states may grant privileges to their own citizens that are not accorded to out-of-state citizens — a state may require residency for voting, for example, or for attending state universities.

*Extradition.* A fugitive from justice in one state who is found in another state "shall on demand of the executive authority of the state from which he fled, be delivered up to be removed to the state having jurisdiction of the crime." Although fugitives are usually returned upon the request of the governor of the state in which the crime has been committed, under unusual circumstances extradition is sometimes refused. There is no formal method to compel a state to return a fugitive from justice.

*New States.* Congress is given the authority to admit new states to the Union, but no new state can be created within the jurisdiction of an existing state or formed from a combination of two or more states without the consent of the state legislatures involved as well as of Congress.

*Guaranteeing Republican Government.* The guaranty clause requires the United States to "guarantee to every state in this Union a republican form of government, and [to] protect each of them against invasion; and on application of the legislature [of the state] or of the executive (when the legislature cannot be convened) against domestic violence." In the early years of the Republic, Congress delegated to the president the authority to send troops to protect states against domestic violence under the terms of this constitutional provision.

*Article V: Amending the Constitution*

The Constitution establishes two methods of amendment. First, Congress may by a two-thirds vote in both houses propose amendments that are submitted to the states. In order for an amendment to be added to the Constitution, three-fourths of the state legislatures or conventions must approve it. All constitutional amendments that have been adopted have been proposed by Congress, and all but one have been submitted to the legislatures of the states. Only the Twenty-first Amendment, which repealed the Eighteenth Amendment (Prohibition) in 1933, was ratified by state conventions.

The second method of amending the Constitution, which has not yet been used, requires Congress, upon the application of two-thirds of the state legislatures, to call a special constitutional convention for proposing amendments, which must then be ratified by two-thirds of the legislatures or conventions of the states.

Although twenty-six amendments have been added to the Constitution, many of them significantly changing its original provisions, more important constitutional change has occurred as a result of judicial interpretation and governmental practices. The ambiguity of many parts of the Constitution has provided great leeway for the courts, the president, and Congress in constitutional interpretation.

*Article VI: The Supremacy Clause*

The penultimate article of the Constitution is one of its most important:

This Constitution, and the Laws of the United States which shall be made in Pursuance thereof; and all Treaties made, or which shall be made, under the Authority of the United States, shall be the supreme Law of the Land; and the Judges in every State shall be bound thereby, any Thing in the Constitution or Laws of any State to the Contrary notwithstanding.

The supremacy clause unequivocally binds state judges to the terms of the Constitution and requires them to respect the authority of the national government and constitutional prescriptions regarding the states. Within its sphere of action, the national government is supreme.

*Article VII: Ratification of the Constitution*

The framers of the Constitution carefully provided for its ratification by state conventions rather than state legislatures, recognizing that many legislatures were dominated by advocates of states' rights who had vested interests in preserving state power. Article VII states that: "The ratification of the conventions of nine states, shall be sufficient for the establishment of this Constitution between the states so ratifying the same."

### The Bill of Rights

The Bill of Rights was not part of the original Constitution, but between the proponents of the new government and delegates to state ratifying conventions an informal understanding was struck that a bill of rights would be added as a condition of ratification. Some Federalists considered a bill of rights to be redundant, providing for rights that everyone recognized already existed under natural law as well as in the common law that had been inherited from England. Many state political leaders, however, held that the citizens of states would be best protected by a separate bill of rights that would enumerate freedoms and individual rights that could not be curtailed by the national government (see Chapter 2).

## Perspectives on the Constitution

The theoretical underpinnings of the Constitution were forcefully and eloquently explained by Alexander Hamilton and James Madison in a series of essays that appeared in the newspapers of New York City between October 1787 and August 1788. Hamilton initiated the articles, which were written in the form of letters to the people of New York, and wrote fifty-four of the eighty-five essays that were published. James Madison wrote twenty-six essays, while John Jay, a prominent New York lawyer and political leader who was to become the first chief justice of the Supreme Court, contributed five articles. Collectively the essays were published in one volume entitled *The Federalist,* which, along with the debates of the convention, became an authoritative source on the meaning of the Constitution.

The Constitution can be viewed from one of two broad perspectives. First, it can be seen as incorporating James Madison's explanation of the constitutional plan that he developed at the convention and supported in *The Federalist.* Madison emphasized the importance of constitutional limits on government. Second, the Constitution can be interpreted from the strict Federalist perspective of Alexander Hamilton, who helped to shape it at the Convention and who described its grand design in *The Federalist.* Hamilton emphasized the importance of constitutional powers over the limits on government. He viewed the Constitution as a device that would enable the government, particularly the president, to act forcefully in the national interest.

## The Madisonian Model of Constitutional Government

James Madison was a strong nationalist, believing, as did Alexander Hamilton and a majority of the delegates to the Constitutional Convention, that the supremacy of the national government over the states was critical to the survival of the Union. But at the same time he was suspicious of political aspirations, which he believed could easily lead to demagoguery. Unbridled governmental power would, in Madison's view, inevitably pose a threat to the cherished liberties that had been won on the bloody battlefields of the Revolutionary War.

*Preventing Tyranny of the Majority.* The Founding Fathers recognized that democracy could degenerate into anarchy if the will of the majority were unchecked. The tyranny of the majority, which in its worst expression was nothing more than mob rule, was as much to be feared as an overweening monarch — in the view of some delegates, it constituted an even greater danger to the polity. Madison stated the concern of delegates about the possible tyranny of the majority when he told them that the purposes of the Constitution were, first, "to protect the people against their rulers, [and] secondly, to protect the people against the transient impressions into which they themselves might be led."[5] Direct popular control over government would be insufficient to guard against potential abuses of power, for headstrong majorities might trample upon the rights and interests of minorities. Madison stressed that citizens should always be aware of the possibility of betrayal of their trust by government, arguing that an "obvious precaution against this danger would be to divide the trust between different bodies of men, who might watch and check each other.[6] Like most delegates to the convention, Madison was concerned about the unbridled rule of the majority. He wanted to help create a governmental obstacle course that would restrain the majority from taking ill-considered, unjust, and unfair actions that would trample upon minority interests and rights.

*The Separation of Powers as a Limit on Government.* The Madisonian model of government stresses the importance of the separation of powers as an automatic device to prevent tyranny of the majority and the abuse of governmental power. The president checks Congress, and the legislature is divided into two bodies that check and balance each other. Madison did not refer to the role of the Supreme Court as a check upon either Congress or the president, and the Constitution contains no specific provision for

[5]Farrand, ed., *Records*, 1:421.
[6]Ibid.

judicial review. In general, Madison stressed the need to balance a wide range of interests in government; no one interest was to dominate. Popular and state interests would be represented in the House and the Senate, respectively.

Madison summed up his views on the separation of powers in *The Federalist* (No. 47): "The accumulation of all powers, legislative, executive, and judiciary, in the same hands, whether of one, a few, or many, or whether hereditary, self-appointed, or elected, may justly be pronounced the very definition of tyranny." He was quick to point out, however, that the principle of separation of powers did not require the three branches of government to be absolutely independent of one another. In fact, if the checks and balances system were to work, each branch must have some control over the acts of coordinate branches. For example, the president was given veto authority over congressional laws, subject to an override by a two-thirds vote in Congress. At the same time, Congress shared various executive powers, including the authority to make treaties and appointments to the Supreme Court.

A careful reading of Madison's views at the convention and in *The Federalist* reveals that the Madisonian model is one of internal governmental limits and checks on the one hand, and of extensive national powers over the states on the other. Madison wanted a national government that would be forced to operate with restraint in response to the temporary and passionate demands of popular majorities advancing their own interests at the expense of minority rights and interests. But he also wanted a national government that had the incentive and the ability to act swiftly, rationally, and with firmness to advance the national interest.

## The Hamiltonian Model of the Constitution

The Constitution, viewed from a Hamiltonian perspective, considers the separation of powers more important as a buttress of the presidency and the Supreme Court than as a source of checks and balances among the three branches of government. Differences between the Madisonian and Hamiltonian models of government derived from the Constitution are differences of degree rather than kind, but they nevertheless reflect important contrasting opinions on the way in which the government under the Constitution is supposed to work. Hamilton emphasized the importance of executive power, and he also stressed the significance of the independence of the Supreme Court and its implicit authority to overrule acts of Congress. He saw the separation of powers as expanding rather than limiting executive power, on the basis of the independent authority and constituency given to the president.

*The Separation of Powers as Support for a Strong Executive.* Perhaps the best synthesis of Hamilton's views on the separation of powers can be found in his discussions in *The Federalist* of the presidency (No. 70) and of the Supreme Court (No. 78).

Hamilton opened his discussion of the separation of powers by reiterating a point he made at the convention: "There is an idea, which is not without its advocates, that a vigorous executive is inconsistent with the genius of republican government. The enlightened well-wishers to this species of government must at least hope that the supposition is destitute of foundation; since they can never admit its truth, without, at the same time, admitting the condemnation of their own principles." Hamilton then went on to state the fundamental premise of his model of government: "Energy in the executive is a leading character in the definition of good government. It is essential to the protection of the community against foreign attacks; it is not less essential to the steady administration of the laws, to the protection of property against those irregular and high-handed combinations, which sometimes interrupt the ordinary course of justice, to the security of liberty against the enterprises and assaults of ambition, of faction, and of anarchy." Hamilton found that the "ingredients which constitute energy in the executive are: unity; duration; and the adequate provision for its support; competent powers." And the "ingredients which constitute safety in the republican sense are: a due dependence on the people; a due responsibility."

The Constitution, largely because of Hamilton's efforts, provided for both an energetic and a responsible executive. The unity of the presidency, its independent powers, and indirect popular election that did not depend upon Congress guaranteed that it would possess the attributes of energy and safety which Hamilton sought. While Madison considered the separation of powers to be a critical check upon ill-advised popular majorities and the evil effects of faction, Hamilton saw in the powerful presidency that he considered the separation of powers to have established the answer to good government and control of faction. Not only could the president check the legislature through his veto power, but he also could take independent action to advance the national interest.

## The Supremacy and Scope of National Power

Regardless of the differences between James Madison and Alexander Hamilton over interpretations of the separation of powers, both agreed that there should be no question about the formal authority of the national government over the states and about the wide scope allowed for national authority. Both men stressed the importance of granting to the federal government the broadest powers politically feasible to achieve the purposes of the Union. In the 1980s, well over a century after the end of the Civil War — a century that has witnessed the steady growth of national power in relation to that of the states — it is difficult to comprehend that at the time of the framing of the Constitution the states were little nations, possessing virtually all of the authority of nation-states. Curtailing the sovereignty of the states with their own consent was a major, almost miraculous achievement of the Constitutional Convention. The adoption of the Constitution, however, did not settle the issue of the proper balance of national and state authority, which remained a controversial issue until well into the twentieth century. Even after constitutional questions were settled in favor of the national government, political debate continued over how far the national government should intrude into the affairs of the states.

Most of the important formal powers of the national government are enumerated in Article I. The seeming explicit enumeration of powers, however, is far from clear. For example, Congress has the authority to regulate commerce among the states. But what does that mean? Can Congress use this formal authority to regulate *intrastate* commerce, or does it have authority only over commerce between the territorial boundaries of the states? Legal battles were fought over such issues on numerous occasions during the nineteenth and much of the first half of the twentieth centuries as states challenged the constitutionality of federal laws on the grounds that they exceeded the authority of Congress.

Supreme Court decisions on the extent of congressional authority have had a profound effect on national policies. The Court, for example, severely limited the Sherman Anti-Trust Act of 1890 in a series of decisions and, during one of its most controversial periods, struck down Franklin Roosevelt's early New Deal legislation, by contesting Congress's authority to enact it.

Both Madison and Hamilton agreed that the powers enumerated in Article I should be loosely or flexibly construed to give Congress the widest latitude to choose the appropriate means of carrying out its responsibilities. Both, for example, would have supported Chief Justice John Marshall's opinion in *Gibbons* v. *Ogden* (1824), which broadly interpreted the commerce power of Article I to give Congress the authority to regulate all commercial matters that affected commerce among the states.

Hamilton's arguments for expansive national powers were raised in a practical context in 1791 after Congress had passed its first legislation creating a national bank. Nothing could be dearer to Hamilton's heart than a national bank. George Washington had appointed him the first secretary of the treasury, a position he held with relish and which he considered made him responsible for the financial stability of the new republic.[7] After Congress passed the bank legislation, President Washington, apparently doubtful of its constitutionality, requested the views of Hamilton and Jefferson on the matter. Predictably, there was no doubt in Hamilton's mind that the law was constitutional. Reiterating the views he had previously expressed in *The Federalist* and applying them to the legislation, Hamilton wrote to the president:

It is conceded that *implied powers* are to be considered as delegated equally with *expressed ones*. Then it follows, that as a power of erecting a corporation may as well be *implied* as any other thing, it may as well be employed as an *instrument* or *means* of carrying into execution any of the specified powers, as any other *instrument* or *means* whatever. The only question must be in this, as in every other case, whether the means to be employed, or, in this instance the corporation to be erected, has a natural relation to any of the acknowledged objects or lawful ends of the government. Thus a corporation may not be directed by Congress for superintending the police of the city of Philadelphia, because they are not authorized to *regulate* the *police* of that city. But one may be erected in relation to the collection of taxes, or to the trade with foreign nations, or to the trade between the states, or with the Indian tribes; because it is the province of the federal government to *regulate* those objects, and because it is incident to a general *sovereign* or *legislative* power to *regulate* a thing, to employ all the means which relate to its regulation to the best and greatest advantage.[8]

In contrast to Hamilton, Jefferson took the strict constructionist stance in his letter to the president:

I considered the foundation of the Constitution as laid on this ground: That "all powers not delegated to the United States, by the Constitution, nor prohibited by it to the states, are reserved to the states or to the people.". . . To take a single step beyond the boundaries thus specially drawn around the powers of Congress, is to take possession of a boundless field of power, no longer susceptible of any definition.

The incorporation of a bank, and the powers assumed by this bill, have not, in my opinion, been delegated to the United States by the Constitution.[9]

Jefferson thus narrowly interpreted the constitutional powers of the national government, finding nowhere in Article I the explicit or implied authority to incorporate a national bank.

Hamilton's views prevailed in 1791 when Washington agreed with him

---

[7]The Treasury Department building at the White House end of Pennsylvania Avenue is guarded by a statue of Alexander Hamilton, whose stern countenance serves as a reminder to those within that they should act responsibly and conservatively to protect the solvency and credibility of the nation in financial affairs.
[8]Gerald Gunther, *Cases and Materials on Constitutional Law,* 9th ed. (Mineola, N.Y.: The Foundation Press, 1975), p. 101.
[9]Ibid., p. 100.

on the constitutionality of the legislation and signed the bill creating the first Bank of the United States. Chief Justice John Marshall also supported an expansive view of national power, affirming the constitutionality of the Bank of the United States in the famous case of *McCulloch* v. *Maryland* (1819) on the grounds that the national government must have the broadest possible authority to carry out its responsibilities. But the historic decisions of the early nineteenth-century Marshall Court did not settle once and for all the question of the scope of national power in relation to that of the states. The Supreme Court did not finally and fully accept the doctrines of the Marshall Court that underlay expansive and almost unlimited national power to regulate the economy until the late 1930s (see Chapter 3).

## Conclusion

The Constitution has from the outset been a frugal and flexible document subject to varying interpretations depending on the political interests of the interpreters. Ultimately, political forces have a lot to do with constitutional interpretations. The Supreme Court itself is not an isolated body, but rather is deeply if indirectly involved in politics. Often cases appealed to the Court, and those accepted for review by it, reflect ongoing and important political controversies.

The ebb and flow of politics throughout American history has reflected and emphasized many views of the Constitution, including the contrasting approaches Madison and Hamilton took to the separation of powers and checks and balances. The politics of much of the nineteenth century largely favored the Madisonian approach, with the power of the president balancing that of Congress. Even during most of the Civil War Congress was the dominant body, and it often acted in ways that gave credence to Madison's concern that aggressive legislatures might put the checks and balances system out of kilter.

While the nineteenth century may have belonged to Madison, the political trends of the twentieth century have favored a strong and independent Hamiltonian presidency, capable in times of crisis of rising above the limiting effects of the separation of powers to govern in the national interest effectively and with dispatch. The "imperial presidency," which stresses the importance of the prerogative powers of the president over checks and balances as well as the need for cooperation with Congress, is distinctly Hamiltonian in character. Times of crisis in American history have produced presidents who have acted independently to deal with national crises. Abraham Lincoln, Woodrow Wilson, and Franklin D. Roosevelt, for example, established important precedents for vigorous and independent presidential actions, precedents that were later followed by such presidents as Harry S. Truman, Lyndon B. Johnson, and Richard M. Nixon.

The strong presidency that characterized American politics from the New Deal through the Nixon administration came under attack once again as a result of what were considered to be Nixon's excessive grabs for power in both foreign and domestic policy as well as his staff's attempt to cover up the Watergate affair. The resurgent Congress of the 1970s reflected the cyclical nature of the balance of power between the president and Congress.

The same separation of powers that has produced independent and powerful presidents has also forged a political system characterized by checks and balances that has on occasion even stalemated governments. Even the strongest presidents have been frustrated by an assertive Congress.

The survival of the nation and the supremacy of the national government were goals strongly supported by Hamilton and Madison. The flexibility of the Constitution they helped to draft has provided a basis for forceful presidential action to meet national crises while at the same time it has established checks and balances that have prevented the president from becoming a constitutional dictator. In the long run, it has served the broad purposes of constitutional democracy — effective but limited government.

## Suggestions for Further Reading

Beard, Charles A. *An Economic Interpretation of the Constitution.* New York: Macmillan, 1913. In this controversial work, the author argues that the Constitution was written by an economic elite to protect its financial interests.

Farrand, Max. *The Framing of the Constitution of the United States.* New Haven: Yale University Press, 1913. A brief work covering the highlights of the Constitutional Convention by the editor of the definitive volumes on the convention proceedings that feature Madison's notes.

Hamilton, Alexander, Madison, James and Jay, John. *The Federalist Papers.* New York: New American Library, 1961. Originally published as newspaper articles in 1787–88. The best current edition of *The Federalist* is that by Clinton Rossiter.

Rossiter, Clinton. *1787: The Grand Convention.* New York: Macmillan, 1956. A lucid writer provides an absorbing account of the Constitutional Convention and the subsequent ratification campaign.

Wills, Garry. *Explaining America: The Federalist.* Garden City, N.Y.: Doubleday, 1981. The author gives his view of the "real" Madison, stressing the Virginian's support of a strong national government.

————. *Inventing America.* Garden City, N.Y.: Doubleday, 1978. An innovative and challenging account of the origins of the Declaration of Independence.

# chapter 2

# Civil Liberties and Civil Rights Under the Constitution

The Bill of Rights, which every citizen now takes for granted, was not part of the original Constitution of 1787. Its omission did not mean that the delegates to the Constitutional Convention considered civil liberties and civil rights to be of minor importance; quite the contrary was the case. The men who drafted the Constitution assumed the existence of inalienable civil liberties and civil rights, and many believed these rights to be based on a natural law that was superior to the laws of men. Theoretical considerations aside, all of the delegates had been molded in one way or another by the Anglo-American legal tradition which up to the time of the writing of the Constitution had strongly emphasized the importance of independent rights and liberties of citizens that could not be curtailed by government.

The framers of the Constitution, like all American colonists, assumed that the rights of Englishmen did not stop at the borders of Great Britain, but followed them to the shores of America. The delegates to the convention of 1787 could cite chapter and verse from the Magna Charta of 1215, the English Bill of Rights of 1689, and the numerous common law precedents that upheld the rights and liberties of citizens. It was the assumption of the existence of pervasive civil liberties and civil rights possessed by all citizens that made the addition of a separate bill of rights to the Constitution seem redundant, superfluous, and even dangerous because it would imply a national authority to curtail rights and liberties that were not specifically included in the bill of rights.

## Civil Rights in the Original Constitution

Although the Founding Fathers failed to add a separate bill of rights to the original Constitution, some protections of civil rights were included. The national government was prohibited from suspending the writ of habeas corpus "unless when in cases of rebellion or invasion the public safety may require it" (Art. I, sec. 9). Neither Congress nor state governments were permitted to pass bills of attainder or ex post facto laws (Art. I, sec. 9, 10).[1] In Article III, sec. 2, the Constitution provides for jury trials "of all crimes" and that "such trials shall be held in the state where the said crimes shall have been committed." This section guarantees the right to a jury trial to persons accused of crime by the *national* government.

### The Debate over the Bill of Rights

The failure of the framers of the Constitution to include a separate bill of rights, which was barely discussed during the convention proceedings, caused concern among some of the political leaders in the states. After all, the states had in their own constitutions extensively set forth the rights of their citizens. Why should not the federal government do the same? Opponents of the Constitution used the lack of a separate bill of rights as an argument against its adoption, and even proponents of the Constitution suggested that it would be wise to add a bill of rights.

The closeness of the ratification campaigns in several states made the promise of the advocates of the new Constitution to draft a bill of rights an important trade-off for votes in the ratifying conventions of several states. Many of the delegates to the first Congress considered themselves to be under an obligation to honor promises that had been made during the ratification campaigns. In his first inaugural address, President Washington called on Congress to consider carefully the addition of a bill of rights to the Constitution. Under the leadership of James Madison, Congress rose to the occasion, drafting twelve amendments, ten of which were finally submitted to the states for ratification to become the Bill of Rights of the new national government.

---

[1]The *writ of habeas corpus* is a court order to an arresting officer requiring the defendant to be brought before the court with a statement of why the defendant is being held in custody. Although the Constitution authorizes the suspension of the writ of habeas corpus in cases of rebellion of invasion where the public safety requires it, congressional laws or presidential actions suspending the writ are subject to judicial review. A *bill of attainder* is legislation that convicts and punishes a person. An *ex post facto law* retroactively makes a particular act a crime that was not a crime when it was committed or, subsequent to the commission of a crime, increases the punishment for it. Ex post facto laws by definition impose criminal penalties. Retroactive civil laws are not prohibited by the Article I, sec. 9 proscription upon ex post facto laws.

*Drafting the Bill of Rights*

Today the Bill of Rights is not only taken for granted; its provisions are considered by most citizens to embody historical, traditional, and immutable rights and liberties. But just which rights and liberties were to be included was a highly debated topic.

During the drafting of the Bill of Rights by the first Congress, the question of its applicability to the states themselves was not explicitly raised. It was clearly the intent of the drafters of the Bill of Rights, however, that its provisions would apply only to the national government. The debates in the first Congress focused solely upon questions concerning the proper limit of national government. Significantly, the Senate defeated a House proposal which provided that "no state shall infringe the right of trial by jury in criminal cases, nor the rights of conscience, nor the freedom of speech or of the press." The rejection of this provision unequivocally proves the intent of the first Congress to apply the provisions of the Bill of Rights only to the national government. The First Amendment sets the tone for the entire Bill of Rights in its opening words: "*Congress* shall make no law . . ." (emphasis added).

Twelve amendments to the Constitution were approved by Congress in 1789 and sent to the states, where the first ten amendments were ratified by the requisite three-fourths of the states in 1791.[2]

## An Overview of the Bill of Rights

*The First Amendment: Freedoms of Speech, the Press, Religion, and the Rights of Assembly and Petition*

The First Amendment embodies fundamental liberties which many consider to be the most important in the Bill of Rights. The amendment provides that

Congress shall make no law respecting an establishment of religion, or prohibiting the free exercise thereof; or abridging the freedom of speech, or of the press; or the right of the people peaceably to assemble, and to petition the Government for a redress of grievances.

The First Amendment guarantees of freedom of speech, the press, assembly, and petition are essential underpinnings of the democratic process. The

---

[2]Connecticut, Massachusetts, and Georgia failed to ratify the amendments. On the one hundred fiftieth anniversary of the adoption of the Bill of Rights in 1941, the legislatures of these three states voted their approval of it.

fundamental importance of the freedom of speech and of the press led the Supreme Court to nationalize them early, making them applicable as safeguards against state action under the due process clause of the Fourteenth Amendment, which provides that no state shall deprive any person of life, liberty, or property without due process of law. The opinion in *Gitlow* v. *New York* (1925) and the ruling in *Near* v. *Minnesota* (1931) defined the "liberty" of the due process clause to include the freedom of speech and of the press.

In addition to guaranteeing freedoms essential to the democratic process, clauses of the First Amendment on religion proscribe Congress from passing legislation that would establish an official government church or aid a particular religion, and from interfering in the free exercise of religion through legislation that would prevent people from practicing their religious beliefs. The freedom to practice religion is not absolute and may be curtailed on the basis of a compelling governmental interest. For example, the Constitution does not require Congress to exempt all persons from the draft who claim a religious conscientious objection to war. The conditions of conscientious objector status set by Congress do interfere with the free exercise of some religions.

### *The Second Amendment: The Right to Bear Arms*

The Second Amendment states that

A well regulated militia, being necessary to the security of a free State, the right of the people to keep and bear arms, shall not be infringed.

This amendment was passed because of the fear that Congress might disarm the state militias.[3] One of the more controversial provisions of the Constitution was the Article I power of Congress to regulate state militias, with the provision that the appointment of militia officers would be reserved to the states as well as the authority of training the militia in accordance with the discipline prescribed by Congress. Alexander Hamilton wrote (*The Federalist*, No. 29) that if it were "possible seriously to indulge a jealousy of the militia upon a conceivable establishment under the federal government, the circumstance of the officers being in the appointment of the states ought at once to extinguish it. There can be no doubt that this circumstance will always secure to them a preponderating influence over the militia."

The states did not accept Hamilton's argument that they would have

---

[3]The word "state" in the amendment is used in the generic sense and does not refer to the states of the Union. This does not affect the intent of the amendment, however, which was to protect the states against federal action disarming their militias.

nothing to fear from national control over their militias, which many state leaders felt might lead to a standing national army without any countervailing force in the states. Elbridge Gerry of Massachusetts spoke to this point in his defense of the Second Amendment in the first Congress:

What, Sir, is the use of a militia? It is to prevent the establishment of a standing Army, the bane of liberty. Now, it must be evident, that under this provision, together with their other powers, Congress could take such measures with respect to a militia, as to make a standing army necessary. Whenever governments mean to invade the rights and liberties of the people, they always attempt to destroy the militia, in order to raise an army upon their ruins.[4]

Since the intent of the Second Amendment was clearly to prevent national disarmament of state militias, to what extent is the *constitutional* authority of Congress to regulate guns limited? Clearly, Congress cannot regulate guns in such a way as to disarm state militias. But there would seem to be no constitutional impediments to general gun control legislation aimed at protecting individuals against violence. For example, in *United States* v. *Miller* (1939), the Court upheld the National Firearms Act, which required the registration of certain types of guns including sawed-off shotguns, against a Second Amendment challenge that it violated the individual's rights to bear arms. Justice McReynolds wrote for the Court that in the absence of evidence that the possession of a sawed-off shotgun "at this time has some reasonable relationship to the preservation or efficiency of a well-regulated militia, we cannot say that the Second Amendment guarantees the right to keep and bear such an instrument. Certainly it is not within judicial notice that this weapon is any part of the ordinary military equipment or that its use could contribute to the common defense."[5] The *Miller* ruling did not answer the question of the extent to which individuals have a Second Amendment right to bear arms that ordinarily would be appropriate to military forces. Since the *Miller* case is the only one pertaining to the constitutionality of a federal law challenged on Second Amendment grounds, some doubt remains regarding the validity of comprehensive federal gun control legislation.

## The Third Amendment: Limits on Quartering of Soldiers

The eighteenth-century fear of standing armies in the colonies and the new states was amply justified, since such armies had been employed by Great

[4]Cited in A.F. Dick Howard, *Commentaries on the Constitution of Virginia* (Charlottesville: University Press of Virginia, 1974), p. 273.
[5]*United States* v. *Miller*, 307 U.S. 174, 178 (1939).

Britain to suppress colonial resistance and enforce unpopular laws. The Third Amendment was directed at the unpopular British practice of quartering soldiers in private homes, an exploitation of citizens that both nationalists and states' rights advocates agreed was intolerable. The Third Amendment provides that

No Soldier shall, in time of peace be quartered in any house, without the consent of the owner, nor in time of war, but in a manner to be prescribed by law.

The Third Amendment has not required judicial exposition or comment because there is no ambiguity in nor has there been any debate over its terms.

### The Fourth Amendment: Protection Against Unreasonable Searches and Seizures

The Fourth Amendment is deeply rooted in the Anglo-American legal tradition. It was a common practice in Great Britain, beginning in the fourteenth century, to have agents of the government conduct searches of homes and persons to ferret out materials that were, in the view of the king and his ministers, seditious and against the public interest. The unbridled power of the king to authorize searches and seizures was curbed somewhat after the Glorious Revolution of 1688 and the establishment of parliamentary supremacy.

After 1688 the English government, with the support of the monarchy, began to limit governmental authority to search and seize because unreasonable searches and seizures were considered to be a violation of the fundamental rights of English citizens. The enforcement of tax laws through abusive searches and seizures was specifically curbed by Parliament in the eighteenth century. Parliamentary action did not establish standards limiting searches and seizures generally, however, and the common law courts took it upon themselves to develop common law standards that would restrict searches and seizures that had been authorized by the king and Parliament.

While Englishmen in Britain were given increased protection by the courts against unreasonable searches and seizures, their compatriots in the American colonies were increasingly subjected to searches and seizures by agents of the British government seeking to enforce customs and tax laws. Great Britain was attempting to impose its rigid mercantile system of economic controls over the colonies through whatever means it considered necessary, regardless of the "rights" of the colonist. Officers of the Crown in the colonies conducted searches for smuggled goods simply on the basis of the authority derived from their commissions. When they met opposition, they obtained "writs of assistance" issued by colonial governors or courts under the authority of Parliament in the name of the king. The authority of Parliament to issue such writs was directly challenged in the Colony of Massachusetts in the famous Writs of Assistance case in 1761. A group of Boston merchants employed James Otis, a brilliant young lawyer, to argue their position that the writs should not be issued. Otis told the colonial court that the writs violated the fundamental constitutional rights of Englishmen and that Parliament had no authority to authorize them. The writs were issued, although Otis had persuaded some of the justices to his side, and they continued to be granted until the outbreak of the Revolutionary War.

The colonial experience with arbitrary searches and seizures by agents of the Crown in violation of what the colonists considered to be fundamental principles of English law was the historical background of the Fourth Amendment, which provides that

The right of the people to be secure in their persons, houses, papers, and effects, against unreasonable searches and seizures, shall not be violated, and no Warrants shall issue, but upon probable cause, supported by Oath or affirmation, and particularly describing the place to be searched, and the persons or things to be seized.

The Fourth Amendment requirement for search warrants establishes an important judicial check upon the search and seizure actions of police and government officers. Although the initiative for searches and seizures always lies with police agents, they must obtain court approval before acting. Although courts more often than not readily grant police requests for search warrants, the involvement of the courts prevents totally independent police action. Perhaps the most important limitation of all on searches and seizures is that evidence that a court finds was obtained through unreasonable search and seizure is inadmissible in both federal and state court.[6]

The Fourth Amendment, like most constitutional provisions, contains a great deal of ambiguity. What is a "search and seizure"? What is an "unreasonable" search and seizure? Both of these questions have been answered in contrasting ways by different courts and justices. For example, in *Olmstead v. United States* in 1928, Chief Justice Taft wrote the Court's majority opinion holding that wiretapping did not constitute a "search" under the terms of the Fourth Amendment. To be covered by the Fourth Amendment, declared Taft, a search must be accompanied by the seizure of physical objects or the physical entry into the premises that are searched. The case itself

[6]The Supreme Court extended the full protection of the Fourth Amendment to the states in *Mapp v. Ohio*, 367 U.S. 643 (1961).

involved, in the words of the Court, a massive conspiracy to sell liquor unlawfully. The discovery of the conspiracy was made through wiretapping. Four justices dissented in separate opinions. Justice Louis Brandeis wrote one of his most famous dissents, in which he linked the Fourth Amendment protection against unreasonable searches and seizures with the Fifth Amendment safeguard against compulsory self-incrimination. He stated:

When the Fourth and Fifth Amendments were adopted, the "form that evil had theretofore taken" had been necessarily simple. Force and violence were then the only means known to man by which a government could directly effect self-incrimination. It could compel the individual to testify — a compulsion effected, if need be, by torture. It could secure possession of his papers and other articles incident to his private life — a seizure effected, if need be, by breaking and entry. Protection against such invasion of "the sanctity of a man's home and the privacies of life" was provided in the Fourth and Fifth Amendments by specific language.[7]

After noting the original conditions that led to the Fourth Amendment defense against unreasonable searches and seizures and the Fifth Amendment protection against self-incrimination, Brandeis pointed out that the Fourth and Fifth Amendment safeguards should be extended to meet new problems of government invasion of privacy: "Subtler and more far-reaching means of invading privacy have become available to the government. . . . Discovery and invention have made it possible for the government, by means far more effective than stretching upon the rack, to obtain disclosure in court of what is whispered in the closet."[8] Brandeis concluded that

The makers of our Constitution undertook to secure conditions favorable to the pursuit of happiness. They recognized the significance of man's spiritual nature, of his feelings, and of his intellect. They knew that only a part of the pain, pleasure, and satisfactions of life are to be found in material things. They sought to protect Americans in their beliefs, their thoughts, their emotions, and their sensations. They conferred, as against the government, the right to be let alone — the most comprehensive of rights and the right most valued by civilized men. To protect that right, every unjustifiable intrusion by the government upon the privacy of the individual, whatever the means employed, must be deemed a violation of the Fourth Amendment.[9]

Brandeis particularly emphasized that the Fourth Amendment proscription upon unreasonable searches and seizures may buttress the Fifth Amendment

---

[7]*Olmstead v. United States*, 277 U.S. 438, 473 (1928).
[8]Ibid.
[9]Ibid., p. 478.

protection against self-incrimination. Under such circumstances the Fourth Amendment should be broadly interpreted to limit government action.

The disagreement among the justices in the *Olmstead* case reflected the contrasting ways in which the Fourth Amendment could be interpreted. Disagreement over the reach of the Fourth Amendment continued. In *Katz v. United States* (1967) the Court, with Justice Black registering the only dissent, extended the safeguards of the Fourth Amendment to require search warrants before police officers can eavesdrop, even in semipublic places (in this case a telephone booth). Justice Black, dissenting, would have strictly interpreted the Fourth Amendment. Taking a position similar to that of the majority in the *Olmstead* case, he argued that the Fourth Amendment protections cover only objects that can be physically seized. Black's dissent concluded that eavesdropping on a conversation held in a telephone booth cannot in any literal sense be considered a "search and seizure."

The question concerning the extent to which searches and seizures can be conducted with and without warrant has not been definitively answered by the Supreme Court. The *Katz* ruling somewhat ambiguously extended the shield of the Fourth Amendment to electronic eavesdropping, but at the same time it permitted such eavesdropping and, by implication, wiretapping if law enforcement officers first obtain a warrant. The Supreme Court and the lower federal judiciary continue to grapple with the problem of defining Fourth Amendment standards on a case-by-case basis.

### The Fifth Amendment: Grand Juries, Double Jeopardy, Self-Incrimination, Due Process, and Eminent Domain

The Fifth Amendment is one of the most comprehensive and eclectic parts of the Bill of Rights. It is best considered by breaking it down into its component parts.

*Grand Juries.* First, it provides for grand juries:

No person shall be held to answer for a capital, or otherwise infamous crime, unless on a presentment or indictment of a Grand Jury. . . .

The grand jury, one of the oldest institutions in Anglo-American law, is a jury of inquiry in criminal cases that hears evidence presented by the government prosecuting officer to determine whether or not a presentment should be made or an indictment returned. A *presentment* is a written notice of an offense, based on reasonable grounds for believing that the individual named has committed it, and is made by the grand jury on its own motion. An *indictment* is also a written accusation charging a person with having committed a criminal act, but, unlike the presentment, an indictment is made at the request of the government and usually framed first by the prosecuting officer. Grand juries do not try persons, their function being limited to accusing individuals of crimes. The proceedings are secret, and only the government is represented. The term *grand* jury is derived from its greater size relative to the ordinary trial, or *petit,* jury. At common law, grand juries consisted of not fewer than twelve nor more than forty-three persons. In American practice these numbers have been altered by statute in some states. The ordinary *petit* jury consisted of twelve persons, but this number has also been altered by statute in some states.

While the grand jury is an ancient common law institution, the right to indictment by a grand jury remains one of the handful of provisions of the Bill of Rights that have not been nationalized under the due process clause of the Fourteenth Amendment and made applicable to state action.[10] The Supreme Court has not changed Justice Cardozo's opinion in *Palko* v. *Connecticut* (1937) that the right to indictment by a grand jury, although of "value and importance," is not a "principle of justice so rooted in the traditions and the conscience of our people as to be ranked as fundamental," nor is it "implicit in the concept of ordered liberty."[11]

The Fifth Amendment requires grand jury indictment,

except in cases arising in the land or naval forces, or in the Militia, when in actual service in time of war or public danger. . . .

The Supreme Court has construed the exemption to the grand jury requirement to extend only to persons serving in the military forces. Civilian dependents or employees of the military cannot be tried for capital crimes by military tribunals, but must be given the full protection of the Bill of Rights.[12]

*Double Jeopardy.* In addition to the grand jury safeguard in capital cases, the Fifth Amendment provides protection against double jeopardy:

[No person] shall . . . be subject for the same offense to be twice put in jeopardy of life or limb. . . .

---

[10]The other parts of the Bill of Rights that have not been nationalized under the due process clause of the Fourteenth Amendment are: trial by jury in civil cases; prohibition against excessive bail and fines; the right to bear arms; and the Third Amendment prohibition of the quartering of troops in private homes.
[11]*Palko* v. *Connecticut,* 302 U.S. 319, 325 (1937).
[12]See *Kinsella* v. *United States ex rel Singleton,* 361 U.S. 234 (1960); *Reid* v. *Covert,* 354 U.S. 1 (1957).

The double jeopardy provision of the Fifth Amendment applies only to criminal cases, and, until 1968, the protection against double jeopardy under the Fifth Amendment extended only to federal crimes.[13] What constitutes "double jeopardy" is not always easily answered. A defendant is put into jeopardy when he or she has been indicted and brought to trial. If the defendant is acquitted, or if the prosecutor agrees to a dismissal of the case, the defendant cannot be tried again. The double jeopardy restriction, however, does not prevent the retrial of a defendant if the jury was unable to reach a verdict during the first trial. Moreover, the double jeopardy shield does not prevent both the federal government and the states from separately trying an individual who has committed an offense that violates both federal and state laws. A person may also be subject to civil proceedings in addition to a criminal trial for the same offense.

*Self-Incrimination.* Perhaps the most historic and widely cited provision of the Fifth Amendment is its protection against self-incrimination:

[No person] shall be compelled in any criminal case to be a witness against himself. . . .

The Fifth Amendment safeguard against self-incrimination has a long and complicated history. The origin of the privilege dates to the twelfth century and arose from disputes between the monarchy and the church. The Crown in its struggle with the church sought to limit the authority of bishops to compel testimony from citizens of the realm with regard to alleged offenses. The privilege against self-incrimination, however, did not become operative in the common law until centuries later. During the sixteenth and seventeenth centuries it was not an uncommon practice to use torture to extract confessions from alleged criminals. But by the end of the seventeenth century the privilege against self-incrimination was incorporated into the common law largely as a result of an action of Parliament that voted to overturn a conviction by the king's council of the Star Chamber on the ground that the court had violated the individual's right to refuse to testify against himself.[14] Although the privilege against self-incrimination had deep historical roots, until 1964 the Supreme Court did not consider it to be one of those fundamental and historic rights required to be included under the due pro-

---

[13]The double jeopardy safeguard of the Fifth Amendment was incorporated into the due process clause of the Fourteenth Amendment in *Benton* v. *Maryland*, 392 U.S. 925 (1968).
[14]See Erwin N. Griswold, *The Fifth Amendment Today* (Cambridge: Harvard University Press, 1955), p. 3.

cess clause of the Fourteenth Amendment as a limitation upon state action.[15] The protection against self-incrimination as strictly interpreted by the courts applies only to criminal cases. A major question regarding the reach of the Fifth Amendment self-incrimination shield was raised during the 1950s when congressional investigations by the House Committee on Un-American Activities and by Senator Joseph McCarthy, chairman of the Government Operations Committee, cast a broad net to catch and expose communist subversives. Many witnesses before these congressional committees refused to answer questions on grounds of self-incrimination as well as on First Amendment grounds of freedom of speech, the press, and association. Congressional questioning could not only expose a witness to possible criminal prosecution for violation of subversive control statutes, but also cast a chilling effect upon the willingness of persons to express political views or join associations that might possibly be considered subversive. Regardless of the claims of witnesses to the contrary, their rights before congressional committees conducting legitimate investigations are determined by Congress, not by the courts. The rules of congressional committees may and usually did permit witnesses to "take the Fifth" in their refusal to answer questions. On more than one occasion, however, frustrated committee chairmen and members sought contempt citations to be voted by Congress against what they considered to be obstreperous witnesses. Several rulings by the Supreme Court did require that committee investigations have a legitimate legislative purpose, but the Court did not extend the self-incrimination protection of the Fifth Amendment to witnesses before congressional committees.[16]

Congress has passed legislation that under certain circumstances — for example, in connection with narcotics violations — allows federal prosecutors to grant immunity from both federal and state prosecution in return for compelled testimony. Once immunity is granted to a person he or she may not refuse to answer questions.

*Due Process.* After the self-incrimination clause the Fifth Amendment includes the due process clause, which provides that no person shall

be deprived of life, liberty, or property, without due process of law. . . .

The due process clause of the Fifth Amendment should be contrasted with the due process clause of the Fourteenth Amendment, which provides that

[15]See *Mallory v. Hogan*, 378 U.S. 1 (1964); and *Murphy v. Waterfront Commission of New York Harbor*, 378 U.S. 52 (1964).
[16]See *Watkins v. United States*, 354 U.S. 178 (1957); and *Barenblatt v. United States*, 360 U.S. 109 (1959).

*no state* may deprive a person of life, liberty, or property without due process of law. As we will see below, the due process clause of the Fourteenth Amendment has been interpreted to include all of the protections afforded by the Fifth Amendment due process clause and many more as well.

The phrase "due process of law" is highly indefinite, requiring judicial interpretation for clarification. The difficulty comes from the fact that judges and legal scholars often define due process in contrasting ways. What, then, is the meaning of the due process clause in the Fifth Amendment? In one of the few cases in which the Supreme Court attempted to define the meaning of due process, *Murray's Lessee* v. *Hoboken Land and Improvement Company* (1856), Justice Curtis wrote:

The words "due process of law," were undoubtedly intended to convey the same meaning as the words, "by the law of the land," in Magna Charta. . . . The Constitution contains no description of those processes which it was intended to allow or forbid. It does not even declare what principles are to be applied to ascertain whether it be due process. It is manifest that it was not left to the legislative power to enact any process which might be devised. The article is a restraint on the legislative as well as on the executive and judicial powers of government, and cannot be so construed as to leave Congress free to make any process "due process of law" by its mere will. To what principles, then, are we to resort to ascertain whether this process, enacted by Congress, is due process? To this the answer must be twofold. We must examine the Constitution itself, to see whether this process be in conflict with any of its provisions [such as the Bill of Rights]. If not found to be so, we must look to those settled usages and modes of proceeding existing in the common and statute law of England, before the emigration of our ancestors, and which are shown not to have been unsuited to their civil and political condition by having been acted on by them after the settlement of this country. . . . [T]hough "due process of law" generally implies and includes . . . regular allegations, opportunity to answer, and a trial according to some settled course of judicial proceedings . . . yet, this is not universally true.[17]

The formula for determining the content of the Fifth Amendment due process clause announced by Justice Curtis in the *Murray's Lessee* case allowed the Court broad discretion in developing due process standards. The Court was to refer to the Constitution, the Bill of Rights, and "those settled usages and modes of proceeding existing in the common law and statute law of England" to define due process. Using such an approach, the definition of due process arrived at by the Court would necessarily contain a highly subjective element.

The inclusion of the due process clause in the Fifth Amendment implies that the framers of the Bill of Rights thought that "due process of law" had

[17] *Murray's Lessee v. Hoboken Land and Improvement Company,* 18 Howard 272, 276–80 (1856).

a meaning that went beyond the procedural protections included in the other parts of the Bill of Rights. For example, the Fifth Amendment incorporates the protection against self-incrimination directly before the due process clause. Unless the due process clause is to be thought of as being completely redundant, due process presumably was intended to mean something different from the procedural safeguard against self-incrimination and the other procedural protections of the Bill of Rights. The Supreme Court, however, has generally interpreted *procedural* due process in the Fifth Amendment as essentially embodying the procedural protections that are stated elsewhere in the Bill of Rights. But the Court has, at times, gone beyond the explicit provisions of the Bill of Rights in interpreting Fifth Amendment due process. It has held, for example, that the due process law gives aliens the right to a hearing in deportation cases.[18]

Although the due process clause of the Fifth Amendment is largely redundant in the protection of procedural rights, since such rights are included in other parts of the Bill of Rights, a conservative Supreme Court did in the early twentieth century use the due process clause to review the *substantive* content of congressional legislation and overturn it when the Court felt that Congress had intruded upon the liberty and property rights of individuals. For example, in *Adkins* v. *Children's Hospital* in 1923, the Court overturned a congressional statute that prescribed minimum wages for women in the District of Columbia on Fifth Amendment due process grounds. The Court ruled that the law interfered with the constitutional freedom of contract, which was a liberty guaranteed by the due process clause. The *Adkins* case was an example at the national level of due process review which reached to the substance of legislation to determine its fairness. Substantive due process review, which essentially involves the Court in making legislative judgments, has been exercised primarily over state laws under the due process clause of the Fourteenth Amendment. The subjectivity of substantive due process review comes from the wide range of possible interpretations of the word "liberty" and "property" in the due process clause. In giving substance to these words, the Court essentially has to exercise its own judgment without grounding its opinions in explicit provisions of the Constitution, such as the Bill of Rights, or in historic customs, traditions, and common law precedents, all of which are used to define procedural due process.

A development of major importance in the interpretation of the due process clause of the Fifth Amendment was the Court's decision in *Bolling* v.

---

[18]In *Wong Yang Sung v. McGrath*, 339 U.S. 33 (1950), the Court stated that since deportations may deprive aliens of liberty and even of life, they must be given due process, which requires a hearing before an impartial administrative judge or tribunal.

*Sharpe* in 1954 to include equal protection of the laws as part of due process. The Court, essentially employing the method of substantive due process review, defined "liberty" of due process to include equal protection. Equal protection of the laws is explicitly guaranteed in the Constitution only in the Fourteenth Amendment, which governs state rather than national action. In the *Bolling* case the Court held that the Fourteenth Amendment equal protection clause was incorporated in the due process clause of the Fifth Amendment, a ruling that extended equal protection to national action.

*Eminent Domain.* The final provision of the Fifth Amendment states that no

private property [shall] be taken for public use, without just compensation.

The just compensation clause restricts the government's power of eminent (prominent, superior) domain (territory). This is the power all governments have to control the territory of the state for public use in the public interest. In time of peace, for example, the power of eminent domain is used primarily by state governments to take private property for public highways. In time of war, the national government may find it in the public interest to seize territory for the common safety. The power of eminent domain is based upon the ultimate authority of the sovereign to deploy any and all of the state's wealth in cases of public necessity and safety. The power of eminent domain applies only to private property, since the government automatically has control over its own property.

The Fifth Amendment does not limit the power of eminent domain, but it does require that the government pay "just compensation" when it takes private property for public use. Generally what constitutes "taking" private property is clear, as when the government seizes the land of an individual and transfers title to itself. The courts have not defined the taking of private property to include government action that indirectly reduces the value of such property — for example, government regulatory measures that reduce the rates of return that individuals could otherwise receive from their property are not covered by eminent domain. Most government regulation reduces the profit-making opportunities of private individuals in some way, but clearly the government could not function if it were to compensate citizens for the indirect effects of controlling the environment, food and drugs, consumer product safety, health and safety in the workplace, and so on.

Perhaps because the Fifth Amendment limitation upon the power of eminent domain was taken for granted as a proper control of government it was the first provision of the Bill of Rights to be incorporated under the due process clause of the Fourteenth Amendment in 1890.[19]

### *The Sixth Amendment: The Rights of the Accused in Federal Criminal Trials*

The Sixth Amendment prescribes the fundamental rights of those accused of federal crimes. First,

> In all criminal prosecutions, the accused shall enjoy the right to a speedy and public trial, by an impartial jury of the State and district wherein the crime shall have been committed, which district shall have been previously ascertained by law. . . .

*Speedy Trial.* The Sixth Amendment's requirement that jury trials take place in the state where the crime was committed repeats the jury trial provision of Article III. The delegates at the Constitutional Convention considered the right to a trial by jury in criminal cases to be so important that they included it as one of the very few civil rights explicitly protected by the Constitution. The reaffirmation of the right to a jury trial in the Sixth Amendment stresses the late eighteenth-century view of the primary importance of the right to a jury trial. It is interesting, however, that the fundamental right to a jury trial that was so widely accepted at the time the Constitution was adopted was not applied by the Supreme Court in its interpretation of the due process clause of the Fourteenth Amendment until 1968.[20]

In *Duncan v. Louisiana* (1968), the Court finally ruled that the right to a jury trial was a fundamental principle of liberty and justice, and essential to a fair trial. The *Duncan* decision overruled prior decisions of the Supreme Court that had supported the authority of the states to dispense with jury trials in criminal cases. The decision to incorporate the right to a jury trial under the Fourteenth Amendment due process clause was not unanimous. Justice Harlan, joined by Justice Stewart, strongly dissented from the majority opinion. Considerations of federalism were paramount to the dissenting justices, who argued that the Supreme Court should not fasten on the states "federal notions of criminal justice."[21] The major point stressed by the dissenting justices was not that the right to a jury trial was unimportant, but that the states should be granted leeway in legislating their own criminal procedures to try cases falling within their jurisdictions. The dissenters particularly objected to the way in which the Supreme Court selec-

---

[19]*Chicago, Milwaukee and St. Paul Ry. Co. v. Minnesota*, 134 U.S. 418 (1890).
[20]*Duncan v. Louisiana*, 391 U.S. 145 (1968).
[21]Ibid., p. 173.

tively incorporated certain provisions of the Bill of Rights under the due process clause of the Fourteenth Amendment while excluding others. The Court had not conclusively proven, Harlan argued, that the right to a jury trial was any more or less "fundamental" than other provisions of the Bill of Rights that had not yet been incorporated.

The majority opinion in the *Duncan* case clearly signalled a new approach by the Supreme Court to the whole question of incorporating provisions of the Bill of Rights under the due process clause of the Fourteenth Amendment. The opinion itself, supporting the right to a jury trial, virtually completed the process of incorporating the procedural protections of the Bill of Rights under the Fourteenth Amendment. Moreover, the *Duncan* opinion firmly signalled that the Supreme Court was going to interpret the procedural protections afforded by the Fourteenth Amendment due process clause primarily in terms of the Bill of Rights, applying federal protections derived from the Bill of Rights to the states. The Court's approach was intended to establish consistency between federal and state jurisdictions in constitutionally guaranteed criminal procedures.

The jury trial provision of the Sixth Amendment, seemingly simple on its face, is in certain respects difficult to interpret. For example, what exactly constitutes the right to a "speedy" and "public" trial?

The Supreme Court squarely confronted the question of the right to a speedy trial in *Klopfer v. North Carolina* (1967). The appellant, a professor of zoology at Duke University, had been indicted by the State of North Carolina for criminal trespass after he had taken part in a sit-in demonstration at a Chapel Hill restaurant. Klopfer was tried after his indictment, but the jury failed to agree on a verdict and the judge declared a mistrial, which gave the state the opportunity to try the professor again or drop all charges against him. However, the state prosecutors were apparently unable to make up their minds on whether or not to proceed to a second trial, and after a year had passed the defendant demanded to be tried forthwith or have his case dismissed. The state court denied the professor's request to have action taken one way or another on his case and instead granted the state prosecutor's motion to place the indictment on an inactive status that would allow the state to prosecute the defendant at any future time. Klopfer claimed that his Sixth Amendment right to a speedy trial was violated by the North Carolina procedure, which, at the time, was allowed by thirty states. The defendant appealed to the North Carolina Supreme Court, which ruled against him, declaring that the right to a speedy trial did not compel the state to prosecute a defendant. Klopfer took his case to the Supreme Court, which reversed the North Carolina decision on the ground that it violated the speedy trial provision of the Sixth Amendment. Chief Justice Warren wrote the opinion for a unanimous Supreme Court, stating that the delay and uncertainty caused by the North Carolina procedure deprived the defendant of his life and liberty without due process of law that was guaranteed by the Fourteenth Amendment. "The pendency of the indictment," declared Warren, "may subject [the defendant] to public scorn and deprive him of employment, and almost certainly will force curtailment of his speech, associations, and participation in unpopular causes. By indefinitely prolonging this oppression, as well as the 'anxiety and concern accompanying public accusation,' the criminal procedure condoned in this case by the Supreme Court of North Carolina clearly denies the petitioner the right to a speedy trial which we hold is guaranteed to him by the Sixth Amendment of the Constitution of the United States."[22]

*Public Trial.* The Supreme Court has had more difficulty in interpreting the public trial requirement of the Sixth Amendment than in defining the right to a speedy trial. The Burger Court in particular has been unable to agree on exactly what constitutes the right to a public trial. Under certain circumstances the right to a public trial is clear and unequivocal: The Court has held, for example, that a person is deprived of the right where a criminal trial is conducted by a court that is entirely closed to the public.[23]

Undoubtedly the most difficult question confronting the Court with regard to the Sixth Amendment's right to a public trial concerns the extent to which public trials may be curtailed in the interests and at the request of criminal defendants themselves, on the grounds that prejudicial press accounts would deny them their Sixth Amendment right to trial by an impartial jury. Not only does the defendant have the right to a fair trial under the Sixth Amendment, but the state, acting as prosecutor, also has an interest in guaranteeing criminal defendants fair trials.

The Sixth Amendment's guarantee of a fair public trial may conflict with the freedom of the press guaranteed by the First Amendment. The right of the press to cover criminal trials is not absolute, and may be curtailed in the interest of justice. Courts must balance the rights of defendants against the First Amendment freedom of the press in cases where the right of the press to cover a criminal trial freely is challenged. In 1966 the Supreme Court reversed the murder conviction of Dr. Sam Sheppard, who had been accused of killing his wife, on the ground that the media coverage of the trial created an atmosphere of severe prejudice to the defendant.[24] Justice Clark wrote

---

[22]*Klopfer v. North Carolina*, 386 U.S. 213, 222 (1967).
[23]See *In re Oliver*, 333 U.S. 257 (1948). But a defendant's right to a public trial is not absolute and may be curtailed by the state for a number of compelling reasons, one of which is the protection of witnesses, including young witnesses in rape cases, and undercover agents.
[24]*Sheppard v. Maxwell*, 384 U.S. 333 (1966).

the opinion of the Court reversing the conviction, pointing out that from "the cases coming here we note that unfair and prejudicial news comment on pending trials has become increasingly prevalent. Due process requires that the accused receive a trial by an impartial jury free from outside influences. Given the pervasiveness of modern communications and the difficulty of effacing prejudicial publicity from the minds of the jurors, the trial courts must take strong measures to insure that the balance is never weighed against the accused."[25] Clark concluded that trial judges must take all necessary measures to prevent an atmosphere of prejudice to criminal defendants. The *Sheppard* decision did not hold that trial judges should censor press accounts of criminal trials, but merely that they should take necessary action to deter the media from prejudicing the jury. The courts stressed in the *Sheppard* case that trial judges have a wide range of options available to them to prevent the media from undermining fair trials without having to resort to outright censorship.

The Burger Court confronted the question of the constitutionality of direct trial court censorship of the press in *Nebraska Press Association* v. *Stuart* in 1976. The case involved a particularly brutal crime in which six members of a family were murdered in cold blood. The crime attracted widespread media coverage that resulted in pretrial publicity that was prejudicial to the defendant. The trial court judge issued an order that prohibited public release of any testimony given or evidence produced at the preliminary hearing of the murder case. The Nebraska Press Association challenged the order in the higher state courts, but the order was sustained with certain modifications that listed the pretrial events allowed to be reported. The final restrictive order detailing exactly what the press could and could not report from the pretrial hearing was a clear example of prior censorship of the press. On appeal to the Supreme Court, the order was overturned. Chief Justice Burger wrote the majority opinion for the court in the *Nebraska Press Association* case, stressing that since the Nebraska trial court had not invoked closure at the outset of the pretrial proceedings the pretrial hearing was open to the public and to the press, making the restrictive order one of prior censorship of what could be reported. Nothing proscribed the press, Burger declared, from reporting events that transpire in the courtroom.

There was an implication in Chief Justice Burger's opinion that under certain circumstances the Supreme Court might uphold the closure of pretrial proceedings in order to ensure justice to a criminal defendant. The Court did not confront the question of closure in the *Nebraska Press Association* case, however, and the issue of the extent to which trial judges

[25]Ibid., p. 351.

could close pretrial proceedings remained open. While the majority opinion suggested that the closure of pretrial proceedings might under certain circumstances be justifiable, Justices White, Brennan, and Stevens wrote separate concurring opinions that stressed their view that prior censorship of the press is not justified under any circumstances. The three concurring justices agreed that trial judges have the authority to take adequate measures to deal with prejudicial press accounts of criminal trials without having to resort to the extreme measure of censorship of the press. Such measures might include warning newspapers to check the accuracy of their accounts or suggesting to the media that it not publish or broadcast prejudicial stories and material that was not introduced during the hearing. Disobedience of judicial warnings not to engage in out-of-court statements prejudicial to defendants may be punishable as contempt if it is found that the actions of the media constitute a clear and present danger to the conduct of a fair trial. Judicial warnings and citations for contempt may have an adverse effect upon media coverage of trials, but they do not constitute direct censorship of the press.

The constitutionality of the closure of a pretrial criminal proceeding came before the Court in *Gannett Company v. DePasquale* in 1979. Justice Stewart delivered the opinion of the Court, declaring that the public does not have an independent constitutional right to insist upon access to a pretrial judicial proceeding when the accused, the prosecutor, and the trial judge all have agreed to the closure of that proceeding in order to ensure a fair trial. The issue, Stewart stated, "is whether members of the public have an enforceable right to a public trial that can be asserted independently of the parties in the litigation."[26] Stewart pointed out that while there is a strong societal interest in public trials, "there is a strong societal interest in other constitutional guarantees extended to the accused as well. The public, for example, has a definite and concrete interest in seeing that justice is swiftly and fairly administered. . . . Similarly, the public has an interest in having a criminal case heard by a jury, an interest distinct from the defendant's interest in being tried by a jury of his peers."[27] He went on to point out, however, that the public interest in the constitutional guarantees of the Sixth Amendment does not give the public a constitutional right to enforce those guarantees. Moreover, under the Sixth Amendment, the public does not have a constitutional right to attend a criminal trial, although there is a common law rule of open proceedings that "permits and even presumes open trial as a norm."[28] "But," continued Stewart, "even if the Sixth and Fourteenth

[26]*Gannett Company v. DePasquale*, 443 U.S. 368, 382–83 (1979).
[27]Ibid., p. 383.
[28]Ibid., p. 385.

Amendments could properly be viewed as embodying the common law right of the public to attend criminal trials, it would not necessarily follow that the petitioner would have a right of access under the circumstances of this case. For there exists no persuasive evidence that at common law members of the public have any right to attend *pretrial* proceedings; indeed, there is substantial evidence to the contrary."[29]

The *Gannett Company* decision was a highly controversial one, supported by only five justices, three of whom — Burger, Powell, and Rehnquist — felt compelled to write separate concurring opinions of their own because they did not fully agree with the reasoning of Justice Stewart, who had delivered the opinion of the Court. Chief Justice Burger emphasized that the Court's opinion applied only to pretrial processes, a point that he did not feel was entirely clear in Stewart's opinion. Powell stressed the point that excluding all members of the press from the courtroom, which was done by the lower trial court in the *Gannett Company* case, "differs substantially from the 'gag order' at issue in *Nebraska Press*, as the latter involved a classic prior restraint."[30] Justice Rehnquist would have gone further than his colleagues in the majority in support of the authority of trial courts to exclude the press. Rehnquist stated that "the trial court is not required by the Sixth Amendment to advance any reason whatsoever for declining to open a pretrial hearing or trial to the public."[31]

Justice Blackmun, joined by Justices Brennan, White, and Marshall, wrote a vigorous dissenting opinion in the *Gannett Company* case. He contended that the Sixth and Fourteenth Amendments guarantee the right to a public trial not only to the accused but also to the public. The Sixth Amendment, although on its face securing the right to a public trial only to the accused, does not "permit the inference that the accused may compel a private proceeding simply by waiving the right" to a public trial.[32] Blackmun did not suggest that the Sixth Amendment imposes an absolute requirement that courts be open at all times; however, trial courts should impose rigid standards to justify the closure of criminal proceedings. The standards that Blackmun would have applied required the accused to demonstrate to the satisfaction of the trial judge that irreparable damage to the defense would result from the proceedings being open, and moreover to support the conclusion that alternatives to closure would not adequately protect the defendant's right to a fair trial. Finally, Blackmun would have required the

[29]Ibid. Emphasis added.
[30]Ibid., p. 399.
[31]Ibid., p. 404.
[32]Ibid., p. 418.

accused to demonstrate that closure would be effective in protecting against the perceived harm.[33]

The *Gannett Company* decision was widely perceived by the press to constitute a significant threat to its right of access to criminal trials. The pessimistic view of the press was supported by the actions of trial judges throughout the country, who began to issue closure orders in pretrial and even trial proceedings that would never have been given before the *Gannett Company* decision. Chief Justice Burger went to great lengths to explain what he perceived to be the limited nature of the decision, emphasizing that it pertained only to pretrial and not to trial hearings.

The Sixth Amendment's provision for a public trial by an impartial jury requires the trial court not only to conduct criminal proceedings in a non-prejudicial atmosphere, but also to guarantee a jury that is not selected on the basis of gender discrimination. In the 1975 case of *Taylor* v. *Louisiana*, the Supreme Court invalidated a state jury selection system that excluded women, holding that women are "sufficiently numerous and distinct from men and . . . if they are systematically eliminated from jury panels, the Sixth Amendment's fair cross-section requirement cannot be satisfied."[34] A century earlier the Supreme Court had used the equal protection clause of the Fourteenth Amendment to proscribe racial discrimination in jury selection by invalidating a state law that limited eligibility for juries to white males who were twenty-one years of age or older.[35] Generally, where state action is concerned, the equal protection clause has been relied on more often than the Sixth Amendment to prevent discrimination in the selection of juries. In addition to gender and race, nationality and religion are also excluded as criteria for jury selection.

*Local Juries.* After guaranteeing the right to a speedy and public trial by an impartial jury, the Sixth Amendment requires that the trial take place in and the jury be drawn from the state and district where the crime was committed. Like many of the provisions of the Bill of Rights, this part of the Sixth Amendment was included because of the history of dissatisfaction among the colonists with the practices of George III, who had forced colonists accused of committing crimes in America to stand trial in England. The framers of the Bill of Rights were worried that the new national government might be tempted to use the same practice by removing individuals accused of crimes in the states to a separate national jurisdiction. The Sixth Amendment's provision for conducting criminal trials in the district where the

[33]Ibid., pp. 441–42.
[34]*Taylor* v. *Louisiana*, 419 U.S. 522, 531 (1975).
[35]*Shroeder* v. *West Virginia*, 100 U.S. 303 (1880). Contrast *Virginia* v. *Rives*, 100 U.S. 339

crime was committed does not prevent a defendant from seeking to have the trial moved on the ground that it would be impossible to have a fair trial in that community.

*Additional Procedural Rights.* Having prescribed the right to a speedy and public trial as well as the setting of criminal proceedings, the Sixth Amendment grants certain procedural rights to criminal defendants, providing that in all criminal prosecutions the accused shall enjoy the right

to be informed of the nature and cause of the accusation; to be confronted with the witnesses against him; to have compulsory process for obtaining witnesses in his favor, and to have the assistance of counsel for his defence.

The procedural protections afforded to criminal defendants by the concluding clauses of the Sixth Amendment were, in the eighteenth century, considered in the broadest sense to be fundamental to due process of law. Like all of the provisions of the Bill of Rights, however, they were originally intended only to apply within federal jurisdiction. And, as was the case with other procedural protections afforded by the Bill of Rights, the safeguards of the Sixth Amendment were listed separately from the due process clause of the Fifth Amendment. Due process under the Fourteenth Amendment could also be considered separately from the Bill of Rights. According to numerous Supreme Court rulings after 1868, due process in the generic sense did not automatically include the procedural safeguards of the Bill of Rights. The Warren Court, however, in addition to incorporating the right to a speedy and public jury trial under the due process clause of the Fourteenth Amendment, added the remaining procedural protections of the Sixth Amendment as well. In the famous case of *Gideon* v. *Wainwright* in 1963, the Court unequivocally extended the right to counsel in *all* criminal cases to the states under the Fourteenth Amendment due process clause; in 1965 the Court incorporated the right to confrontation of adverse witnesses;[36] and in 1967 it extended the right of accused persons to obtain witnesses in their favor to the states.[37]

The Sixth Amendment rights given to criminal defendants to know the charges against them, to be confronted with adverse witnesses, to have the opportunity to obtain favorable witnesses, and to have the assistance of counsel are essential to making the machinery of justice work. There is a presumption of the innocence of the accused in criminal trials, and defen-

(1880), holding that the mere absence of blacks from a jury did not on its face constitute a denial of equal protection under the Fourteenth Amendment.
[36]*Pointer* v. *Texas*, 380 U.S. 400 (1965).
[37]*Washington* v. *Texas*, 388 U.S. 14 (1967).

dants are given every opportunity to prove their innocence. Criminal proceedings are fundamentally designed to determine accurately the facts of individual cases, facts that pertain to the actions of the accused and to other parties indirectly involved in the case as well.

### The Seventh Amendment: Trial by Jury in Common Law Cases

The Seventh Amendment provides that

In Suits at common law, where the value in controversy shall exceed twenty dollars, the right of trial by jury shall be preserved, and no fact tried by a jury, shall be otherwise reexamined in any Court of the United States, than according to the rules of the common law.

The Seventh Amendment remains one of the few parts of the Bill of Rights that has not been incorporated under the due process clause of the Fourteenth Amendment as a fundamental right. It applies to *civil* suits at common law, not to suits arising out of statutory law. While the Seventh Amendment gives parties to civil common law suits the right to trial by jury where the value of the controversies exceeds twenty dollars, a jury may be waived with the consent of both parties.

### The Eighth Amendment: Prohibition of Excessive Bail, Fines, and Cruel and Unusual Punishments

The Eighth Amendment provides that

Excessive bail shall not be required, nor excessive fines imposed, nor cruel and unusual punishments inflicted.

The excessive bail and fine safeguards of the Eighth Amendment have been applied by the Supreme Court at the federal level to prevent setting of bail at a figure higher than is reasonable to ensure the presence of a defendant at his or her trial. In determining the reasonableness of bail a court may take into account, for example, such considerations as the reputation of the offender and his or her ability to pay. Bail may be denied for some crimes, such as those for which the penalty is death. Moreover, bail may be denied if the court considers that under no circumstances will it ensure the presence of the accused at trial. Bail may also be denied to persons the courts feel will commit other crimes pending their trials. While the excessive bail provision applies to federal jurisdiction, it has not been extended to the states under the due process clause of the Fourteenth Amendment.

The Eighth Amendment prohibition upon excessive fines has rarely raised a controversy in the courts. The Supreme Court has held that the failure to pay a fine due to indigency cannot be used as a reason for sentencing a defendant to prison.[38] Moreover, the Court has ruled that indigents cannot be detained for failure to pay a fine for an offense that is not otherwise punishable by imprisonment.[39]

By far the most important provison of the Eighth Amendment is its prohibition upon the infliction of cruel and unusual punishments. This prohibition generally pertains to the sentencing of criminal offenders and to punishments suffered after incarceration.[40]

The framers of the Eighth Amendment inserted the cruel and unusual punishment prohibition to ban punishments such as branding and whipping, which still existed in certain parts of the country at the time the Bill of Rights was adopted. It was clearly the intent of the framers of the amendment to prevent torture and other forms of "barbarous" punishment, but they did not intend to abolish what was obviously the most extreme example of a "cruel" punishment — capital punishment. Capital punishment was not "unusual" at the time the Eighth Amendment was framed, and was an accepted punishment in the states for murder, rape, and other crimes as well. In an early death penalty case, Justice Black wrote a concurring opinion expressing his view of the intent of the Eighth Amendment with regard to capital punishment:

The Eighth Amendment forbids "cruel and unusual punishments." In my view, these words cannot be read to outlaw capital punishment because that penalty was in common use and authorized by law here and in the countries from which our ancestors came at the time the amendment was adopted. . . . Although some people have urged that this Court should amend the Constitution by interpretation to keep it abreast of modern ideas, I have never believed that lifetime judges in our system have any such legislative power.[41]

Justice Black's view that the Eighth Amendment does not apply to capital punishment was accepted by the Court until its historic decision in *Furman*

---

[38]*Williams v. Illinois*, 399 U.S. 235 (1970).
[39]*Tate v. Short*, 401 U.S. 395 (1971).
[40]In *Ingraham v. Wright*, 430 U.S. 651 (1977), a majority opinion by Justice Powell joined by Justices Burger, Stewart, Blackmun, and Rehnquist specifically stated that the Eighth Amendment applied only to those convicted of a crime and did not cover the disciplinary corporal punishment of public school children; however, Justice White, joined by Brennan, Marshall, and Stevens, dissented, declaring that the Eighth Amendment prohibition upon cruel and unusual punishment should not be restricted to those convicted of crimes but should prohibit all barbaric punishments regardless of the nature of the offense for which the punishment was given. The dissenters would have applied the Eighth Amendment to the disciplinary spanking of schoolchildren.
[41]*McGautha v. California*, 402 U.S. 183, 226 (1971).

v. *Georgia* in 1972. The *Furman* case, in which the petitioner had been convicted of murder during a burglary and sentenced to death, was joined with two other cases, one in Georgia and the other in Texas, in which the defendants had been convicted of rape and sentenced to death. All of the defendants were black, and the women in the rape cases were white.

The Supreme Court invalidated the death sentences in the *Furman* and related cases, but the grounds for invalidation varied and each of the majority justices wrote a separate opinion. The dissenters were also unable to agree on the constitutionality of the death penalty, and they too wrote separate opinions expressing their views.

Justice Douglas, one of the five justices in the majority that invalidated the death penalty, stated that it was cruel and unusual punishment to apply the death penalty selectively to minorities as was the case in the states involved in the *Furman* case. Justice Brennan declared that the cruel and unusual punishment provision of the Eighth Amendment was not limited to torture and other forms of punishment that were considered cruel and unusual at the time the amendment was adopted. Arbitrarily subjecting persons to capital punishment — which had not been proven to serve any penal purpose — was, concluded Brennan, an affront to human dignity that violated the Eighth Amendment. Justice Stewart agreed with his colleagues in the majority that the capricious way in which the death penalty was imposed made it cruel and unusual punishment. Justice White voted to invalidate the death penalty because in the states involved in the *Furman* and related cases, Georgia and Texas, the death penalty had been so infrequently used that it could not be demonstrated to serve the purpose of criminal justice. Finally, Justice Marshall flatly stated that the death penalty violated the Eighth Amendment because it was excessive, unnecessary, and morally unacceptable.

Chief Justice Burger led the four dissenting justices, whose separate opinions sounded a strong tone of judicial self-restraint. Joining Burger in dissent were Justices Blackmun, Powell, and Rehnquist, all of whom argued that regardless of whether or not members of the Court considered the death penalty to be personally distasteful, it was not the proper role of the Supreme Court to prevent the states from imposing the death penalty, which clearly was not considered to be cruel or unusual at the time the Eighth Amendment was adopted. They concluded that the death penalty was no more cruel in the twentieth century than it had been at the time the Eighth Amendment was adopted; therefore, there was no constitutional justification for overturning the use of the death penalty in the states.

In addition to finding the capricious imposition of the death penalty a violation of the Eighth Amendment, the Court has found other punishments to be impermissibly cruel and unusual. Long before the *Furman* case in

1972, the Court held in a bizarre case that it was cruel and unusual punishment to subject a person to the process of execution a second time, after the first execution failed because of technical difficulties.[42] In other cases not related to the death penalty, the Court has invalidated on Eighth Amendment grounds a state law making narcotic addiction a crime punishable by a short term in jail[43] and overturned a congressional statute that prescribed the loss of citizenship as part of the punishment for members of the armed forces who had been convicted and dishonorably discharged for desertion during wartime.[44] The Court has also reviewed prison conditions and practices to determine whether or not they are in conformity with judicial standards required under the Eighth Amendment. For example, the Court has ruled that the deliberate indifference of prison officials to the serious medical needs of a prisoner is cruel and unusual punishment.[45]

### The Ninth Amendment: Rights Retained by the People

The Ninth Amendment was added to the Bill of Rights to answer one of the most important objections that was raised during the debate over the inclusion of a separate Bill of Rights in the Constitution. One of the principal arguments of Alexander Hamilton and others who opposed a separate Bill of Rights was that it would imply the authority of the national government to abridge rights that were not explicitly enumerated in a Bill of Rights. The Ninth Amendment expressly bars such an inference:

The enumeration in the Constitution, of certain rights, shall not be construed to deny or disparage others retained by the people.

The Ninth Amendment was based on the concepts, widely held in the eighteenth century, of natural law and natural rights. Thomas Jefferson articulated in the Declaration of Independence the general philosophy that all men "are endowed by their Creator with certain inalienable rights." Jefferson listed life, liberty, and the pursuit of happiness as the most fundamental of natural rights, among others that went far beyond those he had explicitly put into the Declaration of Independence. Jefferson's views reflected those of most eighteenth-century Americans, who assumed the existence of natural rights that were conferred by the "laws of nature and of nature's God"

---

[42]*Louisiana ex rel Francis v. Resweber, Sherf et al.,* 329 U.S. 459 (1947) held that it was cruel and unusual punishment to reschedule a convicted murderer for electrocution after the first attempt had failed because the apparatus malfunctioned and did not deliver sufficient electric current to result in death.
[43]*Robinson v. California,* 370 U.S. 660 (1962).
[44]*Trop v. Dulles,* 356 U.S. 86 (1958).
[45]*Estelle v. Gamble,* 429 U.S. 97 (1976).

and not by government. Jefferson and others considered a separate Bill of Rights important simply to reinforce the protection of citizens against governmental intrusion into clearly important areas of civil liberties and civil rights. But the framers of the Bill of Rights did not intend that its enumeration would be inclusive of all natural rights and liberties, a point that was made explicit by the Ninth Amendment.

The concepts of natural law and natural rights, accepted at the time the Constitution and the Bill of Rights were framed and adopted, pose difficulties for those who later interpret and implement law. Defining the content of natural law and the natural rights derived from it is necessarily a highly subjective process. The framers of the Constitution apparently did not want to grapple with the issue of enumerating the rights and liberties of citizens apart from the very few rights they included in the main body of the Constitution, on which there was no disagreement. James Madison and his colleagues in the first Congress recognized that the Bill of Rights was only a partial listing of the fundamental rights and liberties of citizens.

The Supreme Court has periodically recognized that there is a universe of rights that extends beyond the explicit provisions of the Bill of Rights. The due process clause of the Fourteenth Amendment in particular has been used not only to incorporate most of the provisions of the Bill of Rights, but also, in several important cases, to extend the right of privacy, a right that was not enumerated in the Bill of Rights. The right of privacy was defended in *Griswold* v. *Connecticut* (1965), in which the Court ruled that a Connecticut statute that made it a criminal act to prescribe or even to use birth control devices was an unconstitutional invasion of personal privacy. Justice William O. Douglas wrote the majority opinion in the *Griswold* case, citing the Ninth Amendment as justification for extending rights to citizens that were not part of the Bill of Rights. Douglas stated that the

guarantees in the Bill of Rights have penumbras, formed by emanations from those guarantees that help give them life and substance.... Various guarantees create zones of privacy. The right of association contained in the penumbra of the First Amendment is one.... The Third Amendment in its prohibition against the quartering of soldiers "in any house" in time of peace without the consent of the owner is another facet of that privacy. The Fourth Amendment explicitly affirms the "right of the people to be secure in their persons, houses, papers, and effects, against unreasonable searches and seizures." The Fifth Amendment in its self-incrimination clause enables the citizen to create a zone of privacy which government may not force him to surrender to his detriment.[46]

[46]*Griswold v. Connecticut*, 381 U.S. 479, 484 (1965).

In the *Griswold* case the Court used the due process clause of the Fourteenth Amendment to incorporate a new right of privacy that had never before been explicitly upheld against intrusion by the states.

Justice Goldberg emphasized the importance of the Ninth Amendment in granting the Court freedom to go beyond the Bill of Rights in defining the protections afforded to citizens:

The Ninth Amendment to the Constitution may be regarded by some as a recent discovery and may be forgotten by others, but since 1791 it has been part of the Constitution which we are sworn to uphold. To hold that a right so basic and fundamental and so deep-rooted in our society as the right of privacy in marriage may be infringed because that right is not guaranteed in so many words by the first eight amendments to the Constitution is to ignore the Ninth Amendment and to give it no effect whatsoever. Moreover, a judicial construction that this fundamental right is not protected by the Constitution because it is not mentioned in explicit terms by one of the first eight amendments or elsewhere in the Constitution, would violate the Ninth Amendment, which specifically states that "The enumeration in the Constitution, of certain rights, shall not be construed to deny or disparage others retained by the people."[47]

The *Griswold* case was a launching ground for a major debate in constitutional law regarding the authority of the Supreme Court to go beyond the Bill of Rights in defining the due process clause of the Fourteenth Amendment. Justice Black, dissenting, became the leading spokesman for the point of view that the Court should limit itself to upholding only those rights that were explicitly enumerated in the Bill of Rights. Black took the historically questionable position that the Ninth Amendment was "intended to limit the federal government to the powers granted expressly or by necessary implication."[48] The Ninth Amendment, concluded Black, should not be used in combination with the due process clause of the Fourteenth Amendment to limit state action beyond the constraints expressly stated in the Bill of Rights.[49]

The Ninth Amendment was again used by some of the justices of the Supreme Court as a basis for supporting the interventionist approach of the Court in recognizing a right to personal privacy that included, within limits,

[47]Ibid., pp. 491–92.
[48]Ibid., p. 520.
[49]Black had consistently taken the position that the due process clause of the Fourteenth Amendment fully incorporated the provisions of the Bill of Rights. In the context of the 1940s and 1950s Black's position — in contrast to that of Justice Frankfurter, for example — was considered to be one of judicial intervention. Frankfurter, unlike Black, favored only selective incorporation of certain provisions of the Bill of Rights as part of due process under the Fourteenth Amendment.

the right to abortion. Justice Blackmun's opinion for the Court in *Roe* v. *Wade* stated that the right of privacy, "whether it be founded in the Fourteenth Amendment's concept of personal liberty and restrictions upon state action, as we feel it is, or as the district court determined in the Ninth Amendment's reservation of rights to the people, is broad enough to encompass a woman's decision whether or not to terminate her pregnancy."[50] Justice Blackmun was pointing out that the Ninth Amendment could be used as a basis for the Court's decision, although the majority of justices in the *Roe* case held that the abortion statutes under consideration invaded the liberty that was protected by the due process clause of the Fourteenth Amendment. In a concurring opinion, Justice Douglas noted that the Ninth Amendment "obviously does not create federally enforceable rights. . . . But a catalog of these rights includes customary, traditional, and time-honored rights, amenities, privileges, and immunities that come within the sweep of 'the blessings of liberty' mentioned in the Preamble to the Constitution. Many of them, in my view, come within the meaning of the term 'liberty' as used in the Fourteenth Amendment."[51]

### The Tenth Amendment: The Reserved Powers of the States

The Tenth Amendment was added to the Bill of Rights to assuage the fears of the advocates of states' rights. The amendment provides that

The powers not delegated to the United States by the Constitution, nor prohibited by it to the States, are reserved to the States respectively, or the people.

The Tenth Amendment adds nothing to the intent of the framers of the Constitution, which clearly was to establish a national government with enumerated and implied powers while reserving to the states all powers that were not delegated to the national government. The Constitution, however, did not explicitly provide a reserved powers clause guaranteeing to state governments all those powers not delegated to the national government. Reassurances by proponents of the Constitution during the ratification campaign, stating that the new national government would be limited to those powers defined in the Constitution, were not accepted by advocates of states' rights and by those fearful of an overbearing national government. Alexander Hamilton, for example, pointed out that the "powers delegated by the proposed constitution to the federal government are few and defined. Those which are to remain in the state governments are numerous and in-

---

[50]*Roe v. Wade*, 410 U.S. 113, 153 (1973).
[51]Ibid., pp. 210–11.

definite." Hamilton, perhaps the strongest nationalist of the time, was nevertheless willing to declare unequivocally that "the powers reserved to the several states would extend to all the objects which, in the ordinary course of affairs, concern the lives, liberties, and properties of the people, and the internal order, improvement, and prosperity of the states."[52]

The proponents of states' rights, during the debate over the Tenth Amendment, attempted to limit more explicitly the authority of the national government by restricting its powers to those "expressly" delegated by the Constitution. The nationalists, led by Madison, defeated the end-run attempt by the champions of states' rights in the first Congress, for they recognized, as they had during the Constitutional Convention itself and the ratification campaign, that a viable national government had to be given the flexibility to employ whatever means were necessary and proper for the implementation of its enumerated powers.

While the Tenth Amendment was a redundant addition to the Constitution, it was later to be cited from time to time by the Supreme Court and by the advocates of states' rights as an important limitation on the authority of the national government. In the early twentieth century the Court used the Tenth Amendment to support the doctrine of dual federalism, which held that the national government could not use its authority under Article I to invade the reserved powers of the states. For example, an attempt by Congress in 1916 to regulate the conditions of child labor in the states by using its commerce power to prevent the shipment in interstate commerce of goods produced by children under proscribed conditions was invalidated by the Court in *Hammer v. Dagenhart* in 1918. The Court simply held that control over the conditions of production was a matter of local concern and fell within the sphere of the reserved police powers of the states that could not be invaded by the national government.[53] The doctrine of dual federalism survived until the middle of Franklin D. Roosevelt's second term. The Court had earlier frustrated many of the major programs of the New Deal and in some cases used the Tenth Amendment as the basis for its decisions. In 1936 the Court overturned a major piece of New Deal legislation regulating the conditions of agricultural production on the grounds that the power to regulate agriculture was reserved to the states.[54]

The Court's abandonment of the doctrine of dual federalism after 1937 was a return to the nationalist position on the scope of federal power that had been taken by Chief Justice John Marshall at the outset of the nineteenth century. In a number of wide-ranging opinions, Marshall rejected the

[52]*The Federalist,* No. 45.
[53]*Hammer v. Dagenhart,* 247 U.S. 251 (1918).
[54]*United States v. Butler,* 297 U.S. 1 (1936).

argument made by the proponents of states' rights that the Tenth Amendment limited the authority of the national government to powers that had been expressly enumerated in the Constitution. In *McCulloch* v. *Maryland* (1819) and in *Gibbons* v. *Ogden* (1824), he argued that Congress has the authority not only to employ whatever means it considers necessary to implement its enumerated powers, but also to exercise exclusive jurisdiction in cases of conflict between federal and state laws. The abandonment by the Supreme Court of the doctrine of dual federalism in 1937 was accompanied by a return to the firm nationalistic tone of the opinions of the Marshall Court.

## The Process of Nationalization of the Bill of Rights

The preceding overview of the Bill of Rights lists the dates for the inclusion of particular rights under the due process clause of the Fourteenth Amendment, making them applicable to state action. Most of these provisions were not finally incorporated under the Fourteenth Amendment until the end of the Warren Court era in 1968. The process of incorporation was a gradual one that reflected shifting views on the Supreme Court and changing responses to what were considered by many justices to be conditions in the states requiring judicial intervention rather than self-restraint.

### Applying the Bill of Rights Under the Due Process Clause

The process of nationalization involved the Court in a delicate and often controversial process of applying its own values in defining the content of the due process clause of the Fourteenth Amendment. The intent of the congressional framers of the Fourteenth Amendment was very likely to make the entire Bill of Rights applicable to the states under the amendment's privileges and immunities clause, which provided that no state "shall make or enforce any law which shall abridge the privileges or immunities of citizens of the United States."[55] Five years after the adoption of the Fourteenth Amendment in 1868, however, the Supreme Court in the historic *Slaughterhouse Cases* ruled that the amendment's privileges and immunities clause did not in any way alter the constitutional balance between the national

---

[55]The Radical Republicans in Congress who authored and sponsored the Fourteenth Amendment stated explicitly that the privileges and immunities clause incorporated the entire Bill of Rights as a limitation upon the states. Even those in Congress who opposed the Fourteenth Amendment agreed that its privileges and immunities clause would have the effect of nationalizing the Bill of Rights. Historical evidence, however, does not clearly establish that the state legislatures that adopted the amendment agreed that it would nationalize the Bill of Rights.

government and the states that had existed before the amendment was adopted.[56] The "privileges and immunities" of citizens of the United States, the Court held, consisted of the same privileges and immunities that had originally been incorporated into the Constitution, such as the privilege to possess property. The Court concluded that the rights of citizens insofar as they were exclusively within state jurisdictions were determined solely by state constitutions and laws. The effect of the *Slaughterhouse* opinion was to establish two classes of citizens: those of the United States on the one hand and those of the states on the other. The rights and obligations of each class of citizen were determined, respectively, by the federal Constitution and laws and by state constitutions and laws.

The *Slaughterhouse* decision essentially struck the privileges and immunities clause from the Fourteenth Amendment as a viable weapon for judicial protection of civil liberties and rights. When the Court was challenged in the twentieth century to extend the protection of the Bill of Rights to the states, the means it had for doing this was the due process clause of the Fourteenth Amendment, unless it chose explicitly to overrule the *Slaughterhouse* decision and resurrect the privileges and immunities clause. The Court found the due process clause to be easily adaptable to applying the Bill of Rights within state jurisdictions; moreover, by using the admittedly vague concept of due process the Court had discretion to impose its own interpretation of exactly what constituted Fourteenth Amendment due process. The due process clause readily accommodated the ebb and flow of judicial opinion concerning how far the standards of the Bill of Rights should apply to the states (see Figure 2.1).

The process of incorporation of most of the provisions of the Bill of Rights was a long and often tortuous one. In deciding whether or not to incorporate certain provisions under due process, the Court was essentially engaging in substantive due process review. That is, the Court frequently injected its own values into its definitions of what constituted "liberty," just as it had in determining under what circumstances "property" could be regulated under the due process clause. For example, when the Court decided in *Gitlow* v. *New York* that the "liberty" of the Fourteenth Amendment incorporated the First Amendment guarantee of freedom of speech and of the press, it was simply applying its own notions of what the Fourteenth Amendment due process clause should protect. Moreover, the Court's method of giving procedural substance to the due process clause was as subjective as its formula for determining liberty and property rights.

In the first half of the twentieth century the Court declared that its standard for determining what freedoms and rights were to be included under

---

[56]*Slaughterhouse Cases*, 16 Wallace 36 (1873).

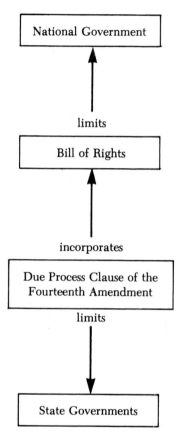

**Figure 2.1.** *The Application of the Bill of Rights. The Bill of Rights limits state action only through the due process clause of the Fourteenth Amendment.*

the due process clause was whether or not a freedom or right was fundamental to the protection of liberty and justice, historical, and "implicit in the concept of ordered liberty." The standard for applying due process that the Court began to develop as early as 1908, in *Twining* v. *New Jersey,* at first resulted only in a highly selective process of incorporation of the Bill of Rights.[57] By the time of the benchmark case of *Palko* v. *Connecticut* in 1937, in which Justice Cardozo spelled out the selective incorporation approach that had become and was to remain the basis of interpreting the due process clause by a majority of justices, only a few of the safeguards of the Bill of Rights had been incorporated.[58] These included all the freedoms of

[57] *Twining* v. *New Jersey,* 211 U.S. 78 (1908).
[58] *Palko* v. *Connecticut,* 302 U.S. 319 (1937).

the First Amendment, with the exception of the right of petition; the eminent domain safeguards of the Fifth Amendment; a watered down right to counsel drawn from the Sixth Amendment that applied only to capital cases; and a general right to a fair trial based on the Seventh and Eighth Amendments, but not fully applying their provisions. The long process of incorporating most of the remainder of the Bill of Rights was finally completed in 1968.

During the incorporation process there were frequently sharp disagreements on the Court regarding the proper formula to be used in defining Fourteenth Amendment due process. The selective incorporation approach, articulated by Justice Cardozo in the *Palko* opinion, was the most widely accepted and required that the definition of the various components of the Fourteenth Amendment due process clause be drawn explicitly from the provisions of the Bill of Rights. Usually this meant that the incorporation of a provision of the Bill of Rights would make it applicable to the states in the same way that it applied in federal jurisdiction. The incorporation of the right to privacy under due process in the *Griswold* decision in 1965 added an important new dimension to the selective incorporation formula under which the Court expressed its willingness to go beyond the Bill of Rights in defining due process. This approach has been described as "selective incorporation *plus*."[59]

A more flexible and subjective approach to defining due process than resulted from selective incorporation was advocated by Justice Felix Frankfurter and a minority of the Court as the Bill of Rights was gradually being nationalized.[60] The Frankfurter approach has often been referred to as one of "natural law," under which due process was defined on the basis of the same general standards used in selective incorporation — namely, the fundamental, historical, and essential nature of a freedom or right. The Bill of Rights would not itself be used as the major reference point in the process of definition. Under the Frankfurter method, a right or freedom would be incorporated under the Fourteenth Amendment not because it was in the Bill of Rights, but because regardless of the Bill of Rights it could be considered of a fundamental nature.[61]

---

[59] Henry J. Abraham, *Freedom and the Court*, 3rd ed. (New York: Oxford University Press, 1977), pp. 97, 100–102.

[60] Ibid., pp. 97–99.

[61] An excellent and interesting example of the Frankfurter approach may be found in *Rochin v. California*, 342 U.S. 165 (1952), in which Frankfurter wrote the Court's opinion holding that stomach-pumping to produce evidence for a criminal trial was a violation of due process because the conduct "shocks the conscience," and offends even "hardened sensibilities." The methods were "too close to the rack and the screw to permit of constitutional differentiation."

Another minority approach to defining Fourteenth Amendment due process was espoused by Justice Black, who argued that it was the clear intent of the framers of the Fourteenth Amendment to apply the Bill of Rights to the states and that therefore all the provisions of the Bill of Rights should be incorporated under the due process clause. Black forcefully argued against the position that more freedoms and rights than were explicitly included in the Bill of Rights could be extended to the states under the rubric of due process. His dissent in the *Griswold* case argued that since there was no express right to privacy in the Bill of Rights, the Connecticut birth control law — which Black considered to be "uncommonly silly" — could not be invalidated on the ground that it violated a right of personal privacy that was protected by due process of law.

The essential completion of the incorporation of the Bill of Rights by the end of the Warren Court era in 1968 did not finally resolve controversy over the meaning of due process within and without the Court. In the middle decades of the twentieth century, federalist considerations were an important basis for judicial self-restraint in limiting the extension of the protections afforded citizens at the national level to the states. The Warren Court's adoption of the incorporation-plus approach in the *Griswold* case raised the possibility of the Court's becoming a super legislature over the states in important areas of public policy. The Court's decision to invalidate state abortion laws in *Roe* v. *Wade* in 1973, on the grounds that they violated personal privacy protected by the Fourteenth Amendment, was heralded by many as a defense of freedom of choice but criticized by some as an outrage. The political controversy over the abortion decision continued into the 1980s, when right-to-life groups pushed for a constitutional amendment that would overturn the Court's decision.

The history of incorporation continually involved the Court in controversies regarding the extent to which national standards should control the states. The incorporation-plus position that has been taken by the Court has extended the controversy to involve the question of how far the justices may go in imposing their interpretation of due process of law beyond what is explicitly part of the Bill of Rights.

## A Note on Equal Protection of the Laws

The Bill of Rights does not explicitly require equal protection under the laws. The constitutional prescription of equality is first found in the Fourteenth Amendment equal protection clause, which provides that "no state shall . . . deny to any person in its jurisdiction the equal protection of the laws." The principle of equality was first applied to the states to protect the newly freed blacks from discrimination. Requirements for equal protection are also found in the Thirteenth Amendment, prohibiting slavery and involuntary servitude, and in the Fifteenth Amendment, forbidding the government to deny citizens of the United States the right to vote "on account of race, color, or previous condition of servitude."

With the exception of the privileges and immunities clause in the original Constitution, which, in the words of Alexander Hamilton, was designed to ensure the "equality of privileges and immunities to which the citizens of the Union will be entitled,"[62] equal protection did not exist as an operative concept before it became an explicit part of the Fourteenth Amendment in 1868. The framers of the Constitution assumed that all citizens would be equal before the law; they did not consider it necessary to state or even discuss the obvious. Insofar as the framers discussed equality, they were concerned with the equality of the vote of each state in the Senate, the equality of representation in the House based on population, and the equality of states in voting for the president. The issue of equality at the Constitutional Convention, then, focused upon the equality of states, not of citizens, except insofar as they were represented by states. The framers of the Constitution knew, in the words of South Carolina delegate Charles Pinckney, that among the people of the United States "there are fewer distinctions of fortune and less of rank than among the inhabitants of any other nation. Every freeman has a right to the same protection and security and a very moderate share of property entitles them to the possession of all the honors and privileges the public can bestow. Hence arises a greater equality, than used to be found among the people of any other country, an equality which is more likely to continue."[63]

While the states are required to provide equal protection under the Civil War amendments, particularly the Fourteenth, and under the privileges and immunities clause of Article IV, sec. 2, equal protection standards have been extended to the national government as well.[64] In *Bolling* v. *Sharpe* (1954), the Court found an equal protection command in the due process clause of the Fifth Amendment.[65] Again, in *Wesberry* v. *Sanders* (1964), the Court held that the requirement of Article I, sec. 2 that representatives be chosen "by the people of the several states" means "that as nearly as is practicable one man's vote in a congressional election is to be worth as much as another's."[66]

[62]*The Federalist*, No. 80.
[63]Farrand, ed., *Records*, 1:398.
[64]Under the privileges and immunities clause, states are required to grant equal treatment under their laws to citizens of other states. See, for example, *Toomer* v. *Witsell*, 334 U.S. 385, 395 (1948).
[65]*Bolling* v. *Sharpe*, 347 U.S. 497 (1954).
[66]*Wesberry* v. *Sanders*, 376 U.S. 1, 7–8 (1964).

The standards of equal protection, which have been principally developed and applied under the Fourteenth Amendment equal protection clause for the states and under the due process clause of the Fifth Amendment for the national government, have varied over time. Until the Warren Court era the states were given broad discretion to enact laws that treated separate groups of people differently. Federalist considerations were paramount in the minds of most justices in reviewing state actions challenged on equal protection grounds. The interventionist stance of the Warren Court radically altered the way in which equal protection was judicially determined.

### How the Problem of Equal Protection Arises

A potential problem of equal protection arises when legislation treats two groups of people differently in pursuit of a particular legislative goal. For example, benefits under the Social Security system may not be allocated to men and women on the same basis, reflecting a congressional premise that the economic needs of men and women differ. In a section of the Social Security law that was declared unconstitutional in 1975, Congress provided greater benefits to women than to men similarly situated.[67] A variety of provisions of federal and state laws have granted women greater economic benefits than men in the same position. This results in "unequal treatment" in the generic sense but is not necessarily in violation of constitutional standards of equal protection applied by the courts. For example, the Court has upheld tax exemptions for widows that were not granted to widowers[68] as well as exempting women from jury duty unless they volunteer.[69] Increasingly, however, the unequal treatment of men and women in law has been disallowed by the Supreme Court. In addition to eliminating gender differentiation in the Social Security law, the Court has voided laws that exclude women from being appointed administrators of estates,[70] deny military dependency allowances to the male spouses of female members of the armed

---

[67] *Weinberger v. Weisenfeld*, 420 U.S. 636 (1975).

[68] *Kahn v. Shevin*, 416 U.S. 351 (1974), upheld a Florida law giving more favorable tax exemptions to widows than to widowers on the grounds that the legislative classification was substantially related to a legitimate legislative goal, namely remedying the subordinate economic position of women in society.

[69] *Hoyt v. Florida*, 368 U.S. 57 (1961), sustained a Florida law that exempted women from jury duty but required men to serve on the grounds that the separate treatment of men and women was justified because "woman is still regarded as the center of home and family life." Ibid., pp. 61–62.

[70] *Reed v. Reed*, 404 U.S. 71 (1971).

services,[71] and require husbands but not wives to pay alimony following divorce.[72]

The process of differentiating groups of people in legislation is one of *classifying* these groups for the purposes of the law. Since the decision of the Warren Court in *Brown* v. *Board of Education* in 1954, racial classifications have been overturned, even those designed to remedy the effects of past discrimination.[73] In the *Brown* case itself the Court unanimously declared unconstitutional the de jure segregation of the races in seventeen southern and border states. Other classifications in law that the Court has viewed with suspicion but has not always voided include the separate classification and differential treatment of "illegitimate" children,[74] aliens,[75] and poor people.[76]

Strengthening equal protection of the laws has been a major movement in both federal and state courts since the era of the Warren Court, which extended from 1953 to 1968. The Warren Court was particularly anxious to protect the right of racial minorities to equal treatment under the law. Complementing the decisions of the Supreme Court during the Warren period were congressional and presidential actions that vastly extended equal protection of the laws under the Civil Rights Act of 1964, the Voting Rights Act of 1965, and a major affirmative action program initiated by President Lyndon B. Johnson. Under affirmative action the government required its own agencies, as well as groups in the private sector receiving federal funds, to take measures to remedy the effects of past discrimination. Affirmative action programs became commonplace throughout the federal bureaucracy and among universities, labor unions, and private employers to encourage

---

[71]*Frontiero* v. *Richardson*, 411 U.S. 677 (1973).

[72]*Orr* v. *Orr*, 440 U.S. 268 (1979).

[73]*Regents of the University of California* v. *Bakke*, 438 U.S. 265 (1978).

[74]See, for example, *Labine* v. *Vincent*, 401 U.S. 532 (1971), which upheld a Louisiana law subordinating the rights of acknowledged illegitimate children to legitimate children and relatives of the parents in claims upon an estate left without a will; and *Weber* v. *Aetna Casualty and Surety Co.*, 406 U.S. 164 (1972), which overturned a Louisiana workers' compensation law subordinating the claims of illegitimate to those of legitimate children.

[75]See, for example, *Gram* v. *Richardson*, 403 U.S. 365 (1971), which voided a state law that denied welfare benefits to all noncitizens and to aliens who had not resided in the country for a period of fifteen years; and *In re Griffiths*, 413 U.S. 717 (1973), invalidating a New York law that limited permanent positions in the state civil service to American citizens.

[76]In *San Antonio* v. *Rodriguez*, 411 U.S. 1 (1973), the Court sustained a Texas law under which the property tax was used by local communities as the basis of financing public education. The law had been challenged as a violation of the equal protection clause of the Fourteenth Amendment on the grounds that it operated to the disadvantage of the poorer school districts.

the hiring of blacks and other racial minorities as well as women — groups that had been subject to past discrimination.

Both the Supreme Court and the political arms of government retreated from the firm commitment to affirmative action made by the Court, Congress, and the president in the 1960s. The 1978 *Bakke* decision in particular questioned the very basis of affirmative action by holding that the medical school of the University of California at Davis could not establish quotas for the admission of members of racial minorities. Such a practice, stated the Court's majority, was unconstitutional "reverse discrimination" against whites. The conservative approach of the Burger Court toward equal protection was complemented by that of the Reagan administration, which moved immediately to soften affirmative action programs in the federal government and the private sector. The Reagan administration also opposed the continuation of provisions of the Voting Rights Act of 1965, which authorized the Justice Department to intervene actively within state and local jurisdictions to prevent discrimination in voting.

While there has been a shift away from governmental activism in affirmative action and other areas of equal protection, the fundamental right to equality under the laws remains an outstanding feature of the American polity, one that has strengthened democracy and constitutional government.

## The Role of the Bill of Rights in Constitutional Democracy

Ironically, although the Bill of Rights was not included in the original Constitution, it has become — in combination with the Fourteenth Amendment, under which most of its provisions have been nationalized — an indispensable part of our constitutional democracy. It protects the vital freedom of expression without which democracy would be a sham. It guarantees that those accused of crime will be innocent until proven guilty through procedures that conform to due process of law. And the unique right to equal protection, added in the Fourteenth Amendment as a limit on the states, and also made applicable to the national government after it was incorporated in the Bill of Rights under the Fifth Amendment due process clause, has helped to ensure equal opportunity to all regardless of race or gender in a nation with an unfortunate history of racial and, often, gender discrimination.

The Bill of Rights was meant to stand above the temporary, passionate, and often misguided whims of political majorities. At the extreme, a lynch mob or its equivalent can be viewed as the embodiment of democracy, representing after all a unanimous vote for immediate action. But the Constitution requires, even in the absence of the Bill of Rights, a fair trial by an impartial jury for those accused of crime. Above all, the rights of the individual must be respected before the government can take action.

Respect for the rights of minorities prevents the government from suppressing unpopular political views. Freedom of political expression is explicitly complemented by religious freedom and, implicitly, has been extended to literary expression as well.

The Bill of Rights is an important underpinning of limited government under the Constitution, but it does not exist in a vacuum, nor are its provisions automatically applied to protect individual freedoms and rights. Individuals and groups must become politically active not only in pursuing litigation in the courts but also by pressuring legislatures and executives to uphold their constitutionally-granted freedoms and rights. Like all parts of the Constitution, the Bill of Rights is dynamic, not static, and over time its meaning and application depend on political forces. Fortunately, over the long term, these have favored enhancement rather than restriction of the cherished liberties and rights that distinguish our constitutional democracy.

## Suggestions for Further Reading

Abraham, Henry J. *Freedom and the Court.* 4th ed. New York: Oxford University Press, 1982. The author discusses the development of civil liberties and civil rights through an examination of leading Supreme Court cases.

Higginbotham, A. Leon, Jr. *In the Matter of Color.* New York: Oxford University Press, 1978. An award-winning study of the role of law in the subjugation of black Americans during the colonial period.

Kluger, Richard. *Simple Justice.* New York: Random House, 1977. The history of school desegregation from the adoption of the Fourteenth Amendment in 1868 to the *Brown* cases in 1954 and 1955.

Orfield, Gary. *Congressional Power: Congress and Social Change.* New York: Harcourt Brace Jovanovich, 1975. An examination of the legislative politics of civil rights legislation.

Sindler, Allan P. *Bakke, Defunis, and Minority Admissions.* New York: Longman, 1978. An absorbing account of the *Bakke* case and the history of affirmative action.

Woodward, C. Van. *The Strange Career of Jim Crow.* New York: Oxford University Press, 1957. A brief account of the background and flavor of segregation as it was practiced in the South.

*chapter* **3**

# The Dynamics of the Federal System

The history of American politics is to a very large extent a reflection of the changing balance between national and state power. The struggle for freedom in America began with the colonies' effort to free themselves from England's yoke. Although the colonial governments were legally directly under the control of the British government, in practice the enormous distance in space and time between the mother country and America enabled the colonies to have wide discretion in determining how they were to govern themselves. The quest for freedom that drew the colonists to America was nurtured on its shores, and eventually led to the Revolution and the Declaration of Independence.

## Original State Sovereignty

The Revolution and the Declaration of Independence reflected the desire of the former colonies that had now become independent states to retain their sovereignty as states. The Declaration of Independence is somewhat misleading in its title: "A Declaration by the representatives of the United States of America in Congress assembled." While the Declaration seems to be referring to a union of the states, in fact each of the states considered itself an independent, sovereign body. The signing of the Declaration represented approval by the states themselves as well as a mutual pledge by its signers to support its principles and the boycott and embargo actions that already had been taken against Great Britain. Although the signing was a tentative first step toward union, Garry Wills points out that "the 'we' of the Declaration is neither the 'we the people' of the Constitution nor the 'we as individuals' who signed as a promise of observing the embargoes. The Declaration speaks for the thirteen United *States*. These new *states* pledged to each other their honor, that honor accruing to sovereignties as they take their 'free and equal station' with other nations."[1]

## The Articles of Confederation

Although the Articles of Confederation, submitted to the states by Congress in 1777 and finally ratified by all states in 1781, moved tentatively and timidly in the direction of establishing a central government, they left the sovereignty of the states largely untouched. Under the Articles, all national governmental authority resided in a Congress in which each state had one vote. The powers delegated by the Articles to the national government were very limited and did not include the authority to tax or to regulate commerce. Given their recent experience with Great Britain, whose taxes and commercial regulations upon the colonists had led to so much unhappiness that it was a major cause of the break with the mother country, the states had no intention of relinquishing these powers to the national government.

The lack of an explicit executive and judicial authority under the Articles was a major weakness, to say the least, in the national government, but it would have been unthinkable at such an early stage in the development of the new government to create the kind of strong executive authority that eventually emerged under Article II of the Constitution. Too many colonists perceived a strong executive as a threat to their fundamental rights of life, liberty, and property.

The weakness of the national government under the Articles was reflected in their provision that "each state retains its sovereignty, freedom and independence, and every power, jurisdiction and right, which is not by this confederation expressly delegated to the United States, in Congress assembled." The inclusion of this caveat was a victory for the advocates of states' rights. Its terms provide an interesting background to the debate that occurred after the adoption of the Constitution over the proper interpretation of the authority of Congress under Article I. It was clearly the intent of the Federalists at the Convention to allow the extension of congressional authority beyond the explicit powers of Article I to incorporate whatever reasonable means Congress considered necessary to execute its powers. The Articles of Confederation were based upon the acceptance of the supremacy of states' rights, whereas the Constitution was unequivocally nationalist in its thrust.

[1]Garry Wills, *Inventing America* (Garden City, N.Y.: Doubleday, 1978), p. 340.

The Constitutional Background of Federalism   **71**

*The Emergence of the Union*

From the perspective of the 1980s it is easy to forget that the emergence of a real union of the states came only after long and bitter conflict between proponents of national power and advocates of states' rights. It is remarkable that in the atmosphere of the postrevolutionary period, when state sovereignty was widely accepted without question, a constitution clearly nationalist in tone was drafted in the first place and ratified by the states. It took men of vision — not just men of property out to protect their interests, as Charles Beard claims — to embrace the nationalist cause as the failure of the government under the Articles of Confederation became increasingly evident. The need to provide for a strong national defense, which could only come about through the common action of the states, was an important motivating factor in the adoption of the Constitution, as was the evident need for the national regulation of commerce among the states and with foreign nations. Under the Articles the states continued to act as free and independent nations, but they had already become too intertwined commercially to permit each to go its own way. Foreign commercial and military threats to the interests of the individual states could be met only by the establishment of a national government capable of ensuring the national defense and the regulation of foreign commerce.

As the federal system evolved, it was profoundly shaped by the development of constitutional doctrines of federalism and by changing political forces.

## The Constitutional Background of Federalism

*Definition of Federalism*

Federalism is defined as a system in which there is a constitutional division of authority between a central government and, collectively, constituent units that in the United States are the individual states.[2] Federalism contrasts with a unitary form of government in which all constitutional authority remains with the national government (see Figure 3.1). The constitutional division of authority between national and constituent units in federal or unitary systems does not have to be based on written constitutions, but rather may stem from parliamentary legislation. In Great Britain, for example, which is a unitary government, the actions of Parliament are supreme, and insofar as they affect the basic structures of government and determine the rights and liberties of the British people, they form the un-

---

[2] The constituent units in federal systems are referred to in different ways. In the Canadian system, for example, the constituent units are called provinces.

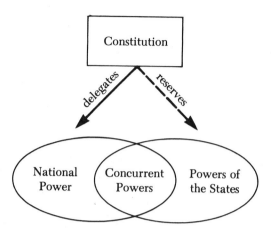

**Figure 3.1.** *Federalism. Under federalism the Constitution delegates powers to the national government and reserves the remaining powers for the states. States may exercise powers concurrently with the national government, such as the regulation of commerce and taxation, when the exercise of state power does not undermine national supremacy or the effective exercise of national power.*

written constitution of the country. Laws of Parliament may also determine Commonwealth relationships, and, in the case of Canada, the British–North American Act of 1867 became the "constitution" of Canada. The Canadian government remains without a formal written constitution similar to that of the United States. Whether by formal constitution or informal constitutional arrangements adopted through statutory law, all the federal systems of the world — which consist primarily of systems arising from former British colonies — grant by law a degree of governmental autonomy to constituent units.[3]

The constitutional division of authority between national and state governments in a federal system is one in which the states independently or concurrently with the national government exercise substantial powers. In the focus of our study, the United States, the constitutional powers granted to the federal government by the delegates at the Constitutional Convention represented the extreme to which the nationalists could go in strengthening the central government while securing the support of convention moderates and advocates of states' rights. While Alexander Hamilton boldly suggested

[3]Federal systems that were former British colonies, in addition to the United States, are Australia, Canada, India, Malaysia, Nigeria, and Pakistan. The British West Indies, New Zealand, and Rhodesia tried federalism but failed. The only former self-governing British colonies that never tried federalism are Burma and the Union of South Africa.

the possibility of abolishing the states altogether, neither he nor any of the other delegates saw such a course of action as a practical possibility.

## Establishing Federalism

The constitutional overview given in Chapter 1 stresses the nationalistic character of the Constitutional Convention and the fact that both James Madison and Alexander Hamilton, whose views of the Constitution are used to reflect two contrasting ways in which the Constitution may be interpreted, agreed fundamentally on the principle of national dominion over the states. Madison was as much a nationalist as Hamilton in advocating a strong national government in relation to the states.

The Madisonian and Hamiltonian perspectives reflected the views of an overwhelming majority of the convention delegates. After all, the convention had been called specifically to remedy deficiencies in the Articles of Confederation and to strengthen the weaknesses of the federated government under the Articles, particularly in relation to the regulation of commerce and providing for the common defense.

## Federalism in the Constitution

The Founding Fathers were intent on establishing the supremacy of the national government within its own sphere, defined by the constitutional authority that was given to Congress, the president, and the judiciary. Considered to be highly innovative and almost radical at the time was the power given to the national government to act directly on the citizens of the states without having to use state legislatures as intermediaries. As James Madison was careful to point out, however, direct national power "extends to certain enumerated objects only, and leaves to the several states a residuary and inviolable sovereignty over all other objects" (*The Federalist*, No. 39).

State power is protected by the constitutional apparatus in several ways. Most important is the federal character of the Senate, in which each state has two senators regardless of population. Large and small states are thus equally represented, the result of the "Great Compromise" that prevented the convention from dissolving at the last minute and ultimately saved the Constitution. The states also act as entities in the Electoral College, which continues to buttress their importance as geographical and demographic units in choosing the president even though electors are duty bound to ratify the popular vote in their states. Finally, states must recognize constitutional amendments, giving state legislatures a critical voice in the process of constitutional change.[4]

As with all parts of the Constitution, the provisions governing federalism are highly flexible and have been subject to changing interpretations. Ultimately the balance of national and state power was to be determined by the political process in which the Supreme Court necessarily performed an important role as its interpretations of the boundaries of national and state power responded to evolving political pressures.

## How the Constitution Shapes the Federal System

The Constitution determines the formal relationships between the national government and the states, and governs the formal linkages among the states themselves. Constitutional interpretation over the almost two centuries since the birth of the Republic has of course profoundly affected the constitutional standards that govern the federal system.

### Early Constitutional Interpretation of Federalism

The Federalist framers of the Constitution clearly intended to create a government with powers adequate to deal with the scope of national concerns, and with supremacy over the states within the sphere of national power. The intentions of such key convention figures as Alexander Hamilton, James Madison, and Edmund Randolph that have been discussed at length above were unequivocally in support of a dominant national government, although there were naturally disagreements among these and other members of the Convention on the proper scope and reach of national power.

The early interpretation of the Constitution by the Supreme Court before and during the era of the Federalist Chief Justice John Marshall articulated and implemented the principles of the flexibility and completeness of congressional authority coupled with national supremacy. The opinions of Chief Justice Marshall in *McCulloch* v. *Maryland* (1819) and in *Gibbons* v. *Ogden* (1824) completed a trend in Court rulings that upheld the broad construction of congressional power under Article I and the supremacy of national over state law. The Court left no doubt that it would uphold Article VI of the Constitution, which states that "this Constitution and the laws of the United States which shall be made in pursuance thereof; and all treaties made . . . under the authority of the United States, shall be the supreme law of the land; and the judges in every state shall be bound thereby, anything

---

[4]The Constitution also provides for the approval of constitutional amendments by state conventions, a method that was used only once.

in the Constitution or laws of any state to the contrary notwithstanding." The Supreme Court made it clear that it would not only uphold national law and void state legislation contrary to it, but would also extend its jurisdiction to state courts to assure the compliance of state judges with national law.[5]

The early rulings of the Supreme Court that supported national power made it clear that, although the intentions of the framers of the Constitution were clearly in favor of a strong national government, the ambiguity of much of the language of the Constitution opened the way to state challenges to national power. It was not too difficult for the advocates of states' rights to construct a constitutional rationale that supported a weak rather than a strong national government. Even the supremacy clause itself, which on its face seemed to be an absolutely clear statement of the predominance of national law, could be construed narrowly, as it was by the lawyers speaking for the states in the *McCulloch* and *Gibbons* cases, to extend only to those powers of Congress *explicitly* mentioned in Article I. The proponents of states' rights simply argued that the sphere of state sovereignty encompassed many of the powers that the Federalists included under Article I on the basis of the necessary and proper clause. The plain language of the Constitution did not resolve many of the questions concerning the proper boundaries of state and national power. What were considered the reserved powers of the states became a matter of constitutional interpretation.

Constitutional prescriptions extended beyond the delineation of national power and the supremacy of national law. Article I, sec. 10 prohibits states to enter into "any treaty, alliance, or confederation," or to grant letters of marque and reprisal that authorize private citizens to equip their ships with arms to attack enemy ships. Moreover, states are forbidden to coin money or to issue bills of credit. States cannot "pass any bill of attainder, ex post facto law, or law impairing the obligation of contracts, or grant any title of nobility."

The Constitution forbids the establishment of trade barriers among the states, providing that "no state shall, without the consent of the Congress, lay any imposts or duties on imports or exports, except what may be absolutely necessary for executing its inspection laws."

Finally, Article I provides that "no state shall, without the consent of Congress, lay any duty of tonnage, keep troops, or ships of war in time of peace, enter into any agreement or compact with another state, or with a foreign power, or engage in war, unless actually invaded, or in such imminent danger as will not admit of delay."

While the Constitution prohibits certain state acts, it also defines national

---

[5]See, for example, *Chisholm v. Georgia,* 2 Dallas 419 (1793).

obligations to the states in several areas. Congress was forbidden to prohibit the importation of slaves until 1808, although the national legislature was authorized to impose a tax or duty upon the importation of slaves not to exceed ten dollars per person. Congress has the authority to admit new states to the Union, "but no new state shall be formed or erected within the jurisdiction of any other state; nor any state be formed by the junction of two or more states, or parts of states, without the consent of the legislatures of the states concerned as well as of the Congress" (Art. IV, sec. 3).[6] The guaranty clause of the Constitution also clarified the duties of the national government to the states, providing that "the United States shall guarantee to every state in this Union a republican form of government, and shall protect each of them against invasion; and on application of the legislature, or of the executive (when the legislature cannot be convened) against domestic violence" (Art. IV, sec. 4).

The Constitution defines certain relationships among the states themselves as well as between the states and the national government. According to Article IV, "full faith and credit shall be given in each state to the public acts, records, and judicial proceedings of every other state." Congress has the authority by general legislation to "prescribe the manner in which such acts, records, and proceedings shall be proved, and the effect thereof."

In regulating interstate relationships the Constitution also provides that the "citizens of each state shall be entitled to all privileges and immunities of citizens in the several states" (Art. IV, sec. 2). States were obligated to respect the laws of other states regulating crime and slavery.

The early interpretation of the Constitution by the Supreme Court through the era of Chief Justice John Marshall focused primarily on defining the extent of the authority of Congress and of the federal courts over the states as well as on establishing the principle of national supremacy in domestic affairs, leaving delicate questions of interpretation of the constitutional provisions regulating federalism to a later time, when appropriate cases and controversies arose. Marshall did consider one other aspect of federalism under the Constitution when, on two occasions, he used the provision forbidding the state impairment of the obligation of contracts to invalidate state laws.[7]

Marshall broadly interpreted the proscription of the contract clause in a way that limited state action even more than the framers of the Constitution

---

[6]Five states have been formed out of other states with the consent of their legislatures and of Congress: Vermont from New York (1791); Kentucky from Virginia (1792); Tennessee from North Carolina (1796); Maine from Massachusetts (1820); and West Virginia from Virginia (1863).

[7]*Fletcher* v. *Peck,* 6 Cranch 87 (1810); *Dartmouth College* v. *Woodward,* 4 Wheaton 518 (1819). Chief Justice John Jay, acting as federal circuit court judge, had earlier used the contract clause to void a Rhode Island statute.

had intended. The clause was put into the Constitution essentially because the framers did not want property rights to be overturned by popularly elected majorities in state legislatures, and it was aimed at debtor relief laws that had been passed by many states. Marshall held in *Fletcher* v. *Peck* (1810) that the contract clause prohibition extended beyond the protection of private contractual rights to public contracts as well.[8] In *Dartmouth College* v. *Woodward* (1819), Marshall reaffirmed the Court's position that the contract clause did not govern private debtors and creditors only, but rather precluded the legislature of New Hampshire from abrogating what in effect was a public contract.[9]

While the early Supreme Court, and the Marshall Court in particular, upheld national power and broadly interpreted the constitutional proscription of state impairment of contracts, two years before his death Marshall's opinion in *Barron* v. *Baltimore* (1833) held the protections of the Bill of Rights inapplicable to the states. The ruling did not excite the great interest that had been aroused by such major cases as *McCulloch* and *Gibbons,* which to both the nationalists and the advocates of states' rights involved crucial questions of constitutional law and vital state interests. Given the historical context within which the Bill of Rights was framed and adopted, there was virtually no rationale that Marshall could have used to support a decision contrary to his ruling in the *Barron* case. Neither the framers of the Constitution nor the congressional contingent led by James Madison that drafted the Bill of Rights had intended that it limit state action. The constitutional ambiguity surrounding questions of national power and supremacy involved in earlier decisions of the Marshall Court did not pertain to the question of applicability of the Bill of Rights to the states. Although Marshall had little choice but to make the ruling he did, the constitutional historian Charles Warren found it "a striking fact that this last of Marshall's opinions on this branch of law should have been delivered in limitation of the operation of the Constitution, whose undue extension he had been so long charged with seeking."[10]

While the Marshall Court and its predecessor had resolved the major constitutional question of the reach of national power and its supremacy over the states, other important aspects of constitutional provisions pertaining to federalism remained to be clarified. The Court had yet to face questions concerning the extent to which it could become involved in political

[8]The Marshall Court ruled in the *Fletcher* case that the contract clause prevented the Georgia legislature from rescinding a previous act that had granted land titles.
[9]Marshall did not extend the prohibitions of the contract clause to include all public contracts, but only those that affected property interests.
[10]Warren, *The Supreme Court in United States History,* vol. 2 (Boston: Little, Brown & Co., 1922):240–41.

controversies relating to the constitutional charge to the national government that it guarantee states a republican form of government. And, in other areas, it would have to decide on questions of the supremacy of national government in foreign affairs in cases that did not arise until the twentieth century. Throughout its history the Supreme Court has also had to refine and expand the doctrines of the Marshall Court governing the reach of national power and the supremacy of national law. Moreover, the Court has continually confronted cases requiring the resolution of conflict among the states.

Finally, although *Barron* v. *Baltimore* made the issue of the applicability of the Bill of Rights to the states temporarily moot, the passage of the Fourteenth Amendment in 1868 laid the groundwork for major developments in constitutional law that placed the Court squarely in the center of what seemed to be an endless controversy over the meaning of the due process and equal protection clauses. Perhaps the most significant aspect of the constitutional law of federalism in the twentieth century was the gradual inclusion of the protections of the Bill of Rights in the Fourteenth Amendment's due process clause, making them applicable to state action. The early interventionist approach of the Marshall Court in expanding national power under Article I, particularly in the regulation of commerce, was more than matched by the activist Warren Court in the 1950s and 1960s when it applied national standards of civil liberties and civil rights to the states under the Fourteenth Amendment.

## The Development of Constitutional Standards Governing Federalism

### Restricting National Power

The strong support given to doctrines of nationalism by the Supreme Court through the era of Chief Justice Marshall was not continued after Marshall's death in 1835. Marshall had interpreted the Constitution in support of strong national regulation of commerce, but the Court was soon to define the commerce power of Congress more narrowly, in a way that vastly expanded the sphere of state sovereignty.[11] The post–Marshall Court also re-

---

[11]See, for example, *New York* v. *Miln,* 11 Pet. 102 (1837), in which the Court upheld five to two as a legitimate exercise of the state police power a New York law that required ships' masters to report specified data about passengers on vessels arriving at New York ports; and *Cooley* v. *Board of Wardens,* 12 Howard 299 (1851), which upheld a Pennsylvania statute regulating pilots in the Port of Philadelphia on the grounds that the subject of the regulation was local in character. The *Cooley* case in particular changed the Court's interpretation of the commerce clause that had provided the basis for sweeping national power in *Gibbons* v. *Ogden,* 9 Wheaton 1 (1824). Under the *Cooley* test, national power could

duced the reach of national power that had prevailed during the Marshall era under the contract clause by narrowly interpreting the clause to allow states greater freedom to take action that changed contractual obligations.[12]

The trend in constitutional interpretation after the Marshall era, which supported expanded state police powers and powers to regulate commerce concurrently with the national government, continued with certain mutations well into President Franklin D. Roosevelt's New Deal in the 1930s. The Court adopted standards that not only expanded state power in relation to the national government, but that also expanded the sphere of private corporate rights in relation to both the states and the national government at the turn of the twentieth century. The decision of the Supreme Court in *Lochner* v. *New York* in 1905 reflected what could be called a new approach to federalism, one that supported the fragmentation of power not only among the states but among corporate interests as well. In the *Lochner* case the Court held that a New York law prohibiting bakery employees from working more than ten hours a day or sixty hours a week violated the "freedom to contract" of both employers and employees. The right to contract, stated the Court, is one of the fundamental liberties protected by the due process clause of the Fourteenth Amendment. While the liberty to contract, concluded the Court, is not absolute, any state interference with the exercise of the right must be demonstrated to be a fair, reasonable, and appropriate use of the state police power.[13]

The 1905 ruling began the so-called *Lochner* era of substantive due process, during which the Supreme Court imposed its interpretation of due process on both national and state legislatures to limit the scope of economic regulation.[14] While more state and federal laws were upheld than struck

---

not extend to objects of commerce that were local in nature and demanded a diversity of local regulations. Under the *Gibbons* doctrine, on the other hand, the test was not whether the objects of regulation were local or national in character, but whether the matter regulated affected interstate commerce in any way.

[12]See *Charles River Bridge* v. *Warren Bridge*, 11 Peters 420 (1837), in which Chief Justice Taney upheld wide state powers to take action in the public interest even when they affected private interests based on the state charter. Taney's opinion was in marked contrast to Marshall's doctrine in the *Dartmouth College* case and in *Fletcher* v. *Peck*, which bound states to honor the terms of contracts they had entered into in the past.

[13]*Lochner* v. *New York*, 198 U.S. 45 (1905). The *Lochner* case was a classic example of the Court's using a "substantive due process" formula to overturn a state law. The substantive due process approach involved the Court in reviewing state laws under the due process clause of the Fourteenth Amendment and national laws under the due process clause of the Fifth Amendment to determine whether, in the view of the Court, they were "reasonable." Under the substantive due process approach, the Court imposed its values on state and national legislatures.

[14]Substantive due process was also employed in the nationalization of the protections in the Bill of Rights as well as in the extension of civil liberties and rights beyond the explicit provisions of the Bill of Rights (see Chapter 3).

down during the period after the *Lochner* decision, the Court's substantive due process approach did act as a limit on both national and state governments. The states as well as the national government were subject to close judicial scrutiny of laws regulating working conditions and setting rates that could be charged by railroads as well as of other types of economic regulation. Both national and state sovereignty suffered, and a new sovereignty of economic interests began to emerge that, if the trend had continued, could have led to a new form of federalism.

### The End of the Lochner *Era: Resurgence of National Power*

The crisis of the Depression, and the concomitant political development that saw a reinvigorated and more broadly based Democratic party rise under the leadership of Franklin D. Roosevelt, brought an end to the *Lochner* era and the interventionist approach of the Supreme Court in reviewing economic legislation at both national and state levels. During Roosevelt's first term in office, the Supreme Court, under the leadership of Chief Justice Charles Evans Hughes, valiantly fought against what it considered an excessive expansion of national power over the states and private interests. The Hughes Court at first wanted to continue a decentralized federal system that emphasized state sovereignty and private economic rights. In one prominent New Deal case, *Schechter v. United States* (1935), a unanimous Supreme Court struck down the keystone of the early New Deal program, the National Industrial Recovery Act of 1933. The principal reason for declaring the law unconstitutional was that it exceeded the commerce power of Congress.[15] Hughes, who wrote the majority opinion, ruled that Congress could not, as it had in the Recovery Act, regulate business activities that only indirectly affected interstate commerce.

While the *Schechter* case was an extreme one, involving an extraordinarily sweeping national law that had become unpopular by the time the *Schechter* decision was handed down, the strict constructionist approach of the Court that was used to overturn the NIRA was also used to nullify less controversial New Deal legislation.[16] By the end of his first term, Roosevelt and his advisers were planning a political coup against the Supreme Court, which involved a court-packing scheme that would allow the president to

---

[15]Another major consideration of the Court was its conclusion that the NIRA delegated excessive legislative authority to the president and therefore violated the principle of separation of powers, which requires that primary legislative authority reside in Congress.
[16]The Roosevelt administration itself had become disenchanted with the NIRA and was not unhappy to see the political controversy in which it had become embroiled settled in one stroke by the Court's decision.

appoint one new justice for each justice over seventy years of age.[17] Roosevelt's plan was submitted to Congress after his overwhelming victory in 1936. Although it had no chance of passage, since it was seen by conservatives and many liberals alike as an unwarranted attack on judicial independence, the Supreme Court could not help but realize that its insistence on narrowly interpreting federal power during a time of national emergency made it increasingly resented and placed it in political jeopardy. Finally, in a series of decisions beginning in 1937, a majority of the Court supported both New Deal and state legislation regulating economic activity that it would have declared unconstitutional on the basis of the standards it had applied during the early New Deal.[18]

The New Deal was a watershed both for constitutional law and the politics of federalism. Although the Marshall Court had bolstered a strong national government, the support for national authority by subsequent Courts weakened. The Supreme Court now came full circle to champion once again expansive federal power in the economic sphere over states, private individuals, and corporate interests. The constitutional law of federalism was complemented by political developments that reflected a widespread national trend toward an increased role for the federal government in policymaking affecting state and local interests. The states' resources had been inadequate to meet the crisis of the Depression, which demanded a national solution — a full use of national powers and resources to cope with problems of unemployment, social security, labor relations, and economic regulation. The decline of state sovereignty and power that the New Deal represented in both constitutional law and in politics was much later to be temporarily halted, although a predominant national government has remained the central feature of American federalism into the 1980s.

## Constitutional Doctrines Affecting Federalism After the New Deal

The year 1937 marked the end of the Supreme Court's application of the substantive due process formula in reviewing national and state legislation in the economic sphere. This shift paved the way for the expansion of na-

---

[17]In 1936 there were six septuagenarian justices. If Roosevelt had been authorized to appoint one new justice for each of them, he could have had enormous influence on the Court's philosophy and approach.

[18]See, for example, *National Labor Relations Board* v. *Jones and Laughlin Steel Corporation*, 301 U.S. 1 (1937), which upheld the National Labor Relations Act of 1935 on the grounds that it was properly based on the commerce power of Congress; and *West Coast Hotel Company* v. *Parrish*, 300 U.S. 379 (1937), in which the Court upheld the validity of a Washington state minimum wage law on the grounds that it was within the state police power. Significantly, Chief Justice Hughes wrote the majority opinions in both cases.

tional power over the states, an expansion based largely on the commerce power, and gave the states freedom to regulate their own economic affairs provided their laws did not conflict with federal legislation.

While the post-1937 Court allowed the federal government to regulate virtually every facet of economic activity on the basis of the commerce power, state sovereignty did not die completely. In the 1970s the Burger Court held that under certain circumstances it could act as a limit on the commerce power of Congress. The Court noted in *Fry* v. *United States* (1975) that federal power cannot be exercised "in a fashion that impairs the states' integrity or their ability to function effectively in a federal system."[19] The *Fry* case involved a challenge to the application to state employees of a national wage freeze under the Economic Stabilization Act of 1970. The employees contended that the act interfered with sovereign state functions in violation of the Tenth Amendment. Although the Court upheld the law on the grounds that it was emergency legislation designed to reduce rather than increase pressure on state budgets, it warned that it would not permit unwarranted national intrusions into the sphere of state sovereignty. Exactly what constituted state sovereignty remained undefined.[20]

A majority of the Burger Court temporarily applied the concept of state sovereignty to limit the national commerce power in *National League of Cities* v. *Usery* in 1976.[21] As in the *Fry* case, *National League of Cities* challenged federal legislation as a breach of state sovereignty. Congress had broadened the coverage of the Fair Labor Standards Act by extending its wage and hour provisions to state employees. The National League of Cities contested the law on the grounds that it intruded on the states' performance of essential governmental functions. Justice William Rehnquist wrote the Court's opinion sustaining the challenge. Rehnquist noted the plenary authority of Congress under the commerce clause, citing Marshall's opinion in *Gibbons* v. *Ogden,* but he also emphasized that "there are limits upon the power of Congress to override state sovereignty, even when exercising its otherwise plenary powers to tax or to regulate commerce."[22] Rehnquist concluded that extension of the wage and hour provisions of the Fair Labor Standards Act to state employees invaded the sovereign authority of the states to determine the wages paid to their employees. The national legislation also unconstitutionally interfered with the power of states to deter-

[19] *Fry* v. *United States,* 421 U.S. 542, 547–48n (1975).
[20] Justice William Rehnquist dissented in the *Fry* case, asserting that the national law improperly interfered with the exercise of traditional state functions involving the determination of pay for public employees.
[21] *National League of Cities* v. *Usery,* 426 U.S. 833 (1976). Overruled in *Garcia* v. *San Antonio Metro.,* 83 L ed. 2nd 1016 (1985).
[22] Ibid., p. 842.

mine how they will deliver governmental services to their citizens. Although overriding considerations of national policy may support federal legislation that invades state sovereignty, as the Court found in the *Fry* case, in *National League of Cities* v. *Usery* Rehnquist found no compelling reason to uphold the federal legislation.

The *National League of Cities* ruling was controversial both within and without the Court. Justice William Brennan, joined by Justices White and Marshall, wrote a strong dissenting opinion emphasizing that the broad reach of the commerce power, which had been supported in a long line of cases beginning with *Gibbons* v. *Ogden,* supported the federal legislation. The three also argued that the Court should exercise judicial self-restraint in reviewing cases concerning the proper balance between national and state power. A reasonable exercise of the national commerce power should be upheld, for it is not the responsibility of the judiciary to determine the structure of the federal system. Their view became law in the 1985 Court *Garcia* v. *San Antonio Metro.,* overruling the *Usery* case. In the economic sphere, the Court's ruling in *Schechter* v. *United States* in 1935 was the last major decision upholding a commerce clause challenge to the exercise of national power on the grounds that Congress had exceeded its Article I authority.

*Judicial Activism in Defining National Standards for Civil Liberties and Civil Rights*

Although after 1937 the Court allowed the political process to resolve the balance of national and state power in the sphere of economic policy, the Court was to become an active force in applying national standards of civil liberties and civil rights to the states. The New Deal marked a shift from the states to the national government in the balance of power in economic policymaking. This shift in the federal system was, after the Court adopted a posture of self-restraint, the result of political demands on the president and Congress to take action to meet the national economic emergency. National economic policy was determined by the president and Congress, not by the courts. In the sphere of civil liberties and civil rights, however, the Supreme Court became the focal point of policymaking that was ultimately to alter the constitutional landscape of the federal system in a profound way.

The nationalization of civil liberties and civil rights was a slow process that began with the court's declaration in *Gitlow* v. *New York* in 1925 that the freedom of speech and press guaranteed by the First Amendment applied to the states. The *Gitlow* decision itself, however, gave the constitutional benefit of the doubt to the New York legislature in reviewing its criminal anarchy statute that had been challenged in the case. The result was that the Court upheld the New York law. In 1931, in *Near* v. *Minnesota,* the

Court for the first time overturned a state law that was found to violate the national standard of freedom of the press guaranteed by the First Amendment that was part of the "liberty" protected by the due process clause of the Fourteenth Amendment.

The process of nationalizing civil liberties and civil rights that began with the *Gitlow* and *Near* cases did not continue in earnest until the era of the Warren Court. When Chief Justice Earl Warren retired in 1968, most of the protections of the Bill of Rights had been nationalized under the due process clause of the Fourteenth Amendment, and the Court had adopted a substantive due process stance that it now was applying to the sphere of civil liberties and civil rights. This position laid the groundwork for the expansion of national standards even beyond those defined in the Bill of Rights. In *Griswold v. Connecticut* the Court in 1965 held that a Connecticut birth control statute violated a national right to privacy — one that was not explicitly spelled out in the Bill of Rights, but which could be implied from it. In 1973, in *Roe v. Wade,* the Burger Court was to use the newly articulated right to privacy as the basis for its decision granting women the right to obtain abortions. The *Roe v. Wade* decision signalled that the Burger Court was not going to turn the clock back to the time when the Court had cited considerations of federalism as the basis for judicial self-restraint in applying national standards of civil liberties and civil rights to the states.

## The Politics of Federalism

Political forces have helped shape the constitutional context within which the federal system functions, and they have also informally shaped intergovernmental relations. The politics as well as the constitutional law of federalism reflect the ebb and flow of forces and themes of centralization and decentralization. The politics of the colonies, the Revolution, and the Articles of Confederation reflected strong forces of decentralization. In contrast, the Constitutional Convention of 1787, the Constitution itself, and its early interpretation by the Supreme Court through the Marshall era represented the politics of nationalism and the centralization of power.

### A Historical Perspective

While the Constitution and its early interpretation were remarkable victories for the proponents of a dominant national government with broad powers, the nineteenth century was characterized by the dominance of the states rather than the national government over the political and economic life of the country. The constitutional underpinnings of a strong national government could not alone support such a government without the acquiescence and coalescence of political forces moving in the same direction. The politics of the nineteenth century, as well as the dispersed and decentralized economic system of the period, buttressed state sovereignty and the fragmentation of political power.

The victory of the North in the Civil War established the authority of the Union, but it did not lead to an immediate expansion of national power. The states dominated the federal system after the Civil War as they had done before. The apparent congressional intent behind the Fourteenth and Fifteenth Amendments, to extend national policies of civil liberties and civil rights to the states, was not realized until a century after the amendments had been ratified. The constitutional law and politics of the post–Civil War period put aside the amendments and, with respect to some provisions, temporarily nullified them.

Throughout the nineteenth century the components of the political process were largely decentralized and dispersed. The principal interest groups were privilege-seekers focusing on state legislatures for such largesse as corporate charters and land grants. The state legislatures had more bounty to distribute to private interests than did Congress. It was not until post–Civil War industrialization and the development of national economic interdependence that national business, labor, and agricultural interest groups arose to lobby the national as well as the state governments. The nationalization of interest groups was not completed until well into the twentieth century.

The political parties of the nineteenth century also furthered the decentralization of the federal system. While the philosophies of the parties were often oriented to national problems, their organizations were state and local rather than national in character. The disintegration of national parties began after the demise of the original Federalist and Republican (Jeffersonian) parties that had reflected, respectively, the nationalist and states' rights views of the Constitution. Neither the Federalist nor the Republican party was national in scope, and both were dominated by political elites that determined the positions of the parties and selected their leaders primarily on the basis of congressional caucuses of party members. The Democratic party of Andrew Jackson was the first to approximate a national party drawing a broad membership and nominating its candidate for president by a convention, which was considered to be far more democratic than nomination by "King Caucus," the meeting of the members of the party holding congressional office. Although the Democratic party and the opposition Whig party developed a high degree of party uniformity on national issues, the organizations of both were necessarily confederations of state and local interests. It was these interests that dominated not only the parties, but the Congress as well. Their representatives gathered once every four years to nominate candidates for the presidency, but the seeming unity of the parties in presidential election years belied their real diversity.

Similarly, the parties of the twentieth century remained essentially broad confederations of state and local interests, even as they developed more comprehensive party programs dealing with national issues. American parties have from the very beginning helped to aggregate political interests, but the political and economic diversity of the country, reflected in the constitutional structure of federalism, have always fostered the dispersion and decentralization of power.

The centrifugal forces of the nineteenth century continually changed the character of the party system. There was no lasting coalition of interests that could form the base of a long-term national party. From the beginning of the Republic until the Civil War, the country saw parties come and go, with no single party reflecting purely national interests. The Federalists and the early Republicans were replaced by the Jacksonian Democrats and the Whigs, which in turn metamorphosed into other parties. The split between the North and the South over the issue of slavery profoundly affected the party system as the Civil War approached, splitting the Democrats into northern and southern factions and giving rise to several new parties. The most important of these was the Republican party, which held its first national convention in 1856 and which four years later nominated as its candidate for the presidency Abraham Lincoln.

The post–Civil War period saw the parties shift once again in organization and policy orientation in response to the war itself. These changes solidified the Democratic party in the South, which became its most important base of support. The Republican party that had led the nation to victory was to dominate the national political scene with very few interruptions until the election of Franklin Roosevelt in 1932, and the Grand Old Party also developed effective political machines that dominated the politics of the rising urban areas as well as the northern states. The party founded solely to oppose slavery became, by the turn of the twentieth century, largely the party of corporate interests, which it advanced at national, state, and local levels of government.

The industrialization and general economic advance of the country began to shape the character of the Democratic and the Republican parties. In the nineteenth century the Democrats were rooted in the agrarian sections of the country, but gradually the party began to reflect the interests of factory workers as well, both in small cities and larger urban communities. A pooling of interests that began to develop between farmers and workers in opposition to corporate interests was represented by the Democratic party that elected Roosevelt. During the New Deal the axis between farmers and labor became the base of the Roosevelt coalition that transformed what had once been a minority party into a dominant national party that was to prevail for decades to come.

### Changing Patterns of Federalism: The New Deal and Centralization of Power

The politics of the New Deal fundamentally altered the character of the federal system. The Great Depression was an economic emergency that was national in scope and clearly required national action. Roosevelt moved quickly to meet the emergency, and he was eventually successful in securing the passage of legislation to channel federal funds to the states to deal with unemployment and with welfare problems generally. The states and localities had demonstrated their inability to cope with the massive unemployment, which required a vast expansion of governmental assistance. The Social Security Act of 1935 marked the beginning of federal legislation that gradually took income security and welfare responsibilities away from the states and located them unequivocally in the hands of the national government.

The Social Security legislation of the New Deal represented an important shift in power that took place in the federal system during the Roosevelt's first two administrations. New and more subtle forms of federal taxation complemented the income tax to bolster the federal treasury at the expense of the states, and to create what Daniel P. Moynihan refers to as a predominantly federal fisc.[23] Beginning with the New Deal, the federal government did not hesitate to use its superior revenue-raising power to dominate many facets of state and local government. Federal grant-in-aid programs were instrumental in the progressive increase in federal power over the states. Categorical grant programs are those in which the federal government stipulates conditions that state and local governments must meet in order to receive federal funds. Until the early 1970s, federal aid was channelled to the states solely through categorical grant programs, which grew from 30 in 1938 providing $800 million of aid to the states to 379 by 1968 dispersing $15.2 billion of aid. The categorical grant programs exemplified the centralism that was the backbone of federal policy from the New Deal through the Great Society of Lyndon B. Johnson, which was later reduced somewhat by the revenue-sharing policies of the Nixon administration; however, the "New Federalism" of the Nixon era was unable to stem the tide of centralization through categorical grants because of the interest on

[23]Daniel P. Moynihan, "The Future of Federalism," in *American Federalism: Toward a More Effective Partnership* (Washington, D.C.: Advisory Commission on Intergovernmental Relations, 1975).

the part of many members of Congress in continuing them. More than a hundred categorical grant programs were added during the decade of the 1970s concurrently with a growth in federal aid through revenue-sharing.[24]

While the centralism of the New Deal changed the nature of inter-governmental relations by shifting relatively more power to the national government than it had previously exercised over the states, state and local — particularly urban — governments continued to grow in importance and assumed many new responsibilities of their own. Cities such as New York and Los Angeles represented the trends and problems of urban government in dozens of other communities throughout the nation. Just as the national government had expanded during the New Deal in response to political demands that it cope with the problems of the Depression, state and local governments expanded to meet the pressing needs of their communities. Beginning in the 1960s, resurgent state and local governments challenged the national government for a greater share of public revenues. The new stirring among state and local governments resulted first in the increased centralism of the Johnson administration and, second, in a reaction to the increasing dominance of the federal government that led to the New Federalism of the 1970s.

## The Changing Federal System of the 1960s

The federal system in the 1960s reflected a new and more focused centralism than was represented by the New Deal. The problems of state and city governments in such areas as welfare, education, rapid transit, crime, assistance to the elderly, and even sewage were studied and restudied by an army of federal and state bureaucrats, by such research groups as the Brookings Institution, and by advisory commissions and congressional committees. At first there seemed to be an abiding faith that, whatever the problem, it could be solved by professional analysis and federal-state cooperation, which would use federal resources to solve state and local problems. No area was considered off limits to federal jurisdiction. During the years of Johnson's Great Society programs, the federal government boldly moved into the most cherished sphere of state sovereignty, education, to implement by the use of the categorical grant technique policies formulated at the national level.

---

[24]The nature of federal aid to state and local governments is detailed in the yearly reports of the Advisory Commission on Intergovernmental Relations, Washington, D.C., which also issues valuable periodic reports on various aspects of intergovernmental relations.

As the federal government forthrightly — or, as some would say, arrogantly — created programs to deal with poverty, health, urban renewal, and a host of other problems in local communities, the politics of federalism became chaotic. Each new linkage between the federal bureaucracy and its local counterparts, established in order to bring about federal-state cooperation in the dozens of areas that the national government had entered for the first time, created a new bureaucratic power base and intensified political conflict within and among bureaucratic enclaves. Power seekers at the local level built political constituencies of their own to give them leverage at both state and national levels of government. Local political leaders were often infuriated by upstart challengers whose constituencies had been fueled by federal funds. The federal Office of Economic Opportunity, for example, spawned local community agencies that frequently challenged mayors and other members of local political establishments. The famous "Model Cities" program, under which the federal government sought to eliminate urban blight and encourage city planning, was another example of an area in which intense bureaucratic rivalries developed. The principal federal department involved, Housing and Urban Development, encouraged local participation in city planning without defining how it was to be accomplished. Inevitably, "citizen participation" was transformed in various ways into the development of political constituencies representing the viewpoints of bureaucrats and politicians. The same kind of confusion and conflict that surrounded the poverty program administered by the Office of Economic Opportunity accompanied HUD's Model Cities program.

The centralism of the 1960s ultimately produced more confusion than coordination in intergovernmental relations. The many attempts by federal bureaucrats to dictate local policies, and particularly their encouragement — tacit or otherwise — of local political leaders with their own constituencies capable of challenging both the elected and non-elected local political establishments, resulted in a backlash from many regular state and local politicians. Both the president and Congress were the recipients of widespread demands from governors, mayors, and other local political leaders to reduce the power of the federal government, and of its bureaucracy in particular, in state and local affairs. State and local political establishments quite naturally wanted to be in charge of programs administered within their jurisdictions. At the same time, they wanted the federal government to put unrestricted funds at their disposal. Their demands ultimately resulted in what the Nixon administration called "revenue sharing." Nixon's sponsorship of the program helped him to gain important support from state and local leaders that helped to nudge him into the White House after the very close election of 1968.

*The "New Federalism" of the 1970s*

The New Federalism of Richard M. Nixon's first term called for a revitalization of state and local governments, which meant a reduction in the direct control of the federal government over local programs. State and local governments still wanted federal funds, but without the kinds of strings that were attached in the categorical grant programs. At first a major goal of proponents of the New Federalism was to remove the increasing welfare burden of state governments that was beginning to cripple their finances. They hoped to do this by federalizing welfare through a family assistance plan that would provide direct grants to welfare recipients who met federal standards. The keystone of the New Federalism was revenue sharing, which was to include both the general provision of undesignated federal funds to state and local governments and special revenue sharing that consolidated major federal grant programs under which earmarked funds would go to the states, but without burdensome federal controls.

The New Federalism was conservative in tone, aiming at equipping state and local governments to meet traditional responsibilities, such as welfare, which had grown and changed in ways that made it impossible for state and local governments with limited resources to meet them. The conservatism of the New Federalism nicely fit the philosophy of the Republican party; many Democrats as well, having become disenchanted with the failure of the liberal programs of the Great Society, saw value in the restoration of local initiatives and means to cope with public responsibilities.

Although early proponents of the New Federalism and of revenue sharing looked for a distinct reduction in the role of the federal government in state and local affairs, the forces of centralization kept pace with those of decentralization. During the 1970s almost a hundred new categorical grant programs were added, and by the end of the decade these programs constituted 72 percent of total federal aid. This was a reduction from the past, when categorical grant programs encompassed all federal aid to the states; however, the continued importance of categorical grants made it clear that centralism would remain the dominant characteristic of intergovernmental relations.

The New Federalism stressed the importance of local governments at the expense of the states, particularly urban areas whose pressures for aid were felt and answered by Washington. The bypassing of state governments during the 1970s was even more thoroughgoing than it had been during the years of the Great Society programs, when the standard method of federal aid involved grants to states that in turn might be dispensed to local governments.

## Washington Politics and Federalism

Washington politics is essentially a centripetal force in the federal system. The aims of Washington politicians and administrators are primarily to draw into their vortex as much power as possible, which does not mean ignoring state and local interests but does mean retaining in Washington as much control as possible over the largesse of the federal government. Local constituencies are built to support power on Capitol Hill and in the administrative agencies downtown. Although this encourages the dispersion of power within Washington, it does not lead to the relinquishing of power by political actors in Washington to their local counterparts. The centripetal force exerted by the Washington community was a major reason that, despite their best efforts, the Republican presidencies of Richard Nixon and Gerald Ford did not succeed in subordinating the categorical grant programs to the revenue sharing of the New Federalism. Neither Nixon nor Ford had a Republican Congress, but even if they had had one, it is doubtful that Republican chairmen of powerful committees on Capitol Hill would have played the Washington power game differently from the way the Democrats did. In general, revenue sharing does not allow congressmen to claim credit for benefits distributed to local districts — credit that is often a major reason for their reelection. Ronald Reagan's block grant program, similar to revenue sharing, was not unanimously embraced by Republican committee chairmen in the Senate. Congress significantly scaled down Reagan's proposals by excluding many major categorical grant programs.

The Constitution provided the basis for the centralization of power in Washington. The balance that Madison saw in the Constitution between national and state interests was clearly skewed, with a little help from the Federalists, in favor of national over state power. Both the power and the political ability of Washington politicians to bypass state governments in building local power bases is rooted in the Constitution. The Founding Fathers saw clearly that if the states were made the intermediaries between the government and the people, meaningful national power would be a fiction. By providing government with the authority to act directly on the people, the framework for an eventually dominant national government was constructed. The coalescence of constitutional and political realities doomed the New Federalist movement of the 1970s from the start.

## Federalism in the 1980s

The struggle between the forces of centralization and of decentralization, which has always been a part of American politics, continues in the 1980s, but without the intensity that accompanied the political conflict over the Great Society programs of the 1960s or the New Federalism of the 1970s. The issue of the proper balance between the national government and state and local governments has receded, to be replaced by political debate over such pressing concerns as inflation, unemployment, energy, and foreign and military policies.

Neither Democrats nor Republicans particularly stressed issues pertaining to intergovernmental relations in their presidential and congressional campaigns in the 1980s. The party platforms did not contain planks that covered federalism per se, instead dealing with the issue of intergovernmental relations primarily through platitudes rather than specific recommendations. The Republicans opposed the federalization of welfare and generally supported state and local initiatives. The Democrats advocated somewhat greater national action to deal with state and local problems, but, like the Republicans, did not raise problems of intergovernmental relations to a major level of debate.

The view of the proper balance of power between national, state, and local governments remains in limbo under the Reagan administration. At the same time, the usual power struggles over who is to administer federal programs continue, as do the programs themselves that are rooted in Congress and the bureaucracy. The trend toward centralization of power may be temporarily halted or slowed but most of the categorical grant programs spawned by previous administrations and Congresses remain in effect and will continue to buttress the centralism of the federal system.

## Federalism and Constitutional Democracy

The Founding Fathers and later Alexander Hamilton and James Madison, foreign observers of the American political scene such as Alexis de Tocqueville and James Bryce, politicians, and political theorists have debated and analyzed the federal system from all angles. De Tocqueville reemphasized Hamilton's observations in *The Federalist* that, although federal forms of government had existed before, American federalism was unique because of the authority the states granted to the national government to carry out its laws on the people directly, without the intervention of state governments. The Constitution created a strong national government in its own time, and it made possible even greater centralization of national power over the states in the future. The wide scope of the powers of Congress enumerated in Article I, in combination with the necessary and proper powers clause, makes national authority virtually limitless, subject only to political constraints and judicial interpretation.

As James Madison pointed out, federalist ideas of governmental structure contributed to the intricate constitutional system of limited government (*The Federalist*, Nos. 10, 39). Not only would state sovereignty be retained in certain spheres, but also the existence of the states as multiple political units would help to control the harmful effects of factions opposed to the national interest. Divisive interests would be isolated in what James Bryce called "politically watertight compartments" — the states.[25] Finally, by dividing power between the national government and the states, federalism contributed to the balance of power so ardently sought by the framers of the Constitution.

State governments continue to play a vital political role, as do the thousands of local governments throughout the country. But the nationalization of politics that has occurred in the twentieth century, rooted in Franklin Roosevelt's New Deal centralism and later spurred by a national press and media that focused public attention more on the national than on state and local political arenas, has made federalism and state power less significant. As the Founding Fathers would have wanted, national power has expanded to meet the increasingly common political concerns of the people. Federalism is an important but no longer dominant feature of the pluralistic politics that has always characterized the American polity.

[25]James Bryce, *The American Commonwealth* (New York: G.P. Putnam's Sons, Capricorn Books, 1959), 1:85. Bryce's treatise was first published in England in 1888.

## Suggestions for Further Reading

Banfield, Edward C. *The Unheavenly City*. Boston: Little, Brown, 1968. An examination of the social, political, and economic problems of cities and their role in the federal system.

Diamond, Martin. "The Federalist's View of Federalism." In *Essays in Federalism,* edited by George C.S. Benson, pp. 21–64. Claremont, Calif.: Institute for Studies in Federalism of Claremont Men's College, 1961. A discussion of the meaning of federalism to the Founding Fathers.

Grodzins, Morton. *The American System*. Chicago: Rand McNally, 1966. A classic treatment of federalism that argues that there has always been an extensive overlapping of functions between national and state governments.

Pressman, Jeffrey L., and Wildavsky, Aaron B. *Implementation*. Berkeley and Los Angeles: University of California Press, 1973. A case study of the ways in which federalism affects the implementation of public policy.

Reagan, Michael D., and Sanzone, John G. *The New Federalism*. New York: Oxford University Press, 1981. An overview of federalism, including grants-in-aid, revenue sharing, and block grants.

Riker, William H. *Federalism: Origin, Operation, Significance*. Boston: Little, Brown, 1964. A comparative study of the theoretical and practical aspects of federalism.

*part* **II**

# The Political Process

# Political Parties, Elections, and the Electorate

Political parties are, in democratic theory at least, the cement that holds the political process together and gives it meaning. The Constitution was not framed with parties in mind, and in fact the Founding Fathers viewed political parties with suspicion. One of James Madison's principal arguments in support of the Constitution was that the system of federalism and the separation of powers would prevent any one faction from controlling the apparatus of the national government. Faction, to Madison, included both political parties and interest groups.

## The Problem of Faction

### Madison's View

Madison defined faction as "a number of citizens, whether amounting to a majority or minority of the whole, who are united and actuated by some common impulse of passion, or of interest, adverse to the rights of other citizens, or to the permanent and aggregate interest of the community." He declared that one of the great advantages of the Constitution and the Union established under it would be "its tendency to break and control the violence of faction. The friend of popular governments never finds himself so much alarmed for their character and faith as when he contemplates their propensity to this dangerous vice."[1]

Madison told his countrymen that under the new Constitution factions would not be able to control the national government because the Republican principle of representation would disperse and refine factional de-

---

[1] *The Federalist*, No. 10.

mands. No one group would be able to elect a sufficient number of representatives to control Congress. Moreover, the checks and balances at the national level would prevent unbridled majority rule, which would eliminate the possibility of any one party's dominating the governmental process.

Madison also viewed federalism as an important check on faction. "The influence of factious leaders," he wrote, "may kindle a flame within their particular states, but will be unable to spread a general conflagration through the other states; a religious sect may degenerate into a political faction in a part of the Confederacy; but the variety of sects dispersed over the entire face of it must secure the national councils against any danger from that source. A rage for paper money, for an abolition of debts, for an equal division of property, or for any other improper or wicked project, will be less apt to pervade the whole body of the Union than a particular member [state] of it, in the same proportion as such a malady is more likely to taint a particular county or district than an entire state."[2]

The anti-party bias of the framers of the Constitution reflected in *The Federalist* was understandable at the time. The process that had led to the framing of the Constitution had been one of constant tension between centripetal and centrifugal forces — between the nationalists who dominated the Philadelphia convention and the advocates of states' rights who saw in the proposed Constitution a threat to their interests. The new nation was faced with the possibility of disintegration, and faction was at the time a direct threat to the national interest embodied in the Constitution. In the view of the Founding Fathers, the nation simply could not afford the luxury of uncontrolled pluralism of interests. Pluralistic disintegration was the vice that the Constitution was supposed to cure, not by eliminating faction but by constructing a government in which faction could not dominate the policymaking process.

While the Constitution and the theory underlying it contain an anti-party bias, none of the provisions of the Constitution directly limit the growth of parties in any way. The First Amendment enumeration of the freedom of speech, of the press, and of association and the right to petition government for redress of grievances created an environment in which both parties and interest groups could and did flourish.

Madison recognized that although faction may be undesirable, constitutional government requires preservation of the liberty essential to the existence of parties and interest groups: "Liberty is to faction what air is to fire,

[2]Ibid.

an aliment, without which it instantly expires. But it could not be less folly to abolish liberty, which is essential to political life because it nourishes faction, than it would be to wish the annihilation of air, which is essential to animal life, because it imparts to fire its destructive agency."[3]

The Federalist and Republican parties emerged in the decade after the founding of the Republic, and from that day to the present, political parties have always been at the center of national political life, helping to aggregate interests, shape public policies, provide leadership, and offer choices to the people during elections that have helped to channel popular aspirations into governmental policies. Parties have not by any means been the perfect instruments for organizing the collective will of a majority of the nation and translating it into public policy, but given the pluralism of the polity, the parties have gone about as far as they can in directing clashing interests and opposing views of the role of government and the policies that should prevail.

## The Liberal–Democratic Model of Party Government

The skeptical eighteenth-century view of parties as factions antagonistic to the national interest gave way in the nineteenth and twentieth centuries to a recognition by many theorists that effective parties are essential to democracy. There is some tension between the premises of constitutional government and what is best termed the liberal-democratic model of party government, in which parties assume a pivotal position in the political process.

As the somewhat elitist government of eighteenth-century America began to emerge as the representative democracy of the nineteenth century, it was inevitable that parties developed to reflect, shape, and capitalize on the demands of an ever-increasing and diverse electorate. Jacksonian democracy marked the beginning of a new era of party politics, in which a mass electorate would be courted by political leaders who found it both necessary and profitable to build party organizations to compete effectively in the political marketplace.

As political parties became a prominent fixture in democratic politics, serving the power-oriented goals of politicians and raising the political aspirations of large numbers of people, democratic theorists began increasingly to concern themselves with defining the appropriate role of parties in the democratic polity. Parties could no longer be simply dismissed as undesirable factions opposed to the national interest.

[3]Ibid., No. 101.

## The Role of Parties

What should the role of parties be in democratic government? This question has been eloquently answered by theorists of the liberal-democratic model of government, in which the parties are an an integral part of the government, acting as the primary force shaping public policy. At the same time, parties bridge the gap between the government and the people by providing the electorate with alternatives at election time. In the liberal-democratic model the function of parties is primarily to allow the electorate to make a rational choice among alternatives in public policy. Parties become, in a sense, modern-day instruments of the Enlightenment ideals of rationality and progress. The model assumes that the individual voter is rational and both desirous and capable of making political choices based on an accurate and informed assessment of individual interests.

For some theorists, party government is at its best "government by discussion," assuming the existence of a rational and responsible electorate as well as of political leaders who recognize that their fate at the polls will be determined by the attractiveness to the voters of the policies they present.[4] This model of government contrasts sharply with the modern public relations approach to political campaigning, which is based on the premise that the electorate is irrational and will merely choose among images of candidates rather than rationally consider issues of public policy in voting.

## Stages of Discussion

Four stages of discussion occur in the ideal party model of government. First, it is the responsibility of each major political party to formulate and to sharpen issues of public policy for debate and for consideration by the electorate. The first stage occurs within the party organization, among party activists. At this stage interest groups make their demands known, testifying, for example, before the platform committees of the parties on such issues as civil rights, the minimum wage, and a wide range of economic and social concerns. In the party model, interest groups channel their demands through political parties, which have a virtual monopoly over the presentation of major policy proposals within government. Because the demands of the political system are to be channeled first to the parties and then to government, public policy deliberations have a consistency, continuity, and

[4]For the best elaboration of the liberal-democratic model of party government, see Sir Ernest Barker, *Reflections on Government* (London: Oxford University Press, 1942). Barker's book was a passionate defense of democracy against the challenge of fascism, which posited a theory of government that ridiculed the premises and practices of democracy.

visibility that they do not have where groups outside the parties have free rein to pressure the institutions of government. The model assumes disciplined party organizations in which the members, once elected, strive to achieve the goals of the party and always vote together in the legislature in support of party programs. If the model were strictly followed in the United States, for example, the Republican majority in the Senate would consistently support the programs of President Reagan, who himself would base his legislative recommendations on the policies that had been agreed on at the Republican National Convention. The first stage of discussion would thus be completed at the party conventions if the model worked ideally in American politics.

Once the parties have agreed on the platforms to be presented to the public, the electorate begins the next stage of discussion, in which voters are given a chance to analyze the contrasting programs of the parties on the basis of rational presentations of issues by party candidates. The electoral process extends the arena of debate from the parties to the voters. If the parties carried out their task of formulating contrasting policy proposals, rational choice by the electorate of whichever party program seemed best to meet the interests of individual voters would be possible. Theoretically, serious debates are to take place among party candidates, from which all relevant information to make a rational electoral choice is given to the voters. Once the electoral process is completed, the electorate chooses one party or the other by voting for its candidate.

The third stage of discussion comes about after the election at the governmental level in Congress and the executive. Together the members of the majority and minority parties tailor their legislative agendas to the party programs that have been agreed on in the preceding party and electoral stages of discussion. Ideally, the executive is of the same party as the majority of the legislature and acts as a leader in setting the agenda and guiding legislation through Congress. Members of the legislature in the minority act collectively as an *opposition party*, criticizing the policies of the majority and recommending proposals of their own based on their party's platform in order to sharpen national political debate and make the electorate aware of alternatives to the policies of the majority.

## Parties as Policy Instruments

Party government stresses the role of parties at all stages of the policy process. It is the parties that collectively formulate policy proposals, set the legislative agenda, and determine the timing of legislative enactments. It is the parties that make electoral choice meaningful through legislation and executive actions that are responsive to the choices made by voters. Disciplined parties are necessary bridges between the people and the government over which the electorate transmits its will to government, and they serve as the mechanism for making policy responsive to the electorate's decisions at the ballot box. In a two-party system with single-member districts, the party that wins usually represents a majority of those who vote. Party government therefore means the rule of the majority, thus differing with the constitutional structuring of separation of powers and federalism as well as with the concept of "concurrent majorities," the domination of the political process by different majorities of interest groups in separate policy spheres.

Why are political parties so essential to the realization of majority rule? The assumption is that only political parties can give the necessary degree of definition, coherence, and unity to the process of formulating and implementing policies based on majority choice. Without parties, the selection of candidates becomes haphazard, and although individual candidates may run their campaigns on the basis of policy issues, once elected they will, without party support, be powerless in the maze of government to implement their promises to the electorate. Therefore, although political campaigns may raise policy issues, where political parties do not function in a disciplined manner the public is deceived if it thinks that candidates can meaningfully connect policy preferences with government action.

In the American system, however, party backing is not necessary for elected politicians to exercise power. Especially in foreign and military affairs the president has independent prerogative powers that enable him to act independently in many instances. On Capitol Hill inter-party coalitions often enact laws.

Although the president can take foreign policy initiatives without congressional approval, in the domestic sphere the support of both Congress and the bureaucracy is required if the White House is to have a strong policy impact. In foreign policy, the president is the supreme power, and his authority has been recognized by the Court.[5] But even in foreign policy it behooves a president desirous of maintaining his power to seek the approval of Congress for major foreign policy actions, as Johnson did in securing passage of the Gulf of Tonkin Resolution that gave him carte blanche to engage in military action in Vietnam; and as Reagan did on most of his controversial Central American policies.

White House leadership in foreign policy, however, is usually respected if not always acclaimed by Congress. For example, Carter's recognition of the mainland Chinese government after Nixon and his secretary of state, Henry Kissinger, had paved the way, raised a storm of criticism on Capitol Hill.

---

[5]See, for example, *United States v. Curtiss–Wright Corp.,* 299 U.S. 304 (1936).

This was led by Senator Goldwater and others who felt that the United States had betrayed Taiwan, its trusted ally. But the recognition of the People's Republic of China, once made by the White House, was not revoked. Even Reagan, a staunch supporter of Taiwan who had during the 1980 campaign strongly criticized Carter's recognition of Communist China, was persuaded to continue the formal ties between mainland China and the United States that had been established with great effort.

In the ideal model of party government, a major function of the party is to bind the executive and the legislative branches. This takes place readily in parliamentary systems such as that of Great Britain, where the executive is the cabinet, a committee of the majority party in the legislature. American parties are too diversified, however, to bring about easy cooperation between the president and Congress, and the constitutional system of separation of powers virtually guarantees conflict rather than agreement between the White House and Capitol Hill. The occupants of each end of Pennsylvania Avenue have different political constituencies and interests that often clash. The president and powerful members of Congress are constantly striving for power, and the struggle more often than not transcends party lines. President Reagan found soon after his election that he could not rely on the Republican majority in the Senate, in which the senior members of his own party had assumed committee chairmanships. For example, Senator Orrin Hatch from Utah, the chairman of the Labor and Human Resources Committee, did not support all of Reagan's proposals for cuts in social programs, including aid to the handicapped. Republican Senator Robert Dole, the new chairman of the powerful Finance Committee, was highly skeptical of Reagan's tax cut proposals because of the likelihood, in Dole's view, that they would increase budget deficits. Reagan represented a particular group within the Republican party, and the Republican members of Congress were by no means all Reaganites. The party label continued to be an insufficient glue to bind its members together when Reagan pushed for a major overhaul of the entire tax system in 1985. Many Senate Republicans became his most formidable opponents.

## Parties and the Electoral Process

It is interesting and insightful to contrast the American party process with the ideal model of party government to determine the extent to which parties have contributed to the achievement of rational and responsible politics. The focus of our analysis will be upon the national presidential and congressional parties. It should always be remembered, however, that there are literally hundreds of "parties" throughout the United States that, although they are classified as Democrats or Republicans, have separate constituen-

State and local parties

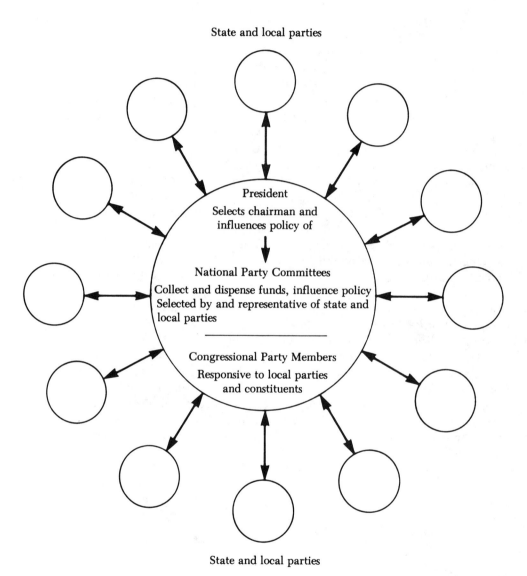

State and local parties

**Figure 4.1.** *National Political Parties. National parties are confederations of national, state, and local interests.*

cies and often contrasting policy orientations (see Figure 4.1). State and local leaders in New England, for example, whether Republicans or Democrats, have little in common with their party brethren in Texas on the critical policy issue of energy. The New England states are consumers of energy, whereas Texas, particularly in its more rural parts, is a producing state. Even within Texas, however, Democrats and Republicans are split on the energy issue, those from such consuming areas as Houston favoring the regulation of oil and natural gas prices, while representatives from producing areas support deregulation of the energy industry.

## Presidential Parties

From the earliest days of the Republic, presidential politics have been, every four years, the focus of the attention of voters throughout the country. More recently, because of the attention the media give to the game of presidential politics, the race for the presidency seems to be a continual one that begins within weeks after an election. The incumbent apparently begins immediately to prepare for victory in the next election, while challengers test the political waters and begin to line up backers and establish organizations they hope will propel them into the lead in the race for the presidential nomination of their party.

Capturing the presidency is, in the minds of politicians, equivalent to winning the Nobel Prize. The White House is the grand prize for members of the victorious party as well, since it elevates the power and status of party adherents who have supported the winning candidate.

Because of the importance of the presidency to each party, both Republicans and Democrats have national organizations that have been primarily oriented to bringing the diverse elements of the party together once every four years for the purpose of electing the president. In recent years, the national organizations have also increased party strength throughout the country by providing financial support and political expertise to party candidates.

## Congressional Parties

Two types of parties are associated with Congress. First, there are the parties of Capitol Hill — the Democratic and Republican caucuses, steering committees and committees on committees, leaders who perform various tasks from assigning party members to committees to scheduling legislation for floor debate and votes. Because Congress is both constitutionally and politically separated from the president, the White House cannot assume its party members on Capitol Hill will follow the president's lead. Parties do not easily bridge the wide gap that separates the executive and legislative branches at the two ends of Pennsylvania Avenue. The president's success on Capitol Hill depends on his persuasive ability with members of both parties.

In addition to the national congressional party organizations, each member of Congress has in effect his or her own "party," consisting of loyal followers and members of the electorate that support the congressman's reelection. Although with virtually no exceptions congressmen run on the Republican or Democratic ticket, they are careful to gear their organizations and styles to the particular needs and desires of their constituents. Political free enterprise characterizes congressional elections, which see members going their separate ways to court constituents. Whether or not congressmen support the president or the national congressional party organization will finally depend not on party label, but rather on the independent judgment of the individual legislator regarding whether or not such support will benefit his or her reelection chances.

We are left, then, with a party system that reflects the pluralism of our politics. Ticket splitting is a growing phenomenon among voters, who often ignore party labels and vote for the candidate whose style they like and who they think will best represent their interests.

## Reforming the Party System

How can the disparate American party system be made democratically more effective? Politicians have addressed this question from the early days of the Republic, and in the twentieth century political scientists have also tried to answer it. The nineteenth century witnessed the expansion of the democratic base of political parties: grass-roots movements began to affect the selection of party candidates, while caucuses and primaries expanded to allow rank-and-file voters to participate in nominating their party's candidates for offices at all levels of government. Every state now requires political parties to hold a primary for the direct selection of gubernatorial, congressional, and senatorial nominees. Democracy has also arrived in the nomination of presidential candidates as the vast majority of delegates to national nominating conventions are selected directly by party members voting in primaries or caucuses.

### The Dispute over Reform of the Presidential Nominating Process

Pressures from lower-echelon party leaders and from activist rank-and-file members have at various times in history forced party elites and power brokers to loosen their control over the presidential nominating process. In the early days of the Republic, presidential candidates were chosen by congressional party caucuses, but as the popular base of the parties expanded party leaders outside of Congress demanded that they too be given a say in determining their party's candidate for the White House. Congressional caucuses were replaced by presidential nominating conventions, the first important one held by the Democratic party in Baltimore in 1832 to nominate the colorful Andrew Jackson for the presidency. Presidential nominating conventions were a major step in the democratization of the nominating process, the first major grass-roots reform of the parties.

As the conventions developed, they too came under fire from party reformers who felt that they were excluded from the selection of convention delegates. Direct primaries, in which party members select delegates, evolved in response to continued demands by party "outs" to be involved in the nominating process for the presidency.

Although party primaries and grass roots caucuses became an important part of presidential nominating politics in the twentieth century, until 1972 and the so-called McGovern revolution in nominating politics, party power brokers — elected party leaders, urban machine bosses, and leaders of pressure groups important in the party — largely influenced who would become a presidential candidate. Harry Truman summed up the opinion of most professional politicians when, early in the election year of 1952, he called primaries "eye-wash."[6]

Eye-wash though primaries may be, for the better part of the century the vast majority of successful nominees were those who entered and won the most primary elections. These candidates did not run in primaries in order to secure delegate votes, which were not there in the first place because of the relatively few primaries in existence as well as the fact that many of them were "beauty contests" in which delegates were not directly chosen. Rather, candidates used primary elections as trial runs to gain credibility with party power brokers as campaigners and vote-getters. Big victories in the primaries, however, could in no way guarantee nomination if a candidate did not have the qualifications the brokers were looking for. For example, in 1952 the folksy, jocular Estes Kefauver, Democratic senator from Tennessee who often wore a coonskin cap on the campaign trail, won 64.5 percent of the primary votes against Adlai Stevenson's 1.6 percent; but Stevenson became the party's nominee because he was Truman's choice and that of other power brokers as well. In the same year, Dwight Eisenhower did not win the primaries, receiving 27.1 percent of the vote against Senator Robert Taft's 35.8 percent; nevertheless, Eisenhower, with the backing of

[6]Nelson W. Polsby, *Consequences of Party Reform* (New York: Oxford University Press, 1983), p. 9.

the mostly liberal eastern establishment of the Republican party, captured the nomination.

*Impetus for Reform.* The Vietnam War, the civil rights movement, and the demographic explosion of the baby boom generation coincided in the 1960s, creating a volatile mix that strained political institutions of all kinds, including the parties. Growing numbers of party members, mostly those identifying with the Democrats, felt they were politically disenfranchised, and they wanted their voices to be heard in the party councils. Increasingly bitter about the Vietnam War, college students were one of the most important groups that mobilized to change entrenched governmental politics. They sought to overturn party status quos that had revoked the power to nominate presidential candidates from grass-roots organizations. Rank-and-file members thought those displeased with the party system should have the opportunity to choose a majority of the delegates to presidential nominating conventions. Those dispossessed of power understandably believed that democracy required majority rule within the party, just as it prevailed in general elections.

The target for change was President Johnson, who in the minds of Vietnam critics was responsible for the war. Equally unacceptable to the proponents of change was the vice-president, Hubert Humphrey, the great liberal who had been responsible for many of the party's most progressive policies and Johnson's choice for the presidency after he announced his decision not to run again in 1968 in the face of growing opposition.

### The McGovern Revolution

The immediate cause of the change in the Democratic presidential party was the strife-ridden convention of 1968 in Chicago. Johnson and the power brokers of the party had been able to control the selection of the majority of the delegates, and they dominated the convention proceedings from the opening gavel to the end. The ability of the power brokers to control the party was facilitated by the fact that only 40 percent of the delegates were selected in seventeen primary states, the remainder being chosen by state committees or conventions that were dominated by state and local party leaders.

The antiwar forces knew that they were defeated before the convention began. They rallied around the minority candidacy of Senator Eugene J. McCarthy of Minnesota, who had boldly challenged Johnson in the New Hampshire primary and who was declared to be the "winner" by the press because of his good showing even though he did not achieve a majority of the votes. Some delegates backed South Dakota Senator George McGovern, who was also a strong opponent of the war. McCarthy ended up with 38.7 percent of the primary vote. Meanwhile Humphrey, who during the 1960 campaign had remarked, "You have to be crazy to go into a primary. A primary, now, is worse than the torture of the rack,"[7] avoided most of the primaries and received only 2.2 percent of the vote. Nevertheless Humphrey became the party's nominee, the choice of its retiring president and its power brokers.

*Selection of Presidential Candidates at the Grass-Roots Level*

The McGovern revolution spilled over to the Republican party as the number of state primaries increased and Republican candidates found that they too would have to run the primary gauntlet in order to gain the nomination of their party. While the Republican party did not go as far as the Democratic in requiring proportional representation and affirmative action in the delegate selection process, it too saw a lessening of the influence of traditional power brokers. The growth of presidential preference primaries has made each election season an open one for challengers wanting to test their skills in running for the presidency. Even incumbent presidents, who in the past were always able to control the party to gain nomination for a second term, can no longer be assured an easy victory at nominating conventions. Incumbent presidents now have to be supported by the grass-roots voters of their own parties to win the necessary number of primaries to gain renomination. In 1976, for example, President Gerald Ford was startled to find Ronald Reagan making an end run around party regulars in an attempt to gain the nomination. Reagan entered the Republican primaries and came within a handful of votes of defeating Ford. The Reaganites used their experience to capture the nomination in 1980.

In 1980 the incumbent, Jimmy Carter, was challenged for renomination by Senator Edward M. Kennedy of Massachusetts. Kennedy was unsuccessful, but he managed to gain 1,225 delegates, largely by running in the party's primaries. Carter, however, came to the convention with 1,981 votes, 315 more than he needed for the nomination. Carter, like Ford before him, had to run in the primaries to retain his power within the party. His grass-roots support in states such as Iowa (which uses caucuses and not primaries), throughout the South, and in major industrial areas such as Pennsylvania guaranteed his renomination, but Kennedy's primary and caucus victories enabled him to control thirteen delegations at the convention. During the roll call of delegates, Kennedy gained uncommitted delegates from eight

[7]Theodore H. White, *The Making of the President, 1960* (New York: Atheneum, 1961), p. 87.

additional states, although his total vote was far short of a convention majority.

### 1984 and Beyond

The beat of reform went on in the Democratic party after the 1980 elections, but its rhythm now echoed the belief of party leaders as well as many rank-and-file members that democratization had gone too far. McGovern's defeat in 1972 and, at least in part, Carter's failure to win reelection in 1980 seemed to prove that presidential candidates chosen at the grass-roots level, without the backing of the party's power brokers, were electorally vulnerable. Kennedy's challenge in the 1980 primaries weakened Carter's support within the party — a situation almost unthinkable before the growth of primaries made even incumbent presidents fair electoral game for ambitious politicians within the party.

*The Hunt Commission.* Every Democratic party convention since 1968 has been followed by the establishment of a commission to investigate delegate selection rules. After the 1976 convention the Winograd Commission provided that 10 percent of the delegates' seats to the convention of 1980 would be reserved for elected party officials. It was not until after the 1980 campaign, however, that Governor James B. Hunt of North Carolina headed a commission that seriously undertook to provide the party's elected officials with a significant voice in the convention. Changes proposed by the Hunt Commission, adopted by the Democratic National Committee in 1982, gave fully 14 percent of the delegate seats in 1984 to members of Congress and state and local party officials. Governor Hunt, like Senator McGovern a decade before, wanted to make the national convention more representative of the party than it had been previously. McGovern's rules had skewed delegate representation in the direction of the rank and file; ironically, Hunt now wanted to restore a balance that would give party leaders their rightful voice. A major goal of the reforms, commented Hunt, was "to nominate a candidate who can win and who, after winning, can govern effectively."[8]

Of the 3,923 Democratic delegates to the 1984 San Francisco convention, 568 "superdelegates" drawn from elected party officials, of which 239 were senators or congressmen, represented a significant swing vote that ultimately helped to clinch the nomination for Walter Mondale. Congressman Edward Boland of Massachusetts remarked, "I've never seen this many

[8]*National Journal,* January 2, 1982, p. 26.

members of Congress before at a convention."[9] Oklahoma's Representative James Jones, who had gained prominence as the highly active chairman of the House Budget Committee during Reagan's first term, added, "The more elected officials participate in the national convention, the more balanced the platform and ticket will be. In the 1970s we learned that delegates to conventions didn't have to face the electorate, and they tended to bring a special interest point of view. But in order to effectively govern, we need to be a centrist party. That's what the members of Congress bring to the convention."[10]

Looking forward to 1988, so-called superdelegates may be a short-lived phenomenon, as may be other changes brought about by the Hunt Commission. The number of delegates selected in primaries dropped from 71 percent in 1980, when 35 primaries were held, to 64 percent in 1984, when only 28 were held. Although Walter Mondale received only 39 percent of the primary vote, with the help of superdelegates and national party rules that increased the percentage of the vote a candidate had to win before being awarded any delegates in a primary, he nevertheless was able to capture the nomination. Gary Hart and Jesse Jackson won 36 and 18 percent, respectively, of the primary vote, but both felt that the new rules had discriminated against them. Jackson was particularly chagrined, having received only 10 percent of the delegates. Pressures from the Hart and Jackson forces led to the creation of yet another group, the Fairness Commission, to investigate the Hunt Commission rules with a view to eliminating discrimination and substantially reducing the number of superdelegates. It appeared that the pendulum would swing yet again back in the direction of an emphasis on grass-roots participation in the 1988 nominating process.

## Effects of Grass-Roots Participation on the Presidential Parties

Running for the presidency has become a marathon. Like all marathons, the race tests the mental, emotional, and physical resources of candidates. Walter Mondale, Gary Hart, and Jesse Jackson sometimes became so physically exhausted during their 1984 race for the Democratic presidential nomination that they garbled and even forgot their messages to the public. The presidential party, once a broadly based but fairly cohesive group of party insiders that had a fair degree of consistency from one election to the next, is now shaped in an ad hoc fashion by the candidates themselves. Presidential parties are becoming candidate parties, organized primarily around the

---

[9]*Congressional Quarterly Weekly Report*, July 21, 1984, p. 1745.
[10]Ibid.

personality and policy preferences of the candidates and only secondarily around the traditional power bastions of the parties. Each candidate has a separate organization that may or may not include party regulars, but is certainly not dominated by them. George McGovern was a party outsider, if one defines the presidential party in traditional terms. His appeal was to the grass-roots electorate of the Democratic party, not to its power brokers. Jimmy Carter, too, was outside the traditional Democratic party establishment — labor union leaders, machine bosses, civil rights leaders, and the leaders of various pressure groups such as environmentalists and consumer advocates. Many of these party regulars jumped on the Carter bandwagon once it became clear that he would be nominated; however, their support was often less than enthusiastic. By 1980 many had turned to Kennedy, who they felt was more in line with the traditional liberal Democratic view of the role of government. Walter Mondale, more than his immediate predecessors, was a candidate of the party's power brokers. Nevertheless, he too had to forge his own organization to battle Hart and Jackson in the 1984 primaries.

The nomination of presidential candidates through the grass-roots electoral process has important implications for the role of presidential parties in the polity. Grass-roots selection of candidates makes the party far more subject to the whims of individual party voters than when power brokers select the nominees, and the voters whose whims must be catered to often represent a minority of the broader electorate that identifies with the party and ultimately will help to elect its candidates. Turnout in primaries generally is notoriously low, rarely going above 40 percent and often falling as low as 25–30 percent of those eligible to participate. Those who do turn out tend to represent the more active members of the party, who often hold more extreme views on issues of public policy than do the majority of voters. The candidates selected in the primary process can easily turn out to be extremists within their own parties, as was George McGovern in 1972. Ronald Reagan, too, was once considered to reflect more extreme views on issues of public policy than were acceptable to moderate Republicans, who backed Gerald Ford in 1976 against Reagan. Reagan's nomination in 1980 was greatly aided by a coterie of enthusiastic supporters who had not represented a majority of the party in the past, but who were cohesive enough to win the Republican primaries easily with the help of a small increment of support from newly converted Reaganites.

The marathon preconvention race for the presidency has narrowed the role of presidential parties in policy development. Many candidates who have tested presidential waters by running in primaries have decried the grass-roots method of selecting party nominees. John Anderson, who made a quixotic run for the Republican nomination in 1980 before he was forced to become a third-party candidate, called the system that required him to shake hands at factory gates at sunrise in order to corral a few votes "a crazy way to select the leader of the greatest nation on earth."

Many candidates wince when asked about their experiences in the grueling race for the presidency. Rarely do they have time to think about "the party" — or about important issues of public policy. They generally do not have the time or the inclination to cast their campaigns in policy terms, to approach the electorate as a rational body interested in making a responsible choice between the parties on the basis of the voters' policy preferences. Issues of public policy generally take a back seat to concerns about image.

Most campaigners and their advisers agree with Marshall McLuhan that "the medium is the message," and they concentrate accordingly on the projection of their personalities rather than the content of issues. Messages to the public are kept simple and catchy in order to attract attention and encourage voters to think superficially rather than in depth about matters of public policy.

Walter Mondale, who immediately began gearing up for the 1984 presidential race after his ticket lost in 1980, has commented that to win the nomination and the White House, the candidate must be "willing to go through fire," something Mondale openly admitted he was not prepared to do when he first revealed presidential ambitions in 1974. The growth of the grass-roots nominating system, said Mondale, "has been malignant almost. It is anarchy."[11] "When you're running for president it's like a series of one-night stands in vaudeville — you have to have a good act every night. The good act may carry you farther than the good program."[12] Mondale concluded:

The feeling that bothered me more than anything else was that we were in the control of events we were unable to stop or do anything about. Experts are coming and telling you what you have to do, what positions you have to take — usually it's what they want. Then there are the people who want you to get a speech coach and cut your hair differently. None of that's very important. What's really important is that the goddamn news media won't pay you much attention until you've become big. You have to spend years on the road until you get enough percentage points in the polls. The national media won't give you a break until then, and their eyes turn glassy when you talk to them about it. They don't want to hear about it. That's because their business isn't electing presidents — it's competing with their competitors. The result is that the nation is denied a look at new leadership. If you want to get on the evening news, you have to escalate your rhetoric in order to merit the time. If you're saying something rational and restrained, that's not news. That's one of the reasons politicians look so bad. They're always saying something wild. The news programs don't want to put someone unknown on because their competitor might be putting someone well known on. It's understandable, but why shouldn't there be some national forum where who our next president might be is considered and among those considered are those who are not well known but who have great merit?[13]

Mondale expressed a different point of view during the 1984 primary campaigns, remarking that the primary process "tests much of the same qualities needed in a president, decision making under fire, the ability to unify and persuade."[14]

There is little disagreement with Washington attorney Fred Dutton's statement that a presidential campaign "is a frenetic, superficial, compulsive, neurotic process."[15] While the campaign does test the physical and emotional stamina of the candidates, their organizations, staff, financial backing, and ability to deal with the media — all of which are important in the proper handling of the presidency — campaigns do not and perhaps cannot raise all of the substantive policy issues that the people would like to know about because, ironically, the people are themselves too involved in the nomination process. Much can be hidden from public view in a political campaign, even many attributes of the personalities of the candidates, which can be glossed over much as their physical appearance can be changed by clever makeup before they appear in front of the television cameras.

## Electoral Choice, Parties, and Public Policy

Although political candidates are important representatives of the parties and their actions significant in terms of the role of the party in formulating and implementing public policy, the parties themselves play an important role in setting the policy agenda that goes far beyond that played by candidates and campaigns. Even though American parties are loosely organized confederations of diverse interests, they have become an important link between the people and government. Parties provide an important arena within which policy issues are debated intensely by political leaders and the representatives of powerful pressure groups.

---

[13]Drew, "Running," pp. 66–67.
[14]*Time*, April 23, 1984, p. 39.
[15]Ibid., p. 82.

*Parties and Issue Identification*

If one were to ask voters in any part of the country whether or not there are differences between the Democratic and Republican parties, the answer would most often be yes. Sixty-nine percent of the electorate clearly identify with one of the two major parties, and of the remaining voters who list themselves as independents a majority lean toward one or the other of the parties (see Figure 4.2). Regardless of regional differences between the parties, Democrats are generally identified with programs aimed at the redistribution of wealth, Social Security, and the use of government as a positive instrument to solve economic and social problems. Everyone "knows" that the Democrats are the party of the people, and the Republicans represent the rich. These perceptions are clichés, and like all clichés they are trite and overused expressions that often have little relationship to the truth. The fact remains, however, that people perceive fundamental differences between the parties. Those who identify with the Democratic party have different viewpoints on many issues of public policy than do those who identify with Republicans. This does not mean that those who identify with one party or the other necessarily vote for the candidates of that party in all circumstances. Ticket-splitting has become a common voting habit, one that is frequently cited as evidence of the decline of party politics.

Party differences over public policy are sharper at the national than at the state or local level. Only at the national level are the parties forced to accomodate wide-ranging and often conflicting interests in drafting their platforms every four years. The disintegration and personalization of presidential parties that began in earnest in the 1970s, together with political campaigns that stress images more than issues, have blurred party policy distinctions in the minds of many voters.

Voters have also been confused about party differences because of the sharp splits within the ranks of each party over important issues of public policy. In the past, for example, southern Democrats were diametrically opposed to their northern brethren on the issue of civil rights. Liberal northern Republicans favored free trade, while midwestern members of the party were isolationist and advocated trade barriers.

*The Background and Basis of Party Policy Differences*

As each party seeks a new identity in the 1980s, party leaders are building upon the past at the same time they are developing new policies for the future.

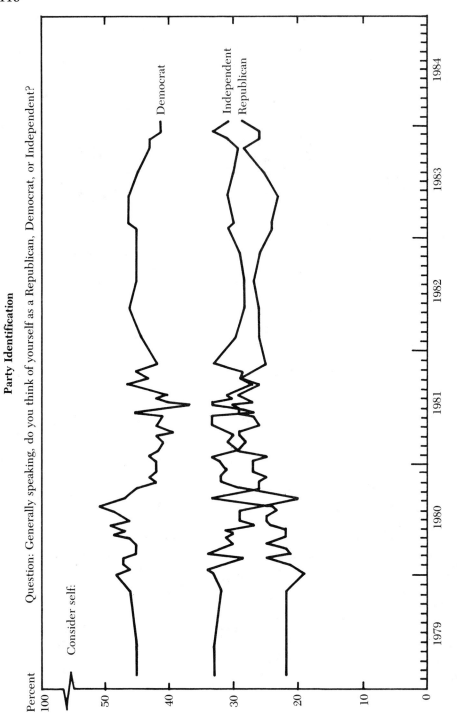

**Party Identification**

Question: Generally speaking, do you think of yourself as a Republican, Democrat, or Independent?

**Figure 4.2.** *Party Identification.*
SOURCE: *Public Opinion,* February/March 1984, p. 31. By permission of American Enterprise Institute for Public Policy Research, Washington, D.C.

*The Democrats.* The origins of the current differences between the two national parties are to be found in the crisis of the Depression and the parties' response to it. FDR formed the so-called Roosevelt coalition within the Democratic party, consisting of laborers, farmers, older Americans, the poor, and liberal intellectuals. The coalition became the basis of Roosevelt's electoral support, returning him to office for an unprecedented four terms. Roosevelt's New Deal programs were responsive to the interests and concerns of each of the groups within the coalition. An underlying assumption of the New Deal was that government should be used to solve economic and social problems. Roosevelt formed a "brain trust" of academic and other experts that encouraged him in his interventionist stance. The New Dealers were what political philosophers have called "positivists," those who believe that government can and should solve human problems. Keynesian economists were also part of Roosevelt's brain trust, urging deficit government spending to stimulate the economy. Roosevelt, who had promised a balanced budget in his 1932 campaign, seized on the Keynesian philosophy as a justification for increased government expenditures to cope with the overwhelming economic problems of the Depression.

*The Republicans.* The Republican response to the New Deal set the tone of future party deliberations and policies for years to come. The Republican party of the 1930s and 1940s was an out-party, excluded from the White House and with a minority in Congress. Just as the Democrats in 1984 had difficulty defining a national party program without an incumbent president to provide leadership, the Republicans of the 1930s and 1940s were a rudderless ship seeking port in the political storm that threatened to destroy the Grand Old Party once and for all. Because the out-party does not have a recognized leader, it tends to fragment into its interests, which are unable to agree on alternatives to the program of the party in power. Roosevelt could well have said, as Reagan did at the outset of his administration, "If you don't like what I am doing you have a responsibility to come up with an alternative to meet the national economic emergency." About all the Republicans did do was attack the New Deal, which they considered, in the words of their 1936 platform, to be a "peril to the nation." Under Roosevelt, they claimed, the powers of Congress had been usurped, the authority and integrity of the Supreme Court undermined, and the rights and liberties of citizens violated. They advocated returning responsibility for the welfare of the community to state and local governments as well as, in words that foreshadowed those of Ronald Reagan and David Stockman, balancing the budget "not by increasing taxes but by cutting expenditures, drastically and immediately." In 1936 Republicans urged, as did Ronald Reagan in his opening address to the nation, that a sound currency be preserved "at all hazards. The first requisite of a sound and stable currency is a balanced budget." The Republican party of the New Deal had not yet articulated the concept of "supply-side" economics, the use of tax cuts to increase incentive for productivity, but they certainly would have agreed with the principle. The roots of the Reagan philosophy of government are to be found in Republican policies of the past, and it is not insignificant that Reagan ordered Calvin Coolidge's pictures to be hung in the Oval Office.

*Party Differences on Foreign Policy.* The national Democratic and Republican parties of the Roosevelt era differed as sharply on foreign as on domestic policy. Isolationism characterized the Republican approach to world affairs, in contrast to Roosevelt's interventionist stance. Foreign policy differences between the parties blurred with the emergence of bipartisan foreign policy after World War II, when both Democrats and Republicans became "cold warriors" who considered the Soviet Union to be the principal threat to world peace and the security of the nation.

*Party Positions on Civil Rights.* The programs of both parties during the 1930s and early 1940s failed to include a civil rights policy. Note should be taken, however, of the women's rights plank in the 1940 Republican platform that favored an equal rights amendment. No such provision was found in the Democratic platform. In 1944 the Democrats picked up the cue, proposing an equal rights amendment to protect the rights of women. Also by 1944 both parties were beginning to pay attention to civil rights, and their platforms included strong statements on the issue. The Republicans in 1944 called for a congressional inquiry into segregation in the armed services and urged the adoption of corrective legislation. They supported a fair employment practices commission, the abolition of the poll tax, and legislation against lynching. The Democrats simply stated: "We believe that racial and religious minorities have the right to live, develop and vote equally with all citizens and share the rights that are guaranteed by our Constitution. Congress should exert its full constitutional powers to protect those rights."

The year 1944 thus marked the beginning of the articulation of civil rights policies by both parties that finally culminated in the passage of the Civil Rights Act of 1964 and the Voting Rights Act of 1965. Beginning with the Eisenhower administration, Republicans proposed a less interventionist role for the federal government in protecting civil rights, but nevertheless always supported the principle of equality under the law. The Republicans were more in favor of leaving the resolution of civil rights issues to the states than were the Democrats. In 1952, however, Republicans did call for federal legislation to end segregation in the District of Columbia.

The Eisenhower period was one of retrenchment for the Democrats, who continued to retain a slim majority of 54 percent of the electorate in congressional, state, and local elections. During the 1950s the Democratic party continued the rhetoric of the Roosevelt administration, doing little to reshape the policy proposals of the New Deal.

### Parties and Policy, 1960–1980

The policy themes of the national Democratic and Republican parties that originated in the New Deal continued with only slight variations in the early 1960s, but the winds of change were being felt by both parties. The comfortable Roosevelt coalition, which in the late 1940s had been threatened by growing southern sentiment opposing the stand of other party groups on civil rights, became even more shaky as the civil rights movement began to grow, reaching a crescendo in the mid and late 1960s. Black and minority support for the Democratic party had been unimportant to Roosevelt, but as these groups participated increasingly in politics they found a more comfortable home in the Democratic than in the Republican party. Most blacks were poor, and did not fit into the establishment circles of the Republicans. The economic programs of the Democrats appealed to blacks because the programs emphasized the importance of federal aid for welfare, education, housing, a minimum wage law, expanded Social Security benefits, and national health insurance. With the exception of many conservative southern Democrats, the party welcomed blacks and minority groups as an important electoral constituency, responding to their needs in the Great Society programs, the Civil Rights Act of 1964, and the Voting Rights Act of 1965.

The expansion of the base of the Democratic party to include blacks and other minorities, and the perception of liberals that the Democratic party was the only available vehicle for important political, social, and economic change, laid the groundwork for the more eclectic party that emerged between 1968 and 1972. The Roosevelt coalition had overexpanded, and it was now threatened unless the party could accommodate the diverse and often contrasting interests it had welcomed under its umbrella. The McGovern revolution was intended to facilitate this accommodation by widening the base of participation in party affairs; the party failed, however, to merge its expanded liberal wing with its conservative and moderate elements in 1972. The McGovern candidacy was considered to be extreme not only by the Republicans, but by many Democrats as well, who crossed party lines to vote for the incumbent, Richard Nixon.

While the Democratic party was changing its base, if not its policy, in the decades between 1960 and 1980, the Republicans too changed their moderate-to-liberal orientation to a highly conservative one. In the early 1960s, Governor Nelson Rockefeller of New York, Senator Barry Goldwater of

Arizona, and Nixon were prominent Republican figures representing, respectively, the liberal, conservative, and moderate wings of the party. Reagan, who was to become governor of California in 1966, was slowly emerging as a new conservative voice. Reagan, first a Democrat who had become a Republican in support of Nixon in 1960, did not formally change his party registration to Republican until 1962. The battles within the Republican party in the early 1960s did not include Reagan, but by 1968 he and his followers had become the conservative wing of the party. It was not until 1980, however, that the Reagan conservatives were able to capture the presidential wing of the party with Reagan's close win over Ford, the incumbent president, in the primaries and at the convention.

### Parties and Policies in the 1980s

Both the Republican and Democratic parties emerged after the 1980 nominating conventions with sharply contrasting social, economic, and civil rights policies that reflected past divergences between the parties. In 1964, Arizona's Senator Goldwater, the Republican nominee, had promised the people "a choice and not an echo." The voters overwhelmingly rejected the conservative Republican, electing Lyndon Johnson by a landslide of the popular vote that was the greatest achieved by any candidate in the twentieth century. In 1980 Reagan too promised a "real choice" to the American people, and once again the electorate voted decisively for change. Whether they were voting for a change of personalities or one of policies was not entirely clear. What they got, however, was a major redirection of government as promised by Reagan. With the help of a Republican Senate and conservative Democrats in the House, who provided a swing vote to give the party a majority, the new president was able to cut taxes and slash governmental expenditures while he enormously increased the defense budget. The Reagan juggernaut left the Democrats in disarray as they groped toward 1984 and the choice of a candidate to run against the extraordinarily popular incumbent.

### Party Trends in the Wake of the 1984 Elections

Ronald Reagan captured 49 percent of the popular vote and the electoral vote of 49 states in his sweeping 1984 victory. Democrats attempted to minimize the importance of the crushing Republican tide by referring to Reagan's win as a personal victory rather than a significant win for the party as a whole. They pointed to the fact that little had changed in the balance of power between the parties at the national and state levels. The Republicans picked up fourteen seats in the House of Representatives, and their already narrow majority in the Senate was reduced to a mere six seats, a loss of two. They gained only one gubernatorial office in the thirteen states that elected governors in 1984, leaving a clear Democratic majority of thirty-four Democratic to sixteen Republican governors. No significant changes occurred in party balances in state legislatures. The election appeared to be one supporting the political status quo as incumbents everywhere were overwhelmingly returned to office.

At virtually no time in American political history have the parties presented a sharper contrast than they did in the 1984 presidential race. Although the platform adopted by the Democrats muted somewhat the liberal ideology of the past, it nevertheless expressed traditional Democratic values rooted in Roosevelt's New Deal and Johnson's Great Society. In his stirring keynote address, New York Governor Mario Cuomo echoed FDR, proclaiming the importance of government in solving economic and social problems. "We believe in only the government we need," said Cuomo, "but we insist on all the government we need."[16]

*The 1984 Democratic Party Platform.* The Democrats sounded the alarm in their 1984 platform warning that a "fundamental choice awaits America — the choice between two futures." After using a great number of words to attack Reagan's programs, the platform presented the Democratic alternatives. Tax reform, deficit reduction, lower interest rates, and economic growth were listed as major goals. The platform emphasized a continued need for government action in education, job training, housing, and rebuilding the roads and bridges of the nation. Although it supported the deregulation of transportation, it also stressed the importance of continuing government regulation in such areas as occupational safety and health, food and drugs, and the environment. The document marked the first time that a campaign platform extensively examined the stand of the opposition party and its alternatives.

Combined with the politics of the convention and the rhetoric of the campaign that followed, the Democratic platform gave the impression more of a party in search of an identity than of one with a clear vision of the future. The coalition of the past that had elected Democratic presidents was in disarray, and more and more voters seemed to be shifting to the Republican party, possibly suggesting that a long-term realignment of voters was on the horizon unless the Democrats could field candidates and present issues that would be widely appealing.

---

[16]*Congressional Quarterly Weekly Report*, July 21, 1984, p. 1783.

*The 1984 Republican Party Platform.* The Republicans took a widely diverging position on every stand the Democrats had adopted. Congressman Trent Lott of Mississippi chaired the platform committee, which was dominated by members of Congress elected by their state parties to serve on the panel. Particularly influential were Jack Kemp of New York, Newt Gingrich of Georgia, and Henry Hyde of Illinois. Together they helped author a document that took strongly conservative positions on the economy and on social issues such as abortion and school prayer. The platform clearly showed the influence of party conservatives, and the few liberal Republicans among the delegates were pushed aside.

### The Meaning of Party Platforms

Former President Ford candidly told David Brinkley during an interview at the 1984 Republican convention that he had never bothered to read the platform on which he ran in 1976. He went on to say that when he was president he never consulted his party's platform before making a decision. In another interview Barry Goldwater, the Republican candidate for president in 1964, declared that he too never took party platforms seriously, noting that he and many of the delegates to the convention disagreed considerably with some of the 1984 Republican platform provisions.

Ford and Goldwater's comments acknowledge the reality that party platforms are not blueprints for governing but expressions of party politics. The positions they assume on policy issues reveal who has power and who does not within the party, and, as such, they are important primarily to the internal rather than to the external political world of parties. Candidates for office rarely if ever refer to platforms, which they often have very little opportunity to influence. In any case, the diverse nature of parties, the umbrella organizations that embrace wide-ranging political interests, has often produced bland platforms that state positions in such general terms that they could have little meaning even if they were taken seriously as a guide to future party action.

Before the convention a broadly representative committee within the party drafts its platform which is then taken to the convention floor for ratification. Delegates to the platform committee are chosen by party organizations around the country as well as the national leadership. The platform committee holds hearings to solicit the views of the different interests within the party. Although ideas from all sources are considered, ultimately the committee chairman and a small group of influential members draft a document that is skewed to reflect their particular ideological views on issues they consider important. The convention must ratify the party's platform, but platform drafters nevertheless have a great deal of discretion in the choice of content and — sometimes almost as important — wording.

Somewhat ironically, it is the fact that platforms reflect internal party politics that makes them particularly important in assessing the future political directions the parties may take. Candidates may not even read the platforms, and once elected they may not consider platform issues to be important in the making of public policy. Platform planks are taken very seriously, however, by party leaders and power brokers as well as by interest groups within the party as reflections of their power in party politics.

## Parties and Voters

While presidential, congressional, state, and local parties go about their business — formulating platforms, providing forums for the debate of issues and arenas for political conflict, defining the rules for selecting candidates in primaries, caucuses, conventions, and committees — the average voter more often than not views them from the outside and is puzzled about their political consequences.

### Changing Voter Attitudes Toward Parties

The decline of political parties is a popular theme among both political scientists and journalists. David Broder, columnist for the *Washington Post*, reflected the views of many of his colleagues when he wrote in 1971 that weak political parties had contributed to a failure of politics in America. "The governmental system is not working," he noted, "because the political parties are not working."[17] Examining electoral trends of the late 1960s, political scientist Walter Dean Burnham observed that "the political parties are progressively losing their hold upon the electorate. A new breed of independence seems to be emerging as well — a person with a better than average education, making a better than average income in a better than average occupation, and, very possibly, a person whose political cognitions and awareness keep him from making identifications with either old party."[18] Burnham concluded, "There is every reason to suppose that twentieth-century American politics has been preeminently marked by the decomposition and contraction of those partisan structures and functions which

[17]David S. Broder, *The Party's Over: The Failure of Politics in America* (New York: Harper & Row, 1971), p. xxiii.
[18]Walter Dean Burnham, *Critical Elections and the Mainsprings of American Politics* (New York: W.W. Norton, 1970), p. 130.

reached their widest, most cohesive form in the decades after the Civil War."[19]

That the United States seems to be evolving a system of politics without parties was reemphasized in 1984 by political scientist Martin P. Wattenberg: "Party coalitions in the United States have undergone a series of processes of decay over the last three decades, increasing the possibilities of *both* short-term and long-term change in the near future. With the weakening of the public's images of the parties, it is no wonder that volatility has become the new catchword of American politics. As the long-term forces that serve to anchor electoral behavior decline, the potential increases for large oscillations in the vote because of short-term issue and candidate factors."[20] Tracing the public's attitude toward political parties from 1952 to 1980, Wattenberg found that the electorate was growing increasing neutral (see Table 4.1). Apparently, a major reason for the growing voter neutrality toward parties is that they are rarely mentioned in the media.[21]

## Conclusion: Parties and Constitutional Democracy

With a constitutional system that discourages political parties more than it encourages them, and in a highly pluralistic society, American parties have performed an invaluable role in the aggregation of political interests throughout the country. They have provided vehicles for broad public choices and for peaceful political change. At critical times in American history, parties have formed and re-formed to articulate the interests of the electorate, altering significantly the course of government action. "Critical" elections — ones in which there are long-term realignments of voters along party lines — have marked significant turning points in the direction of government. The election of Franklin Roosevelt and the Democratic victory in Congress in 1932 is one example of a critical election, and the choice of Ronald Reagan in 1980 and 1984 may be another. The Republican party, long dominated by a white Protestant elite, attracted a far broader cross section of voters in 1980–1984 than it had in the past. Many white Protestants in the South voted for the Republican candidate, as did Catholic and Jewish voters, possibly to form a new Republican coalition. The mood of the nation in the 1980s is distinctly conservative, and the Republican party may become the usual choice of an electoral majority.

Given the nation's tremendous diversity, the parties have done the best

[19]Ibid., p. 131.
[20]Martin P. Wattenberg, *The Decline of American Political Parties, 1952–1980* (Cambridge: Harvard University Press, 1984), p. 131.
[21]Ibid., Chapter 6.

**Table 4.1.** *Trends in the Public's Attitude Toward the Two Major U.S. Parties, 1952–1980 (%)*

| Year | Neutral |
| --- | --- |
| 1952 | 13.0 |
| 1956 | 15.9 |
| 1960 | 16.8 |
| 1964 | 20.2 |
| 1968 | 17.3 |
| 1972 | 29.9 |
| 1976 | 31.3 |
| 1980 | 36.5 |

SOURCE: Martin P. Wattenberg, *The Decline of American Political Parties, 1952–1980.* Copyright © 1984 by Martin P. Wattenberg. Reprinted by permission of the President and Fellows of Harvard College.

that can be expected in bridging the gap between people and government. If the nation ever divides into two clearly contrasting camps, these will undoubtedly be reflected in two fairly disciplined political parties. But the American tradition of individualism, in combination with the almost inevitable continuation of the diversity of interests in the country, will probably prevent political parties in the future from having more distinctive and contrasting policy orientations than they have had in the past. Moreover, the policy differences between the parties have been sufficiently distinctive to offer a real choice to the electorate. The parties have expressed the feelings, often deeply held, of party supporters on broad issues of public policy, and they have helped to set a policy agenda for the nation.

## Suggestions for Further Reading

Burnham, Walter Dean. *Critical Elections and the Mainsprings of American Politics.* New York: W.W. Norton, 1970. An analysis of American voting behavior and political trends.

Burns, James MacGregor. *The Deadlock of Democracy: Four-Party Politics in America.* Englewood Cliffs, N.J.: Prentice-Hall, Inc., 1963. A provocative study of the failure of parties to overcome the separation of powers and govern effectively.

Eldersveld, Samuel J. *Political Parties in American Society.* New York: Basic Books, 1982. The author argues that parties and the party system are alive and well.

Fairlie, Henry. *The Parties: Republicans and Democrats in This Century.* New York: Simon & Schuster, 1978. A lively examination of Republican and Democratic politics.

Key, V.O., Jr. *The Responsible Electorate.* Cambridge: Belknap Press of Harvard University Press, 1966. The author's theme is that a highly rational electorate is often frustrated by manipulative presidential campaigns.

Ladd, Everett Carll, Jr., with Hadley, Charles D. *Transformations of the American Party System.* New York: W.W. Norton, 1975. Political coalitions from the New Deal to the 1970s.

O'Connor, Edwin. *The Last Hurrah.* Boston: Little, Brown, 1956. A best-selling novel, later made into a movie, about an old-time political boss beloved by the people and hated by the Establishment.

# chapter 5

# Interest Groups and Political Participation

Interest groups, like political parties, link people with government. Unlike parties, interest groups do not offer candidates to run for public office. In the United States, at least, interest groups reflect far narrower concerns than do political parties. Parties supply the personnel of government at the highest political levels. Interest groups may back particular political candidates, but more often they seek to avoid identification with one political party to the exclusion of the other. Interest group leaders prefer to play on both sides of the political fence to achieve their political objectives.

The framers of the Constitution viewed interest groups, like political parties, as undesirable factions that should be controlled by constitutional devices. The separate division of powers, representative government, and federalism, all of which were designed to prevent party government, were also thought to be effective constitutional arrangements to disperse the power of interest groups. At the same time, the First Amendment freedom of expression and right to assemble and to petition government for redress of grievances guaranteed a hospitable environment for the proliferation of interest groups.

The Madisonian view that interest groups are opposed to the national interest became representative of the thinking of a large segment of American society. Ironically, while American citizens created and joined interest groups in ever-increasing numbers from the early days of the Republic, pressure groups were often decried as being "selfish" because they advanced their own interests at the expense of those of the general public. The second half of the nineteenth century witnessed the passage of lobbying regulation laws by state legislatures, requiring lobbyists to register and report on their activities. National legislation to control interest groups followed in the twentieth century.

While interest groups have always operated to some degree under a cloud of suspicion, the fact remains that in our pluralistic political system, groups are important channels of communication between people and government. Indeed, some political scientists have suggested that interest groups are the lifeblood of the democratic process because they are the most important vehicles of political participation.

## The Group Theory Model of Government

In sharp contrast to the Madisonian view of groups, a political theory has developed that proclaims that interest groups do, collectively, represent the national interest insofar as that interest can be determined. Group theorists support the view that public policy should be grounded in the demands of relevant interest groups, which together with the government should play a large role in shaping policy that affects them. Group theory is both normative and empirical — that is, it attempts to express both what should be and what in fact exists. Group theorists support the domination of the political process by interest groups that characterizes many spheres of American politics.

Group theorists start with the assumption that in the political process people do not function as individuals but rather through interest groups. Political choice is group choice. Public policy decisions are always made on the basis of the interaction of interest groups with government. An interest group is very broadly defined as an organized or unorganized group of people with a common interest. In the political sphere, an interest group is one whose members share common public policy objectives and generally agree on the means of achieving them. Since, according to group theorists, individuals function only as members of interest groups, group politics becomes an inevitable and desirable part of the democratic process.

Interest groups are involved in government at every turn in the political process. Ronald Reagan immediately raised the opposition of a wide range of interest groups when he proposed far-reaching cuts in federal expenditures and programs that had been enacted in the first place largely in response to group demands. Only weeks after Reagan was inaugurated, coal miners marched in the streets of Washington to protest federal cutbacks in health programs to benefit victims of black lung disease. The dairy farming industry protested cutbacks in dairy supports. Veterans began to mobilize to protect their interests, as did a wide array of other groups that were affected by the sharp budget knife of David Stockman, Reagan's director of the Office of Management and Budget. Interest groups often have close ties with congressional committees and administrative agencies, and it seemed likely that Reagan's program of sweeping budget cuts would be severely modified by Capitol Hill in response to various groups' demands.

### *The Origins of Group Theory: John C. Calhoun's Concept of "Concurrent Majorities"*

Group theorists have always held that factions represent genuine and positive political interests that should be taken into account by government in the policy process. Indeed, one of the main dangers in majority rule is not that factions will control but rather that the power of the majority will override legitimate minority interests.

This viewpoint was one of many eloquently expressed by John C. Calhoun in *A Disquisition on Government,* published in 1853 shortly after his death. Calhoun wanted to construct a theory of government that would ensure that minority interests, such as those represented by the southern states during his time, would not be ignored by the national government. He suggested that all societies are divided into a number of different interest groups, and that the interests of each group are equally legitimate politically and should not be dealt with arbitrarily by government any more than government should deal arbitrarily with individuals. The political interests of the individual are naturally subsumed within the various interest groups of the community. To Calhoun and modern interest group theorists, democracy means group rather than individual participation in public policy formulation. If every person's interests are represented by groups, their argument runs, then the formulation of public policy by groups automatically represents the interests of individuals.

Calhoun was opposed to the development of majority rule and party government. He felt that the division of the country into two major political parties would inevitably produce a major and a minor party, the former dominating the political process completely. Moreover, he thought that as the parties developed they would become more and more detached from the broad interests of the community and would essentially reflect the viewpoints of party elites. As he explained this process,

The government would gradually pass from the hands of the majority of the party into those of its leaders, as the struggle became more intense, and the honors and emoluments of the government, the all absorbing objects. At this stage, principle and policy would lose all influence in the elections; and cunning, falsehood, deception, slander, fraud, and gross appeals to the appetites of the lowest and most worthless portions of the community, would take the place of sound reason and wise debate.[1]

As party leaders become farther and farther removed from the true interests of the community, the possibility of revolution would inevitably increase.

Calhoun's views of the nature and role of political parties suggest a definite conflict between group theory and that branch of democratic theory based on the idea that the only way in which effective democracy can be realized is through party rule. Moreover, although the constitutional model is not based on party rule and is in fact designed to limit the potential power of majorities and to control the influence of parties in government, Calhoun was not satisfied that the constitutional policy-making model sufficiently took into account the diverse interests of the community. He felt that the classical model set up a government in which the numerical majority would determine policy. By numerical majority, he did not necessarily mean a majority of individuals, but a majority formed on the basis of compromises among diverse interest groups. This interest group majority could dominate the branches of national government and force its will on the rest of the community.

Calhoun proposed as a substitute for the constitutional model a system of "concurrent" majority rule (see Figure 5.1). The concurrent majority differs from the numerical majority in that each interest group essentially determines for itself whether to reject or accept any governmental policy affecting it. Calhoun never worked out the details of this system, but it clearly implied that in their spheres of interest minority groups would be able to determine governmental policy. Accepting the premise that all legitimate political interests are represented by groups, the concurrent majority system would bring about the greatest possible freedom for the political interests of the community.

Calhoun was writing at a time when the southern states were struggling to maintain their interests in a government in which they were outnumbered by the states of the North and West. The concurrent majority system so eloquently expressed by Calhoun was very similar to the doctrine of nullification that had gained favor in the South, although not in the rest of the country. According to that doctrine each state, acting independently, could veto legislation that it did not find acceptable. The states were considered to be the major political interest groups.

[1]John C. Calhoun, *A Disquisition on Government* (New York: Political Science Classics, 1947), pp. 41–42.

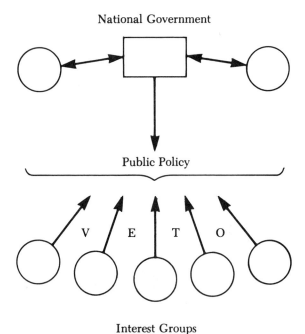

Figure 5.1. *John C. Calhoun's Theory of Concurrent Majority. In Calhoun's concurrent majority theory, each interest group has a veto on national policy affecting it.*

## Modern Group Theory

The most important expression of group theory in modern terms is that of David B. Truman, whose book *The Governmental Process,* published in 1953, has had a profound and lasting effect on the way political scientists view the policy-making process.[2] Drawing on the works of other group theorists, particularly Arthur F. Bentley's *The Process of Government,* which appeared in 1908,[3] Truman asserted that all policy is the result of group interaction, and that this is the only realistic way one can view the political process. Although he did not go so far as to suggest that Calhoun's concurrent majority system was in fact in operation, the tenor of Truman's work was in this direction. Moreover, like Calhoun, he suggested that group de-

[2]David B. Truman, *The Governmental Process* (New York: Alfred A. Knopf, 1953).
[3]Arthur F. Bentley, *The Process of Government* (Chicago: University of Chicago Press).

termination of public policy is the most democratic method of government in channeling legitimate political demands to government.

### *"Potential" Groups*

An important part of the group model of policy formation is the concept of the "potential" interest group. This concept is based on the idea that by definition potential political interests always exist, submerged below the surface of society, which can be activated when people sharing those interests are made aware of the need to take action. It might be possible, for example, to view some of the groups that organized to resist the escalation of the Vietnam War as potential groups whose political awareness finally reached the stage necessary for political activism. Similarly, the consumer and environmental groups that organized in the 1960s and 1970s, exerting a strong force on public policy, reflected interests that had been dormant in previous decades. As long as interest groups remain potential rather than actual they do not directly influence the political process. The possibility that they may organize, however, must always be taken into account by decision makers. Thus, group theorists suggest that even potential groups exert some influence on the policy-making process.

The theory of potential interest groups conveniently solves the problem that is often raised with regard to the group model, that some interests are always better represented in government than others. The group theorists do not deny this; however, they state that if one accepts the existence of potential groups then in fact all interests of society are, by definition, taken into account in one form or another by the institutions of government. It is presumably primarily through the electoral process that potential groups are able to exert influence, since politicians are constantly seeking the "critical mass" necessary for election. There is always a great deal of guesswork among candidates regarding the representative views of their constituents. These views cannot be determined simply by looking at the positions taken by leaders of pressure groups, for the leaders do not always reflect the views of the membership. Moreover, the fact that members of one group generally identify with a number of other groups means that the attitudes of individuals toward the official policy positions taken by the groups with which they identify can always shift.

In reality, it is difficult to accept the group theorists' notion that potential interest groups solve the problem of lack of representation in government of those whose views are not reflected in the positions taken by leaders of powerful organized interests. For example, it was not until Ralph Nader and others began to represent the interests of consumers and to organize consumer groups that the government took consumer interests seriously.

The concern of the government in recent years with environmental matters is also due to the rise of organized pressure groups, such as the Sierra Club, that counterbalance the power of private corporate interests.

*Defining the National Interest*

Interest group theory requires political pluralism. The group model is premised on the idea that the national interest cannot be clearly identified apart from the interests of groups in the political community. This is true by definition if one defines groups in such a way that they take into account the political interests of all individuals. No governmental decision, however, can represent the views of all groups in society, but must compromise among competing interests. In such circumstances, how are those given the responsibility for making final decisions to determine what is correct and proper, or in the public interest?

Assuming equal access to government among groups whose interests are at stake, it seems reasonable that one can fall back on the concept of a procedural ethic to produce the national interest. That is, if every relevant interest has its "day in court," the final decision can be considered the closest approximation to the national interest that is possible in any democratic society as long as it takes into account the views that have been expressed by the groups involved. Even the group theorist, however, might not accept this view, because unless the interests of potential groups are also taken into account in the policy-making process, what emerges cannot be considered the optimum national interest.

The national interest must be more than the sum of the interests of the organized groups of the nation. But by saying this, theorists are adding a mystical dimension to their argument, one which allows the content of the national interest to be hypothesized apart from the interests of identifiable groups. Since no one really knows what constitutes a potential interest group, appealing to the assumed interests of unorganized constituents in making a public policy decision is tantamount to invoking the national interest. When President Nixon stated that the "silent majority" of the American people supported his decisions on Vietnam as well as in certain domestic areas, he was, in the terms of group theory, appealing to a vast potential interest group whose needs had to be taken into account. But in reality no one can know what the "silent majority" is. In fact, the president was embarking on a course of action that he considered to be in the national interest, regardless of the articulated views to the contrary of many organized groups.

Nixon's declaration that a silent majority of the American people supported his actions was not unique to his administration; in fact, presidents both before and after have voiced the same idea. Presidents characteristically believe in what they are doing, assuming that the "silent majority" supports them. As Ronald Reagan initiated his controversial budget-cutting program, 24 percent of the American people expressed disapproval of his presidential performance after he had been in office only two months, the highest disapproval rating ever recorded for a president at the beginning of his first term. The Reagan White House, however, blithely ignored opinion polls, stating that the supportive letters it had received reflected the real views of the people. Reagan, like most presidents before him, undertook a course of action he considered to be in the national interest regardless of the strong political opposition of organized interests and indications of significant popular disapproval as well. The White House counted on the support of the most important interest group of all, the majority of Americans who had elected the president in November. Electoral choice and group preferences rarely coincide, however, as groups seek to pressure government for policies that advance their own interests. The political clout of organized pressure groups often defeats what presidents proclaim to be the wishes of the people.

*Imperfect Mobilization of Political Interests*

Apart from the idea of potential interest groups as a limit on excessive power of organized pressure groups, the group model has also developed other concepts to explain why the interaction of groups does not lead to the domination of the policy process by factions. The most important of these is what E.E. Schattschneider called the "law of the imperfect mobilization of political interests."[4] Based on the fact that individuals are always members of more than one group, this principle states that overlapping group memberships make it impossible for any one group to claim the total loyalty of its members (see Figure 5.2).

For example, doctors working for the Veterans' Administration (VA) have a group identification with both the American Medical Association (AMA) and their employer. On the issue of socialized medicine, the AMA and the VA are in many significant respects opposed to each other. The former has traditionally favored as much freedom of choice as possible for those delivering and receiving medical services, and has supported limited governmental involvement in medicine. The Veterans Administration has generally given an example of socialized medicine in practice, although on a limited

[4]E.E. Schattschneider, *Party Government* (New York: Holt, Rinehart and Winston, 1942), pp. 32–34.

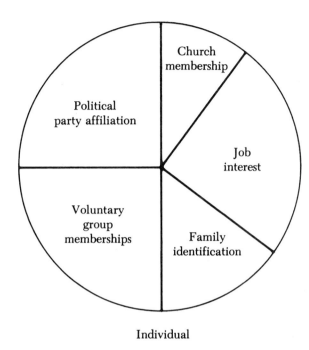

Individual

**Figure 5.2.** *Imperfect Mobilization of Political Interests. Political interests cannot be perfectly mobilized because each person has multiple group memberships and identifications.*

scale. Both the AMA and the VA are interest groups that have vigorously pursued their viewpoints before Congress, the president, and throughout the political system. Neither group, however, can completely claim the loyalty of VA doctors on this particular issue because of the conflicting identifications and values that they hold as a result of membership in both groups.

For group theorists, the existence of overlapping group membership is considered to be the greatest check on factional domination of decision making on a particular policy. A strong argument can be made, however, that this check is ineffective because interest groups do not have to claim the total loyalty of their membership in order to be highly influential in the political process. In fact, the official positions of these groups on political issues are shaped primarily by leaders, not by members. Interest group leaders are more often than not able to convince policymakers that they reflect the views of all members of their group. This can be a serious limitation on the effectiveness of Schattschneider's law of the imperfect mobilization of political interests as a check on group power.

### Countervailing Power

Another concept advanced by group theorists attempting to explain the limited nature of the power of groups is the theory of countervailing power. The essence of this theory is that the power of one group will balance that of another, and throughout the political system groups will tend to check and balance each other (see Figure 5.3). For example, the power of industrial firms will tend to be balanced by that of labor unions, and this will mean that neither will get its way entirely in the political system. Originally advanced in the economic realm by John Kenneth Galbraith in the early 1950s[5] it soon became evident that the theory worked in neither the economic nor the political sphere. The tendency of interest groups is often not to counteract each other, but rather to operate together for mutual benefit. In the economic sphere, for example, the wage demands of labor unions are frequently happily met by management, which simply passes the burden on to the consumer in the form of higher prices.

In the political sphere also, countervailing power is more myth than reality. Each area of public policy has a set of interest groups concerned with it. This set operates within the framework of a political subsystem, in which the particular interests make demands and give supports to various parts of the government that act as conversion structures for the specialized policy area. For example, the Defense Department, in conjunction with the armed services and appropriations committees in the House as well as the president, acts as the focal point of demands from the armaments industry. Policy is formulated within this system, even though its effects have a profound impact on the whole community. The interest groups in the subsystem balance each other to some extent, but they are in accord on the aim to expand the armaments pie so that their piece will be even larger when it is divided. In terms of the political system as a whole, these interests are in effect in collusion to increase the amount of money appropriated for their sphere relative to other areas. Although they are in conflict within their subsystem, this countervailing power does not effectively limit their operation or their influence in the political system.

### Constitutional Checks

Another important way in which interest groups are limited is, of course, by the Constitution. Checks and balances, provisions for extraordinary majorities of greater than 50 percent (e.g., treaties, veto overrides, amendments), and the generally pluralistic character of the governmental apparatus itself are meant to make it difficult for any faction to gain undue

[5]John Kenneth Galbraith, *American Capitalism* (Boston: Houghton Mifflin, 1952).

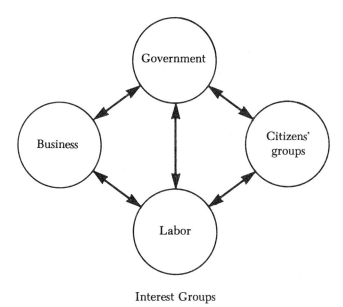

Interest Groups

**Figure 5.3.** *Countervailing Power. The theory of countervailing power asserts that interest groups will check and balance each other.*

power in the policy-making process. But in many cases the very structure of government, which was designed to limit and control factions, has enhanced their influence, since the Constitution provides so many access points at which interest groups can attempt to influence policy. In the original constitutional scheme, these access points were each of the three branches of the government. Because the policy-making process was not fragmented among small units of the government as it is now, interest groups could more easily negate public policy in one branch than bring about the agreement of the three branches of government to make affirmative decisions. The highly specialized nature of policy formulation in our day means that the administrative branch, in conjunction with congressional committees on different areas of policy, can make both affirmative and negative policy decisions. Pressure groups now bring their influence to bear on these bodies. Regardless of what caused the fragmentation of our policy-making process, the modern structure of government greatly increases pressure group influence over what it would be if governmental policy were formulated on the basis of a cohesive majority in Congress led by the president.[6]

[6]Even when cohesive majorities rule, however, pressure groups may determine public policy. See Harry Eckstein, *Pressure Group Politics* (Stanford, Calif.: Stanford University Press, 1960).

On balance, the assurances of group theorists that the pluralism of our system is nothing more than the reflection of a healthy democracy are not convincing. Perhaps we cannot define the national interest, but it is difficult to believe that it never exists apart from the interests articulated by groups. The concept of potential groups is excellent in theory, but potential groups themselves are almost impossible to identify in practice. The groups that are best organized, and that have the most resources and access to decision makers, exert the most power in the political system. The mystical concept of potential interest groups does not explain this away. Those who go along with Calhoun's theory of the concurrent majority would support the idea that the most powerful interests have the greatest say in policymaking. In fact, Calhoun felt that this was the only way in which a political system could be held together; the more powerful interests should be given a larger voice in public policy formulation simply because of their position in the community. This does not produce irresponsible government, but rather government responsible to narrow interests.

Another limit on the democratic nature of group politics is that pressure groups tend to be run by elites, who are often given very broad boundaries within which they can make decisions. Interest group participation in politics means elite control, rather than the formulation of policies by the members of interest groups. There is not necessarily anything wrong with such a system, but interest group politics does not overcome the extraordinary difficulties in bringing about a realization of the democratic ideal.

## The Formal Context of Group Action

The group model of policy formation suggests that interest groups are the focal point of the policy process, subsuming all the legitimate political interests of the community. Members of an interest group, as defined by group theorists, have shared attitudes concerning the goals they want to achieve and the methods of obtaining their objectives. Interest groups can be public or private. The Defense Department is as much an interest group lobbying other branches of the government for its own purposes as is General Motors Corporation. Most discussions of interest groups exclude the public realm, and thereby eliminate an important dimension. Both public and private groups often seek the same kind of objective, focusing on solidifying their position and increasing their power in government.

The activities of both public and private pressure groups are affected by a number of factors. The constitutional structure is based on the premise that factions should be discouraged. The mechanisms of government, especially the separation of powers and the checks and balances system, are designed to make it impossible for any one faction to dominate the policy process. The constitution establishes a pluralistic structure of government, however, which means that public interest groups, in the form of governmental branches with contrasting objectives, are built into the political mechanism. The three branches of government are intended to achieve different goals in response to different constituencies.

Private interest groups are able to exercise influence by gaining access to many parts of government. The establishment of the bureaucracy with broad policy-making powers has led to the most intense political pressures being focused on administrative agencies. The first ingredient, then, in the operation of pressure groups is the pluralism of our governmental structure, reflected by public interest groups, which enables private groups to gain more access to the policy-making process than would be the case in a more unified government.

## The Effects of Federalism

Madison argued in *The Federalist* (No. 10) that the federal structure established by the Constitution would tend to isolate and reduce the power of pressure groups. Actually, though, the structure only enhances the pluralistic nature of the political process and expands the role of groups. First, it creates a large number of governmental pressure groups at state and local levels that would not exist in a unitary form of government. State and local governments have their own power bases, and they exert a strong influence on the national political process for particular policy goals. Today, states maintain paid lobbyists in Washington, and many of the larger cities also have lobbyists whose sole responsibility is to look out for legislation and other government activities affecting the interests of the urban areas they represent.

## Constitutional Protection of Interest Groups

In addition to expanding and encouraging interest group activity, the constitutional system protects the right of private groups to organize and to petition government for redress of grievances. The First Amendment rights mean that the government cannot take action that would curb the normal activities of interest groups.

*Federal Regulation of Lobbying.* The issue of the rights of interest groups was confronted head-on in the case of *United States* v. *Harriss* (1954), when the Court was asked to rule on the constitutionality of the Federal Regulation of Lobbying Act of 1946.[7] The act required the registration with the clerk of the House and the secretary of the Senate of all persons "attempting to influence the passage or defeat of any legislation by the Congress." In the registration form lobbyists were to give their names and addresses and that of their employers, how long they had been employed, how much they were paid, by whom, and for what purposes. They were to list the names of any newspapers or periodicals in which they had caused publications to appear in order to influence directly or indirectly the passage or defeat of legislation. The terms of the act were very broad indeed, and vague enough so that on appeal to the courts the plaintiffs argued that it violated the constitutional requirement of definiteness in the criminal realm.

In its opinion, the Supreme Court ruled that the statute could be upheld as long as its provisions were interpreted narrowly to regulate only those directly involved in lobbying for or against pending or proposed legislation before Congress. Chief Justice Warren made it clear that any attempt by Congress to enact broader restrictions on the activities of pressure groups would be a violation of the First Amendment. Justices Douglas and Black wrote that even narrowly construed, the Federal Regulation of Lobbying Act could "easily ensnare people who have done no more than exercise their constitutional rights of speech, assembly, and press." The majority, however, felt that some limitation on these rights was justified if Congress were to exercise its legislative function in a rational and deliberate way without undue attention to the demands of pressure groups. In the words of Chief Justice Warren,

Present-day legislative complexities are such that individual members of Congress cannot be expected to explore the myriad pressures to which they are regularly subjected. Yet full realization of the American ideal of government by elected representatives depends to no small extent on their ability to properly evaluate such pressures. Otherwise the voice of the people may all too easily be drowned out by the voice of special interest groups seeking favored treatment while masquerading as proponents of the public weal. This is the evil which the Lobbying Act was designed to help prevent.[8]

As long as Congress does not suppress pressure groups but merely circumscribes them and requires that publicity be given to direct lobbying efforts, the requirements of the Constitution are met.

*Campaign Finance Laws.* Aside from requiring the registration of lobbyists and the public reporting of their sources of funds and expenditures, Con-

---

[7] *United States v. Harriss*, 347 U.S. 612 (1954).
[8] Ibid.

gress has prohibited corporations and labor unions from making contributions to or expenditures for the election of any federal official. The corporate spending ban was first enacted in 1907, becoming part of the Corrupt Practices Act of 1925. A ban on union spending was first enacted in 1943 and made permanent by the Taft-Hartley Act of 1947. The prohibitions on corporate and union spending for political campaigns for federal offices was reaffirmed and strengthened in the comprehensive Federal Election Campaign Practices Act, passed in 1971 and amended in 1974 to extend its coverage. In addition to absolutely proscribing corporate and labor union contributions in connection with federal elections, the act limited to a thousand dollars the contributions individuals could make to political campaigns and placed ceilings on the amount of money that candidates for federal office could spend in their election campaigns. Rigid reporting requirements were included in the law, and a federal election commission was established to implement it.

*The Challenge to Campaign Laws.* The Federal Election Campaign Act was challenged on First Amendment grounds in 1976 by then Senator James Buckley of New York, former presidential candidate and senator from Minnesota Eugene McCarthy, and others who argued that the law impinged on their First Amendment freedom of speech and right to associate. The Supreme Court ruled on the case in *Buckley* v. *Valeo* (1976), holding that although the government could control contributions to political campaigns, it could not control spending by campaigns. Spending, stated the Court, is a form of speech that is protected by the First Amendment. At the outset of its opinion the Court stressed that the contribution and expenditure limitations of the law "operate in an area of the most fundamental First Amendment activities. Discussion of public issues and debate on the qualifications of candidates are integral to the operation of this system of government established by our Constitution."[9] "The interests served by the Act," continued the Court, "include restricting the voices of people and interest groups who have money to spend and reducing the overall scope of federal election campaigns. Although the Act does not focus on the ideas expressed by persons or groups subjected to its regulations, it is aimed in part at equalizing the relative ability of all voters to affect electoral outcomes by placing a ceiling on expenditures for political expression by citizens and groups."[10]

The Court reasoned in *Buckley* v. *Valeo* that the restrictions on contributions could be sustained because they would not diminish effective polit-

---

[9]*Buckley* v. *Valeo*, 424 U.S. 1, 14 (1976).
[10]Ibid., p. 17.

ical advocacy. Contribution limits would merely require political candidates and committees to raise funds from a greater number of persons. The expenditure limitation, however, was an unconstitutional impingement on freedom of speech and the right to associate freely because it would operate to reduce the scope of political campaigns and advocacy. The Court concluded that restrictions "on the amount of money a person or group can spend on political communication during a campaign necessarily reduces the quantity of expression by restricting the number of issues discussed, the depths of their exploration, and the size of the audience reached."[11]

While the decision of the Court in *Buckley* v. *Valeo* did not free interest groups to use money as they wished in political campaigns, it significantly expanded the permissible boundaries within which they could function to influence the electoral process. The Court had left no doubt that there were important constitutional limits on the authority of Congress to control the freedom of expression of interest groups and their First Amendment right to associate.

*Protection of Public Advocacy.* The Court continued to expand the constitutional protection of the political advocacy of interest groups by holding that a state public service commission could not forbid a utility to send out with its bills leaflets that advocated particular public policies the utility considered favorable to its interests. The Consolidated Edison Company of New York had sent out with its bills material entitled "Independence Is Still a Goal, and Nuclear Power Is Needed to Win the Battle." The material discussed the benefits of nuclear power, which "far outweigh any potential risk," and assured the reader that nuclear power plants are safe, economical, and clean. The message concluded that only with the development of nuclear power could the energy dependence of the United States be significantly reduced.

The nuclear power advocacy of the Consolidated Edison Company was highly controversial, and it was immediately challenged by the Natural Resources Defense Council, an antinuclear group. The council requested the opportunity to enclose a rebuttal in the next billing, and when Consolidated Edison refused, it went to the Public Service Commission of New York to request that the utility make its billing envelopes available to groups with contrasting views. The commission responded by prohibiting utilities from using bill inserts to discuss political matters, on the grounds that the customers of regulated utilities who receive bills are a captive audience with diverse views who should not be forcibly subjected to the utility's beliefs. The Supreme Court on appeal concluded that "the Commission's suppres-

---

[11]Ibid., p. 19.

sion of bill inserts that discuss controversial issues of public policy directly infringes the freedom of speech protected by the First and Fourteenth Amendments."[12] The Court found that the state had not demonstrated, as it was required to, a compelling interest to justify the restriction imposed by the commission. On the same day the Consolidated Edison case was decided, the Court held that the Public Service Commission could not bar promotional advertising by utilities even if the material advocated a course of action that the state had concluded was against the public interest.[13]

## The Informal Context of Group Action

### The Lack of Disciplined Parties

Another key part of the context within which interest groups operate is the general lack of disciplined political parties in the United States. In many countries, political parties represent very narrow interests, just as pressure groups do; they are factions in the Madisonian sense. In our political system, the absence of such parties is a reflection of the diversity of political forces in the nation. There is no way that ideologically coherent parties can develop out of the political pluralism and the fragmentation of power in the constitutional system. The lack of disciplined parties is not so much a cause of the increased importance of interest groups as an effect of interest group pluralism.

### Laissez-faire Capitalism

Although the Constitution discourages reliance on interest groups as the best influence in shaping public policy, the dominant tendencies in American economic, political, and social development have fostered pluralism. The philosophy of laissez-faire capitalism is analogous to political group theory. The belief that if individuals or groups pursue their own interests and thereby produce what is economically in the public interest is directly equivalent to the interest group theory that the interaction of pressure groups will bring about the closest approximation of the public interest that is possible in a free society.

The capitalist ethic was never fully believed or carried out. It was frequently used merely for propaganda purposes and as a support for the aggressive and often ruthless activities of private enterprise. Nevertheless, the

[12]*Consolidated Edison Co. v. Public Service Commission of New York*, 447 U.S. 530, 544 (1980).
[13]*Central Hudson Gas and Electric Corp. v. Public Service Commission of New York*, 447 U.S. 557 (1980).

theory of capitalism seeped into the crevices of the political system at many points. It has had a strong impact in both the economic and political realms. As groups transferred their practices in the economic sphere to the area of political action, it was only natural to think that the best policy would be produced through group competition.

The ethic of capitalism lends strong support to the idea that competition among pressure groups should be the primary procedure for the formulation of public policy. This ethic is different from group theory in several important respects. It does not recognize the counterbalancing role of government against the forces of the private community. It suggests, rather, that the only legitimate interests are those in the private realm, and that government should be no more than a reflection of the powerful groups of society. Minimal government is the capitalist ideal. Government should intervene only to maintain the rules of the game and to provide minimum needs such as national defense.

## Rise of Voluntary Associations

Pluralism is shaped not only by the way economic groups interact with each other and relate to government, but also by the tendency of individuals in other spheres to organize associations to represent noneconomic interests. Alexis de Tocqueville wrote in *Democracy in America* that the tendency of Americans to form associations for virtually every conceivable purpose was one of the most notable characteristics of our society. "In no country in the world," de Tocqueville maintained, "has the principle of association been more successfully used or applied to a greater multitude of objects than in America."[14]

De Tocqueville emphasized the proclivity of Americans to organize their activities through groups. In many cases these groups performed functions similar to that of government today. Self-reliance and individualism did not mean that individuals stood by themselves, but rather that they organized with their fellows to meet whatever challenges they faced. As it became increasingly evident that voluntary associations could not by themselves handle the complex problems that were arising in nineteenth-century industrial America and that government would have to be expanded, the vast array of private groups formed a reservoir of interests and became the dominating influence in an expanded political process. In de Tocqueville's terms, both interest groups and political parties were examples of voluntary associations in the society that he studied.

[14]Alexis de Tocqueville, *Democracy in America*, vol. 1 (New York: Vintage Books, 1954), p. 198.

## Government Decision Making as a Group Process

Groups have access to government at a number of points, and they are deeply involved in the decision-making processes that shape public policy. Congressional, executive, and particularly judicial procedures encourage and stress interest group participation.

### Group Influence on Congress

Congressional organization and procedures reflect and enhance group power in many ways.

*Fragmented Parties.* Congress is as pluralistic as the political world beyond Capitol Hill, and nowhere is this reflected better than in the lack of disciplined congressional parties. Party organizations are loosely knit on both sides of Capitol Hill, exercising power by consensus rather than by command. Party leaders help to determine policy agendas, but they do so in consultation with powerful committee chairmen who, with their staffs, continue to be predominant. Because Congress does not, through its parties, act as a cohesive and collective force in policymaking, pressure groups can often act in conjunction with the committees that represent their interests to control the content of public policies that affect them.

*Committees as Group Representatives.* The political pluralism that has prevented congressional parties from successfully aggregating wide-ranging interests has encouraged group representation through committees. Private groups are often directly represented on Capitol Hill by committees that act as gatekeepers, choosing what legislation will be proposed affecting their interests. Committees, always seeking to maintain or expand their power within the legislature, are responsible to their policy constituencies, the groups under their jurisdiction, relying on them to provide a political base that is useful in throwing back attacks from outside. For example, forces within Congress as well as outside Capitol Hill periodically seek to reorganize committees, to make them more efficient and responsive to broader political interests (see Chapter 7). When this happens, committees that are attacked mobilize forces within their constituencies to pressure Congress to maintain the status quo. Such tactics usually work, which explains why the number of committees, particularly subcommittees, has grown over the years.

*Congressional Procedures and Group Participation.* Because Congress does not generally act collectively through its parties, its procedures as well as its

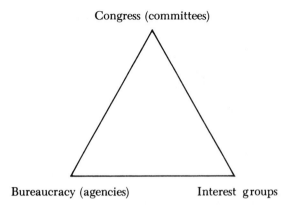

**Figure 5.4.** *The Iron Triangle of Politics. An "iron triangle" connects congressional committees, administrative agencies, and interest groups in mutually supportive arrangements.*

organization enhance group participation. Committees and the groups within their jurisdictions act together as conduits of policy proposals. The views of interested groups are solicited not only in formal hearings, but also informally in conversations with committee chairmen, members, and aides. Private groups, often in conjunction with administrative departments and agencies that frequently represent common viewpoints, supply expert advice to legislators, helping them to draft legislation that takes into account their interests.

*Political Iron Triangles.* The links between congressional committees, private groups, and administrative departments and agencies have often been described as an "iron triangle" (see Figure 5.4). Forged by the incentive to maintain and expand political power, the components of the triangle act collusively to protect their mutual interests. Put perhaps oversimply, private groups help to sustain committees and agencies in return for a favorable consideration of their views. Traditionally, iron triangles have dominated "micropolitical" policy arenas, those in which generally narrow interests are involved. For example, government subsidies to businesses, farmers, and a host of other special interests have been maintained because of the influence of multiple iron triangles. Reagan tried to break the power of iron triangles in many subsidy areas when he came into office in 1981, and again as he embarked on his second term in 1985. White House efforts have succeeded in some policy areas, but the iron triangles are far from dismantled. For example, the House Education and Labor committee spearheaded an effort to restore the cuts in student loans Reagan has proposed in his first term.

**Table 5.1.** *Biggest Spenders of 1984*

| Senate | |
|---|---|
| Jesse Helms (R) North Carolina* | $16,363,390 |
| Jay Rockefeller (D) West Virginia* | $11,736,423 |
| Phil Gramm (R) Texas* | $10,153,877 |
| James Hunt (D) North Carolina | $ 9,530,608 |
| Lloyd Doggett (D) Texas | $ 6,263,000 |
| *House* | |
| Andrew Stein (D) New York | $ 1,739,000 |
| Bill Green (R) New York* | $ 1,163,234 |
| Robert Dornan (R) California* | $ 1,100,000† |
| James Jones (D) Oklahoma* | $ 1,100,000† |
| Stan Parris (R) Virginia* | $   884,049 |
| *Governor* | |
| Rufus Edmisten (D) North Carolina | $ 4,128,141 |
| John Ashcroft (R) Missouri* | $ 3,125,000 |
| Robert Orr (R) Indiana* | $ 3,005,140 |
| James Martin (R) North Carolina* | $ 2,511,825 |
| Kenneth Rothman (D) Missouri | $ 1,863,000 |

SOURCE: *U.S. News & World Report,* December 17, 1984. Copyright © 1984 by U.S. News & World Report, Inc. Reprinted by permission.
*Denotes winner.
†est.
*USN&WR*—Basic data: Campaign committee official estimates

*Electoral Support.* Pressure groups appeal to the reelection as well as to the career incentives of legislators, helping to finance the campaigns of incumbents through political action committees (PACs). Not only do groups contribute directly to the primary and general election campaigns of legislators, keeping within the $5,000 limit imposed by federal law, but they also may spend an unlimited amount on their own to back or oppose candidates. Congressional campaigns are extraordinarily expensive, with amounts approximating half a million dollars not uncommon in House races, and in the Senate at least several million dollars is generally spent (see Table 5.1). Unlike presidential campaigns, congressional election campaigns are not federally financed, primarily because the incumbents who would pass any law authorizing campaign expenditures from the federal treasury know that the lack of federal financing gives them an advantage over challengers because of their greater fund-raising capabilities. Pressure groups held firmly to the adage that a bird in the hand is worth two in the bush, and they prefer to give money to incumbents of both parties, knowing they have greater reelection chances than challengers (see Chapter 7).

The number of political action committees has greatly expanded over the years, making Congress, in the view of cynics, "the best that money can buy" (see Figure 5.5). While the public interest pressure group Common Cause and others have attempted to curtail political action committee contributions to congressional campaigns, both the committees and the groups they represent are integral and important parts of our political process. The Supreme Court has protected the constitutional freedom of groups not only to exist but to spend as much money as they wish for political causes, limiting only the amounts they may contribute directly to political campaigns. No concrete evidence has yet been gathered to prove that past contributions have controlled congressional votes, although legislators themselves agree that it would be naive to suggest they are not well aware of groups that consistently contribute to their campaigns.

### Group Influence on the Executive Branch

While the broad national constituency of the president isolates him somewhat and enables him to deflect special interest pressures, the departments and agencies of the executive branch, even though not elected, are tied to and influenced by private groups in many ways.

*The White House and Special Interests.* Modern presidents are not as beholden to interest groups as they once were. This is because presidents, although the titular heads of their parties, do not rely exclusively on any particular set of party power brokers and the groups they represent to nominate or elect them. Party reforms emphasizing the selection of delegates through primaries and open caucuses have largely pushed aside the party power brokers of the past who met in smoke-filled rooms to choose presidential nominees. Candidates now build their own organizations to capture the nomination and general election, drawing but not depending on broader party resources. They use political consultants and television to build images that will have the widest possible appeal. Although they meet with and solicit the support of groups, too-strong ties to special interests will very likely prevent candidates from forging the kind of national constituency necessary for electoral victory. A fatal flaw in Mondale's run for the White House in 1984 was his open solicitation of and identification with special interests, particularly labor union bosses that had once been so powerful in party councils.

Franklin Roosevelt's New Deal developed an "administrative presidency" stressing executive efficiency and independence from party and special in-

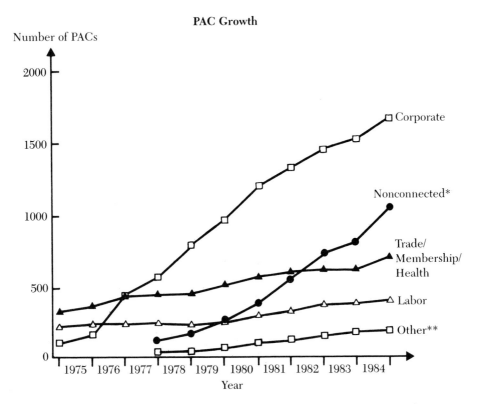

**Figure 5.5.** *PAC Growth*
SOURCE: *Federal Election Commission Record* 11 (March 1985): 6.

terest pressures that set the tone for the future. Roosevelt sought White House control over an expanded executive branch that would enable him not only to influence the course of government, but also to build electoral support independently of his party. A central component of Roosevelt's plan was a new presidential establishment that would help him develop programs and control the growing executive branch. The president dictated to his party and to special interests, rather than having them control him.

From a procedural point of view, Reagan's administration epitomized Roosevelt's ideal of the modern presidency. Reagan drew on the executive office of the president, particularly his staff and the Office of Management and Budget, to rein in the bureaucracy and steer the course of the nation. Budget Director David Stockman, one of Reagan's right-hand men, moved swiftly in the president's first term to slash government expenditures benefiting wide-ranging special interests. Congress, whose committees were more responsive to the concerns of private groups, fought vigorously to restore budget cuts for special interests. At the outset of his second term, Reagan told the people in a radio address to the nation, "Our system of budget making in Congress practically guarantees spending growth." Reagan maintained that the system fostered lobbying by special interests for benefits and to override the national interests, by concentrating great power on a small group of legislators.[15]

Reagan, like both his Republican and Democratic predecessors, attempted to use the full powers of the presidential establishment to mute the influence of special interests. He found, however, as had his predecessors, that governmental decison making in many important areas of public policy remains a group process, not only on Capitol Hill, but in the very executive branch that the modern presidency aimed to control.

*The Executive Branch and Special Interests.* Although nominally most departments and agencies of the executive branch are directly or indirectly under the control of the president, the political reality is quite different. The political iron triangles that link agencies, congressional committees, and special interests provide an independent base of political support for many departments and agencies that enable them to defy or at least deflect presidential commands. Secretaries of major departments and agency heads, for example, will usually fight presidential attempts to cut their budgets and particularly to reduce subsidies to their clientele groups, which are those interests that fall within a department's jurisdiction and provide it with important political support.

The organization and procedures of many executive departments and agencies as well as their political ties enhance interest group influence. Special interests are represented by administrative agencies in much the same way as they are by congressional committees. Departments, such as Agriculture, Commerce, Education, and Labor, were created to give special clienteles their own representatives in the executive branch. The need for special interest representation also spawned such agencies as the Veterans' Administration. Components of the executive branch that were not specifically created to represent special interests, such as the Defense Department,

---

[15] *New York Times,* February 3, 1985.

nevertheless often develop ties with private groups, becoming their governmental emissaries.

Administrative procedures also enhance group influence. Particularly important in this regard are the quasi-judicial procedures used by regulatory agencies to make rules for and resolve disputes between private groups. Congress requires regulatory agencies to hold formal or informal hearings for affected private interests before decisions are made. In some rule-making cases, and more frequently in adjudication of disputes, agencies must make their decisions on the basis of the facts contained in a formal record that is developed by the parties themselves and by the concerned agency. Adverse decisions can be appealed to the federal courts, providing aggrieved parties with yet another way of influencing administrative action. Involved in both administrative proceedings and court litigation are time and expense, resources that are possessed far more by groups than by individuals.

### Use of the Judiciary by Interest Groups

In addition to having access to administrative agencies, private groups shape legislation by bringing cases before the judiciary. The courts cannot initiate cases and controversies because of the limitations placed on them in Article III of the Constitution, but rather must wait for legitimate cases to be raised before they can act. The power of judicial review makes the courts important to private groups in their attempts to control the policy-making process. This authority, not explicitly detailed in the Constitution, nevertheless gives the Supreme Court and lower courts the power to overturn acts of Congress if they are contrary to the terms of the Constitution. Even more important, executive decisions can be overruled if they are unconstitutional or beyond the intent of Congress. Most legislation delegating authority to the bureaucracy gives the courts the power to review administrative decisions within carefully defined boundaries. Within these limits, when private groups want to challenge an adverse administrative action, they will often go to the courts instead of to Congress or the president.

If administrative decisions are usually in favor of the powerful groups in the constituencies of regulatory agencies, why do such groups seek judicial review? Within most economic spheres, particular groups are in conflict with each other over how the largesse of government is to be divided among them. For example, when the Federal Communications Commission grants a lucrative television license, those groups that were in competition for the station may decide to challenge the agency's decision in court, provided they can find legal grounds for judicial review.

## Judicial Response to Group Influence

In the past, powerful economic interests have, from time to time, dominated the judiciary. Although it is difficult to generalize, it can be suggested that over the last hundred years the courts have gone through two stages and now are in a third concerning their approach to reviewing the policy decisions of administrative agencies.

*Interventionism.* In the late nineteenth and early twentieth centuries, the judiciary took a very conservative stance in relation to the bureaucracy, frequently overturning any administrative decisions that were considered in the slightest way hostile to the interests of corporations. For example, railroads used the courts to stymie early efforts by the Interstate Commerce Commission to exert control over them.

*Self-Restraint.* As the bureaucracy began to grow, particularly during the New Deal era, the courts were faced with both political and practical dilemmas in their quest for a working doctrine of judicial review. Politically, strong demands were made on government by a wide range of interests, many of which were not highly organized, to expand the role of government in regulating the economy. Applying conservative doctrines would inevitably lead the courts into controversy. Aside from political problems, the courts also faced a practical dilemma in attempting to deal with the tremendous number of cases that were beginning to arise before administrative agencies. Any attempt to exercise comprehensive judicial review could only cause a breakdown in judicial machinery. Clearly, the best way to avoid both political and practical problems was to exercise judicial self-restraint.

In the political area, the courts developed a doctrine of restraint suggesting that "political questions" were not appropriate for courts to handle. In the review of administrative actions, this meant that policy decisions of agencies would be allowed to stand provided the proper procedural safeguards had been observed. The doctrine of judicial self-restraint in regard to political questions worked to reduce the practical workload of the judiciary, for by circumscribing their sphere of discretion the courts eliminated most of the policy decisions of administrative agencies from their jurisdiction.

*The New Activism.* In the second stage of judicial action, then, the courts became passive rather than active instruments of policy determination. There is evidence that the judiciary is now entering a third stage, characterized by a new activism that is responding to a broader range of influences. Public interest law firms and pressure groups are succeeding in getting the courts to intervene more than they have in the administrative process to force careful consideration of the interests of consumers and of the broader public for formulating public policy. For example, environmental groups have succeeded in delaying administrative action licensing power plants in areas that they consider important to preserve as wilderness, and in postponing pipeline construction and other projects detrimental to the environment. The building of the trans-Alaskan pipeline was delayed for several years by a judicial injunction issued after environmental groups sought to prevent entirely the pipeline's construction, which they felt would have highly adverse environmental effects. More than in the past, the courts are becoming the trustees of the public interest, at least as defined by public interest pressure groups.

## Group Influence on Public Policies

As one looks at the major areas of domestic policy, it is clear that the primary shape of public policy is frequently determined by the interest groups concerned in conjunction with those parts of the government that are their "captives." No way has yet been devised to counterbalance the influence of dominant economic groups; however, these groups do not exercise significant power outside their own economic sphere. For example, Exxon, Mobil, and other large oil companies employ skillful lobbyists in Washington and contribute to the campaigns of sympathetic members of Congress to help shape governmental oil policy. The incentive of the oil industry, which itself is not monolithic, is to foster policies that increase company profits. The power of oil does not reach into the agricultural sphere, where entirely different pressure groups operate to sway decision makers in their favor. Nor are oil and agricultural interests concerned with labor policies, which are the domain of the AFL-CIO, the Teamsters Union, and other powerful labor groups. Powerful economic groups tend to dominate their own policy spheres because of the lack of interest and understanding on the part of the general electorate and outside pressure groups.

When public awareness expands to what were once the exclusive concerns of specialized interests, then these interests no longer have the degree of control over public policy they possessed in the past. The rise of environmental and consumer groups in the 1960s, for example, a movement that expanded in the 1970s, checked the power of corporations to deal with the environment and the consumer as they wished. Ralph Nader mobilized citizens to bring pressure on Congress to enact automobile safety legislation in 1966, and to establish stricter health and safety standards governing unsanitary meat, natural gas pipeline safety, radiation, coal mines, and chemicals. Environmental interests pressured Congress to pass air and water pollution control laws. Labor interests were instrumental in the creation of the Occupational Safety and Health Administration (OSHA), which became the gadfly of large and small businesses throughout the country, constantly tightening safety regulations in the workplace.

Industry groups did not take the attacks of environmental and consumer groups lying down, however, but fought back to elect officials sympathetic to industry views. By the mid-1970s, Congress was awash with members who attacked OSHA as an overbearing and unnecessary government agency reflecting the worst aspects of bureaucratic despotism. The anti-OSHA forces on Capitol Hill received generous support from the business community. In addition to OSHA, conservative members of Congress targeted the Federal Trade Commission (FTC) and the Environmental Protection Agency (EPA) as examples of an excessively burdensome bureaucracy. The election of Reagan in 1980 and 1984, along with a Republican Senate and a House far more conservative than it had been in the past, reflected the victory of private sector economic groups over environmental and consumer interests. Reagan immediately set out to limit both the programs and the agencies, such as OSHA and the EPA, that had been supported by labor and the self-styled "public interest" pressure groups, such as the Nader organization and the environmentalists.

## Group Power in Contrasting Policy Arenas

Although governmental decision making is often a group process, the weight of special interest pressure is greater in some policy arenas than in others. Nevertheless, easy generalizations about group power cannot be made.

Political scientist Theodore Lowi has pointed out that public policy can be divided into three major spheres: redistributive, distributive and regulatory.[16]

### Redistributive Policies

Simply stated, redistributive policies are those that the political community perceives to redistribute wealth, property, rights, privileges, and other benefits from one broad class or segment of society to another. For example, the progressive income tax was originally designed to make the wealthier

[16]Theodore J. Lowi, "American Business, Public Policy, Case Studies, and Political Theory," *World Politics* 16 (July 1964): 673–715. See also Randall B. Ripley and Grace A. Franklin, *Congress, the Bureaucracy, and Public Policy* (Homewood, Illinois: Dorsey Press).

classes pay proportionately more to the government than lower income groups. Such taxes were clearly redistributive in character, and were perceived to be so by the affected groups. Macropolitics distinguishes the redistributive policy arena from others, because the wide impact such policies have gives rise to broad political participation. Outside of government, political parties and coalitions of interest groups take stands on redistributive policies, causing an increase in public awareness and concern about possible governmental actions that will affect the entire community.

Within government, redistributive policies are not left for congressional committees and narrow special interests to determine. Included in the political decision-making process are the president and congressional party leaders and members, who cannot avoid taking stands on all-embracing political issues.

### Distributive Policies

Those policies that are perceived by the political community to have only a short-term and narrow impact are labeled distributive because they involve governmental distribution of subsidies and benefits to special interests. Private groups have their greatest impact in the distributive policy arena, which traditionally has been controlled by "iron triangles" of committees, agencies, and private interests. In contrast to the macropolitics of redistributive policymaking, the distributive arena features micropolitics and a concurrent majority process that gives important interest groups a large influence on what policies will be made.

Although subsidy policies have traditionally been considered distributive, and therefore left to political iron triangles to determine, Reagan made a particularly strong effort to widen the politics of distributive policymaking by heightening public awareness of the real impact such policies have. The president lumped subsidy programs in one package, calling attention to the impact total expenditures for these programs had on the growing federal deficit. The cozy iron triangles that in the past had had enough political independence to determine subsidies found themselves under attack from the president and congressional party leaders who were no longer willing to tolerate committee, agency, and interest group autonomy. Reagan's strategy was a bold and often successful attempt to force Congress to deal with distributive policies at the macropolitical level by making both the public and their representatives aware that the traditional political distinction made between distributive and redistributive policies cannot be justified because in the long run they have the same wide impact.

*Regulatory Policies*

Historically, interest group power has been a feature of regulatory policy-making, which essentially involves governmental determination of permissible group activities in various spheres. The initial phases of regulation involve demands by such macropolitical forces as political parties, interest group coalitions, and sometimes the broader public that the government step in to regulate a particular sector of the community to control what are viewed as the abusive activities of groups within it. In the late nineteenth century, for example, agrarian and populist interests insisted that Congress regulate the railroads, resulting in passage of the Interstate Commerce Act in 1887, which established the Interstate Commerce Commission (ICC) as the regulatory body that would prevent unfair practices and guarantee reasonable rates. Congress has since responded to demands for regulation in a variety of areas by creating independent regulatory agencies as well as regulatory bodies within major executive departments to make rules and adjudicate disputes in their respective policy spheres.

*Pressure Group "Capture" of Agencies.* Ironically, many regulatory agencies became in effect the political "captives" of the very groups they were supposed to regulate. The macropolitics of initial regulation changed to the micropolitics surrounding agencies that, having largely solved the problems that led to their creation, found their political universes narrowed to the regulated groups themselves. Long-established regulatory agencies tended to define the public interest they were mandated to carry out by Congress in terms of the special interests they regulated. More protected than controlled by regulatory bodies, groups such as railroads and airlines lobbied for the continuation of "their" agencies, the ICC and the Civil Aeronautics Board (CAB), respectively. In other areas, powerful economic interests, such as the American Telephone and Telegraph Company (AT&T), were comfortable with the way regulation protected their interests.

*The Struggle for Control of Agencies.* Traditional regulatory politics was much like the distributive arena, distinguished by close ties among congressional committees, agencies, and regulated groups. Beginning with Franklin Roosevelt, however, presidents have attempted to rein in the independent regulatory bodies, which were thought to undermine the efficiency of the administrative presidency. Modern presidents have wanted a unified executive branch in the best Hamiltonian tradition. But Congress, both to buttress its independence from the White House and in response to special interest pressures, continued to support the autonomy of many regulatory agencies against increasingly strong presidential efforts to eliminate or absorb them in the executive branch.

*Deregulation.* The regulatory tide began to change in the mid-1970s, as the White House and congressional leaders began to view deregulation as an idea whose political time had come. Interestingly, neither the White House nor Congress was responding to broad political demands for change in the regulatory system. But influential economists and other students of the regulatory process had for a long time criticized its protection of regulated interests to the disadvantage of the public that it was supposed to protect. Politicians who had no vested interest in the continuation of regulation — those, for example, who were not iron-triangle committee chairmen — saw in deregulation an attractive arena in which they could carry out good public policy and at the same time receive credit for being at the forefront of a major change in the direction of government.

Transportation and banking were the primary foci of a series of congressional bills deregulating industry beginning 1976. Interest groups in these areas found their once comfortable arrangements with government terminated as they were thrown into the free market system where many had to fight for survival. Only one regulatory agency, the CAB, was abolished outright, going out of existence in 1985. But the remaining agencies, such as the ICC, could no longer be viewed as the captives of private groups whose activities were under their jurisdiction.

### Other Policy Arenas

The distinguishing characteristics of defense and foreign policy also affect interest group power in those arenas. A formidable iron triangle in the area of defense procurement is the military-industrial complex, composed of the Armed Services and Defense Appropriation subcommittees of Congress, the Pentagon, and defense contractors who stand to benefit from increased defense expenditures. Private interests lobby vigorously for procurement policies that will benefit them, and in many respects defense expenditure for weapons and supplies is determined by traditional distributive politics that gives dominant power to the Defense Department, the related congressional committees, and private interests.

However, major procurement policy involves the president and broader congressional interests, reducing the power of private groups to determine outcomes. Private groups also find themselves pushed to the background since the president controls major defense and foreign policy initiatives, which on Capitol Hill involve congressional leaders and a majority of members as well.

It is clear from viewing the contrasting characteristics of different policy arenas that the power of interest groups to affect governmental decision making fluctuates from one area to another. Special interests have far less influence in macropolitical policy spheres than they do in micropolitical arenas, which are distinguished by limited political concerns that lead to narrow participation.

## Governmental Interest Groups

The diversity of governmental interest groups is fostered by the pluralism of government at the national, state, and local levels. At the national level, the separation of powers and the checks and balances system mean that there is no unified focus of power. The branches of the government — the president, Congress, judiciary, and bureaucracy — and the groups within them vie for power among themselves.

The greatest source of proliferation of governmental pressure groups comes from the pluralistic character of the executive branch. Departments and agencies represent separate constituencies and have contrasting goals that often tie in closely with those of private groups within their constituencies.

### Executive Branch Assistance to Congress

Rarely is an important piece of legislation passed by Congress without clearance from the administrative agency that will be involved in its implementation. Expert bill drafting is often done by lawyers and other experts in administrative agencies, who provide their services to Congress. Private pressure groups also frequently offer drafts of proposed legislation to congressmen, but they are not as seriously considered as those that come from the administrative branch. One reason for this is that the administrative branch, under the president, is part of the government and is presumed to reflect broad rather than narrow interests.

### Executive Branch Lobbying and Public Relations

Administrative agencies are not supposed to be involved in lobbying activities, and indeed many administrators and legislators alike would not call the constant interaction between the bureaucracy and Congress lobbying. The failure of Congress to recognize that public lobbying poses a problem is reflected in the Federal Regulation of Lobbying Act of 1946, which circumscribes only the activities of private lobbyists. There are laws, however, that specifically prohibit the use of public funds for public relations activities on the part of administrative agencies. Regardless of such legislative proscriptions, many agencies engage in more extensive public relations campaigns than virtually any private group.

For example, the Defense Department has for decades undertaken skillful propaganda programs to aid in recruitment as well as to indoctrinate the public on the importance of the military. Even the individual branches of the Defense Department — the army, air force, and navy — have their own full-time public relations divisions involved in trying to convince Congress and the public, as well as the president, of the unique importance of their particular approach to warfare. Constant pressure is exerted on the legislature, for example, to embark on new shipbuilding programs to support the navy, or to supply funds for the development of new types of aircraft and missiles for the air force and the army.

Although the Defense Department is probably more extensively involved in public relations activity than any other part of the bureaucracy, other agencies as well have initiated propaganda programs to advance their own goals. The Department of Agriculture puts out vast amounts of literature not only to inform its constituency of the nature and importance of the programs that it is involved in, but also to make constituents and legislators aware of the key role the department plays in the maintenance and development of American agriculture. The department lobbies vigorously to shape agricultural legislation before Congress, and it is often the determining force in agricultural policy as it emanates from Congress.

### Presidential Control of Executive Branch Lobbying

When agencies propose legislative programs in Congress, they must go through the Office of Management and Budget (OMB), which is part of the Executive Office of the President. The clearance of all legislative proposals from the administrative branch is an important requirement that has been established by OMB. A forceful presidency can be an extraordinarily powerful force in Congress as well as in the executive branch. But since the president does not have automatic control over the bureaucracy, he can find himself in the same position as other groups when attempting to get administrative agencies to heed his requests.

The president's power and influence are greatest in those areas where he has set forth clear policy positions. He can then exert strong influence on the bureaucracy to fall in line behind his leadership, and this gives him tremendous leverage with Congress. Where the president has not articulated a program, however, the process of clearing proposals through OMB does not enhance the power of the presidency, but merely gives OMB the opportunity to coordinate different requests from within the administrative branch. If it is known that the president does not have a clearly defined position on the proposals of administrative agencies, they are more likely to go directly to Congress, making their desires known informally. They may even go to the president in an attempt to secure his backing. All of this interaction among different parts of the government in the policy-making process should be considered as pressure group activity.

The superior position of the president and the bureaucracy as lobbyists before Congress is derived not only from the fact that they are legitimate parts of the government, but also from the delegation of specific legislative responsibility to the president by Article II of the Constitution as well as to both the president and the administrative branch by Congress. Regulatory agencies are given the specific responsibility of recommending proposals to Congress. They are in this respect the agents of Congress, and in the regulatory field they serve as a primary influence on legislative change. Congress will often wait for recommendations from these agencies before considering any new legislation dealing with regulatory matters. This is not to suggest that regulatory agencies are necessarily more powerful than other parts of the bureaucracy in lobbying Congress, but only that they are considered by Congress itself to be an integral part of the legislative process. This puts them in a better formal position to exert influence. However, informal factors often determine the power of agencies. Such factors include the degree of constituency support for agency proposals, the level of expertise of the agencies as opposed to that of Congress, and whether an agency has the backing of OMB and the president. The same factors that shape the power of regulatory agencies in the legislative process also pertain to other parts of the bureaucracy that do not have the same relationship to Congress.

## Controlling Interest Group Activity

Congressional efforts have been made to restrict the influence of private pressure groups in government. The Federal Regulation of Lobbying Act requires that the receipts and expenditures of lobbyists be reported. Legislation passed in the 1970s to regulate campaign finances limits direct financial contributions to candidates.

### The Ineffectiveness of Legislative Controls

Attempting to control pressure group activity through legislation only touches the surface of the problems that arise in connection with interest group influence in the policy-making process. Requiring the registration of lobbyists, whose numbers have dramatically increased (see Fig. 5.6) and the

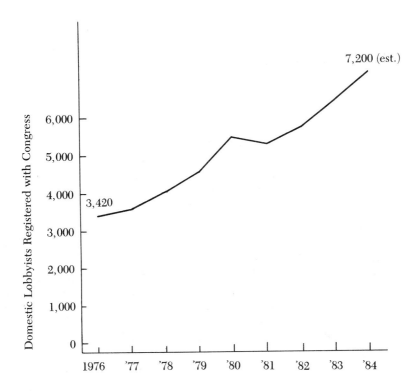

**Figure 5.6.** *Regiments of Lobbyists*
Source: *U.S. News & World Report,* June 17, 1985. Copyright © 1985 by U.S. News & World Report, Inc. Reprinted by permission.

reporting of receipts and expenditures for lobbying activities deals at best with a tiny fragment of pressure group operation. It may provide information for investigative journalists; but even this is unlikely, for those lobbying Congress are careful to keep up appearances in public.

Lobbying legislation does not regulate pressure on administrative agencies and on the president. With regard to Congress, groups have to register and report only if they directly attempt to influence legislation pending before Congress, which is, of course, a matter of interpretation. There is no effective enforcement machinery for the lobbying law, and in recent years no one has been charged with its violation. Even if the law were rigidly enforced, it would not change the nature of the demands made by groups in the policy-making process or their impact — nor, perhaps, should it.

*Public Interest Groups*

To some extent the rise of "public interest" pressure groups has modified the degree of control over public policy exercised by other specialized interests. Examples include environmental policy and legislation protecting the rights of consumers, including requirements for product safety. Without the pressure that has been exerted by public interest pressure groups, laws in these areas would not have been passed. Moreover, public interest groups put continual pressure on administrative agencies to adhere to the letter of the law. They have also used the courts to force administrative agencies to take effective action against private economic groups in these policy areas. Those who have organized public interest pressure groups recognize the legitimacy of our political system and its underlying pluralistic character.

*Common Cause.* One group attempting to change the way governmental duties are carried out by those who occupy elected positions is Common Cause. From its beginning, the hope of Common Cause was that by upgrading the performance of elected officeholders, aiming particularly at members of Congress, and increasing their sense of accountability to the electorate, democratic responsibility would be strengthened and public policy made more responsive to the interests and wishes of the people. Common Cause has consistently lobbied for federal funding of election campaigns, stricter lobbying control legislation, and open decision-making procedures — what are commonly referred to as "government in the sunshine."

*Ralph Nader and the Consumer Movement.* Common Cause is not the only organization that lobbies Congress in the public interest. Ralph Nader, a Princeton and Harvard Law School graduate, stepped to the forefront of public interest lobbyists after he published *Unsafe at Any Speed* in 1965. The book attacked the safety record of the automobile industry, causing General Motors to put private detectives on Nader's trail in an effort to destroy his personal credibility. When the General Motors scheme was uncovered, the corporation, highly embarrassed, abruptly dismissed its hired sleuths, and Ralph Nader went on to organize and lead a very effective consumer movement.

Nader, both individually and through his organization, accomplished more than any other public interest lobbyist in the late 1960s and early 1970s. The publicity Nader gave to the issue of automobile safety was largely responsible for passage of the Motor Vehicle Safety Act in 1966, which mandated vehicle safety standards. Not content with helping solve the problem of automobile safety, Nader expanded his organization, hiring young law school graduates and students who became known as "Nader's Raiders."

Nader assigned his Raiders to investigate the Federal Trade Commission (FTC) in 1968. They found an agency in disarray. Ironically, it was Nixon who, as a result of Nader's investigation, began the reinvigoration of the FTC, which in the late 1970s became a very active and effective agency.

Nader's public interest efforts reached into many other areas. His Raiders found that the Food and Drug Administration (FDA) had approved the use of dangerous chemicals — cyclamates and monosodium glutamate — in the food supply. The resulting publicity resulted in stricter regulation of their use. Nader's legislative victories resulted in stricter controls over natural gas pipeline safety, radiation, coal mines, and air pollution.

As Nader expanded his public interest organization, he created Public Citizen, Inc., and became its executive director. The citizen's interest group engages in wide-ranging activities to support its view of the public interest. Congress Watch constantly monitors Capitol Hill, while other parts of Public Citizen are involved in energy, health, and tax reform policy.

Common Cause, Ralph Nader, and other public interest pressure groups have added an important new dimension to the role of interest groups in the policy-making process. But whether or not such groups can effectively reflect the public interest has been questioned.

## Evaluation of Group Politics

Theodore Lowi has made one of the most important indictments of the group process of politics in recent years.[17] Lowi argues first that the group process of politics runs against the grain of democratic theory and practice. It does not allow for majority rule, or for the establishment of a hierarchy of values within the political system. The values and demands of all interest groups are considered to be of equal merit. This means that "liberal leaders do not wield the authority of democratic government with the resoluteness of men certain of the legitimacy of their positions, the integrity of their institutions, or the justness of the programs they serve."[18] In effect, government cannot hold values different from those of dominant pressure groups. Congress, in the delegation of authority to administrative agencies, frequently gives up its responsibilities and asks the bureaucracy to make rules on the basis of vaguely worded statutory standards.

[17]Theodore J. Lowi, *The End of Liberalism* (New York: W.W. Norton, 1969).
[18]Ibid., p. 288.

### The Failure to Uphold Statutory Standards

The practice of delegating legislative authority supports interest group liberalism because the legislature does not establish adequate standards to guide administrative action. The courts, because of hazily worded statutes, find it difficult to intervene in the process of bureaucratic decision making to force adherence to statutes. In Lowi's view, most of the rules that guide the development of policy by the administrative branch should be laid down by the legislature.

### The Limits of Judicial Review

The Constitution also establishes certain principles of policymaking, but the reluctance of the judiciary to intervene in the administrative process makes even the Constitution an instrument of dubious value in controlling interest group determination of policy. Past doctrines of judicial review, which are based on the concept of judicial self-restraint, have made it difficult for the courts to establish principles to guide administrative action. As a result of the lack of formal rules and procedures, public policy is formulated on the basis of informal bargaining. Lowi suggests that "there is inevitably a separation in the real world between the forms and the realities, and this kind of separation gives rise to cynicism, for informality means that some will escape their collective fate better than others."[19] The expectations of many people about how government should function in contrast to the way it does have caused grave discontent — especially in the last decade, when higher levels of education for a broader segment of the public in combination with an expanded mass media have made it difficult to hide the realities of politics.

### The Drawbacks of Brokered Politics

Lowi indicts the theory as well as the practice of interest group politics. He points out that group theory has falsely propagated a faith that "a system built primarily upon groups and bargaining is perfectly self-corrected."[20] Supposed self-correcting mechanisms, such as overlapping membership, potential groups, countervailing power, and so on, do not in fact operate perfectly, if at all. Moreover, Lowi feels that we would be better off if we leaned toward Madison's distrust of groups as expressed in *The Federalist* rather than toward the more sanguine views of the interest group theorists. Citing Madison's suspicion of groups, Lowi concludes that a "feeling of distrust

[19]Ibid., p. 291.
[20]Ibid., p. 294.

towards interests and groups would not destroy pluralist theory but would only prevent its remaining a servant of a completely outmoded system of public endeavor. Once sentimentality toward the group is destroyed, it will be possible to see how group interactions might fall short of creating that ideal equilibrium."[21] In short, the notion that all is right in the political world as long as interest groups are allowed to function freely should be discarded.

*Defining the National Interest*

Although Lowi's thesis is logical and well argued it does not solve the question of how to replace interest group theory and practice. One can assert what we should be doing, but this is only a small step in helping to bring about those fundamental changes that are necessary to alter the way the system now operates. As Madison acknowledged in *The Federalist*, interest groups or factions will remain an important part of the political system. Pluralism is an inevitable consequence of freedom. Pluralism itself is not bad, but it must always be recognized that control over public policy by concurrent majorities of affected interest groups means by definition that a numerical majority of the people do not shape many of the policies that affect their interests. The national interest is more than the sum of group interests and, as Lowi suggests, should be articulated by the president and members of Congress who have been elected to serve the people. To what degree can the major institutions of government — the presidency, Congress, the courts, and the bureaucracy — be structured in such a way that their creation of policy will not be a simple reflection of pressure group influence? We will treat these questions in the following chapters.

## Conclusion: Constitutional Democracy and Faction

The Madisonian view that faction intrinsically undermines constitutional democracy, by striving to elevate selfish over national interests, has continued throughout our political history in warnings about interest-group corruption of the democratic process. Constitutional attempts to control faction included the separation of powers and the checks and balances system. Moreover, the founding fathers hoped that the decentralization of the federal system would help to disburse and contain the power of factions.

The framers of the Constitution were mostly statesmen who put national interests over private interests, and constructed a government that they hoped would act in the same way. They did not fail to recognize the domi-

---

[21]Ibid., pp. 296–297.

nance of the power incentive that drives all politicians, and attempted to harness it for the public good.

The Founding Fathers also recognized that faction, while undesirable, was inevitable in a free society. The First Amendment freedom of association and the right to petition government for a redress of grievances supports and gives constitutional legitimacy to the political pluralism reflected in the vast array of interest groups.

Whoever defines the national interest and shapes public policy determines the character of the political system. A free government must allow all kinds of groups to organize and pressure for the enactment of public policies in their interests. Criticism from some quarters of the group process of politics is usually nothing more than dissatisfaction with the goals of groups the critics dislike. In the 1980s liberals are concerned with political action committees, and the powers they presumably possess, largely because conservative PACs are on the rise and exerting far more visible power than they have in the past. Before conservatives seriously began to organize their own groups, they too attacked the group process by alleging, for example, that labor unions controlled the Democratic party and its elected representatives.

While different political camps will continue to exchange charges about the unfair influence of their opponents' interest groups and PACs, the group process will remain a healthy and important ingredient of constitutional democracy. Both the formal constitutional structure and political pluralism will prevent any single faction from controlling government.

## Suggestions for Further Reading

Davies, J. Clarence, III. *The Politics of Pollution.* New York: Pegasus, 1970. A case study of the ways interest groups influence federal pollution control legislation.

Fritschler, A. Lee. *Smoking and Politics: Policymaking and the Federal Bureaucracy.* 2nd ed. Englewood Cliffs, N.J.: Prentice-Hall, 1975. One of the best studies of the interaction of Congress, the bureaucracy, and pressure groups in the policy-making process.

Krasnow, Erwin G., and Longley, Lawrence D. *The Politics of Broadcast Regulation.* 2nd ed. New York: St. Martin's Press, 1978. Probes governmental and private interest groups' attempts to influence an agency's determinations of the public interest.

Lowi, Theodore J. *The End of Liberalism.* 2nd ed. New York: W.W. Norton, 1979. Updates the author's views, which criticize the acceptance of interest group power in American politics.

McFarland, Andrew S. *Public Interest Lobbies: Decision Making on Energy.* Washington, D. C.: American Enterprise Institute, 1976. Examines the rise of public interest groups and their role in energy policy.

Truman, David B. *The Governmental Process.* 2nd ed. New York: Alfred A. Knopf, 1971. First published in 1951, Truman's study supports the central role of interest groups in policymaking.

*part* **III**

# The Governmental Process

# chapter 6

# *The Presidency*

Even more than parties and interest groups, the presidency is thought by most citizens to be the focal point of policymaking — witness the tremendous interest in presidential election campaigns, and the relatively large voter turnout compared to that in state and local elections or in elections for congressmen and senators. In our folklore, the president is at the same time king and prime minister. Although the office is often held in higher repute than the incumbent, the occupant of the White House usually gains from the stature of his position. People tend to forget that the president is always involved in the realities of exercising political power, that is, the compromises and deals undertaken in the capacity of a politician, not a king.

The power of the president depends on political skill, on the incumbent's ability to persuade others that it is in their interest to follow the lead of the White House. There is no automatic assurance that presidents have a major influence on the course of public policy. To reach their policy goals, they must not only surmount congressional hurdles but often bureaucratic intransigence as well.

Presidential power is generally aided by having a majority of the same party that occupies the White House in Congress; but there is no unfailing bridge between the two ends of Pennsylvania Avenue based on party loyalty. Even congressional party leaders cannot dictate to their members. Decentralization of power, particularly among committee chairmen, distinguishes Congress and complicates the task of presidential persuasion.

## The Context of the Presidency

*Effects of the Separation of Powers*

The independent powers and separate constituency given to the office of the president in Article II of the Constitution have formed the basis for a vast expansion in presidential prerogatives as the responsibilities of the office increased (see Figure 6.1). Without having to rely on legislative ratification, presidents from Washington to Reagan have taken bold initiatives in both foreign and domestic policy. Like the courts and parts of the bureaucracy, the White House is capable of making decisions without going through the tedious deliberations of the legislative process. Under the Constitution, the presidency is the only political office under the domination of one person.

*Clerk or King?*

One should not overemphasize the powers given to the president by the Constitution, however, because without the necessary political support and acquiescence of other branches of the government, vigorous presidential action can be and has been nullified. Richard Neustadt claims that the Constitution makes the president more of a "clerk" than a king. He is a clerk not in the sense that he is powerless, but rather because the Constitution establishes no clear hierarchical lines of power and responsibility; therefore, all other parts of the government look to the president for leadership, guidance, and help in performing the tasks that they themselves are incapable of carrying out because of the fragmentation of the system. As Neustadt states,

In form all presidents are leaders, nowadays. In fact this guarantees no more than that they will be clerks. Everybody now expects the man inside the White House to do something about everything. Laws and customs now reflect acceptance of him as a great initiator, an acceptance quite as widespread at the Capitol as at his end of Pennsylvania Avenue. But such acceptance does not signify that all the rest of the government is at his feet. It merely signifies that other men have found it practically impossible to do *their* jobs without assurance of initiatives from him. Service for themselves, not power for the president, has brought them to accept his leadership in form. They find his actions useful in their business. But transformation of his routine obligations testifies to their dependence on an active White House. A president, these days, is an invaluable clerk. His services are in demand all over Washington. His influence, however, is a very different matter. Laws and customs tell us little about leadership in fact.[1]

[1]Richard E. Neustadt, *Presidential Power* (New York: John Wiley & Sons, 1960), p. 6.

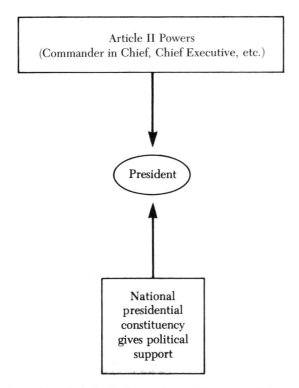

**Figure 6.1.** *The Independent, Unified Presidency. The power of the president is buttressed by independent constitutional authority under Article II and by a nationwide political constituency.*

Just as in many areas the other branches of government need the president in order to take effective action, the president in turn relies on his governmental "constituents" to carry out his order.

### Need for Presidential Leadership

Because of the multiple responsibilities of the presidency, the modern conception of the office is that effectiveness requires strength, vigor, and a positive approach on the part of the incumbent. People expect leadership in their president. Good presidents use the office to its fullest capacity and capabilities. They employ the authority of the office in combination with its political power to initiate and advance important legislation, to attempt to control the bureaucracy, and to take necessary action to deal with foreign and domestic problems. People agree now more than at the time it was written with Alexander Hamilton's statement in *The Federalist* (No. 70) that

> Energy in the executive is a leading character in the definition of good government. It is essential to the protection of the community against foreign attacks; it is not less essential to the study of administration of the laws, to the protection of property against those irregular and high-handed combinations, which sometimes interrupt the ordinary course of justice, to the security of liberty against the enterprises and assaults of ambition, of faction, and of anarchy.
>
> . . . A feeble executive implies a feeble execution of government. A feeble execution is but another phrase for a bad execution; and a government ill-executed, whatever it may be in theory, must be in practice a bad government.

## The President's Powers and Responsibilities

Both the president's powers and his responsibilities have grown enormously over the years. The modern presidency bears little resemblance to the office envisioned by the framers of the Constitution. Even Alexander Hamilton would probably be surprised at the magnitude of modern presidential power and the central role the White House plays in the political system. Constitutional and political changes have supported the growth in presidential power that has in the twentieth century made the office in many respects imperial in character. The imperial analogy has, however, been overdrawn, and a close examination of the powers and responsibilities of the president reveals the limits as well as the strengths of the office.

### Chief of State

The president is our king and prime minister, due to the fact that the Constitution uniquely combines the ceremonial and working functions of the head of government in the same hands. As ceremonial chief of state the president receives foreign leaders at the White House, and he likewise represents the nation when he meets them on his extensive foreign travels.

The president symbolizes the nation in domestic as well as in foreign affairs. As chief of state he must sign all bills and treaties before they become law, a task that can consume many hours of time. Like receiving foreign leaders, signing domestic legislation is highly ceremonial: the president meets with members of Congress in the Rose Garden or the Oval Office to acknowledge their role in passing the legislation and present them with the cherished presidential pens that are later so proudly displayed in congressional offices.

The president also performs a multitude of other ceremonial functions.

When national television focuses on the White House, the president is forever issuing proclamations for holidays and periods such as National Secretaries' Week, kicking off charity drives, lighting the national Christmas tree from the South Portico, presiding over the annual Easter egg hunt, pinning medals on military heroes, receiving Olympic athletes, tossing the coin for the Superbowl (a Reagan first), and hosting state dinners for new members of Congress or the diplomatic corps. The president is the embodiment of the nation as he carries out these and many other ritual responsibilities.

One may well wonder how the president gets anything done in what would appear to be the little time left to him between ceremonies. The answer is that the presidency is not one person, but an institution. Presidents rely on an extensive staff network to help them perform the working responsibilities of their office.

Although ceremonial functions are time-consuming, they add to the strength of the presidency. As long ago as 1867, Attorney General Henry Stanbery argued before the Supreme Court in the famous case of *Mississippi v. Johnson*, which involved a suit that enjoined the president from exercising his authority, "I deny that there is a particle less dignity belonging to the office of the president than to the office of King of Great Britain or any other token seat on the face of the earth. He represents the majesty of the law and of the people as fully and as essentially, and with the same dignity, as does any absolute monarch or the head of any independent government in the world."[2]

As chief of state the president stands above partisan politics. His ceremonial functions constitute a kind of political armor that helps him to deflect criticism. Challenging the chief of state, the political embodiment of the people, can be viewed in some circumstances as an attack on the nation itself. Presidents particularly try to shield themselves from criticisms of military actions they have ordered by wrapping themselves in the chief of state's ceremonial mantle.

*Chief Executive*

The Constitution also makes the president chief executive, requiring him to see that the laws are faithfully executed. The Constitution grants him the authority to appoint "public ministers" as well as gives him the responsibility of overseeing the executive branch. Under the separation of powers the president's executive authority is exclusive, as is the authority of Congress and of the judiciary to make laws and to settle cases and controversies.

---

[2]Cited in Clinton Rossiter, *The American Presidency*, 2nd ed. (New York: Harcourt, Brace, 1960), p. 18.

While the president alone decides how he will execute the laws, the Constitution, through the checks and balances system, actually gives Congress extensive authority to oversee the executive branch. The president cannot appoint public ministers — his cabinet officials — or ambassadors and consuls without Senate approval, and Congress has extended the requirement of Senate advice and consent to thousands of other executive branch jobs. Most presidential appointments are approved, however, making the advice and consent requirement more of a formality than a real hindrance to presidential power.

But because Congress is the law-making body, it determines the organization, procedures, and policies of the executive branch. Under a series of reorganization acts, the first of which was passed in 1939, Congress has delegated to the president the authority to restructure parts of the executive branch subject to legislative veto. Major changes, however, such as the creation or abolition of an executive department, require legislation.

Since Congress sees the executive branch as its agent while the president sees himself as chief administrator, there is a constant tug-of-war between Capitol Hill and the White House to control the sprawling maze of executive departments and agencies that implement government policies. Modern governmental administration is not, as Alexander Hamilton wrote in *The Federalist* (No. 72), "limited to executive details [falling] peculiarly within the province of the executive department." Administrative agencies perform both quasi-legislative and quasi-judicial functions, making rules and regulations that have the force of law at the same time that they adjudicate cases and controversies. In performng these functions agencies are politically and under law as accountable to Congress and the courts as they are to the White House. Presidents strive to achieve the Hamiltonian ideal of a unified executive branch under their sway, but they find inevitably that political and legal obstacles prevent them from truly functioning as chief administrator.

### Commander in Chief

The Constitution makes the president, in Alexander Hamilton's words, the "first General and Admiral of the Confederacy."[3] Even Hamilton's exhalted conception of the presidency did not foresee, however, the extraordinary power the president would have as commander in chief of the armed forces. Scant attention was paid to this provision of the Constitution as the framers inserted it into Article II without debate. The state governors were commanders in chief of their militias, and it seemed obvious that since there was

---

[3] *The Federalist*, No. 69.

to be a national army and navy, the president alone should be commander in chief. Hamilton stressed in *The Federalist* that the authority would amount "to nothing more than the supreme command and direction of the military and naval forces."[4] Congress would have the authority to declare war and to raise and regulate the fleets and armies, thus checking the president's power.

But the Founding Fathers had neglected to define what would be the president's functions as commander in chief, merely bestowing on him the office. By contrast, the Constitution did designate, although in general terms, what the president was empowered to do to carry out his other responsibilities. The vagueness of the clause allowed presidents great leeway in interpreting what would be their authority under it.

Early presidents, usually with the acquiescence of Congress and often under its specific delegation, gradually began to expand their authority as commander in chief. Most presidential actions, however, were taken against Indians and pirates, and there was an understanding that full-scale hostilities against a foreign nation would require a congressional declaration of war.

The crisis of the Civil War and Lincoln's strong assertion of his commander in chief powers set a precedent for the future. Fine distinctions were made between offensive and defensive wars, the latter requiring swift and unilateral presidential action to save the nation. A major 1862 treatise on the war powers, written by the War Department's solicitor, claimed, "Nothing is clearer than this, that when such a state of hostility exists as justifies the president in calling the army into actual service, without the authority of Congress, no declaration of war is requisite, either in form or substance, for any purpose whatsoever."[5]

President Lincoln, on his own initiative, took forceful steps to meet the southern insurrection in the early stages of the Civil War, ordering a blockade of the South, direct military action, and the suspension of the writ of habeas corpus. Although Congress was soon to legitimize Lincoln's actions through legislation, the fact remains that the president had on his own declared war against the South, an exercise of authority that was upheld by the Supreme Court in the *Prize* cases.[6] The Court was careful to declare, however, in a statement that later occupants of the White House sometimes forgot, that the president "has no power to initiate or declare a war either against a foreign nation or a domestic state. But by the *acts of Congress* . . .

[4]Ibid.
[5]Arthur M. Schlesinger, Jr., *The Imperial Presidency* (Boston: Houghton Mifflin, 1973), pp. 63–64, citing William Whiting, *War Powers Under the Constitution of the United States* (1862).
[6]2 Black 635 (1863).

he is authorized to call out the militia to use the military and naval forces of the United States in case of invasion by foreign nations, and to suppress insurrection against the government of a state or of the United States."[7] Moreover, in the famous case of *Ex Parte Milligan,* the Court in 1866 held that the president could not order the trials of civilians by military tribunals even during wartime in localities where the civil courts remained open.[8]

Significantly, the *Milligan* case was decided after hostilities had ended, while the *Prize* cases reached the Court at the height of the Civil War. Neither the Supreme Court nor Congress has been inclined to limit presidential war powers during times of national emergency. Indeed, Congress, beginning in 1798, has passed many laws delegating emergency powers to the president.

Clearly, the president's powers as commander in chief are greatest during wartime, although they perhaps do not extend as far as Franklin Roosevelt claimed in 1942 when in a struggle with Congress he stated, "The president has the powers, under the Constitution and under congressional acts, to take measures necessary to avert a disaster which would interfere with the winning of the war."[9] Almost as an afterthought, he added that "when the war is won, the powers under which I act automatically revert to the people — to whom they belong."[10]

Roosevelt stretched the president's war-making powers far beyond the point to which they had been taken by previous presidents, setting a precedent for an even greater expansion of power in the future. Truman committed American troops to the defense of South Korea without consulting Congress, informing congressional leaders only after the fact that military action had been taken. Presented with communist aggression and with a presidential fait accompli, Congress supported the president, although the Republican Senate minority leader Robert Taft noted that the president had no legal authority to engage American troops abroad. Eventually, as the war turned sour, congressional criticism grew, and when Truman announced that he was going to send four more divisions to Europe to deter possible communist aggression there, Taft supported a resolution that would have required the president to gain congressional approval before he committed troops abroad. Finally passed was a "sense of the Senate" resolution that approved Truman's actions but stated that he should consult Congress before increasing American troop strength in Europe in the future.

Although Congress was critical of Truman, it essentially acquiesced in his expansive view of presidential war powers. And it continued to allow the

[7]Ibid., p. 636.
[8]*Ex Parte Milligan,* 4 Wallace 2 (1866).
[9]Arthur M. Schlesinger, Jr., *The Imperial Presidency,* p. 115.
[10]Ibid., pp. 115–116.

president almost total discretion as commander in chief until the political backlash against the continued presidential escalations of the Vietnam War forced it to take a stand. The War Powers Act of 1973 at least appeared to limit presidential authority by requiring the president to report to Congress within forty-eight hours commitments or a substantial enlargement of combat forces abroad, and terminating such commitments within a sixty- to ninety-day period unless Congress declared war or authorized the continuation of the commitment. Unlike the sense of Congress resolutions of the past, the War Powers Act was legislation that bound the president. In effect, however, the law seems to increase as much as decrease presidential authority. For the first time, Congress explicitly recognized the president's authority to make war and take whatever action he deems necessary to deal with emergency situations. Once troops are commited, it is highly unlikely that Congress, gripped in patriotic fervor, would fail to support the president in the future as it has in the past. Presidents can now cite the law as an affirmation of their war-making powers.

Presidential war-making powers may have a profound impact on domestic policy, affecting civilians as well as the military. The president may decide that curtailment of civil liberties and civil rights is necessary, as when Lincoln suspended the writ of habeas corpus at the outset of the Civil War. Citing his authority as commander in chief, Roosevelt issued Executive Order 9066 in 1942, authorizing the Secretary of War to prescribe military zones that excluded civilians if he deemed "such action necessary or desirable." The order, and subsequent legislation based on it, was used to force Japanese-American citizens from the West Coast into internment camps. The Supreme Court upheld the government's action in *Korematsu v. United States* (1944), acknowledging "the hardships imposed by [the exclusion order] upon a large group of American citizens. . . . But hardships are part of war, and war is an aggregation of hardships."[11] The Supreme Court, however, has not always sustained presidential claims of authority under the commander in chief clause. When President Truman attempted to use it, in combination with his powers as chief executive, to support his seizure of the steel mills to prevent a strike in 1952 on the grounds that it would deter the war effort, the Court overturned him in the historic case of *Youngstown Sheet and Tube Company v. Sawyer.* Justice Hugo Black wrote the majority opinion, which stated in part that "we cannot with faithfulness to our constitutional system hold that the commander in chief of the armed forces has the ultimate power as such to take possession of private property in order to keep labor disputes from stopping production."[12] In a concurring opin-

[11] *Korematsu v. United States,* 323 U.S. 214, 219 (1944).
[12] *Youngstown Sheet and Tube Company v. Sawyer,* 343 U.S. 579, 587 (1952).

ion, Justice Jackson observed, "No doctrine that the Court could promulgate would seem to me more sinister and alarming than that a president whose conduct of foreign affairs is so largely uncontrolled, and often even is unknown, can vastly enlarge his mastery over the internal affairs of the country by his own commitment of the nation's armed forces to some foreign venture."[13]

### Chief Diplomat

The president conducts the nation's foreign affairs, a constitutional responsibility he shares with Congress and particularly with the Senate. But both Congress and the Supreme Court have recognized the president's dominant role. As early as 1816 the Senate Committee on Foreign Relations issued a report stating in part that

> the president is the constitutional representative of the United States with regard to foreign nations. He manages our concerns with foreign nations and must necessarily be most competent to determine when, how, and upon what subjects negotiation may be urged with the greatest prospect of success. For his conduct he is responsible to the Constitution. The Committee considers this responsibility the surest pledge for the faithful discharge of his duty. They think the interference of the Senate in the direction of foreign negotiations is calculated to diminish that responsibility and thereby to impair the best security for the national safety. The nature of transactions with foreign nations, moreover, requires caution and unity of design and their success frequently depends on secrecy and dispatch.[14]

The committee's report recognized, in the formative years of the Republic, the importance of presidential flexibility to conduct foreign affairs. A year after the report was issued, President James Monroe, on his own initiative, negotiated an executive agreement with Great Britain limiting naval forces on the Great Lakes.[15] The White House under Monroe also announced the historic Monroe Doctrine in 1823 without consulting Congress. The first half of the nineteenth century witnessed many such unilateral foreign policy decisions by the president.

Congress asserted itself vigorously in foreign affairs both during and after the Civil War, remaining an active force until World War II. Post-Civil War presidents increasingly resorted to executive agreements to implement major foreign policy decisions that normally would be made through treaties requiring Senate ratification. Nevertheless, presidents ignored Congress at

---

[13]Ibid., p. 642.
[14]Cited in *United States v. Curtiss-Wright Export Corp.*, 299 U.S. 304, 319 (1936).
[15]Arthur M. Schlesinger, Jr., *The Imperial Presidency*, p. 86.

their peril, knowing that they could only go so far in making foreign policy without consulting Congress.

The crisis of World War II swung the pendulum of power back to the White House. Congress, which had tightly held the reins of power, gradually began to delegate more authority to the president to make foreign policy. At the same time, Franklin Roosevelt, who in his first two terms had respected the constitutional role of Congress in foreign policy, began to make decisions on his own. Congress, pushed to the background by the crisis, let Roosevelt have his way.

The presidential ascendency in foreign affairs that Roosevelt asserted continued without important interruptions until Congress, in reaction to the Vietnam War, once again asserted its power in the 1970s. Truman had once characteristically told an audience, "I make foreign policy." But Reagan had a different perspective, remarking in a 1984 news conference that, "in the last ten years the Congress has imposed about 150 restrictions on the president's power in international diplomacy."[16] Congressional interference in the president's conduct of foreign affairs was unprecedented, said Reagan, observing, "Do you know that prior to the Vietnamese War, while this country had only had four declared wars, presidents of this country have found it necessary to use military forces 125 times in our history?"[17]

Two days later, speaking at Georgetown University, Reagan acknowledged the resurgence of Congress that had occurred in the previous decade. "Presidents must recognize Congress as a more significant partner in foreign policymaking," he said, "and, as we tried to do, seek new means to reach bipartisan executive, legislative consensus. But legislators must realize that they, too, are partners. They have a responsibility to go beyond mere criticism to consensus-building that will produce positive, practical and effective action."[18]

The president's power to conduct foreign policy without obstruction by Congress ebbs and flows as it does in other areas of presidential responsibility. The president, however, always initiates foreign policy, which gives him an enormous advantage over Congress. Unlike other congressional committees, the Foreign Relations and Foreign Affairs committees in the Senate and House, respectively, have generally supported presidential initiatives, for their chairmen recognize that the White House is their principal constituent. The president defines their job and in fact gives them the polit-

---

[16]Text of presidential news conference, April 4, 1984, *Congressional Quarterly Weekly Report*, April 7, 1984.

[17]Ibid.

[18]Text of speech made before Georgetown University Center for International and Strategic Studies, April 6, 1984. *Congressional Quarterly Weekly Report*, April 14, 1984.

ical support and backing necessary to sustain their power in the complex world of Capitol Hill.

When all is said and done, the president has, as Justice Sutherland concluded for the Supreme Court during the New Deal when it attempted to curb presidential power in foreign affairs, "plenary and exclusive power . . . as the sole organ of the federal goverment in the field of international relations — a power which does not require as a basis for its exercise an act of Congress."[19]

### Chief Legislator

Both constitutional provisions and, more importantly, political forces have made the president a legislative leader. The Constitution gives him the veto power, which can be overridden only by a two-thirds vote of both houses of Congress — a feat legislators find very difficult to achieve. The president also has the responsibility to recommend legislation to Congress from time to time. "The Constitution," Eisenhower told a press conference in 1959, "puts the president right square into the legislative business."[20]

The first order of business on Capitol Hill as Congress opens its new session each year is the president's legislative agenda. The State of the Union Address sets the tone of the president's program, followed by concrete legislative and budgetary proposals drafted by the executive branch under White House guidance. That Congress is not, however, a passive body in relation to the White House is illustrated by Figure 6.2, which also reveals that presidents are most successful on Capitol Hill in the early years of their administrations. The separation of powers and the lack of disciplined parties foster congressional independence, as presidents find that they cannot count on the votes of their own party members on Capitol Hill.

Powerful presidents, nevertheless, set the tone of government through their legislative programs. Presidents such as Roosevelt, Johnson, and Reagan were indeed chief legislators whose programs changed the face of the nation. Congress remains an independent and proud institution, but powerful and persuasive presidents determine the major items on its legislative agenda.

### Other Presidential Responsibilities

The president's responsibilities extend far beyond his constitutional roles as ceremonial chief of state, chief executive, commander in chief, and chief

---

[19] *United States v. Curtiss-Wright Export Corp.*, 299 U.S. 304, 320 (1936).
[20] Cited in Clinton Rossiter, *The American Presidency*, p. 29.

Percent*

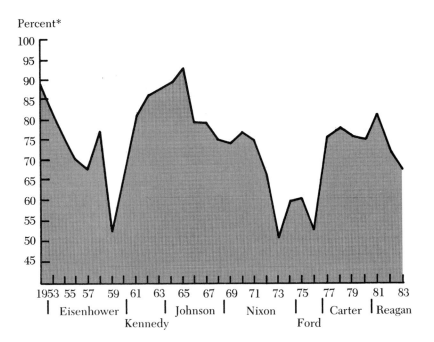

*Percentages based on votes on which presidents took a position.

**Figure 6.2.** *Presidential Success on Votes, 1953–1984*
SOURCE: From *Congressional Quarterly Weekly Report,* Oct. 27, 1984, p. 2803.
Reprinted by permission of Congressional Quarterly Inc.

legislator. Americans have increasingly come to accept Hamilton's view that energy in the executive is the definition of good government. People look to the president to solve their political and economic problems, aggrandizing the role of the White House far beyond constitutional prescriptions or political realities. Since the days of the New Deal and Roosevelt's administrative presidency, which was to stand above politics and efficiently solve the nation's problems, presidential rhetoric has encouraged the belief that, as the sign on Truman's desk stated, "The Buck Stops Here."

A host of political changes since the early days of the Republic account for the acceptance of the Hamiltonian presidency in areas of responsibility that were not prescribed by the Constitution. The modern presidency in particular has been seen as the deus ex machina of a political system that the constitutional separation of powers has often stalemated. The president is expected to rise above the separation of powers and the politics that supports it to act decisively in the national interest. The president, representative of all the people, is ultimately accountable to them for the course of government.

*National Representative.* As the only nationally elected official, the president is the voice of the people and their delegate. The Electoral College continues to give each state a vote equal to the number of its representatives and senators, with three votes allotted to the District of Columbia under the Twenty-third Amendment, but it is the people and not the state legislatures as originally planned who determine the allocation of electoral votes. In each state the presidential candidate who receives the plurality of the popular vote is awarded all the state's electoral votes. Although the Electoral College may skew the popular vote somewhat and even result in the election of a president who has not received a nationwide popular majority, all presidents take very seriously their role as representative of all of the people.

*Party Leader.* The people choose the president, but his party nominates him and without its backing there would be no chance for victory at the polls. Both popular election and the rise of parties have involved presidents in politics from the earliest days of the Republic to an extent not foreseen or desired by many of the Founding Fathers. Hamilton remarked at the Constitutional Convention that ideally the president should be "an elected monarch for life." Other delegates, fearing faction and popular majorities, wanted to remove the president from direct popular election, and the Electoral College was the method chosen to achieve this end (see Figure 6.3).

The electors, chosen by methods prescribed by the state legislatures, were to meet in their states to cast votes for the person best qualified to be president. Originally, the candidate receiving the greatest number of votes, provided it was a majority, became president, and the person who received the second largest number of votes became vice-president. A tie in electoral votes for president threw the election into the House of Representatives, where each state cast one vote, a majority deciding the outcome.

The division of the Electoral College along party lines made the original system unworkable. The Founding Fathers had not taken into account the possibility of party politics entering presidential races. But by 1796 the two-party system was already well established, and in that year the congressional caucus of Federalists named John Adams as its candidate, while the Republicans nominated Thomas Jefferson. Electors of both parties were encouraged to vote for their presidential candidates, but the vice-presidential race was left open. The outcome was that a majority of Federalist electors chose John Adams for the presidency, but Thomas Jefferson came in second, resulting in a Federalist president and a Republican vice-president.

**1984 Electoral Votes by States**

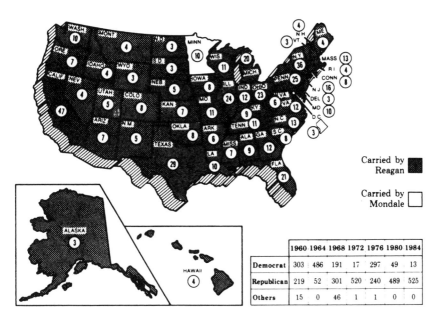

| | 1960 | 1964 | 1968 | 1972 | 1976 | 1980 | 1984 |
|---|---|---|---|---|---|---|---|
| Democrat | 303 | 486 | 191 | 17 | 297 | 49 | 13 |
| Republican | 219 | 52 | 301 | 520 | 240 | 489 | 525 |
| Others | 15 | 0 | 46 | 1 | 1 | 0 | 0 |

**Figure 6.3.** *The President's Electoral Vote Constituency. The electoral vote often does not reflect the popular vote. In 1984 Reagan received 59 percent of the popular vote, but won all but one state and the District of Columbia in the electoral college.*
SOURCE: From *Congressional Quarterly Weekly Report*, Nov. 10, 1984, p. 2893.
Reprinted by permission of Congressional Quarterly Inc.

The situation became even more intolerable in 1800 when the parties nominated candidates for the presidency and the vice-presidency, ensuring a tie in the Electoral College if the party electors voted as a block as the electors of the majority party gave an equal number of votes to their presidential and vice-presidential nominees. The appearance of parties on the presidential scene virtually guaranteed that every presidential election would have to be decided by the House of Representatives, which is what happened in 1800 when Republican electors voted in equal numbers for Thomas Jefferson and Aaron Burr, the party's nominees for president and vice-president. The tie vote threw the election into the House of Representatives, controlled by the Federalists, many of whom supported Burr only in order to prevent their archenemy Jefferson from going to the White

House. A deadlocked House of Representatives played politics for thirty-five ballots as the states, voting as units, refused to allow the constitutionally mandated majority to emerge to decide who would become president. Finally, Alexander Hamilton — no friend of Burr and in fact soon to be killed by him in their notorious duel — threw his support to Jefferson and persuaded enough of his Federalist colleagues to abstain from voting to enable Jefferson to win.

Presidential politics had come of age in 1800, and the debacle of that year caused the passage of the Twelfth Amendment, requiring electors to designate their choices for president and vice-president separately and providing that the person receiving the greatest number of votes in each category, if a majority of the Electoral College, would become president or vice-president. Ratified in 1804, the Twelfth Amendment was an acknowledgment that presidential elections could no longer be separated from party politics. State legislatures had provided for the direct election of electors, and voters then as now took into account party affiliation when choosing electors to vote for the president.

From the early days of the Republic, the president was the titular head of his loosely knit party organization, using his influence to advance party interests and goals. Before the passage of the Pendleton Act of 1883, which created the civil service system that awarded governmental jobs on the basis of merit and not politics, the president under the "spoils system," was able to fill all posts in the executive branch with loyal party followers. However, civil service laws only gradually eroded presidential patronage power; it was not until the end of Franklin Roosevelt's administration that most of the civil service was protected under a merit system that prevented the removal of most lower-echelon government employees solely for political purposes. The White House continues, however, to appoint thousands of top-level executive branch officials.

The President advances party interests in many other ways: he helps to raise funds and campaign for party candidates, for example, and his programs put an indelible stamp on the party, defining it in the eyes of the electorate.

The president also influences the party's organization. He chooses the chairman of the party's national committee, and he has traditionally controlled the national nominating convention. Party reforms have, however — particularly on the Democratic side — made it more difficult even for incumbent presidents to dictate their renomination and direction of the party. Senator Edward Kennedy of Massachusetts did not hesitate to run against Jimmy Carter in 1980, openly challenging what in the past would have been the uncontested claim of an incumbent president to be renominated.

Regardless of the fluctuating power the president may have over his party, he remains the chief Republican or Democratic spokesman. Attending to party affairs is but one more time-consuming presidential responsibility.

*Manager of Prosperity.*[21] Franklin Roosevelt promised the American people that he, as president, would take swift and decisive action to cure the economic ills of the Great Depression. No longer would the fate of the economy be left to the "invisible hand," those market forces that in classical economic theory were supposed to balance supply and demand, producing prosperity in the long run while tolerating short-term economic disruptions.

During the 1930s Congress willingly and even eagerly delegated vast authority to the president to cope with the Depression. The president was indeed to be the manager of the nation's prosperity. In 1946 the Full Employment Act, which created the Council of Economic Advisors in the Executive Office of the President, reaffirmed the White House's role in maintaining economic prosperity. The council reports yearly on the state of the economy to the president as well as to the Joint Economic Committee on Capitol Hill that was also created by the Full Employment Act.

Presidents have been given the responsibility of maintaining a healthy economy, but they do not in reality have the power to curb inflation, high interest rates, unemployment, levels of production, trade deficits, and a host of other economic conditions. Carter, for example, was blamed for the high level of inflation and interest rates that were, at least in part, caused by the Arab oil embargo during the Nixon administration and the Organization of Petroleum Exporting Countries (OPEC) cartel. The Vietnam War also contributed heavily to the inflation of the 1970s, a cause again predating the influence of the 1970s presidents. Reagan took credit for the drop in inflation, interest rates, and unemployment in the 1980s, but in many respects the Reagan White House was the beneficiary of events beyond its control, such as lower oil prices in the early years of the decade brought about by a world oil glut.

Although presidents are unable to affect most areas of the economy, they nevertheless are held accountable for prosperity because of the economic and political legacy of the Great Depression and the New Deal. When large numbers of debt-ridden farmers faced bankruptcy in the mid-1980s, they turned to both the president and Congress for help; but it was the failure of the White House to take action that they blamed for their plight. At farm rallies around the country David Stockman was hung in effigy because of his proposals to cut government-supported farm loans. The White House

---

[21]Presidential scholar Clinton Rossiter first used this phrase to describe the president's economic role; see *The American Presidency,* p. 38.

did finally take some remedial steps to help the farmers, but in the view of many it was too little and too late.

The president's role as manager of prosperity, now so firmly embedded in our political system, will undoubtedly continue to frustrate future occupants of the White House. With virtually no influence on the economy, presidents will yet be held responsible for its unfortunate twists and turns or claim the credit for healthy economic conditions they could not have planned.

## The Institutional Presidency

Clearly, the president cannot single-handedly carry out his many responsibilities. Created in 1939, the Executive Office of the President augmented his personal staff and provided him with specialized agencies to advise and assist him. What is so aptly described as the administrative presidency came of age under Franklin Roosevelt, who was particularly concerned with using the executive branch efficiently to develop and carry out programs necessary to meet the crisis of the Great Depression. Roosevelt appointed a special President's Committee on Administrative Management in 1937 to advise him on how he could most effectively carry out his responsibilities. The panel believed that principles of "scientific management," widely accepted in public administration circles at the time, required a vast expansion in presidential staff agencies.

Following the advice of his committee, Roosevelt created the Executive Office by executive order, using the authority Congress had given to him under the 1939 Reorganization Act, which allowed the president to reorganize the executive branch subject to congressional veto. The Executive Office marked the creation of a presidential bureaucracy that has expanded over the years.

The White House staff and the Office of Management and Budget (formerly the Bureau of the Budget) constitute the core of the Executive Office, which also contains a number of other agencies assisting the president and acting on his behalf (see Figure 6.4).

### The Office of Management and Budget (OMB)

Many Washington insiders consider the Office of Management and Budget to be the most powerful agency in the Executive Office of the President. The Bureau of the Budget, originally created in 1921 by the Budget and Accounting Act and placed in the Treasury Department, was transferred to the Executive Office in 1939, becoming the most important component of the

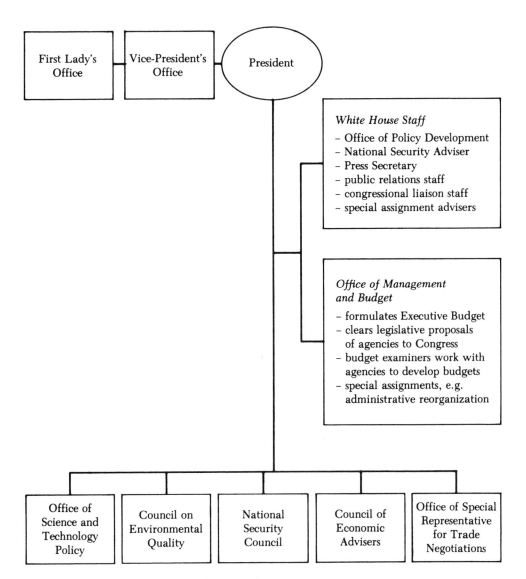

**Figure 6.4.** *The Executive Office of the President.*

new presidential bureaucracy. Because it continued to have some responsibility to Congress under statutory law, President Nixon decided to reorganize it in 1970 to establish formally an agency now entirely under presidential control; after heated debate, Congress accepted Nixon's reconstructed Office of Management and Budget reluctantly.

The office helps the president perform his responsibilities as chief executive and chief legislator. Its budget director, appointed by the president, and a staff of four hundred professionals oversee the complicated task of formulating the executive budget each year, allocating proposed expenditures for the dozens of programs carried out by executive departments and agencies. Examiners work with administrative agencies to formulate their budgets for the coming fiscal year. The examiners follow White House guidelines, making certain that agency budgets do not exceed the limits imposed by the president. OMB's role is to coordinate the agencies' budgets within the executive budget. No executive department or agency any longer, as was previously the practice, submits its budget directly to Congress, but rather must first clear it with OMB, and it is then incorporated in the broad executive budget. Congress, of course, has the final say on budgeting allocations, but it respects both the president's political position and the work that has gone into the budget. Congress, responsive to its own political constituencies, tinkers with the president's budget and generally makes only minor changes.

Legislative as well as budgetary clearance is a responsibility of OMB. The Executive Department and agency legislative proposals, including testimony scheduled to be given before congressional committees on legislation, must be cleared with OMB, which acts as the president's representative. OMB's legislative clearance coordinates the wide-ranging legislative proposals of the executive branch with the president's program.

OMB also helps the president to carry out his executive and legislative responsibilities by assisting him in his role as chief administrator. Before OMB and its predecessor the Bureau of the Budget were given the power of budgetary and legislative clearance, it was common practice for administrative agencies to take their budgets and legislative proposals directly to Congress. On more than one occasion presidents found out what "their" executive departments were doing by reading the newspapers! Franklin Roosevelt reported an incident that was not atypical:

When I woke up this morning the first thing I saw was a headline in the New York Times to the effect that our Navy was going to spend two billion dollars on a shipbuilding program. Here I am, the commander-in-chief of the Navy having to read about that for the first time in the press. Do you know what I said to that?

No, Mr. President.
I said, 'Jesus Chr-rist!'[22]

Roosevelt's experience was not uncommon before and even after the Bureau of the Budget was given clearance responsibilities. It took a long time for major departments and powerful agencies to accede to the wishes of the president that they clear their proposals with the Bureau of the Budget. Powerful departments and agencies found it relatively easy to go around the Executive Office, respecting the formal clearance requirements but informally establishing channels of communication to advance their views with influential committee and subcommittee chairmen. As presidents increasingly made it known that they would not tolerate bureaucratic end runs to Congress, budgetary and legislative clearance began to work effectively to bring those executive branch activities under White House control. The establishment of OMB as a direct arm of the president made even the most powerful and independent agencies respect the clearance process.

### The White House Staff

The personal staff of the president, always his closest and most trusted political advisors, formally became part of the Executive Office when it was created in 1939. More than with other parts of the Executive Office, the power and role of the White House staff depends largely on presidential style and the president's approach to his job. For many years the White House office remained small and its influence relatively weak in comparison with that of recent presidential staffs. Surrounding the president were a chief of staff, a press secretary, and a few aides whose responsibilities were loosely defined.

The gradual bureaucratization and expansion of the White House staff culminated after Nixon took office in 1969. Although Nixon followed in the footsteps of his predecessors, he saw the role of the president in even grander terms, requiring tighter White House reins on the executive branch. Somewhat ironically, Nixon carried Roosevelt's concept of the administrative presidency to its logical extreme. Inside the White House he carefully divided his staff's areas of responsibility among domestic, foreign, and national security policymaking. The source of all policy initiative was to be the White House, and the executive branch was expected to fall into line. The staff viewed itself as an extension of the president himself, as top aides

---

[22]Marriner S. Eccles, *Beckoning Frontiers*, ed. Sidney Hyman (New York: Alfred A. Knopf, 1951), p. 336.

John Ehrlichman and H.R. Haldeman wielded power in the name of the president. Henry Kissinger, advisor on national security, completely dominated foreign policymaking — ignoring the State Department, which did not come into its own again until Kissinger himself was named secretary of state.

## The National Security Council

Kissinger operated in conjunction with another component of the Executive Office, the National Security Council (NSC), which was created by the National Security Act of 1947. The NSC, consisting of the president, vice-president, secretary of state, secretary of defense, and director of the Office of Emergency Preparedness, is convened by the president when he needs useful advice on foreign and military policy matters. But in fact, during critical foreign policy crises the president convenes whatever group of advisors he thinks most appropriate, which may or may not include the members of the NSC; he does not rely on the formal mechanism of the NSC for foreign policy advice.

## The Council of Economic Advisors

Established in 1946, the Council of Economic Advisors aids the president in planning economic policy. This three-member agency issues a yearly economic report to the president and the Congress assessing the state of the economy. The Joint Economic Committee of Congress works with the council to coordinate White House and Capitol Hill efforts in economic planning. The council's placement in the Executive Office of the President reflects the expectation that the president serve as "manager of prosperity," a presidential role assumed by the White House during Franklin Roosevelt's administration. Roosevelt and his brain trust accepted Keynesian economics, which proclaimed that the government should have a central role in managing prosperity. While the supply-side economics of the Reagan administration rejects the Keynesian view, emphasizing instead the role of free enterprise and individual initiative in bringing about economic prosperity, there is little doubt that it is the White House and not the private sector that is blamed if unemployment, inflation, and low productivity continue to plague the economy.[23]

---

[23]Supply-side economics assumes that individual and corporate tax reductions will stimulate the supply of goods by providing an incentive for investment and productivity. The Keynesian school, on the other hand, supports tax reduction when an increase in demand is deemed desirable to raise the level of economic activity. Keynesians, in contrast to advocates of supply-side economics, support a far greater role for the government in the stimulation of economic activity through governmental expenditures.

## Other Executive Office Components

Other agencies within the Executive Office that assist the president include the Office of Science and Technology Policy, the Council on Environmental Quality, the Intelligence Oversight Board, and the Office of the Special Representative for Trade Negotiations. These components of the Executive Office reflect presidential responsibilities for the policy areas they cover. The Office of Science and Technology Policy, for example, advises the president on science policy and has direct ties to the scientific community, which is largely responsible for its existence. The Council on Environmental Quality, created by the National Environmental Policy Act of 1969, gives the president direct responsibilities in environmental policymaking. The president's pivotal role in trade negotiations is performed with the assistance of his special representative in that area.

Since the creation of the Executive Office in 1939, the White House staff and OMB have remained its most important components. The White House staff in particular has grown to become one of the largest and most important parts of the office. Presidential promises to reduce the size of the federal bureaucracy, a goal that has never been achieved, have never been seriously applied to the presidential bureaucracy — the Executive Office. Republican as well as Democratic presidents have seen in their personal staff and agencies of the Executive Office a necessary and important underpinning of the power of the White House. In the political battles of the Capitol, the presidential bureaucracy is often pitted against the regular bureaucracy and narrow iron triangles of congressional committees, agencies, and pressure groups.

The White House staff always contains one or two persons who are particularly close to the president, giving him political advice and sometimes acting in his name in relations with other parts of the government and the private sector. In the Carter administration, White House Chief of Staff Hamilton Jordan was the president's closest advisor in domestic policy. The personal friendship between the two men supported Jordan's power both within and without the presidential bureaucracy. In the Reagan administration, presidential counsel Edwin Meese III and White House Chief of Staff James A. Baker III emerged in Reagan's first year of office as the president's spokesmen. Both men went on to Cabinet posts, Meese becoming attorney general and Baker secretary of the treasury.

In addition to the press secretary and the president's close personal advisors, the White House staff consists of a national security advisor (who may or may not be close to the president) and a domestic policy group. Moreover, there is an extensive staff to deal with congressional liaisons.

Regardless of how the White House staff is organized, it has clearly become the dominant force in the Executive Office. Carter, who ran on a promise that he would reduce the size of the federal bureaucracy and the Executive Office as well, actually increased his staff from that of Nixon and Ford. Regardless of presidential proclamations — usually before or immediately after the election and during the first months of new administrations — that "cabinet government" will be practiced, it is the presidential bureaucracy and especially the White House staff that overshadows the cabinet. As presidential administrations progress, the cabinet tends to split into individual fiefdoms, with cabinet secretaries striving to strengthen and solidify their own power — sometimes against the White House. Presidents tend to view the federal bureaucracy with suspicion and often distrust, causing them to increase the numbers and the powers of their own personal bureaucracy. Republican presidents especially have a difficult time with the largely Democratic career bureaucracy. Nixon expanded the Executive Office more than any president had before him. Ford added to the number of aides in the White House, and although Reagan again promised cabinet government, it seems likely that he too will go the way of his predecessors in relying increasingly on the support of the White House staff and other components of the Executive Office.

The presidency has become institutionalized in the Executive Office. Members of both the president's personal staff and the regular agencies of the Executive Office often act in the president's name to become in effect an invisible presidency — one that may not always act in the best interests of the president or of the country. Although the press keeps an eagle eye on what goes on within the confines of the White House and the presidential bureaucracy, it is not always possible to ensure the accountability of the men and women who work for the president, who often can and do act on their own initiatives.

The White House staff in particular is an arena of power in which the players sometimes go to any lengths to elevate their personal status. The atmosphere of the White House tends to breed, as one notorious former aide wrote, "blind ambition."[24] Reagan aide Michael Deaver observed that "people will kill to get an office in the West Wing."[25] Having an office close to the president's Oval Office in the West Wing symbolizes power. George Reedy, a particularly astute political observer with long Washington experience on Capitol Hill and in the Johnson White House, has written: "Below the President is a mass of intrigue, posturing, strutting, cringing, and pious 'commitment' to irrelevant windbaggery. It is designed as the perfect setting for the conspiracy of mediocrity — that all too frequently successful collec-

[24]For an account of an admittedly extreme situation, but one that is nevertheless highly instructive, see John Dean, *Blind Ambition* (New York: Simon & Schuster, 1976).
[25]*New York Times*, March 5, 1985, sec. A.

tion of the untalented, the unpassionate, and the insincere seeking to convince the public that it is brilliant, compassionate, and dedicated."[26] Reedy concluded that the White House is and has always been "an ideal cloak for intrigue, pomposity, and ambition."[27]

Although members of the president's staff can exercise a great deal of power on their own, ultimately they are responsible to the president when he makes his wishes clear. Perhaps the greatest problem of the institutionalized and bureaucratic presidency is not the exercise of independent power by staff members, but their sycophancy in relation to the president himself. The president needs good and independent advice, which means staff members that will tell him if in their view he is embarking upon the wrong course of action. But whether presidential staffs are the "best and the brightest," or merely mediocre, they consistently seem unable in the environment of the White House to criticize a president who is bent on a particular course of action. "For a thousand days I would serve as counsel to the President," wrote John Dean about the Nixon administration, and "I soon learned that to make my way upward, into a position of confidence and influence, I had to travel downward through factional power plays, corruption, and finally outright crimes. Although I would be rewarded for diligence, true advancement would come from doing those things which built a common bond of trust — or guilt — between me and my superiors. In the Nixon White House, these upward and downward paths diverged, yet joined, like prongs of a tuning fork pitched to a note of expediency. Slowly, steadily, I would climb toward the moral abyss of the president's inner circle until I finally fell into it, thinking I had made it to the top just as I began to realize I had actually touched bottom."[28] Thomas E. Cronin writes, "Can a lieutenant vigorously engaged in implementing the presidential will admit to the possibility that what the president wants is wrong or not working? Yet a president is increasingly dependent on the judgment of these same staff members, since he seldom sees some of his cabinet members."[29] Cabinet secretaries, too, if they are close to the president, may find it difficult to challenge what they consider to be a wrong course of action. It was not until the waning days of the Johnson administration that Secretary of Defense Robert McNamara began to dissent from the president's stubborn pursuit of the Vietnam War, only to find himself suddenly appointed head

[26]George E. Reedy, *The Twilight of the Presidency* (New York: New American Library, 1971), p. xiv.
[27]Ibid.
[28]John Dean, *Blind Ambition*, p. 21.
[29]Thomas E. Cronin, "The Swelling of the Presidency: Can Anyone Reverse the Tide?" reprinted in *American Government: Readings and Cases,* ed. Peter Woll (Boston: Little, Brown, 1981), p. 355.

of the World Bank. Johnson appointed Clark Clifford as secretary of defense in the expectation that he would support the Vietnam War, only to have Clifford tell him that the war could not be won. The government needs more men like Clark Clifford, but regrettably they are rarely to be found in the political arena.

## The Presidency as an Instrument of Policy Innovation

In most areas of public policy the president cannot make significant innovations unless there is substantial support both within and without the government for such action. Broadly based forces of change focus on the presidency; this is what led to the election of Roosevelt in 1932. It is when the presidency is riding the crest of a wave of change, such as occurs after critical elections in which major shifts take place in voter alignments from one party to the other, that the White House can be a catalyst in forging new directions in public policy. Elections are not critical because large parts of the public have specific ideas on policies they want to see put into effect, but because voters feel that a new approach is needed, one different from the policies the party in power has supported.

### *Franklin D. Roosevelt and the New Deal*

The electorate was, to say the least, discontented, in 1932 because of the Depression, and people naturally blamed the inaction of President Hoover. A variety of proposals were made to Hoover by experts both inside and outside government as to how he might meet the crisis of the Depression, but those who were unemployed and marching in the streets did not know of these, nor did they have specific policy recommendations of their own. They only wanted to see Hoover out of office and someone — anyone — in to replace him. At such times the president must offer leadership to shape new programs, although this is no guarantee that they will be accepted by Congress, the Supreme Court, or the bureaucracy.

Franklin Roosevelt was the major force behind the New Deal, but it took a long time before New Deal legislation was accepted by Congress and the Supreme Court. Once Roosevelt's "honeymoon" with Congress was over in 1933, he met increasing resistance to his proposals in the legislature. Although a large majority of the voters supported the president, as revealed in his landslide election in 1936, they were supporting the man more than the specific content of his policy proposals. Regardless of Roosevelt's continuing frustrations on the domestic front in policy innovation, there is little doubt that it was his tenacity in the pursuit of his goals that brought the New Deal from the realm of ideas to reality.

The New Deal program continued even after the election of Dwight Eisenhower in 1952. Eisenhower's election did not mark a long-term shift of the electorate to the Republican party, nor did Eisenhower's approach represent a major ideological contrast to many New Deal programs. Public policy, particularly monetary and fiscal policy, took a more conservative turn during the Eisenhower years, but it was not Eisenhower's intent to use the White House to make radical changes in governmental policy.

*Post–New Deal Initiatives: John F. Kennedy and Lyndon B. Johnson*

After the relative cautious Eisenhower administration, the Kennedy and Johnson years produced significant White House initiatives in domestic and foreign policy that changed the political face of the nation. Johnson's Great Society programs in particular put the federal government in a dominant position over the states in controlling economic and social policy. Presidential initiatives in civil rights, which admittedly sprang from the nationwide civil rights movement of the 1960s, changed the nation's political character. It was Johnson, for example, who issued the executive order based on Title VI of the 1964 Civil Rights Act that established affirmative action programs throughout the federal government and in private institutions receiving federal funds. Although Johnson declared that his order was based on Title VI, in fact the language of Title VI barring discrimination in federally funded programs in no way explicitly provides for "reverse discrimination," which affirmative action requires.

Johnson's initiatives in domestic policy were more than matched by his foreign policy, which was concentrated almost solely on the pursuit of the Vietnam War. No president in history has had a greater impact upon foreign relations.

*The Conservative Tide: Richard M. Nixon and Ronald Reagan*

In the decade following the Johnson administration, perhaps the most significant presidential policy innovation was that of Richard Nixon in opening relations with the People's Republic of China. President Jimmy Carter carried the Nixon initiative to its logical conclusion by recognizing the government of mainland China, but it was Nixon who, with the help of his astute and politically skillful secretary of state, Henry Kissinger, made history by reversing the policy of nonrecognition that had prevailed for over two decades.

Ronald Reagan's victory in the 1980 presidential election promised major White House initiatives to alter drastically the course of domestic policy. The conservative tone of the Reagan administration was at the opposite end of the political spectrum from the Democratic New Deal policies that had governed the nation since the 1930s. Reagan's "new beginning" represented an effort to end the dominant role of the federal government in economic and social policy. Reagan was the first Republican elected since the New Deal who seriously undertook a program to reduce radically federal expenditures, taxes, and government regulation of the economic and social life of the country. Like presidents before him, however, Reagan found that presidential prerogatives in domestic affairs are extremely limited. Major policy innovation cannot be carried out without the cooperation of Congress, the bureaucracy, and the courts.

## Presidential Prerogative Powers

Today the president, although frustrated in many of his domestic pursuits, nevertheless possesses the power of life and death over the nation. This is a true paradox, because with relative ease a president can involve the United States in a major war that might mean the destruction not only of this country, but of all mankind; however, he often cannot secure the passage in Congress of the most trivial legislation, or necessarily receive the support of the bureaucracy for implementing his own policy initiatives.

These far-reaching prerogative life and death decisions reflect a distinctly personal attribute of presidential power, for they are often dependent solely on the man, his perceptions of the world, and his character. Perhaps the most important current issue in relation to presidential power and policy-making pertains to this area where the president acts in a personal capacity to shape the course of the nation.

Presidential discretion in the military and foreign policy spheres is generally accepted, but this general compliance has been punctuated from time to time with complaints that the president has too much power. During the twentieth century, the actions of any president that has involved the United States in war have been attacked by various groups. Woodrow Wilson was subject to criticism for leading the country into World War I, and the initiatives taken by Franklin Roosevelt to aid our allies against Germany before World War II were criticized by various isolationist groups as inappropriate and exceeding the constitutional authority of the office. One of the main campaign issues in 1952 was the Korean War; the Republicans implied that once again the Democratic "war party" had improperly led the United States into foreign involvement.

## The Korean Decision

President Truman's decision to send troops to Korea without consulting the United Nations or Congress was at first generally accepted by congressional leaders. But as the war dragged on, American commitments and casualties in Asia began to mount, and so did criticism of the president's discretionary authority. In January of 1951 Senator Robert Taft, in a major Senate speech, accused the administration of formulating defense policy since the end of World War II without consulting either Congress or the people. Taft asserted that without authority the president had "involved us in the Korean War and without authority he apparently has now adopted a similar policy in Europe." A few days after Taft's speech Republicans in the Senate introduced a resolution that expressed the sense of the Senate that American ground forces should not be sent to Europe in the absence of a congressional policy relating to the issue.

In characteristic style, Truman contended that he could and would send troops wherever he wanted without consulting the legislature. The controversy over the scope of presidential authority and discretion in military and foreign policymaking was a precursor of the dispute over presidential initiative in Vietnam. Johnson's decisions were based on clear historical precedents, as was the political feedback.

## The Vietnam Decision

The Vietnam War once again gave rise to extensive discussion in Congress about the proper role of the legislature in the exercise of the war power. Although quick to give Johnson his Gulf of Tonkin Resolution, many congressmen later regretted their vote, for it was widely interpreted as giving the president blanket authority to pursue whatever military action he wished in Southeast Asia. Johnson himself used the resolution as a reminder to legislative critics that he was pursuing the war with the consent of Congress.

The mounting congressional criticism of Johnson's Vietnam policies continued into the Nixon administration. Nixon's decision to invade Cambodia in 1970 and Laos in 1971 provoked particularly heated congressional opposition, which in turn led to increased efforts to curb the president's power to make war.

## The War Powers Resolution

The most serious congressional incursion on the war-making authority of the president occurred in November of 1973, when Congress overrode Nixon's veto of the War Powers Resolution, first passed by Congress in October. Under terms of this resolution, the president "in every possible instance" must consult with Congress before involving U.S. armed forces in hostilities. The resolution requires regular presidential consultation with Congress during war to keep the legislature informed of presidential actions. When the president orders troops into hostilities without a declaration of war from Congress, he must within forty-eight hours submit to the Speaker of the House and to the president pro tem of the Senate a report setting forth the circumstances necessitating the introduction of U.S. armed forces, the constitutional and legislative authority under which such introduction took place, and the estimated scope and duration of the hostilities or involvement. After this report is submitted to Congress, the president must terminate the use of U.S. armed forces within sixty days unless Congress has declared war or given other specific authorization for the use of armed forces, or has extended by law the sixty-day period or is physically unable to meet as the result of an armed attack on the country. The initial sixty-day period during which the president may take independent action cannot be extended by Congress under the resolution for more than thirty additional days. President Nixon's veto of the bill was overridden by a vote of 284–135 in the House and 75–18 in the Senate, indicating strong congressional sentiment to limit the president's war-making powers.

Ironically, although the War Powers Resolution was designed to restrict presidential discretion to make war, it may have had the opposite result. For the first time in history Congress recognized in the resolution presidential authority to commit troops abroad. The resolution would not have prevented, for example, Truman's unilateral action in sending troops to Korea, or Johnson's commitment of armed forces in Vietnam. During the Reagan administration the resolution had no effect whatever on the president's decision to send marines to Lebanon or to invade Grenada. Although Reagan did run into some verbal rhetoric by congressional Democrats opposing his actions, presidents are virtually assured of support from Capitol Hill when they undertake military actions on their own initiative.

Not only is the War Powers Resolution an ineffective check on the war-making powers of the president, but it is also constitutionally questionable under the separation of powers. The resolution gives Congress power to veto presidential actions, which may if challenged be viewed as an unconstitutional legislative interference in executive affairs.[30]

---

[30]The Supreme Court has held the legislative veto to be unconstitutional under other circumstances. See *Immigration and Naturalization Service v. Chada*, 462, U.S. 919 (1983).

## The Role of the President in Constitutional Democracy

Our system of government as originally constructed had a negative orientation, designed to prevent the effective exercise of governmental authority. The intricate intermeshing of the various branches of the government that was required in the policy-making process was meant to limit potentially "evil" influences on government emanating from factions and demagogic individuals who were more concerned about their own interests than about the national interest. However, a government intended to work inefficiently if at all obviously could not meet the wide range of responsibilities that inevitably were placed on it, nor could it produce effective government during critical periods. The bureaucracy developed to take over expanded governmental responsibilities, and the powers of the presidency grew to provide leadership and effective decision making in times of crisis.

In the area of foreign and military affairs, the presidency does not conform to traditional constitutional restraints. Although the Constitution did foresee in part that the president would have to have wider discretionary powers in the foreign than in the domestic sphere, nevertheless the authority to declare war clearly resided with Congress, and the Senate was to advise and consent on treaties and ambassadorial appointments. A major question for the future of the presidency is how our governmental system can balance the need for power with constitutional requirements of responsibility and constraints. In the domestic arena, unless stronger parties develop that will bring about closer links between the White House and Congress, the president will be severely curtailed in his legislative activities. Moreover, the bureaucracy will inevitably place constraints on the ability of the president to shape and implement public policy. Even in parliamentary governments with a strong two-party system, such as that of Great Britain, the administrative branch exercises wide discretion in policymaking.

Although the presidency is usually called an institution, the fact remains that the White House is more a reflection of the man who holds the office than of its bureaucratic components. It is an extension of the president's preferences and inclinations in most critical areas of decision making. Each president shapes the institution more than it shapes him, particularly in the conduct of foreign policy.

In the middle of the 1980s, the presidency continues to be the focus of national attention and hope. The widely perceived abuses of presidential power that occurred in the foreign policy sphere during the Johnson administration and in both the domestic and foreign policy areas in the Nixon years brought the presidency as an institution into temporary disrepute. The resurgence of congressional power in the 1970s as a result of the Watergate affair and Nixon's secret bombing of Cambodia may be only temporary. The same forces that have increased presidential responsibilities and powers in the past will continue to support the authority of the White House. National crises, both foreign and domestic, have been a major cause of the "imperial" presidency. Americans will continue to expect the president to be the initiator of broader public policy changes. Reagan's overwhelming electoral victories represented the hope in the hearts of many people that the presidency would once again be able to sustain economic prosperity, and reduce the burden of an overbearing government.

## Suggestions for Further Reading

Cronin, Thomas E. *The State of the Presidency.* 2nd ed. Boston: Little, Brown, 1980. A comprehensive and fresh interpretation of the modern American presidency.

Crouse, Timothy. *The Boys on the Bus.* New York: Random House, 1973. A superb book on the activities and antics of the press during a presidential campaign.

Hess, Stephen. *Organizing the Presidency.* Washington, D.C.: The Brookings Institution, 1976. A detailed analysis of the institutional presidency and of the way the White House has been organized from Franklin D. Roosevelt to Richard M. Nixon.

Lowi, Theodore J., *The Personal President: Power Invested, Promise Unfulfilled.* Ithaca, N.Y.: Cornell University Press, 1985. The author argues that the increasingly personal, plebiscitary presidency undermines political stability and the constitutional system.

Neustadt, Richard E. *Presidential Power: The Politics of Leadership.* Rev. ed. New York: John Wiley, 1976. The presidency viewed by an insider, who argues that presidential power does not extend beyond the ability to persuade.

Rossiter, Clinton. *The American Presidency.* New York: Harcourt, Brace, 1956. A classic work on the powers and responsibilities of the presidency.

Schlesinger, Arthur M., Jr. *The Imperial Presidency.* Boston: Houghton Mifflin, 1973. The author criticizes the escalation of presidential power against the backdrop of the Nixon administration.

# chapter 7

# Congress

Every two years, after elections are held for the House of Representatives and the Senate, those who have been elected to Congress for the first time bring with them a high sense of mission. They hope to influence new directions in public policy. Not only do they hold the institution of Congress in high regard, considering it to be the primary influence on public policy in government, but they also feel that their individual roles can be significant within the framework of the legislature. After all, doesn't the Constitution designate Congress the primary legislative body? And doesn't legislation mean public policy? No other branch of government is given direct legislative authority by the Constitution.

## The Constitutional Context of Congress

*The Formal Structure of Congress*

The formal constitutional provisions governing Congress shape it in many ways. The bicameral division of the legislature inevitably causes internal conflict between the House and the Senate. Different constituencies for the two legislative branches, different powers, and different terms of office, reinforce bicameralism (see Figure 7.1). These legislative differences make it difficult for Congress to develop a unified legislative policy.

Originally, the major reason for the bicameral legislature was to secure the representation of differing interests — of the states in the Senate, the people in the House. It was not until 1913, with the adoption of the Seventeenth Amendment, that the Senate was elected directly by the people; previously, senators were selected by state legislatures. The indirect selection of the Senate, in combination with longer tenure and a slightly older age

The Bicameral Congress

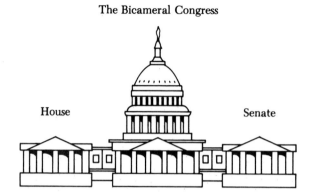

| *House* | *Senate* |
| --- | --- |
| • two-year term | • four-year term |
| • smaller, equal constituencies (local) | • larger, unequal constituencies (state) |
| • 435 members | • 100 members |
| • unique constitutional powers:<br>  – originates tax bills (Ways and Means Committee important)<br>  – impeachment | • unique constitutional powers:<br>  – advice and consent on many presidential appointments (judiciary and foreign relations committees important)<br>  – tries impeached officers; convicts by a two-thirds vote<br>  – approves treaties by a two-thirds vote (Foreign Relations Committee important) |
| • Rules Committee important | • Rules Committee plays minor role |
| • limited debate | • unlimited debate unless sixty senators vote cloture |
| • unequal power among members | • greater equality among senators |
| • committee and subcommittee chairmen more powerful | • committee and subcommittee chairmen less powerful |
| • staff less powerful | • staff very powerful |
| • greater specialization of members | • senators must deal with more policy areas |

Figure 7.1. *The Bicameral Congress: House and Senate Differences*

qualification (senators must be thirty years of age, representatives twenty-five), was intended to give the Senate a more conservative cast than the House.

In *The Federalist* Hamilton and Madison argued that the House and the Senate were to have different policy orientations and responsibilities. Direct election and a two-year term of office rendered the House continually dependent on the interests of local constituents. The Senate, on the other hand, was able to act in a more deliberate fashion; it could give greater thought to important issues of public policy, particularly in foreign affairs, and where necessary check rash actions by the House. The most important objects of federal legislation within the purview of the House were the regulation of commerce, taxation, and regulation of the militia (*The Federalist*, No. 56).

## Constitutional Division of Power

Under the terms of the Constitution, all bills for raising revenue must originate in the House; the House thus has powerful initiative that often determines the course of tax policy. The real balance of power between the House and the Senate in tax policy is not determined by the Constitution, however, but by the political skills of the respective chairmen of the Ways and Means Committee of the House on the one hand, and the Senate Finance Committee on the other. By proposing amendments to tax legislation, the Senate can in effect initiate tax policy.[1] Power over tax policy may thus shift from the House to the Senate, depending on the political astuteness of the tax chairmen. Democratic Ways and Means chairman Wilbur Mills skillfully guided tax legislation through many Congresses. His replacement by the less effective Democratic Congressman Al Ullman of Oregon allowed Senator Russell Long of Louisiana, Democratic chairman of the Senate Finance Committee, to become the dominant Capitol Hill power in tax legislation. Beginning in the Ninety-seventh Congress, the House Ways and Means Committee again returned to powerful control under the chairmanship of Chicago Democratic Congressman Dan Rostenkowski of Illinois, a protégé of House Speaker Tip O'Neill. Rostenkowski seemed likely to restore the dominance of the House. On the Senate side, the elections of 1980 dethroned Russell Long and put in his place Kansas Republican Robert Dole, an often acerbic but nevertheless able senator. Although Dole promised to work closely with ranking minority member Long, it seemed improbable

---

[1]Article I, sec. 7 of the Constitution specifically authorizes the Senate to propose amendments to the legislation: "All bills for raising revenue shall originate in the House of Representatives; but the Senate may propose or concur with amendments as on other bills."

that the Senate Finance Committee would command the respect of the House to the same degree that it had under Long's chairmanship.

In addition to providing for House initiation of revenue legislation, the Constitution assigns different tasks to the two sides of Capitol Hill in other areas as well. Most importantly, the Senate is the predominant power in foreign policymaking. The Constitution gives the upper body exclusive authority to advise and consent on treaties made by the president and to approve ambassadorial appointments. The prestige of the Senate Foreign Relations Committee is tied directly to the constitutional role of the Senate in foreign policy. The power of the committee ebbs and flows in response to the need for and effectiveness of presidential power in foreign affairs. During times of crisis, the president tends to dominate foreign policy. Since World War II the leading position of the United States in world affairs has generally increased presidential power relative to that of the Senate in foreign policymaking. The foreign policy arena is one of almost constant crisis — cold war, hot wars, and continuing world instability. Because the Constitution allows the president greater prerogative authority in foreign affairs, the White House has overshadowed Congress in foreign policymaking far more than in the domestic sphere.

Another difference in the roles assigned to the House and the Senate is that the Constitution gives the House the authority to impeach presidents and other civil officers, while the Senate is to try impeachments, which require a two-thirds vote for conviction. The Senate has the authority to advise and consent on presidential appointments of not only ambassadors but also Supreme Court justices, "public ministers" — which means cabinet members — "and all other officers of the United States, whose appointments are not herein otherwise provided for, and which shall be established by law: but the Congress may by law vest the appointment of such inferior officers, as they think proper, in the president alone, in the courts of law, or in the heads of departments."[2] The constitutional power of the Senate to advise and consent on appointments has given it an important role in shaping the executive branch. Congressional legislation has extended the requirement of senatorial approval of appointments far beyond those designated in the Constitution to include hundreds of top-level bureaucratic officials.

*Judicial Interpretation of Policy-Making Authority Under Article I*

The Constitution can be interpreted as both a negative and a positive document — that is, the powers of the national government can be seen as

[2]Constitution of the United States, Article II, sec. 2.

either limiting or extending its authority. With few exceptions, the course of American constitutional interpretation by the Supreme Court was set by Chief Justice Marshall in the early nineteenth century. In such famous cases as *McCulloch* v. *Maryland* (1819) and *Gibbons* v. *Ogden* (1824), a "loose" rather than "strict" constructionist view was taken of the Constitution, and particularly of the implied powers clause, which gives the legislature all authority that is "necessary and proper" to implement its enumerated powers.[3] Although from time to time in American history the Supreme Court has limited the authority of Congress, the major trend of judicial decisions has been toward permitting Congress to do whatever it wishes, provided that there is no clear violation of the Bill of Rights.

It was during the New Deal era that the most serious challenge to congressional authority occurred, when the Supreme Court ruled several important pieces of New Deal legislation unconstitutional for exceeding the enumerated powers of Congress. The era of the New Deal was not the only time that the Supreme Court struck down legislation because it was beyond congressional authority, but it was the most serious judicial threat to the actions of the political branches of government — Congress and the presidency — based on the idea of constitutional restraint.

After the election of 1936 and Roosevelt's attempt to change the composition of the Supreme Court, a more liberal Court interpreted the Constitution more loosely, thus upholding New Deal legislation. What is or is not constitutional is a matter of subjective opinion on the part of the Court, and proponents of the New Deal argued vigorously that their standards of constitutionality were as valid as those of the justices. The latter, they held, interpreted the Constitution in line with their conservative orientation.

In the early phase of the New Deal, such important legislation as the Agricultural Adjustment Act of 1933 and the National Industrial Recovery Act of 1933 were invalidated as having gone beyond the authority of Congress. However, in the historic case of *National Labor Relations Board* v. *Jones and Laughlin Steel* (1937), Chief Justice Charles Evans Hughes and Justice Owen J. Roberts switched to the liberal side of the Court, thus giving the New Deal a victory.[4] At issue in the case was the Wagner Act (National Labor Relations Act) of 1935, which, on the basis of the commerce clause, extended federal regulatory power to deal with labor disputes that burdened or obstructed interstate commerce. The National Labor Relations Board (NLRB) was created with the authority to issue cease and desist orders that would be enforced through the courts against business firms that were found guilty of engaging in "unfair labor practices." The terms of the act

---

[3] *McCulloch v. Maryland*, 4 Wheaton 316 (1819); *Gibbons v. Ogden*, 9 Wheaton 1 (1824).
[4] *National Labor Relations Board v. Jones and Laughlin Steel*, 301 U.S. 1 (1937).

did not extend merely to businesses involved in transporting goods across state lines; they also included manufacturing firms that were antecedent to and separate from the process of transporting goods.

In cases previous to *National Labor Relations Board* v. *Jones and Laughlin Steel,* the Court had held that such extensions of federal regulatory power were beyond the authority of Congress under the commerce clause. After upholding the extension of regulatory power in labor relations, the Court went on to support New Deal legislation in agriculture on the basis of the commerce clause. Early New Deal legislation in this field had been declared unconstitutional because Congress had based it on its authority to tax and to provide for the general welfare.

The New Deal settled once and for all the controversy over whether the boundaries of congressional authority in domestic legislation were to be narrow or broad. It also revealed that in reality this is a political, not a constitutional, question, decided not by the Supreme Court operating in a vacuum, but by the ebb and flow of political forces. Roosevelt's unrelenting pressure on the Supreme Court, backed by his enormous popular support, caused it to reverse its position.

A month before the *Jones and Laughlin* decision, the Court had indicated a more liberal stance in *West Coast Co.* v. *Parrish.* Harold L. Ickes noted the case in his diary:

The Supreme Court yesterday did a complete somersault on the question of minimum wages for women. It reversed itself on the *Adkins* case decided in 1923, in which the Court declared unconstitutional a law establishing minimum wages for women. . . .
. . . I do not know just what the effect on public opinion will be, or on the Court fight, but it seems to me that it is an admission on the part of the Supreme Court of charges that we have made to the effect that it hasn't been following the Constitution, but has been establishing as the law of the land, through Supreme Court decisions, the economic and social beliefs of the judges of the Court. It seems to me that on the whole, the effect will be to weaken the prestige of the Court in public estimation because when it was under fire, the Court ran to cover. For my part, I would have had more respect for the Court if it had gone down fighting and smiling after the manner of Justice McReynolds [who wrote a vigorous dissenting opinion]. Hughes and Roberts ought to realize that the mob is always ready to tear and rend at any sign of weakness.[5]

*Policymaking Based on Treaties.* Another and rather esoteric area in which the authority of Congress has been challenged is in relation to its power to implement treaty provisions. Congress, in addition to having the authority to carry out its enumerated powers, may "make all laws which shall be

---

[5]*Harold L. Ickes, The Inside Struggle* (New York: Simon & Schuster, 1954), pp. 106–107.

necessary and proper for carrying into execution . . . all other powers vested by the Constitution in the government of the United States, or in any department or officer thereof." The treaty-making power is an example of authority vested by the Constitution "in the government of the United States, or in any department or officer thereof," on the basis of which Congress can enact laws. Article VI of the Constitution provides in part that

This Constitution, and the laws of the United States which shall be made in Pursuance thereof; and all Treaties made, or which shall be made, under the Authority of the United States, shall be the supreme Law of the Land. . . .

Since treaties and the Constitution are equally legitimate sources of authority, can Congress in pursuance of the treaty pass laws that would be unconstitutional solely on the basis of its enumerated powers?

In *Missouri v. Holland* (1920), the Supreme Court held that Congress can make a law to put into effect the provisions of a treaty that would be unconstitutional in the absence of the treaty.[6] However, the law in the *Missouri* case did not violate a specific provision of the Constitution. The Court has held that Congress cannot use a treaty or an executive agreement (treated as a treaty by the Supreme Court) as authority to pass a law that violates an explicit provision of the Constitution.

In *Reid v. Covert* (1957), the Court, after citing the language of Article VI, which makes treaties the supreme law of the land along with the Constitution, pointed out that

There is nothing in this language which intimates that treaties and laws enacted pursuant to them do not have to comply with the provisions of the Constitution. Nor is there anything in the debates which accompanied the drafting and ratifications of the Constitution which even suggests such a result. . . . It would be manifestly contrary to the objective of those who created the Constitution, as well as those who are responsible for the Bill of Rights — let alone alien to our own entire constitutional history and tradition — to construe Article VI as permitting the United States to exercise power under an international agreement without observing constitutional prohibitions. In effect, such construction would permit amendment of that document in a manner not sanctioned by Article V. The prohibitions of the Constitution were designed to apply to all branches of the national government and they cannot be nullified by the Executive or by the Executive and the Senate combined. . . .[7]

The *Reid* case involved an executive agreement between the United States and Great Britain that provided that U.S. military courts would have ex-

[6]*Missouri v. Holland*, 252 U.S. 416 (1920).
[7]*Reid v. Covert*, 354 U.S. 1, 21 (1957).

clusive jurisdiction over criminal offenses committed in Great Britain by American servicemen or their dependents. Violations of British laws by Americans would be tried by court-martial. The case appealed the decision of a court-martial trial that had convicted the wife of a serviceman of murdering her husband. Court-martial trials do not provide the full protections of the Bill of Rights, and on this basis the Supreme Court upheld a lower district court judgment that Mrs. Covert (the wife) should be released from custody. Provisions for court-martial trials established by Congress cannot be extended to civilians on the basis of executive agreements because such action would violate the Bill of Rights.

*The Effects of Judicial Interpretation of Article I.* Today, the issue of constitutional limitations on Congress is dormant. Controversy over such limitations has in the past always resulted from political rather than legal factors — that is, from the conservative orientation of the Court, which led to its curbing what it considered the too liberal policies of Congress. Certainly from the standpoint of the Constitution itself it is difficult to foresee how Congress might be limited in the future. Except for clear violations of the Bill of Rights, constitutional restraints on the legislature are largely irrelevant. Congress has been able to use the war power, the power to tax and to provide for the general welfare, and the commerce clause to justify virtually any legislation expanding the role of the federal government.

Although the Court has not, since the New Deal, interpreted the Constitution to restrict congressional authority beyond the constraints of the Bill of Rights, the Madisonian model of the separation of powers frequently limits the ability of Congress to act. The legislature is checked not only by the president, but also by the internal checks and balances of bicameralism, the separate constituencies and powers of the House and the Senate.

## Committees: The "Little Legislatures" of Capitol Hill

Committees are the keystone of the legislative process (see Figure 7.2). Congress, like most legislative bodies, has organized itself in committees in order to provide the requisite specialized division of labor and to meet demands for representation by special interests that span the political landscape, from agriculture, labor, and business to veterans, the elderly, and Indians.

Legislative efficiency and responsiveness, however, are not the only reasons for the decentralization of Congress in over three hundred committees and subcommittees. Another reason behind the dispersion of committees on Capitol Hill is the personal quest for power by both congressional members and staffers.

Power on Capitol Hill — which is in large part the reputation for power

This graphic shows the most typical way in which proposed legislation is enacted into law. There are more complicated, as well as simpler, routes and most bills fall by the wayside and never become law. The process is illustrated with two hypothetical bills, House bill No. 1 (HR 1) and Senate bill No. 2 (S 2).

Each bill must be passed by both houses of Congress in identical form before it can become law. The path of HR 1 is traced by a solid line, that of S 2 by a broken line. However, in practice most legislation begins as similar proposals in both houses.

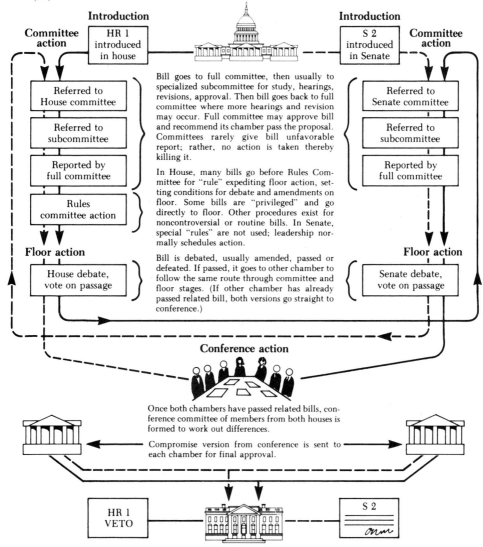

**Introduction**

**Committee action**

HR 1 introduced in house

Referred to House committee

Referred to subcommittee

Reported by full committee

Rules committee action

**Floor action**

House debate, vote on passage

Bill goes to full committee, then usually to specialized subcommittee for study, hearings, revisions, approval. Then bill goes back to full committee where more hearings and revision may occur. Full committee may approve bill and recommend its chamber pass the proposal. Committees rarely give bill unfavorable report; rather, no action is taken thereby killing it.

In House, many bills go before Rules Committee for "rule" expediting floor action, setting conditions for debate and amendments on floor. Some bills are "privileged" and go directly to floor. Other procedures exist for noncontroversial or routine bills. In Senate, special "rules" are not used; leadership normally schedules action.

Bill is debated, usually amended, passed or defeated. If passed, it goes to other chamber to follow the same route through committee and floor stages. (If other chamber has already passed related bill, both versions go straight to conference.)

**Introduction**

S 2 introduced in Senate

**Committee action**

Referred to Senate committee

Referred to subcommittee

Reported by full committee

**Floor action**

Senate debate, vote on passage

**Conference action**

Once both chambers have passed related bills, conference committee of members from both houses is formed to work out differences.

Compromise version from conference is sent to each chamber for final approval.

HR 1 VETO

S 2

Compromise version approved by both houses is sent to President who can either sign it into law or veto it and return it to Congress. Congress may override veto by a two-thirds majority vote in both houses; bill then becomes law without President's signature.

**Figure 7.2.** *How a Bill Becomes a Law. Committees play a dominant role in the legislative process.*
SOURCE: *Guide to Congress*, November 1976 (Washington, D.C.: Congressional Quarterly, Inc.), p. 345. By permission.

— is acquired by members of Congress when they become chairmen of standing committees or subcommittees. Staffers who become chief counsel or chiefs of staff for committees are also placed above their peers in power and status. Increasing the number of committees gives both congressmen and their aides expanded opportunities to enhance their political reputations.

### A Map of Committees

There is a hierarchy of committees on Capitol Hill. The standing committees, which are the permanent committees that do not formally "rise" at the end of a legislative session but continue from one session to another, have final power over all legislation. They are divided into subcommittees, many of which have in effect become little different from standing committees themselves in terms of their permanency and power (see Tables 7.1 and 7.2). The legislative jurisdictions of the fifteen standing committees of the Senate and nineteen standing committees of the House are determined by the rules of each body. Subcommittees and their jurisdictions are created and determined by the standing committees. Additionally, both the House and the Senate have select or special committees that have been created to do specific tasks. Generally, select committees are investigative in nature and do not have the authority to report legislation, but some are little different from regular standing committees. For example, the select intelligence committees of the Senate and the House have legislative and budgetary authority over the Central Intelligence Agency, the Federal Bureau of Investigation, and other parts of the intelligence community.

*Assignment to Committees.* New members of Congress seeking committee assignments make their requests known to the appropriate party committees. In the Senate, the Democratic Steering Committee, chaired by the floor leader, determines the assignment of new members as well as transfers from one committee to another. There are, in addition to the floor leader, twenty-one Democrats on the Steering Committee, making it directly representative of close to half of all Democratic senators. Senate committee assignments by Republicans are made by the party's Committee on Committees, chaired by the party's floor leader, who runs the committee with the help of fifteen Republican colleagues.

On the House side, assignments to the standing committees are made by the Democratic Steering and Policy Committee and by the Republican Committee on Committees. The Speaker appoints members of select committees in the House, but in the Senate they are appointed in the same manner as standing committees.

**Table 7.1.** *Ninety-ninth Congress (1984–1985), U.S. House of Representatives*

| Standing and select committees | Number of subcommittees |
|---|---|
| Agriculture | 8 |
| Appropriations | 13 |
| Armed Services | 7 |
| Banking, Finance and Urban Affairs | 8 |
| Budget | 0; 8 task forces |
| District of Columbia | 3 |
| Education and Labor | 8 |
| Energy and Commerce | 6 |
| Foreign Affairs | 8 |
| Government Operations | 7 |
| House Administration | 6; 1 task force |
| Interior and Insular Affairs | 6 |
| Judiciary | 7 |
| Merchant Marine and Fisheries | 6 |
| Post Office and Civil Service | 7 |
| Public Works and Transportation | 6 |
| Rules | 2 |
| Science and Technology | 7 |
| Select Aging | 4 |
| Select Children, Youth and Families | 0; 3 task forces |
| Select Hunger | 0; 2 task forces |
| Select Intelligence | 3 |
| Select Narcotics Abuse and Control | 0 |
| Small Business | 6 |
| Standards of Office Conduct | 0 |
| Veterans' Affairs | 5 |
| Ways and Means | 6 |
| Total:  27 | Total:  139 |

## The Role of Committees

The standing committees of Congress have jurisdiction over major spheres of public policy and the administrative departments and agencies that implement policy. The most prestigious committees — the House Appropriations and Ways and Means committees, the Senate Foreign Relations and Judiciary committees, and the predecessors of the Armed Services committees of both parties — date to the early days of the Republic. The most important responsibilities given to Congress by the Constitution have been

**Table 7.2.** *Ninety-ninth Congress (1984–1985), U.S. Senate*

| Standing and select committees | Number of subcommittees |
|---|:---:|
| Agriculture, Nutrition and Forestry | 6 |
| Appropriations | 13 |
| Armed Services | 6 |
| Banking, Housing and Urban Affairs | 5 |
| Budget | 0 |
| Commerce, Science and Transportation | 8 |
| Energy and Natural Resources | 5 |
| Environment and Public Works | 5 |
| Finance | 8 |
| Foreign Relations | 6 |
| Governmental Affairs | 6 |
| Judiciary | 8 |
| Labor and Human Resources | 6 |
| Rules and Administration | 0 |
| Select Ethics | 0 |
| Select Indian Affairs | 0 |
| Select Intelligence | 0 |
| Small Business | 7 |
| Special Aging | 0 |
| Veterans' Affairs | 0 |
| Total: 20 | Total: 89 |

delegated to these committees. Members seeking to build their Washington careers around the goal of personal power ardently strive to join committees such as Appropriations or Ways and Means because they represent the constitutional role of the House in the broader political system. In the Senate, the unique powers of the Judiciary and Foreign Relations committees make them choice assignments for senators who want to achieve power and status in the body.

*Serving Member Goals.* There is always a committee that serves the goals of members, whether they be striving for reelection, power, or good public policy.[8] House members who have been unsuccesful in their attempts to join the Appropriations or Ways and Means committees may turn to the House Administration Committee, which has the authority to rule the budgets of

[8] See Richard F. Fenno, Jr., *Congressmen in Committees* (Boston, Little, Brown, 1973), p. 1 and passim.

every committee of the House, including the allotting of travel expenses for the much-sought-after foreign junkets, with an iron hand. The House Administration Committee came into its own under the chairmanship of Ohio Democrat Wayne Hays, who was proud of his reputation as the "meanest son-of-a-bitch on the hill."[9] Hays used the committee's power over office allowances, travel vouchers, telephone service, and office space to reward his friends and punish his enemies. From 1971 to 1976, when he was forced to resign when it was revealed that he kept his mistress, Elizabeth Ray, on the public payroll, Hays thoroughly enjoyed his reputation for power in the House.

Members of Congress who have reelection as their primary goal — mostly freshman congressmen — seek membership in "pork-barrel" committees in which they can claim credit for particular benefits to constituents. Agriculture, Interior and Insular Affairs, Merchant Marine and Fisheries, Post Office and Civil Service, and Public Works and Transportation are good reelection committees. Appropriations subcommittees, have also been used by members to channel public funds to their districts. And particularly in the House, the Armed Services Committee was used effectively by its former chairman, South Carolina Democrat L. Mendel Rivers, who funnelled so much military money into his Charleston district that 35 percent of the employment payroll in the district came from military installations or defense industries. At the same time, Rivers was one of the most powerful members of the House, virtually equivalent to the secretary of defense. His example illustrates that both reelection and power may be achieved in one stroke by ingenious members who have chosen their committees and built their congressional careers carefully.

## Basic Types of Committees

*Appropriations and Authorization (Legislative) Committees.* There are basically two types of committees in Congress — appropriations and authorization — that have different kinds of authority in the legislative process. Appropriations committees, as the name implies, designate just how much money will be spent to implement programs that have been passed by authorization or legislative committees, which have jurisdiction over particular areas of policy, such as agriculture, defense, and veterans' affairs. They may authorize money to be spent in the areas over which they have jurisdiction, but they cannot guarantee that the levels of authorization will be the same as the budgets finally approved by the appropriations committees.

---

[9]Marguerite Michaels, "The Biggest Bully on Capitol Hill," *New York Magazine,* March 8, 1976, p. 39.

The appropriations committees can stymie the implementation of any program simply by refusing to appropriate adequate funds. The prestige of the appropriations committees of both the House and the Senate is indicated by the fact that the most senior members of both bodies serve on them. The chairmanships of the committees are the most sought-after in Congress.

## Reform of the Congressional Committee System

Important changes in the committee system began to occur in the 1960s and culminated in the 1970s. Reforms were enacted to disperse greater power among rank-and-file members in the House and, more importantly, to increase the number and power of subcommittees so that a greater number of members could get a piece of the action.

### The Trend Toward Decentralization in the House

Ironically, the decentralization of power in the House as well as in the Senate in the 1970s resulted from a feeling among party members that the major committee chairmen were unrepresentative of a cross section of party views. Many party members thought that party responsibility would be increased it if became more difficult for a small clique of party leaders to rule Capitol Hill. During the 1950s and early 1960s the Democratic party on both sides of Capitol Hill was largely controlled by a conservative southern minority who did not reflect the views of either the majority of the congressional Democratic party or the national Democratic party. The Democratic Study Group, composed of liberal members of the House, was formed in 1965 to work on a strategy to break the control of conservative Democrats, but it was not until 1973 that the group began to see the fruits of its efforts.

*Evolution of the Rules Committee.* One of the major bastions of conservative strength in the House was the Rules Committee, traditionally chaired by conservative southern Democrats. The power of the Rules Committee was formidable, for it essentially had a veto over what legislation would reach the floor and controlled the terms of debate that would be allowed on legislation. Although there were ways to bypass the Rules Committee through a suspension of the rules by a two-thirds vote or a discharge petition that required a majority vote, they were rarely used.[10] Even the most

---

[10]Another complicated method of bypassing the Rules Committee was the "calendar Wednesday procedure," used successfully only twice, under which committee chairmen could place bills that had been reported from their committees on a special calendar that was called each Wednesday. A bill passing on the Wednesday it was called became law without going through the Rules Committee.

powerful Speakers, such as Texas Congressman Sam Rayburn, who led the House between 1940 and 1961 with the exception of four years of Republican rule (the Eightieth Congress, 1947–48, and the Eighty-third Congress, 1953–54), found the Rules Committee to be an important obstacle to leadership. For his part, Rayburn succeeded in weakening the committee somewhat by enlarging it, but it was not until 1973 that the Democratic Speaker was given the power to select the Democratic members of the Rules Committee. The weakening of the Rules Committee in 1973 marked the beginning of a major trend toward decentralization of party power in the House.

*Subcommittee Bill of Rights.* The Ninety-third Congress (1973–74) pursued its reform of the committee system by passing a "subcommittee bill of rights," which prevented the chairmen of standing committees from arbitrarily controlling the budgets and staffs of subcommittees. Moreover, the parent standing committees could not without good reason remove jurisdiction over important legislation from subcommittees.

*Democratic Assignment to Committees.* As the reforms of the Ninety-third Congress continued, the Democrats removed the power of appointing committee members from the Democratic members of the Committee on Ways and Means, where it had been lodged in the past, and gave it to an expanded Democratic Steering and Policy Committee of twenty-four members — three chosen by the Democratic Caucus of all Democrats in the House, twelve elected by regional groups of House Democrats, and nine appointed by the Speaker. Democratic committee chairmen are first nominated by the Steering Committee and then approved by the larger Democratic Caucus. The caucus flexed its newly acquired muscles at the beginning of the Ninety-fourth Congress in 1975, voting to unseat the powerful senior chairmen of the Agriculture, Armed Services, and Small Business committees.

*Republican Changes.* Although the Republicans were a persistent minority in the 1960s and 1970s, they too decentralized party power in the House. The Republican Conference was revived, led by Illinois Congressman John Anderson, and adopted the practice of voting by secret ballot on the Republican committee nominees selected by the Republican Committee on Committees. Formerly, seniority was not required for a congressman to become a ranking member of a committee or, if the Republicans were in a majority, its chairman. Republicans, like Democrats, were not permitted to hold more than one position of party leadership in the House.

### Senate Committee System Reform

The winds of change in the House that led to a decentralization of power swept to the north side of Capitol Hill and modified the Senate as well. The adjustments made by the Senate, however, were more subtle and informal than those of the House.

*The End of the Senate Establishment.* Prior to the 1970s the Senate had long been dominated by an "establishment," an inner corps of senators, mostly southerners, who had seniority and who determined the norms of the body. The Senate establishment was a collegial elite, an inner club of senators who liked each other and who had the same values of hard work, reverence for the institution, courtesy, and respect for colleagues. Members of the clique did not have to be of any particular ideological persuasion, but they did have to conform to the norms of the Senate that had been developed by its senior members over the years.[11]

The decade of the 1970s saw far greater turnover in the Senate than had occurred in the past. As early as 1970, newly arrived freshman senators began to demand a greater voice in Senate proceedings, a voice that had traditionally been denied them until they had served an apprenticeship of at least several years. The Senate freshman class of 1970 formed its own caucus and made it known that new senators would not remain silent while their senior colleagues controlled the institution and received its choice plums in the form of committee chairmanships and staff allotments.

*Changing Norms.* By the mid-1970s, the iron grip that the old Senate establishment had had on the body had loosened to the point that freshman senators of the majority party were customarily given subcommittee chairmanships and staffs of their own. Moreover, newcomers to the body were not expected to serve a long apprenticeship before they could actively participate in Senate proceedings. Many of the norms of the Senate, however, remained and were adopted by a new group of senators who were rapidly on the way to becoming a new Senate establishment, one more open than the inner clique of the past, but that nevertheless required senators to uphold many of the traditional values in order to be accepted.

A major difference between the old and the new inner cliques was the ability of freshman senators to become part of the establishment. Democratic Senator John Glenn of Ohio, for example, immediately made his mark in the Senate and was accepted by powerful colleagues as one of their

---

[11]The Senate establishment is described in William S. White, *Citadel: The Story of the United States Senate* (Boston: Houghton Mifflin, 1956); and Donald R. Matthews, *U.S. Senators and Their World* (Chapel Hill: University of North Carolina Press, 1960).

own, a Senate insider. During the same period South Dakota Senator James Abourezk took a different path and became a Senate maverick, which automatically placed him outside the newly emerging inner club of the 1970s. As Abourezk approached the end of his first term in 1978 he decided not to seek reelection, publicly proclaiming that he had been excluded from the Senate elite and did not feel that he could be effectual in the body.

*Spreading Power.* The opening up of the Senate establishment reflected a decentralization of power that required Senate leaders to cultivate their party colleagues carefully in order to wield power effectively. No longer could a small group of senators determine the course of Senate action. The passage of Senate Resolution 4 in 1977, which reorganized the committee system and gave junior senators more staff than they had been able to claim before, crystallized the changes in Senate leadership. The 1977 reforms limited the number of committee chairmanships that could be held by any one senator as well as the number of committees on which senators could serve. The result of the resolution was to spread power more evenly throughout the body. The reforms themselves were initially pushed by junior senators, who were able to garner enough support to defeat strong opposition from such powerful members as Russell Long of Louisiana, John Stennis of Mississippi, Abraham Ribicoff of Connecticut, and other committee chairmen who saw in the reforms a threat to their power in the Senate.

## Congressional Parties, Caucuses, and Special Groups

In the Congress of the 1980s, party leaders in both the House and the Senate have had to rely on their powers of persuasion more than ever before to achieve party cohesion in the numerous stages of the legislative process, which extend from committee to floor. The parties of Congress, although not disciplined, represent an integrative force that is often in direct conflict with the dispersed and individualistic committees. The effective exercise of power by party leaders requires that headstrong committee chairmen be kept in line, a task that even the most skillful congressional leaders have been unable to accomplish consistently.

While it is difficult to maintain party discipline in Congress, members of both parties vote along party lines more than 65 percent of the time. This indicates that party ideologies do mean something, and that the leaders of the congressional parties have a higher degree of success than is generally attributed to them in marshalling their forces. Fairly elaborate leadership organizations characterize the parties on both sides of Capitol Hill, with the most prominent position being the Speaker of the House, who is chosen by the majority party in that body (see Figures 7.3–7.6).

**Democrats**

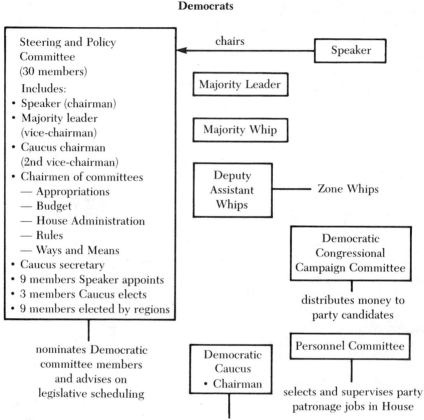

nominates Democratic
committee members
and advises on
legislative scheduling

distributes money to
party candidates

selects and supervises party
patronage jobs in House

ratifies Steering Committee nominations of committee members and chairmen
  or may substitute own nominations and appointments
nominates Speaker
helps to set party policies
determines committee size and procedures, and ratios of Democrats to
  Republicans

**Figure 7.3.** *House Democratic Leadership.*

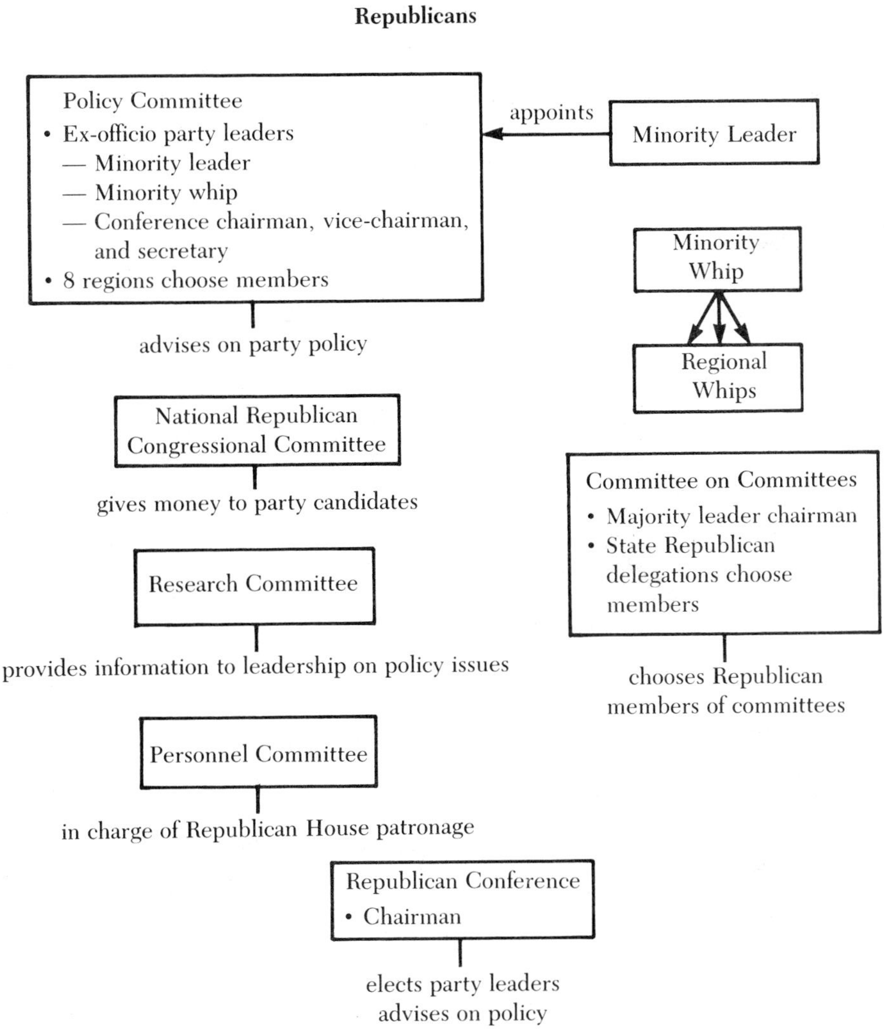

**Republicans**

Figure 7.4. *House Republican Leadership.*

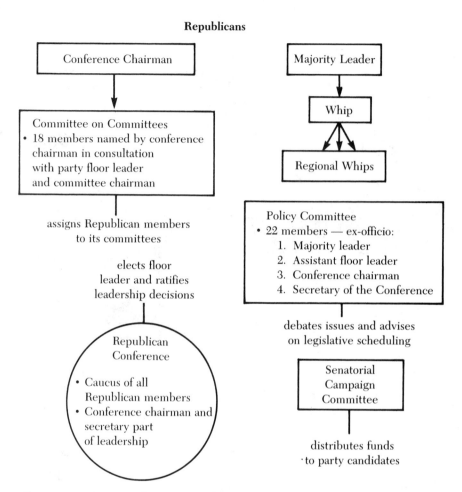

**Figure 7.5.** *Senate Republican Leadership.*

## The Speaker of the House

The Speaker of the House, a constitutional office, is in his own right one of the most powerful politicians in Washington.[12] That power can be greatly enhanced through astute political persuasion. Because the Speaker is chosen by a majority of the House, he is the first-ranking leader of his party. On the Democratic side, the Speaker chairs the Steering and Policy Committee

[12]Article I, sec. 2 provides that members of the House of Representatives "shall choose their speaker and other officers. . . ."

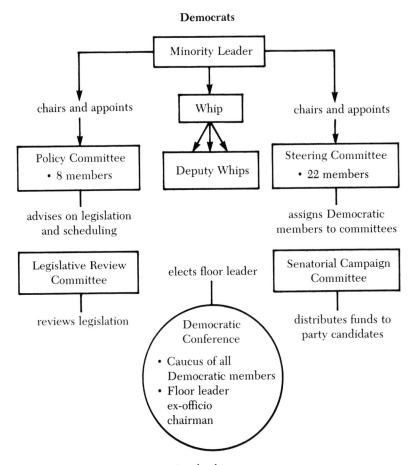

**Figure 7.6.** *Senate Democratic Leadership.*

and appoints nine of its twenty-four members. Through this committee, which controls scheduling of legislation as well as Democratic committee assignments, the Speaker has the greatest influence of any member of the House in setting the legislative agenda. Knowing that the Speaker is the key to success in the House, presidents carefully court him to help their legislative programs survive the complicated legislative maze on Capitol Hill. The Speaker not only determines the scheduling of legislation on the floor, but also controls the Rules Committee through which most legislation must pass and appoints the House members of conference committees to meet with their Senate counterparts to resolve legislative differences between the two sides of Capitol Hill. Not to be overlooked as an important adjunct of the Speaker's power is his authority to determine Capitol office and parking spaces and to select who will travel with him on foreign junkets.

The Speaker of the house has always had seniority, which means that he comes from a "safe" district. In the twentieth century no Speaker has been defeated at the polls. House Speaker Tip O'Neill represented the Eighth District of Massachusetts, which includes Cambridge and parts of Boston, from 1953 to 1986. O'Neill, the classic Massachusetts "pol," became Speaker in 1977.

*Party Floor Leaders*

Assisting the Speaker is the House majority leader, an important position that is usually a stepping-stone to the speakership itself. Both the majority and minority floor leaders have the responsibility of marshalling the troops on important party issues. The floor leaders have their own staffs as an adjunct of their offices, an important emolument and symbol of power in the House. The floor leaders are in touch with each other and with the Speaker in guiding the legislative agenda, and they communicate regularly with other party members, particularly the chairmen of key committees, to improve the chances for party cohesion. Democrat James Wright of Texas was elected to the House in 1954 and decided in 1976 to run for majority leader, an election he won by the narrowest of margins. The Republican floor leader, Robert Michel of Illinois, was elected in 1956 and rose through the ranks of the party to become minority leader in the Ninety-seventh Congress. Michel had chaired the congressional campaign committee and served as party whip before he replaced Arizona Congressman John Rhodes, who voluntarily stepped down, as minority leader in 1981.

*Senate Floor Leaders.* The Senate majority leader informally holds many of the powers of both the Speaker and the majority leader of the House. He does not preside over the Senate, but rather closely directs parliamentary proceedings on important matters through informal consultation with the presiding officer.[13] The powers of the majority leader extend as far as his ability to persuade his colleagues to support him and his party's position. Effective majority leaders stress the importance of collegiality and lead by consensus, not by command. The majority leader, with the assistance of a parliamentarian and staff aides, assigns legislation to committees and determines what legislation will be brought to the floor for debate and vote. Standing opposite the majority leader, the minority leader attempts to bring

---

[13]The presiding officer of the Senate is the vice-president, the president pro tempore, or more commonly an acting president pro tempore. Senators rotate as acting president pro tempore over the Senate.

about as much cohesion as possible among his party colleagues. Both majority and minority leaders are judged by their fairness and efficiency — qualities that are usually necessary to be elected to the leadership positions in the first place.

*Party Whips*

Assisting the majority and minority leaders in both the House and the Senate are the majority and minority "whips," who monitor the moods of colleagues in an effort to bring about as much party cohesion as possible. In the House, the majority whip is appointed by the Speaker when the Democrats are in control or by the majority leader on those rare occasions when the Democrats have been in the minority. House Republicans, when they are a minority, elect their chief floor whip. In the Senate, both majority and minority whips are elected by caucuses of the respective parties.

*Stepping-Stone to House Leadership.* The position of whip in the House has been an important stepping-stone in the Democratic party to the higher party posts of majority leader and Speaker. At the opening of the Ninety-seventh Congress, for example, Illinois Congressman Dan Rostenkowski had the choice of becoming chairman of the Ways and Means Committee or majority whip. Rostenkowski had strong ambitions to become Speaker and knew that becoming whip would put him on the right track — as it had others before him, like Tip O'Neill, whom the then Speaker Carl Albert had chosen to become whip in 1971. However, Rostenkowski finally decided to take the Ways and Means chairmanship after strong persuasion by O'Neill, who wanted the politically astute Illinois congressman to head the most important committee in the House.

On the Republican side, the whip is elected by the party conference or caucus of its members, and the position may also be a stepping-stone to higher party posts. For example, Illinois Republican Bob Michel, who became minority leader in 1981, had been elected as Republican whip in 1974.

Both parties in the House have a number of subordinate whips that are appointed and elected by party leaders to help bring about a semblance of party discipline. The Democrats and Republicans, respectively, have zone and regional whips chosen by state delegations in the major geographical areas of the country.

*Senate Whips.* The position of whip is less significant in the party organization of the Senate than in that of the House. Both parties elect their whips in the Senate, and party whips have on occasion been in sharp conflict with party leaders. For example, Louisiana Democrat Russell Long, when he was party whip from 1965 to 1969, openly challenged the majority leader, Montana Democrat Mike Mansfield. Although the position of whip is not generally a stepping-stone to the majority of minority leadership posts in the Senate, Robert Byrd, who defeated Edward Kennedy for the whip position in 1971, used the post to cultivate party support that led to him becoming majority leader in 1976.

### Party Committees, Caucuses, and Conferences

The party organizations of both the House and the Senate are assisted by special party committees and by caucuses or conferences of party members.

*Party Committees in the House.* The House Democratic Steering and Policy Committee, controlled by the Speaker, selects Democratic committee members, subject to final approval by the Democratic caucus. The position of chairman of the caucus has been important in the party hierarchy since the resurgence of the power of the caucus in the early 1970s. On the Republican side of the House, a party Committee on Committees, chaired by the minority leader, makes Republican committee assignments. The Republican conference, which is the caucus of all Republican members, must approve committee assignments. The position of chairman of the conference, held in 1985–1986 by New York Congressman Jack Kemp, is an important party post, although not equivalent in power to the caucus chairman on the Democratic side.

*Senate Party Committees.* The Senate also has party committees that make committee assignments, the Democratic Steering Committee and the Committee on Committees. The Democratic Steering Committee in the Senate is chaired by the Democratic leader, but the Republican leader does not chair the Committee on Committees.

*House and Senate Party Committees.* Other party positions of importance in Congress are the House and the Senate Campaign Committees for each party, policy committees (merged with the Steering Committee in the House Democratic organization), and several minor committees. The party policy committees were an outgrowth of the Legislative Reorganization Act of 1946 and were established to aid the parties in developing and coordinating party programs. The policy committees are most effective as party instruments when they are chaired by party leaders, as is the Democratic Policy Committee in the Senate. The Republican Senate Policy Committee, however, does not include the party's floor leader.

The House Democrats have developed the most effective party policy committee by merging it with the Steering Committee and placing it under the control of the Speaker and majority leader. The Democratic Steering and Policy Committee can provide leadership while at the same time it represents a cross section of party views by including ex officio nine of the most important party leaders of the House. In addition to the Speaker and majority leader, the Steering and Policy Committee includes the party whip as well as the chairmen of the Appropriations, Budget, Rules, and Ways and Means committees. When the Democrats are the minority party, the ranking members of these important committees are represented on the Steering and Policy Committee.

The committees and party organizations of Capitol Hill are the principal vehicles through which the members of Congress play out the constant and continuous drama of legislative politics. The vast number of committees and subcommittees reflects the forces of decentralization, while the parties strive to bring some cohesion and meaningful ideological debate to Congress. The forces of change on Capitol Hill have favored the fragmentation rather than the integration of power. The iron fist of party leaders has been replaced by kid gloves. Even committee chairmen, especially in the House, have had to relinquish some of their power to subcommittee chairmen as the result of the subcommittee bill of rights and other procedural rules.

The dispersion of power on Capitol Hill has resulted not only from rules changes and the explosion of subcommittees, but also from the formation of special groups and "caucuses" that reflect special interests.

## The Caucuses and Special Groups of Congress

Special interests exist within Congress as well as outside it. Primarily a phenomenon of the House of Representatives, members have organized caucuses, coalitions, and groups to represent special interests and points of view as well as, more importantly, to become a basis for exercising power in Congress. Over fifty special groups have been formed in the House, including the Black Caucus, the Congressional Hispanic Caucus, the Congresswomen's Caucus, the Environmental Study Conference, the Textile Caucus, and the Steel Caucus. One of the most interesting groups is the congressional Tourism Caucus, formed in 1979 to promote tourism throughout the United States. Two hundred fifty members of Congress are part of the Tourism Caucus, making it by far the largest special group in Congress. The Tourism Caucus is the envy of other groups, as it boldly holds fundraisers to fill its treasury. At its first fundraiser, fifty-seven groups contributed the maximum amount of a thousand dollars each for tickets to a lavish dinner. The fundraiser brought in over two hundred thousand dollars, which members of Congress may not use directly but which pay a large staff that is generously given space in House office buildings.

*Caucus Organization.* Admittedly, most of the caucuses on Capitol Hill are not as rich or as effective in shaping policy touching their interests as is the Tourism Caucus, but all of them employ staffs that use House offices, usually in one of the "annexes" down the street from the Rayburn Building on the south side of Capitol Hill.

Legislators who chair important caucuses receive recognition within and without Congress. The chairman of the Black Caucus, for example, is considered by the president to be a representative of black opinion and is invited to the White House to discuss presidential programs affecting black interests. The chairwoman of the Women's Caucus has high visibility among women's groups and is the spokeswoman for the interests of one segment of the women's community on Capitol Hill.

*Special Groups.* Caucuses do not directly impinge on congressional parties, but other groups have been formed that do. The Democratic Study Group became an important component of the Democratic party in the House after it was established in 1956 to represent the views of liberal members. Liberal Republicans created the Wednesday Club in the Eighty-eighth Congress (1963–64). Understandably, the Wednesday club has had little influence in the largely conservative Republican party, a conservatism that was greatly strengthened in the 1980s.

The Democratic Forum, created after the 1980 elections, is composed of conservative Democrats, mostly southerners, who temporarily joined with House Republicans to form a majority on critical issues. Texas Democrat Charles Stenholm became the group's leader. As the early Reagan budget proposals were sent to Capitol Hill, the forty-four-member Forum held the balance of power, a strategic position of strength from which it could effectively negotiate both with the members of its own party and with the Republicans. By 1986 the Forum's power had declined and its members decreased in number.

The expansion of caucuses and special groups in Congress is consistent with the trend toward decentralization of power that has made it so difficult for party leaders to maintain even a semblance of discipline.

### The Growing Role of Staff

Like all modern institutions, Congress has a bureaucracy of its own composed of aides, or "staffers" as they are known on Capitol Hill, who assist members in many ways. Staffers are often tantamount to surrogate congressmen, performing constituent service functions, generating legislative ideas, organizing and orchestrating legislative hearings, handling the media, and giving advice to the representatives or senators for whom they work.

The multiple responsibilities of members of Congress, particularly senators, allow them little time to deal directly and personally with the myriad matters that come before them. Often they scarcely have time to think, let alone act. They are occupied from dawn until dusk and beyond with meetings of all kinds — from breakfasts with staffers, interest group leaders, and on rare occasions at the White House to committee hearings followed by luncheons and afternoon committee sessions or floor proceedings. Multiple committee assignments complicate the picture, and staffers are relied on to keep representatives and senators abreast of what is going on in committee rooms and on the floor. Effectiveness on Capitol Hill requires a member to have a good staff, and legislators often judge each other by the quality of the aides who represent them in Congress.

Sometimes staffers seem more powerful than the members themselves. Senator Ernest Hollings of South Carolina, when he was chairman of the Legislative Appropriations Subcommittee, voiced the view that staffs may control members more than the other way around: "There are many senators who feel that all they are doing is running around and responding to the staff. My staff fighting your staff, your staff competing with mine. It is bad. . . . Everybody is working for the staff, the staff, the staff; driving you nutty. In fact, they have hearings for me all of this week. . . . Now it is how many nutty whiz kids you get on the staff to get you magazine articles and get you headlines and get all of the other things done."[14]

The Legislative Reorganization Act of 1946 spurred the growth of congressional staff by providing funds for both committee and personal aides. By giving members expert advice, staffers were to help Congress meet the challenge of what was viewed from Capitol Hill as an overly powerful executive branch. The number of congressional aides has grown steadily ever since (see Figure 7.7). As what Michael Malbin has called "unelected representatives" who work behind the scenes, staffers are perhaps the most significant internal influence on congressional politics and policies.[15]

## The Congressional Budget-Making Process

Capitol Hill has always been the scene of a tug-of-war between the forces of decentralization and centralization. The expansion of committees, cau-

---

[14]Cited in Harrison W. Fox, Jr. and Susan Webb Hammond, *Congressional Staff: The Invisible Force in American Lawmaking* (New York: Free Press, 1977), pp. 4–5.
[15]Michael J. Malbin, *Unelected Representatives* (New York: Basic Books, 1980).

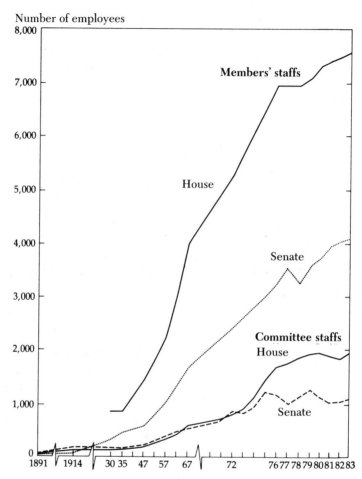

**Figure 7.7.** *Staff of Members and of Committees in Congress, 1891–1983*
SOURCE: Norman J. Ornstein et al., *Vital Statistics on Congress*, 1984. Reprinted by permission of American Enterprise Institution for Public Policy Research.

cuses, and special groups and coalitions has fragmented the legislative process. Party leaders have struggled against these centrifugal tendencies with only limited success. Party leaders, particularly in the House, strongly supported the new congressional process created by the Budget and Impoundment Control Act of 1974 in the hope that it would make Congress more effective as a collective body, as opposed to what had been the overriding power of the executive in the formulation of the national budget. However, the attempt to integrate and centralize the congressional budget-making process threatened the power of both the appropriations and the authorization committees that had always had free rein in determining budgetary allocations.

### The Budget and Impoundment Control Act of 1974

At first sponsored by only a small group of leaders in the House and the Senate, the Budget Act of 1974 finally passed overwhelmingly after it had been sufficiently amended to assure committee chairmen that their traditional powers would not be threatened.

*The Impoundment Issue.* Both external and internal politics shaped the Budget Act. The immediate impetus for the legislation was the struggle between the Democratic Congress and the Nixon White House, which saw the president vetoing congressional appropriations bills and impounding funds that Congress had appropriated for a wide range of programs. The president's impoundment authority was based on a series of antideficiency acts that were passed in the 1880s to allow the president to prevent the expenditure of funds that would lead to deficits in the federal budget. The impoundment authority was first used extensively during the Truman administration, when the president ordered substantial impoundments of defense appropriations. Although previous impoundments had raised the ire of Capitol Hill, the extent of Nixon's impoundments, coupled with the fact that a Republican president was defying a Democratic Congress, precipitated congressional action to end the president's impoundment authority.

*Charge of Congressional Irresponsibility.* The impoundment issue of the Nixon administration was linked with the congressional budget-making process because one of President Nixon's major rationales for impounding funds was that Congress had acted irresponsibly in authorizing and appropriating expenditures that exceeded government revenues. The argument of the White House was not that a balanced budget was required, but that budgetary planning was necessary that could reasonably determine the revenues and expenditures of the government for upcoming fiscal years. Before the passage of the Budget Act, Congress made little response to the president's challenge, since there was no way to coordinate effectively the congressional committee process that had the final authority to determine governmental revenues and expenditures.

*The Need for Legislative Planning.* Presumably, if Congress could engage in effective budgetary planning to ensure that within limits revenues and expenditures would be balanced, there would be no need for a presidential impoundment authority. The Budget Act revoked the president's impoundment authority and established a new budget-making process on Capitol Hill. Under the law, the president could no longer permanently impound funds without congressional approval. At the same time, the act established an elaborate procedure to encourage responsible budgeting by Congress.

### The Budget Committees and Budget-Making Process

The Budget Act created new budget committees in both the House and the Senate, as well as established a congressional Budget Office to assist all congressional committees in assessing the budgetary implications of their recommendations. The act also introduced a new budget timetable for both the committees and Congress itself in submitting and approving budgetary proposals (see Table 7.3).

*Budget Resolutions.* The budget-making process focuses on the drawing up of two concurrent budget resolutions, the first scheduled for May 15 and the second for September 15, just before the beginning of the fiscal year on October 1. The budget committees formulate the resolutions after receiving the president's budget and the views of the congressional committees. The first budget resolution represents a target for Congress, one that may be and usually is amended extensively as the budget-making process continues over the summer months, leading to the passage of the second and final budget resolution in the fall.

*Budgetary Politics.* On its face, the Budget Act seems to give the budget committees power superior to that of the Appropriations and Authorization committees. However, the congressional politics has dictated far weaker budget committees than the proponents wanted. In the House, the Budget Committee itself was greatly weakened in relation to other committees when it was made a temporary rather than a permanent committee. Members cannot serve for more than four years in a ten-year period, and the Appropriations and Ways and Means Committees control ten of the twenty-five slots on the committee. At the time the Budget Act was being considered, the chairmen and powerful members of the Appropriations and Ways and Means committees made certain that their power would not be threatened by the new House Budget Committee. The Senate Budget Committee was not formally weakened, like its counterpart in the House, but powerful Senate Chairmen — particularly Russell Long of the Finance Committee — did not hesitate to undermine the authority of the new Budget Committee when it threatened their turf.

**Table 7.3.** *Congressional Budget Timetable*

| Deadline | Action to be completed |
| --- | --- |
| 15th day after Congress convenes | President submits his budget, along with current services estimates.* |
| March 15 | Committees submit views and estimates to budget committees. |
| April 1 | Congressional Budget Office submits report to budget committees.† |
| April 15 | Budget committees report first concurrent resolution on the budget to their houses. |
| May 15 | Committees report bills authorizing new budget authority. |
| May 15 | Congress adopts first concurrent resolution on the budget. |
| 7th day after Labor Day | Congress completes action on bills providing budgetary and spending authority. |
| September 15 | Congress completes actions on second required concurrent resolution on the budget. |
| September 25 | Congress completes action on reconciliation process implementing second concurrent resolution. |
| October 1 | Fiscal year begins. |

NOTE: Congress has not always adhered to these deadlines. In recent years, Congress has increasingly fallen behind schedule.
*Current services estimates of the dollar levels that would be required next year to support the same level of services in each program as does this year's budget. The Budget Act originally required submission of the current services estimates by November 10 of the previous year. Since the president was then still in the midst of developing his budget proposals for the next year, Congress later agreed to permit simultaneous submission of the current services and executive budgets in January.
†The budget committees and CBO have found April 1 too late in the budget-making process to be useful; hence CBO submits its report(s) in February, although April 1 remains the date required by law.

The budget-making process mirrors the politics of Capitol Hill, the constant power struggles among committees, staffs, and party leaders. The formalities of the budget-making process that were so easily laid out by the Budget Act do not represent the realities of the process. The budget committees have been unable to control the Appropriations, Ways and Means, Finance, and Authorization committees. The budgetary process is dictated more by the iron triangles of committees, agencies, and pressure groups than by a rational overview of budgetary needs emanating from the budget committees. The centrifugal forces of Capitol Hill dominate budgeting regardless of the best intentions of the proponents of centralized budgeting procedures.

*Budget Committee Strategies.* In the first few Congresses after the Budget Act went into effect, the budget committees were little more than rubber stamps for the far more powerful traditional committees on the Hill. Far from dominating the budgeting process, the House Budget Committee essentially shaped the budget resolutions to accommodate the interests of the most powerful committees in the body. On the Senate side, Budget Committee Chairman Edmund Muskie valiantly fought for control, only to find his efforts constantly undermined by Finance Committee Chairman Russell Long and other chairmen as well, including those of Appropriations, Armed Services, Agriculture, and Veterans' Affairs. The chairmen of the budget committees of the House and the Senate knew that their power could extend only insofar as they were supported by the members of their respective bodies. But those members were more used to and supportive of the power of the regular committees and their prominent chairmen. Even congressmen and senators who had not yet achieved a committee chairmanship knew that the power they ultimately sought would be less significant if precedent were established under which the budget committees could dominate the other committees and subcommittees of Congress.

*Focus on the Federal Deficit.* The Reagan administration's emphasis on the need for responsible budgeting, as well as the overriding emphasis on budgetary problems and the federal deficit, once again put the budget committees and the entire congressional budget-making process in the limelight. The new chairmen of the committees, Democrat James Jones of Oklahoma in the House and New Mexico Republican Pete Domenici in the Senate, basked in the glow. They did not hesitate to use the opportunity to strengthen their power within Congress and visibility outside it. Efforts were made once again to make the budget committees more effective instruments of centralized control. The chairmen wanted more power to deal with specific budgetary items within the jurisdiction of the Appropriations committees. For example, Senate Budget Committee Chairman Domenici wanted to amend the Budget Act to permit his committee to set binding spending limits in particular budgetary areas.

As the House and Senate budget committee chairmen and their staffs looked for ways to increase the power of the budget-making panels, the appropriations committees of both bodies, the Ways and Means Committee of the House, and the Senate Finance Committee began to marshal forces to oppose legislative changes that would reduce their power by limiting their traditional jurisdiction.

*Reconciliation*

The Budget Act of 1974 contained a potentially important provision that gave Congress the authority to change governmental revenues and expenditures by using its budget resolutions to force changes in programs already in existence. Under the reconciliation process, a majority of the House or the Senate instructs appropriations and authorization committees to adjust revenues and expenditures granted by existing law. The budget committees recommend reconciliation resolutions subject to the approval of the House or the Senate.

*Early Use of Reconciliation.* Reconciliation was used for the first time in 1980, for the budget resolution for fiscal year 1981. In the first budget resolution, Congress required committees to trim programs by 4.6 billion dollars and increase revenues by 3.6 billion. President Reagan relied heavily on the process of reconciliation to implement his proposals to bring the federal budget under control. In the Senate, the Budget Committee unanimously supported a reconciliation resolution that instructed fourteen authorizing and appropriations committees to cut $36.4 billion from the fiscal 1982 budget that had been proposed by President Carter in January of 1981. Shortly after the Budget Committee action, in April of 1981, the Senate endorsed the reconciliation resolution by a vote of 88–10, indicating that both Republicans and Democrats strongly supported the idea of governmental savings. Although the reconciliation orders were supported nearly unanimously in the Senate, powerful committee chairmen warned that although they would make the necessary reductions, the specific items that would be eliminated from the budget would be determined at their discretion. The chairmen made this claim even though the Senate in certain cases instructed the committees to make cuts in programs as designated by the Senate.

The House also adopted reconciliation in the first session of the Ninety-seventh Congress in 1981. Unlike the Senate, however, the House incorporated its reconciliation recommendations in its first budget resolution. The Democratic majority in the House, however, while supporting Reagan's proposal for a balanced budget, did not agree with many of his specific recommendations. The reconciliation orders of the House did not cut as deeply into social programs as those passed by the Senate.

*Trends in Budgetary Politics.* The future of the budget-making process on Capitol Hill depends on the political environment and, in particular, on how important a balanced budget is perceived to be. Although congressional politics has occasionally dictated collective action and a strengthening of congressional procedures, as in the passage of the Budget Act itself, more commonly the politics of Capitol Hill supports the decentralization and dispersion of power. The strong Senate action taken at the outset of the Reagan administration to pass the president's budgetary proposals and force the reconciliation of existing programs with the recommendations of the White House was an unusual occurrence. It came about because of the astute leadership of Howard Baker and a temporarily disciplined Republican majority that was able to overcome the normally disintegrative forces of powerful committees linked in the iron triangles of Washington politics. After 1982, however, the budget-making process again began to crumble.

Even on those rare occasions when the House and the Senate act effectively as collective bodies, they must contend with each other before legislation can be completed and passed. The budget-making process requires passage of two concurrent resolutions that reflect the often sharply contrasting views of the House and the Senate. Differing economic assumptions as well as politics on the two sides of Capitol Hill can be a major obstacle to integrated and centralized congressional budgeting. Senate and House conferees have a difficult task in reconciling the views of their respective bodies.

## Congress and the Washington Political Establishment

Congress is generally viewed as an institution accessible and responsive to outside forces, such as public — and particularly constituent — opinion, pressure groups, the presidency, the bureaucracy, and, less directly, the courts. The external world is important to Congress as legislators cope with the complexities of Washington politics while pursuing reelection.

### The President and Congress

Presidential powers and responsibilities profoundly affect the legislature. Under the Constitution, the president is "chief legislator," based on his responsibility to recommend legislation and to provide Congress with a State of the Union message each year as well as on his veto power. The president, especially in the initial stages of a new administration, sets the agenda for Capitol Hill. When the president takes a strong stand on legislative proposals, there is a very good chance of their passage. Effective presidents have been able to achieve an 80–90 percent success ratio on Capitol Hill; less politically persuasive presidents have barely been able to secure the passage of a majority of their proposals.

The president's program, particularly at the beginning of an administration, sets the agenda for Capitol Hill. The legislative recommendations of Ronald Reagan, for example, dominated Congress's agenda in 1981. Legislative debate focused on the president's proposals, and a Republican Senate, along with a conservative coalition of Republicans and Democrats in the House, were favorably disposed toward the White House and initially supported the key budgetary and tax reduction plans of the president.

The president works with Congress through an extensive legislative liaison staff in the White House as well as through the Office of Management and Budget. The White House liaison team courts party leaders on Capitol Hill and powerful committee chairmen. Knowledgeable presidents do not try to push Congress farther than it is inclined to go, withdrawing proposals that have little chance of passage. The president's reputation for power on Capitol Hill can remain intact only if he has creditable success in securing the passage of legislation.

When the president takes a stand on legislation, his powers are imposing. OMB performs a clearance function for all legislative recommendations of administrative agencies, requiring agency proposals to conform to the president's program. Administrators cannot testify before congressional committees without first having their testimony cleared by OMB. They cannot formally transmit legislation to Capitol Hill without OMB approval. The budgets of agencies are shaped by OMB into a comprehensive executive budget that is always the first item on the legislative agenda.

The president has enormous power to deal with Congress, but it would be a mistake to conclude that the White House is the dominant force on Capitol Hill. Congress has interests and powers of its own that easily counterbalance those of the president. Ironically, it is the executive branch itself, apart from the presidential bureaucracy, that often effectively represents and implements legislative views that contrast with those of the White House. The president formally controls much of the operation of the bureaucracy, but informally, agencies develop their own patterns of political support that conflict with those of the president, and they forge avenues of communication with Congress that bypass the White House.

### Congress and the Bureaucracy

From the vantage point of Capitol Hill, the regular bureaucracy — that is, those agencies outside the Executive Office of the President — is an agent of Congress. It is a congressional creation, mandated to carry out congressional programs.

*Administrative Supervision.* Congressional committees are assigned specific oversight functions to review the way agencies are doing their job and determine if they are acting in accordance with congressional wishes. The supervisory function may not always be effectively carried out because members frequently find that it is in their interest to engage in activities more directly related to their principal incentives of reelection and building power within Congress. However, the symbolic recognition of the importance of supervision is a reflection of a strongly held congressional belief that administrative agencies are adjuncts of the legislative and not the executive branch. Washington's iron triangles, formed by congressional committees, agencies, and pressure groups, represent collusive interests that exclude the president.

*Cooperation in Policymaking.* The bureaucracy has a major role in formulating congressional policy. The close cooperation that exists between many parts of Congress and the bureaucracy is a vital component of congressional policymaking. Such cooperation gives administrative agencies access to Congress to influence the legislative process. At the same time, it gives congressional committees avenues of influence over policy implementation by the bureaucracy. Admittedly, the scope of governmental activity and widespread specialization tend to reduce congressional control of administrative policymaking. Even specialized legislative committees with members and staffs of long tenure and great skill in particular areas find it difficult to keep up with the rapidly moving and complex activities of the bureaucracy.

The extent to which administrators consult members of Congress depends on a variety of political factors and personalities. Sometimes very close ties exist, and administrative action is not taken without the prior knowledge of key congressmen. In some instances congressional authorization is sought in advance.

*Administrative Expertise.* An important aspect of the relationship between the bureaucracy and Congress is that agencies are often instrumental in shaping the technical details of legislation that they must administer. As early as 1937, the report of the president's Committee on Administrative Management found that over two-thirds of all legislation emanating from Congress originates in and is often drafted by the bureaucracy. This does not mean, of course, that agencies stand apart as a separate political force dictating the contents of congressional bills. On the contrary, the president and special interests may dictate agencies' positions.

It is difficult to calculate the extent to which congressional autonomy has been reduced with the growth in the power of the presidency and of the administrative branch. Although the president and the agencies may initiate legislation, it is Congress that determines what is finally done. Senate and House have both the power and the inclination to change legislative recommendations coming from the White House and the bureaucracy. It is a foolish president indeed who underestimates the irascibility of Congress. Although the complexities of the modern policy-making process may frequently give legislators the feeling that their understanding of most policy issues is very thin, the same is true for bureaucrats, presidents, and judges. Within or without the legislature, in-depth knowledge of policy spheres can be gained only through specialization.

*Interest Groups and Congress*

Interest groups complete the iron triangles in the Washington power establishment. Private groups and associations of all kinds have always been a prominent feature of the landscape; however, the decade between 1970 and 1980 witnessed an extraordinary increase in the representation of groups in Washington. The city changed from a relatively sleepy southern town to a bustling metropolis crowded with office buildings, restaurants, and sparkling new hotels, all of which were supported by pressure groups and trade associations that had decided a permanent presence in the capital was necessary to protect their interests.

High-paid lobbyists and high-powered lawyers benefitted from the largesse of groups, who found it necessary to hire people with specialized skills to find their way through the maze of Washington politics. Retired or defeated members of Congress are an important part of the core of lobbyists. "A former U.S. Congressman, no matter how capable, is worth more in Washington than any place else — considerably more," declared one representative.[16] Connections and inside knowledge can be sold for a great deal of money. The fact that many former members of Congress are highly paid lobbyists only serves to make the iron triangles of the city more closely connected and more effective bastions of political power.

*Assistance to Legislators.* Interest groups, like the bureaucracy, do not simply exert pressure on Congress; they are frequently an integral part of the legislative process itself. Just as administrative agencies detail employees to work for congressional committees, interest groups put their staffs at the disposal of legislators, who may call on them to supply information, draft legislation, testify at hearings, or provide needed political advocacy for the passage of legislation. Many former staff members of Congress, captivated by Potomac fever and under the gun of high mortgage payments for their Washington condominiums and townhouses, work for interest groups and continue to supply expertise to Congress even though they are no longer

[16]*Congressional Quarterly Weekly Report,* December 27, 1980.

directly employed on Capitol Hill. Members of Congress find comfort in dealing with former colleagues and staffers who understand the needs of elected officeholders.

*Financial Support.* In addition to supplying staff assistance to Congress, through their political action committees pressure groups provide much of the money that supports the campaigns of incumbents seeking reelection. Money and politics are closely connected, and the support given to members of Congress by interest groups is another strong link in the iron triangle of politics.

## Congressmen and Constituents: The Pursuit of Reelection

Most members of Congress, in order to be reelected, must have close ties with their constituents, but such relationships are frequently based on activities that have little to do with their Washington careers. On Capitol Hill, congressmen are primarily interested in demonstrating their power and status in the House or Senate. To do this they may seek prestigious committee assignments, or chairmanships of important committees with large staffs. Other ways of gaining power are through effective legislative work, investigations, or holding party leadership positions such as majority or minority leader, or chairman of the Democratic Caucus or Republican Conference in the House or their counterparts in the Senate. Although Washington careers are oriented to the achievement of internal power, constituency careers pursue the goal of reelection.

### Reelection Activities

The large gaps that frequently exist between Washington and constituency careers do not mean that legislators do not spend a great deal of their time in Washington engaged in activities relating to reelection. They use the emoluments of their offices, particularly their staffs, to remain in contact with voters in their districts and states. Political scientist David Mayhew has written that members of Congress advertise, claim credit, and take positions to strengthen constituency relationships and ensure reelection.[17] Mayhew stresses that they "must constantly engage in activities related to reelection."[18]

---

[17]David Mayhew, *Congress: The Electoral Connection* (New Haven: Yale University Press, 1974).
[18]Ibid., p. 49.

*Advertising.* A member of Congress advertises by "disseminat[ing] one's name among constituents in such a fashion as to create a favorable image, but in messages having little or no issue content. A successful congressman builds what amounts to a brand name, which may have a generalized electoral value for other politicians in the same family."[19] Advertising is particularly necessary for House members, who generally have far less visibility among constituents than do senators. Congressmen advertise through newsletters, opinion columns of newspapers, radio and television reports to constituents, and questionnaires. Members also heighten the public's awareness of them by attending social events, such as weddings and bar mitzvahs, in their districts.

*Claiming Credit.* Legislators also pursue reelection by claiming credit for particular benefits to constituents. Pork-barrel projects and casework are the primary credit-claiming activities of congressmen. Members distribute "pork" to their constituents in the form of dams and buildings.[20] Casework is the handling of specific constituent requests and complaints, largely related to the rulings and activities of bureaucrats who for one reason or another displease voters.

*Taking Positions.* Finally, congressmen seek reelection by taking positions on issues that they think will appeal to constituents. Rarely, however, do legislators take strong stands on issues because of the likelihood of alienating some voters. The "best position-taking strategy for most congressmen at most times is to be conservative — to cling to their own positions of the past where possible and to reach for new ones with great caution where necessary."[21] Safe position taking would include such statements as "I will support Poland if it is invaded by the Soviet Union," "I will support the president," or "the government must take action to reduce unemployment."

---

[19]Ibid.

[20]William Safire traces the term "pork barrel" to the pre–Civil War practice of distributing pork to the slaves from huge barrels. C. C. Maxey wrote in the *National Municipal Review* in 1919: 'Oftentimes the eagerness of the slaves would result in a rush upon the pork barrel, in which each would strive to grab as much as possible for himself. Members of Congress in the stampede to get their local appropriation items into the omnibus river and harbor bills behaved so much like Negro slaves rushing the pork barrel, that these bills were facetiously styled "pork barrel" bills, and the system which originated them has become known as the "pork-barrel system."' *Safire's Political Dictionary* (New York: Random House, 1978), p. 553.

[21]Mayhew, *Congress*, p. 67.

## Reelection Goals and Washington Careers

Because of the importance of advertising, credit claiming, and position taking, it would seem likely that most congressional members would build their Capitol Hill careers by facilitating their performance of these activities. Indeed, Mayhew argues that they do just that — for example, by choosing committees and pursuing legislative goals that enhance their prospects for reelection. As much as members may worry about reelection, however, there is little doubt that a great deal of what goes on in Congress does not directly relate to reelection. Freshman and junior members of Congress generally must pay strict attention to building constituency organizations capable of returning them to office, but even they do not seek assignments only to those committees that will promote their reelection by helping them to channel benefits to their districts or states. Nor do they always pursue legislative goals that are geared to pleasing constituents. Astute freshmen who wish to build their power in Congress are more interested in pleasing the leaders of the congressional parties and the chairmen of powerful committees than they are concerned with shaping their careers primarily in terms of reelection needs.

## Home Style Versus Washington Style

Richard Fenno, Jr. pointed out in a study of the political strategies of House representatives that congressmen pursue reelection goals by building effective constituency organizations and an appealing home style — activities that have little relationship to what members do in Washington.[22] Even David Mayhew would admit that, with the important exception of credit claiming, much of the advertising and position taking done by congressmen is external to what they do to build power on Capitol Hill. Particularly as members gain seniority, based on an effective constituency organization and style, they are freer to pursue carrers oriented toward power and, in Fenno's terms, "good public policy."[23]

The freedom of individual congressmen to pursue power and public policy in Washington without having to worry about the reactions of voters in their constituencies is primarily due to the electorate's lack of knowledge about or interest in the details of what goes on in Congress. Although most of the activities of legislators are a matter of public record, the public rarely

---

[22]Richard F. Fenno, Jr., *Home Style: House Members in Their Districts* (Boston: Little, Brown, 1978).

[23]Richard Fenno lists three primary goals of members of Congress: reelection, power and influence on Capitol Hill, and good public policy. See Richard F. Fenno, Jr., *Congressmen in Committees* (Boston: Little, Brown, 1973).

takes the time to examine the record. Individuals and interest groups are for the most part uninterested in the fine points of the policy issues with which members of Congress deal, or in the byplay of power on Capitol Hill.

Warren E. Miller and Donald E. Stokes demonstrated in one study of constituency influence in Congress that less than 20 percent of the electorate had even read or heard anything about candidates running in their district.[24] Ignorance of representatives' policy positions means that the electorate is not concerned about what policy preferences candidates or incumbents have. As a result,

The communication most congressmen have with their districts inevitably puts them in touch with organized groups and with individuals who are relatively well informed about politics. The representative knows his constituents mostly from dealing with people *who do* write letters, *who will* attend meetings, *who have* an interest in his legislative stance. As a result, his sample of contacts with a constituency of several hundred thousand people is heavily biased; even the contacts he apparently makes at random are likely to be with people who grossly overrepresent the degree of political information and interest in the constituency as a whole.[25]

Constituency influence, then, may help legislators with respect to a narrow set of issues, but it does not give them a well-charted guide for legislative action. In many of their votes on proposed bills they act as Burkean trustees of the interests of their constituencies. They vote in accordance with their perceptions of the needs of the district they represent.

*Interest Representation*

Charles O. Jones's concept of a "policy constituency" explains how congressmen behave in the legislative process.[26] Such a constituency consists of substantial interests from the legislator's district that have knowledge of and are concerned about particular issues of public policy. Jones found in one case study of the House Agriculture Committee that congressmen who have clearly defined policy interests in their districts sought and usually succeeded in getting assignments to committees with jurisdiction over those interests. For example, a representative who had substantial interests in tobacco would be assigned to the Tobacco Subcommittee of the House Agriculture Committee. At the committee stage the representative would work hard to take into account the demands of pressure groups in his or her district. Since

[24]Warren E. Miller and Donald E. Stokes, "Constituency Influence in Congress," *The American Political Science Review* 57 (March 1963):45–56
[25]Ibid., pp. 54–55.
[26]Charles O. Jones, "Representation in Congress: The Case of the House Agricultural Committee," *The American Political Science Review* 55 (June 1961):358–67.

most legislation is given final shape by committees, representatives on policy committees relevant to their districts are in a good position to serve private interests in their constituencies.

## The Role of Congress in Constitutional Democracy

The major constitutional responsibility of Congress is to represent the people while providing a check on the president and the executive branch. Originally, the Senate was to represent the states through its election by state legislatures. Since the adoption of the Seventeenth Amendment in 1913, however, the Senate has been popularly elected, making it too a democratic body. But the constitutional requirement that each state have two senators regardless of population gives to less populous states disproportionate strength in the upper body.

Ironically, Congress has been criticized for being too representative. Electoral politics, writes political scientist Gary Jacobson, gives Congress "great individual *responsiveness,* equally great collective *irresponsibility.*"[27] Members of Congress are individually accountable to their districts or states, which they carefully cultivate to ensure their reelection. Party labels, however, mean little in congressional elections because voters tend to return incumbents, particularly House representatives, who have channeled federal largesse to their districts or served their personal needs through casework. Although party affiliations determine the formal distribution of power on Capitol Hill between the majority and the minority, party leaders cannot dictate policy to rank-and-file congressmen.

Critics of legislative fragmentation nevertheless fail to take into account that Congress can hardly be expected to rise above the pluralistic forces that characterize policymaking. Congress almost perfectly reflects the individualism of American politics, the dispersion of power that the Founding Fathers so ardently desired.

Congress could probably perform its constitutional role better if it were more cohesive, but still it has carried out its basic political responsibilities effectively. It remains a proud and independent institution that, from a historical perspective, has only occasionally succumbed to presidential domination. It continues as the primary legislative body in a system of separation of powers and checks and balances that guarantees limited but also popular government.

[27]Gary Jacobson, *The Politics of Congressional Elections* (Boston: Little, Brown, 1983), p. 189. Italics in original.

## Suggestions for Further Reading

Fenno, Richard F., Jr. *Home Style: House Members in Their Districts.* Boston: Little, Brown, 1978. The way congressmen win reelection is often different from the way they build their Washington careers.

Fiorina, Morris P. *Congress: Keystone of the Washington Establishment.* New Haven: Yale University Press, 1977. Members of Congress, their growing staffs, bureaucrats, and lobbyists have become a Washington establishment that is, in some respects, manipulative and uncontrolled.

Jones, Rochelle, and Peter Woll. *The Private World of Congress.* New York: The Free Press, 1979. The principal goal of members of Congress and their aides on Capitol Hill is internal power and status.

Mann, Thomas E., and Norman J. Ornstein, eds. *The New Congress.* Washington, D.C.: American Enterprise Institute, 1981. Eleven scholars examine changes that have occurred in Congress and their consequences for the policy-making process.

Mayhew, David R. *Congress: The Electoral Connection.* New Haven: Yale University Press, 1974. The organization, procedures, and norms of Congress are designed to ensure the reelection of members.

Redman, Eric. *The Dance of Legislation.* New York: Simon & Schuster, 1973. A lively case study by a former Senate staffer of how a bill becomes law.

# chapter 8

# The Bureaucracy

For both the president and Congress, the bureaucracy is a critical link in the chain of power. Presidents in the twentieth century have viewed the bureaucracy as an integral part of the executive branch, properly subject to their control. At the same time, Congress considers the bureaucracy to be its agent and most administrative agencies as logical extensions of the legislature. Presidents stress that agencies exercise executive functions, while Congress properly points out that the bureaucracy performs legislative tasks as well. And although the president and Congress battle for power over the bureaucracy, the courts, noting the widespread exercise of judicial powers by the bureaucracy, intervene directly in its administrative proceedings through judicial review.

Presidents and politically ambitious congressmen know that the support of the bureaucracy is essential to their power. From William Howard Taft at the beginning of this century to Ronald Reagan, presidents have unsuccessfully attempted to make the bureaucracy an arm of the White House. Their lack of success in bringing the bureaucracy to heel is the result of Washington politics, which makes administrative agencies the central component of a permanent political establishment consisting of powerful members of Congress and a vast array of interest groups. The impervious linkage of congressional committees, agencies, and pressure groups — Washington's iron triangles — has consistently frustrated presidential attempts to dominate the executive branch.

The bureaucracy is a critical part of politics and policy making on Capitol Hill. In most areas the burden of refining and enforcing public policy rests on the bureaucracy. Administrative agencies are the delegates of both Congress and the president to fulfill the broad policy purposes of the legislative and executive branches. Since much of the legislation passed by Congress sets policy guidelines only in very broad terms, it is the bureaucracy that must fill in the details of congressional law and make the concrete decisions that give meaning to governmental policy.

The scope of activity of administrative agencies, their generally large size, and the complexity of the issues with which they deal often restrict administrative accountability to any of the original three branches of the government. Although created by Congress and unable to act without congressional authority, agencies can dominate the legislative process that gave them birth. The expertise of Congress is often no match for that of the bureaucracy, and most of the subject matter with which modern legislation deals is very technical and requires specialized skills for proper formulation. Bureaucratic advice often determines congressional actions. Moreover, through its rule-making powers the bureaucracy legislates independently of Congress, although of course always within the limits of authority laid down by Congress. The content of our laws is sometimes determined more by administrative legislation than by statutory law.

## The Constitutional Context of the Bureaucracy

Although the Constitution does not explicitly establish the bureaucracy, the governmental system it sets up has a profound impact on the structure, functions, and general place that the administrative branch occupies in the political scheme. At the time of the framing of the Constitution there was no discussion of the administrative process as we know it today. Rather, the concept of administration was incorporated under the heading of the executive branch. Executive agencies were to be adjuncts of the presidency — in the words of Alexander Hamilton in *The Federalist* (No. 72), they were to carry out the "mere execution" of "executive details."

The Hamiltonian view, which admittedly favored a strong presidency, was simply that the president as chief executive would have the responsibility and power to control the small executive branch that would be established. Hamilton himself foresaw a vigorous and independent role for the president and the executive branch, and he was not adverse to having the executive dominate the legislature, a practice he indeed later encouraged when he became secretary of the treasury. Nevertheless, Hamilton advanced the theory that the executive branch would not exercise independent political power, but rather would be politically neutral under the domination of the president, and the executive branch acting as a unit would carry out the mandates of the legislature. Hamilton clearly stated what was to be the relationship between the president and the administrative branch:

The persons, therefore, to whose immediate management the different administrative matters are committed ought to be considered as assistants or deputies of the Chief Magistrate, and on this account, they ought to derive their offices from his appointment, at least from his nomination, and ought to be subject to his superintendence.[1]

Since he did not foresee the role of the administrative branch in legislation and adjudication, Hamilton's view was that it should properly be under the control of the president. In the classical constitutional model, the bureaucracy was not to be a primary policymaking branch.

### Presidential Versus Congressional Control of the Bureaucracy

Although Hamilton suggested that the administrative branch should be incorporated into the presidency, the constitutional system itself in many ways supported an independent bureaucracy. Comparing the powers of Congress and the president over the administrative branch, it becomes clear that both have important constitutional responsibilities (see Figure 8.1). Congress retains primary control over administrative organization. It alone creates and destroys agencies and determines whether they are to be located in the executive branch and made responsible to the president or outside it and independent. Congress has created a large and ever-growing number of independent agencies and placed many of their operations beyond presidential control. The president's power to reorganize the executive is delegated to him by Congress.

The power of the purse is critical in exercising control over administrative agencies, and originally Congress was to have this authority to control appropriations. Today the Office of Management and Budget and the president have assumed the initiative in this area, although the centralization of the budgetary process within Congress may restore legislative initiative.

Other ways in which Congress controls the bureaucracy include setting forth the "intent of Congress" to be followed by agencies in exercising policy-making powers. Moreover, Congress can and does interfere in the appointment and removal process for top-level officials. Ministerial appointments are to be "by and with the advice and consent of the Senate" under the terms of the Constitution, and this stipulation has been extended by Congress to include a large number of administrators. Congress may also establish conditions for removal, granting administrators such as those on independent regulatory commissions short-term tenure for specified periods

[1]*The Federalist,* No. 72.

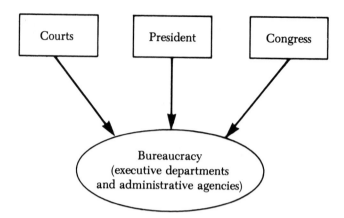

**Figure 8.1.** *The Constitutional Context of the Bureaucracy. Each of the constitutional branches exercises important powers over the bureaucracy.*

of time, during which they may not be removed except for specific causes stated by law. In such cases, Congress excludes political reasons as cause for removal, usually providing that administrators may be dismissed only for malfeasance or moral turpitude.

The antagonism between Congress and the president often results in the legislature's placing numerous obstacles in the path of presidential control of the administrative branch. Such actions counter the trend in public administration circles to allow the president to assume more and more power over administrative agencies, a trend aimed at producing greater efficiency through centralized coordination and planning.

### Quasi-legislative and Quasi-judicial Functions

Administrative agencies exercise all three functions of government. This adds another dimension — to say the least — to the traditional notion of the separation of powers.

*Legislative Functions.* First, administrative agencies performing regulatory functions have been given what effectively amounts to legislative power because Congress was unable, and on many occasions unwilling, to bear the burden of passing concrete legislation to deal with the myriad problems that began to confront government in the late nineteenth century. A mere glance at the Code of Federal Regulations, which is the law developed by administrative agencies based on broad congressional delegations of authority, illustrates the magnitude of the legislative tasks that confront government.

Particularly in recent decades, beginning with the rapid expansion of the role of government during the New Deal, Congress has scarcely been able to deal even with the major problems that confront it. A fragmented and dispersed body especially when there is no powerful presidential leadership, it finds the passage of legislation a very tedious and time-consuming task indeed. For purely technical reasons, Congress must rely on outside agencies to fill in the details of the legislation that it passes in broad outline. It can still be specific in legislation, but it simply does not have the time today to write the regulations formulated by departments such as Health and Human Services, which employs over 120,000 bureaucrats, or agencies such as the Occupational Safety and Health Administration, the Environmental Protection Agency, and numerous other regulatory bodies.

*The Delegation of Authority.* Another important reason why administrative agencies are given such extensive legislative responsibility is that in politically sensitive regulatory areas Congress is motivated to transfer the burden of reconciling intense group conflicts onto the shoulders of bureaucrats, thus relieving members of having to take stands on controversial issues. Until the advent of Ralph Nader and the consumer movement, Congress was more responsive to the influence of powerful private pressure groups in formulating legislation. At the same time, it was buffeted by a certain amount of public pressure, which often came to it under the auspices of the president as a representative of the nation at large. During the New Deal period, administrative agencies were created largely from the recommendations of President Roosevelt and his staff. Many of these agencies were intended to regulate business enterprises. In such cases, recognizing that crisis conditions, presidential demands, and public pressure necessitated the extension of the government's regulatory authority, Congress nevertheless did not have to get into the even more tricky political and technical issues of the content of such regulatory policies. It avoided this simply by delegating legislative authority to administrative agencies under very broad standards. Congress mandates agencies, for example, to act in the "public interest, convenience, and necessity" or to establish "just and reasonable rates." This essentially gives agencies carte blanche in the legislative field. In such circumstances, agencies become the centers of political controversy, subject to the most intense pressure from regulated groups to secure policies favorable to their interests.

*Administrative Adjudication.* Since administrative legislation is generally very complex and technical in nature, the adjudication of disputes arising under it requires expertise and a specialized knowledge of the subject for proper resolution. For this reason Congress has assigned judicial responsibilities to administrative agencies to decide cases and controversies arising under their jurisdiction, rather than giving the courts original jurisdiction. However, in many areas Congress has provided for judicial review after agency decisions are rendered, and this does provide a judicial check on administrative discretion.

In the early twentieth century, another major reason agencies were given adjudicative responsibilities in regulatory and welfare fields was that the courts were not sympathetic toward the purposes of federal and state legislation. The courts, generally conservative in nature, essentially nullified regulatory statutes by their decisions. For example, when the ICC was originally created in 1887, the courts had to act affirmatively before ICC decisions could go into effect. The commission was given no independent judicial powers. A conservative judiciary rendered the ICC a totally ineffective regulatory body during the first decade of its existence, until Congress recognized its plight and granted it judicial power subject only to later court review.

In the area of workmen's compensation, it was common practice for the courts to nullify compensation laws in states where the legislatures had failed to provide for independent workmen's compensation commissions. The courts simply applied old common law rules to workmen's compensation cases, essentially substituting substantive common law standards for those contained in legislation that was in fact passed for the sole purpose of granting more extensive rights to workmen than had prevailed under the common law. The only way to get around the courts in such instances was to grant independent judicial authority to the workmen's compensation commissions, and this violated traditional concepts of the rule of law that required all adjudication to be handled by regular (common law) courts.

Although conservative legal scholars considered administrative adjudication unconstitutional, the courts, faced with political necessity, eventually invented easy rationalizations for the exercise of both legislative and judicial functions by administrative agencies. This occurred despite the fact that there was no constitutional provision for an administrative branch with such powers. Basically, the courts found that as long as primary legislative and judicial powers remain in the hands of Congress and the judiciary, the exercise of "quasi-legislative" and "quasi-judicial" functions by administrative agencies does not undermine the constitutional separation of powers. In the legislative field, provided that Congress clearly states its intent, it is the responsibility of agencies to follow legislative mandates. Filling in the details of legislation is not the same as formulating legislation in the first place.

Rationalizing the placement of judicial functions in the hands of administrators was somewhat more difficult than justifying administrative exercise of legislative functions. The courts essentially solved this problem rhetorically. They held that true judicial power is exercised only by constitutional courts, which must conform to the conditions stated in Article III. In reality, of course, although administrative agencies do not meet the various requirements of Article III, they are extensively involved in adjudication.

## The Political Context of the Bureaucracy

### Agency Response to Political Support

Agencies often develop distinguishable characteristics that shape their orientation toward public policy. Most important is the nature of their political support. "Clientele" agencies, such as Agriculture, Labor, and Commerce, were originally created to serve special interests, not the public interest. It is the job of the Department of Agriculture to protect farmers, not to lower food prices in the cities. The Department of Labor was established to represent the interests of workers directly, just as the Department of Commerce was established to give business interests a voice in government. The public policy positions taken by such departments tend to reflect the views of their clienteles. Moreover, even agencies that were not originally established on a clientele basis tend to serve a narrow set of interests from which they draw political support. Independent regulatory agencies are often characterized as being captives of the groups they regulate. There is little doubt that the railroad industry found a strong voice in government in the Interstate Commerce Commission, as did labor unions in the National Labor Relations Board and broadcasters in the Federal Communications Commission. Nevertheless, regulatory agencies were originally intended not to represent clientele interests but rather to serve the public interest in implementing regulatory policies.

### The President Versus the Bureaucracy

Close executive branch ties to clientele groups and to congressional committees undermine presidential control. The president is to see that the laws are faithfully executed, but departments and agencies frequently draw on independent political support in order to go their own ways. They maintain political lifelines connecting them with Capitol Hill because they have found Congress to be an important ally against presidential efforts to undermine their power and independence.

Although Congress jealously guards its administrative preserve, it has been willing to grant the president authority to reorganize the bureaucracy subject to congressional veto.

*The Reorganization Acts.* The first reorganization act, passed in 1939, permitted presidential reorganization plans to go into effect unless they were vetoed by a simple majority in both houses of Congress. Reorganization acts generally have two-year limits, after which they must be renewed by Congress. When the 1939 act lapsed (during World War II Roosevelt was given absolute authority to reorganize the executive branch under a special War Powers Act), Congress did not renew it until 1949, adopting in that year the provision that a majority vote by a single house might veto presidential reorganization plans. Congress continued to renew the reorganization acts until Eisenhower's second term, when the authority was again allowed to lapse. In 1961 Congress restored the reorganization power to President Kennedy, only to become angered at his attempt to use it to create on his own initiative a new Department of Urban Affairs in 1962, rather than submitting legislation to Congress that would establish such a department. The House vetoed the proposal, and Congress again allowed the authority to lapse. It was not renewed until 1964, and then for only one year. The 1964 law prohibited the president from using a reorganization plan to create a new executive department. This provision has been continued in all subsequent reorganization acts. President Johnson requested permanent reorganization authority in 1965, but the Senate rejected the proposal.

*Unilateral Presidential Actions.* Although Congress does not like to see major changes carried out by reorganization orders, preferring instead legislation requiring affirmative congressional action, determined presidents have made unilateral changes in administrative organization without suffering congressional veto. Nixon used the reorganization power that Congress had reluctantly given him to abolish the Bureau of the Budget and create in its place a new Office of Management and Budget completely under presidential domination. Likewise, he used an executive order to create the Environmental Protection Agency and made major changes in the Executive Office of the President. Congress allowed Nixon's reorganization authority to lapse in 1973 and did not pass a new reorganization bill until Carter requested it in 1977.

*Limits on the President.* Carter set out to reorganize the bureaucracy with a vengeance. He had promised the electorate a major reduction in federal agencies and in the Executive Office of the President. In the end, Carter found that he could not effect most of the reorganizations he wanted because of the opposition of Washington's iron triangles. His proposal for a unified Department of Energy under White House control was drastically altered on Capitol Hill by powerful members of the Senate Governmental Affairs Committee, who were suspicious of excessive presidential power over the bureaucracy. In addition, powerful oil and natural gas interests supported the continued independence of the judicial arm of the new department, which would hear cases involving their interests. The department was a hodgepodge of bureaus and agencies whose relationship to each other was determined by political compromises on Capitol Hill rather than by careful planning in the White House.

*Contrasting Presidential Styles.* Reagan, unlike Carter and many previous presidents, wisely avoided a frontal assault on the structure of the bureaucracy in the initial stages of his administration. Not only had the reorganization authority once again lapsed, but Reagan knew that the politics of reorganization often exhausted the reserves of the White House, reserves that would be better spent on achieving major domestic and foreign policy objectives. Although Reagan had made a campaign pledge to abolish the departments of Energy and Education, he immediately began to hedge his promise after the election. Even if the reorganization authority were renewed, the abolition of major departments would require congressional legislation. Reagan soon shelved his reorganization proposals and put his energy into fighting his major battles on Capitol Hill — those involving his budgetary and tax recommendations.

*The Presidential Spur to Deregulation.* Reagan knew that it is far more difficult to abolish agencies than it is to reorganize them. The Carter administration, in combination with powerful committee chairmen on Capitol Hill, had succeeded in completing the deregulation of the airlines industry that was begun during the Ford administration. Carter's appointee as chairman of the Civil Aeronautics Board aided the president and Congress in their efforts to bring an end to the agency's responsibilities, as the CAB went out of existence in 1985. Congress also passed legislation to deregulate the trucking and railroad industries, significantly reducing the powers of the ICC.

The success of deregulation legislation during the Carter administration resulted from an unusual combination of liberal and conservative forces on Capitol Hill. These forces were headed by particularly astute committee chairmen — especially Edward Kennedy of Massachusetts and Howard Cannon of Nevada, of the Judiciary and Commerce Committees, respectively, who, with efficient staff help, mobilized an outside constituency of economic interests that would benefit from deregulation.

*Breaking the Iron Triangles.* The government's move toward deregulation of the powerful airline, railroad, and trucking industries seemed in many respects to defy the laws of political gravity. Powerful groups in all three industries had long enjoyed a virtual monopoly protected by the government. These economic interests had powerful allies, or so they thought, in the CAB and the ICC. The iron triangles of policy seemed to be working smoothly until outside forces, the White House, and Senator Kennedy committed themselves to breaking those triangles that had supported the airline and the trucking industries since the New Deal, when the CAB was created and the ICC was given the power to regulate trucking. Deregulation of the railroads was another matter, for many carriers supported the congressional plan of deregulation that they helped to shape, which they considered to be a last-ditch effort to make them economically viable. In the end, it was the persistence and skill of White House and congressional proponents of deregulation that resulted in breaking the often impenetrable iron triangles composed of agencies, committees, and pressure groups involved in transportation.

## Constitutional Democracy and Administrative Responsibility

Whether exercising legislative, judicial, or executive functions or some combination of the three, administrators are constantly involved in the formulation of policy.

### Controlling Administrative Discretion

Administrative discretion is a fact of life. Administrators can negate the policies established by legislatures, the directives of chief executives, and even the dictates of the judiciary merely by administrative action or inaction. As the bureaucracy began to expand and flourish during the administration of Franklin Roosevelt, conservative critics considered the central problem of administrative expansion to be the delegation of too much power to agencies. In Britain, the Lord Chief Justice referred to the powers of the burgeoning British bureaucracy as "the new despotism." This cry was echoed in the United States by Herbert Hoover, Roscoe Pound, and numerous other thinkers.

More recently, liberals and conservatives in both parties have united to support legislation to curb administrative discretion. Liberal Democrat Edward Kennedy led the fight for the Freedom of Information Act as well as for legislation that would expand the ability of the public to participate directly in agency proceedings. Liberals and conservatives alike worked to pass the privacy act, which curbs administrative invasions of personal privacy. The legislative veto is more strongly advocated by conservatives, but liberals too have joined in the fight to establish machinery for congressional overrides of administrative rule making. Finally, the deregulation of the transportation industry reduces administrative discretion simply by abolishing many administrative powers. Proponents of deregulation, like advocates of other legislation to curtail administrative discretion, represent views along the entire spectrum of political opinion.

In another context, activists like Ralph Nader worry not that the bureaucracy possesses too much power but that it has too little, and that where it does possess power it often refuses to exercise it, making the bureaucracy inadequate as an effective instrument of regulation and policymaking.

What should be the proper role of the administrative branch in the formulation and execution of public policy? How does it fit into our system of constitutional democracy? If it can negate the will of the other branches of government, can it make the democratic process a sham? Where does the responsibility of the bureaucracy lie?

## The Definition of Responsibility

"Administrative responsibility" means adhering to standards that are considered legitimate within the political system. Administrators who act responsibly are, by definition, acting in conformity with certain criteria. Administrative discretion, and the power of agencies in the policy-making process, complicates administrative responsibility immensely. For example, if administrators exercise discretion, then the only meaningful checks are self-imposed. For decades, since the growth of the bureaucracy as a significant political force, political scientists, politicians, and lawyers have attempted to devise ways of ensuring that the administrative branch is made accountable to standards developed by branches outside the bureaucracy itself. The myth that Congress does not delegate primary legislative authority to the agencies but only creates agencies to act as agents of the legislature conforms to the folklore of our constitutional system. In this way the problem of administrative responsibility is solved rhetorically.

Those who think that the essence of responsibility lies in establishing administrative accountability for each of the original three branches of the government in their respective spheres want to eliminate administrative discretion. Administrators are not to create their own standards of responsibility. Herman Finer, the classic spokesman for creating administrative accountability to the legislature, states the problem as follows:

Are the servants of the public to decide their own course, or is their course of action to be decided by a body outside themselves? My answer is that the servants of the public are not to decide their own course; they are to be responsible to the elected representatives of the public, and these are to determine the course of action of the public servants to the most minute degree that is technically feasible. . . . This kind of responsibility is what democracy means; and though there may be other devices which provide "good" government, I cannot yield on the cardinal issue of democratic government. In the ensuing discussion I have in mind that there is the dual problem of securing the responsibility of officials, (a) through the courts and disciplinary controls within the hierarchy of the administrative departments, and also (b) through the authority exercised over officials by responsible ministers based on sanctions exercised by the representative assembly.[2]

## Accountability to Congress

Administrative accountability to the legislature can be maintained through congressional surveillance of administrative activity. Such legislative surveillance can be through close committee supervision of administrative actions, budgetary controls, and development of sources of expertise for the legislature outside the bureaucracy. In varying degrees, Congress has formally attempted to strengthen itself in all of these ways in the hope that it can better control the administrative branch. The Legislative Reorganization Act of 1946 and that of 1970 were designed to increase the technical proficiency of the legislature as well as to establish a more streamlined committee network to supervise administrative activities. If Congress is to control the bureaucracy, it must have its own independent sources of information and, what is even more important, independent motivation to check and balance the power of the bureaucracy.

One of the principal devices in the checks and balances system of the Constitution was the establishment of separate constituencies for the three branches of the government, so that they would be motivated to act in opposition to each other. If the bureaucracy is to be checked within this system, the branches of government that are to control it must have contrasting interests to those of the agencies. With regard to Congress, administrative agencies and congressional committees are often in close alliance rather than in opposition. The same influences that affect committees operate on agencies. In order for legislative supervision to be effective, congressional committees must be able to oversee administrative action independently. Accountability to the legislature must mean accountability to an independent organization. Congress must reflect a public interest that goes beyond the spheres of specialized interest groups.

Another way in which the legislature can ensure administrative account-

[2]Herman Finer, "Administrative Responsibility in Democratic Government," *Public Administration Review* 1 (1941):335–50, at 336.

ability is to write strict laws in which delegations of authority are clear-cut and provide guidelines for administrative action. This has been recommended by Theodore Lowi in *The End of Liberalism*.[3] He advocates that we return to the *Schechter* rule, which prohibits broad delegation of legislative authority to the president or administrative agencies. Such a solution is impossible, however, because the raison d'être of the administrative process is the need for agencies to fill in the details of legislation passed by Congress, applying their expertise and professional skills to areas where Congress does not have the necessary resources to develop public policy.

The bureaucracy and administrative discretion go together. Of course Congress should strive to make its intent as clear as possible, and both the president and administrators can be kept within the boundaries of this intent through judicial review. But realistically, responsibility to Congress cannot be achieved simply by clearer statutory language. Not only has Congress been generally unwilling to be specific in the enabling statutes of administrative agencies, but once they have been passed it is difficult to get the legislature to amend these statutes to deal with new problems that may arise.

The independent regulatory agencies are considered to be statutory arms of Congress with the responsibility of recommending legislative proposals to meet regulatory needs in their respective areas. Marver Bernstein and others have pointed out, however, that congressional committees rarely respond to the legislative recommendations of these agencies.[4] Judge Henry J. Friendly amusingly cites a French writer in explaining why legislators, regardless of their nationality, prefer not to legislate:

What Dean Rippert has written of the Palais Bourbon could have been written of the Capitol just as well. I commend the entire discussion; here I can extract only a few plums: every man with a privileged position tries to keep it; "when the legislator is asked to legislate, he knows the benefits he will be conferring on some will be matched by burdens on others; he will have his eye fixed on the relative number of his constituents on one side or the other." Moreover, he realizes that "the benefit accorded to some will bring less ingratitude than the loss suffered by others will in resentment"; the optimum is thus to do nothing, since failure will be understood by those desiring the legislation whereas success will not be forgiven by those opposing it. If legislation there must be, the very necessity of a test arouses further opposition, hence the tendency to soften it in the sense of compromise or even of unintelligibility.[5]

[3]Theodore J. Lowi, *The End of Liberalism* 2nd ed. (New York: W.W. Norton, 1979).
[4]Marver H. Bernstein, *Regulating Business by Independent Commission* (Princeton: Princeton University Press, 1955).
[5]Henry J. Friendly, *The Federal Administrative Agencies* (Cambridge: Harvard University Press, 1962), p. 167.

*Accountability to the President*

In public administration circles, the most frequently heard recommendation for limiting administrative discretion is to place the executive branch under the control of the president. Since the development of the scientific management school in the early twentieth century, "principles of public administration" have been fostered in varying forms, one of the most tenacious being that administrative efficiency requires hierarchical control, with one person (in the case of the federal bureaucracy, the president) at the top capable of commanding those below him, and therefore accepting responsibility for what is done. A classic statement of the scientific management position is that by W.F. Willoughby in his *Principles of Public Administration* (1927):

It can be stated without any hesitation that a prime requisite of any proper administrative system is that . . . the Chief Executive shall be given all the duties and powers of a general manager and be made in fact, as well as in theory, the head of the administration.[6]

But does it go without saying that the president is to be, to use Clinton Rossiter's term, "chief administrator"? As Willoughby states, certain advantages flow from this arrangement:

Fundamentally these advantages consist in making of the administrative branch, both as regards its organization and its practical operations, a single, integrated piece of administrative machinery, one in which its several parts, instead of being disjointed and unrelated, will be brought into adjustment with each other and together make a harmonious whole; one that possesses the capacity of formulating a general program and of subsequently seeing that such program as is formulated is properly carried out; one in which means are provided by which duplication of organization, plant, personnel, or operations may be eliminated, conflicts of jurisdiction avoided or promptly settled, and standardization of methods of procedure secured; and finally, one in which responsibility is definitely located and means for enforcing this responsibility provided.[7]

The recommendations of Willoughby and the scientific management school were directly translated into the proposals of the President's Committee on Administrative Management in 1937, and later into the recommendations of the Hoover Commission of 1949.

Many of the same factors that limit Congress's control over the bureaucracy also serve to prevent presidential domination. The size, complexity,

---

[6]W.F. Willoughby, *Principles of Public Administration* (Baltimore: Johns Hopkins University Press, 1927), p. 36.
[7]Ibid., p. 51.

and scope of activity of the agencies preclude control by the president, even with the assistance of the staff of the Executive Office, which was specifically created in 1939 to aid White House supervision of the bureaucracy.

Scientific management theorists supported the idea of presidential control of the bureaucracy for the purposes of administrative efficiency. During the New Deal, liberal Democrats also supported this scheme, which they thought would ensure that the programs of President Roosevelt would be carried out. This gave a political coloration to the concept of presidential control. Liberal supporters of the New Deal, as well as Democratic presidents who endlessly sought increased power over the bureaucracy and a general strengthening of the presidency, were not overly concerned to see the legacy of their efforts pass to President Eisenhower, whom they considered a responsible if somewhat ineffective president. But before Eisenhower came into office, Truman had nevertheless been careful to blanket the New Deal–Fair Deal bureaucrats under civil service regulations so that they could not be removed by an incoming president. This was a common practice of presidents before presidential elections, to prevent the possibility of the opposition party firing unsympathetic administrators.

The Nixon presidency shed a new and disturbing light upon the role of the president as chief administrator. More than any other president before him, Nixon attempted to centralize power in the White House and dominate the executive branch. He vastly expanded the personnel of the Executive Office as well as experimented with a "supercabinet" in January of 1973 — abandoned in May of that year — designed to centralize control over administrative activites in the White House. Administrative agencies were bluntly ordered to impound funds appropriated for programs that did not meet with the approval of the president.

Opposition to the Nixon program led many former supporters of presidential supremacy within the executive branch to reassess their ideas. The Watergate scandal, with its revelations of efforts to achieve total control over the executive branch by a potentially ruthless presidential staff, seemed to raise the specter of a police state. It was, ironically, the opposition of J. Edgar Hoover and the FBI that prevented Nixon from carrying out an extensive plan devised in 1970 of spying on his political adversaries. The Internal Revenue Service also refused Nixon's request to harass those on his "enemy list" by conducting special audits of their returns. In order to carry out the break-in of Daniel Ellsberg's psychiatrist's office, Nixon's staff employed a special group, known as the "plumbers," who operated outside the official bureaucracy. Administrative efficiency under the control of the president can mean carrying out legitimate programs and, in the words of the President's Committee on Administrative Management in 1937, "making democracy work." But at the same time such efficiency can give to the president tools to eliminate political opposition, and thereby to undo the carefully woven design of our democratic government.

### Administrative Independence

Among other things, the Watergate scandal illustrated that an independent bureaucracy is necessary for the maintenance of a system of governmental responsibility. The power of the executive branch is far too extensive to be controlled by any one of the primary branches of government without upsetting the delicate balance of power in the Constitution. The bureaucracy must be maintained as a semiautonomous fourth branch of government that serves to check any potential excesses on the part of the president or Congress. At the same time, administrators are themselves subject to partial control by coordinate branches. Administrative discretion is in the long run never absolute, but the fact of discretion will remain with us. It is an aspect of policymaking in modern constitutional democracy that cannot be entirely eliminated.

Carl Friedrich forcefully argued that in many areas of administrative action the only way to ensure responsibility is through autolimitation — that is, administrative adherence to professional standards.[8] When administrators are not guided by the legislature, the people, or the president, what are they to do when they have been delegated the task of making public policy? Friedrich suggested that they are responsible to "technical standards" that have been developed in the particular policy area, emphasizing the scientific community and its standards of professional conduct. A major problem with Friedrich's argument is that in novel areas there is little agreement within professions on what the best public policy is. Current debates over environmental policy, for example, reflect sharp differences among scientists. When the secretary of the interior must decide whether to authorize the trans-Alaskan pipeline, to push for the development of a trans-Canadian pipeline, or to grant offshore oil leases, he cannot refer to clear-cut professional or scientific standards for guidance. The issues are simply too complex, with conservationists arguing vehemently against the trans-Alaskan plan and the leases while energy specialists, equally reputable in the scientific community, argue for its rapid development. How does an administrator balance the conservation costs of such an energy policy with the benefits to the nation that will accrue from greater energy resources? This is the kind of decision that administrators are again and again forced to make on their

---

[8]Carl J. Friedrich, "The Nature of Administrative Responsibility," *Public Policy* (1940): 3–24.

own, although not without access to the opinions of all other branches of government.

The most important source of administrative responsibility lies in the acceptance by administrators themselves of those procedural standards that have been developed as an integral part of our system of constitutional democracy. These standards require respect for the rights of individuals and of procedural due process as defined with regard to administrative adjudication and rule-making proceedings. It means respect for the mandates of Congress where they have been clearly stated. All points of view must be carefully weighed before policy decisions are made. Above all, the bureaucracy must not be politically neutral when it comes to supporting the values of the system. Fortunately these values have been clearly articulated, and there is no excuse for administrative arbitrariness, unreasonableness, or blind obedience to distorted authority, whether in the White House or the legislature.

## Suggestions for Further Reading

Dodd, Lawrence C., and Richard L. Schott. *Congress and the Administrative State.* New York: John Wiley & Sons, 1979. Examines the close relationships that exist between Congress and the bureaucracy.

Hummell, Ralph P. *The Bureaucratic Experience.* New York: St. Martin's Press, 1977. A provocative analysis of the causes and effects of bureaucracy.

Lewis, Eugene. *American Politics in a Bureaucratic Age.* Cambridge, Mass.: Winthrop, 1977. Traces the implications of the evolving bureaucratic state for democratic values.

Nachmias, David, and David H. Rosenbloom. *Bureaucratic Government U.S.A.* New York: St. Martin's Press, 1980. Analyzes the increasing bureaucracy not only in the executive branch, but also in the presidency, Congress, the judicial branch, political parties, and interest groups.

Seidman, Harold. *Politics, Position, and Power.* New York: Oxford University Press, 1980. Investigates the dynamics of federal organization.

Woll, Peter. *American Bureaucracy.* 2nd ed. New York: W.W. Norton, 1977. Covers the emergence of the federal bureaucracy as a major force in American government and the effect of its role on the constitutional system of checks and balances.

# chapter 9

# The Courts

When Chief Justice Marshall stated in the historic case *Marbury* v. *Madison* (1803) that the last word on interpretation of the Constitution is that of the Supreme Court, an important precedent was established: the High Court held the power and responsibility to make constitutional law. According to Marshall, the entire federal judiciary as well as the Supreme Court have this power and responsibility. Throughout American history the judiciary has from time to time rendered decisions that have had a major impact on the community at large. In this and many other ways it has played a central role in government.

## The Constitutional Context of the Judiciary

### Judicial Review

The federal courts have assumed the authority to declare both state and federal legislation unconstitutional. The Supreme Court has exercised constitutional review far more often over state than over national actions. As of early 1983 it had held only 127 provisions of federal laws unconstitutional in whole or in part out of a total of approximately 88,000 public and private laws that had been passed. By contrast, 1,000 state laws and provisions of state constitutions had been overturned by the Court, 900 of these actions coming after 1870.[1] The Supreme Court has thus not been an important check on Congress during most periods of American history. In maintaining the supremacy of the Constitution and federal law, however,

[1]Henry J. Abraham, *The Judiciary: The Supreme Court in the Governmental Process*, 6th ed. (Boston: Allyn & Bacon, 1983), p. 164.

the Court has unhesitatingly followed Marshall's *McCulloch* doctrine in overturning state legislation that it considers in direct conflict with national law.

*The Reluctance to Raise Constitutional Issues.* Constitutional review is a vital ingredient of the judicial power to shape public policy, but courts raise constitutional issues only when it is thought absolutely necessary to apply the Constitution to resolve a case. Over 99 percent of all cases are settled without having to resort to constitutional review. Courts are significantly involved in the policy-making process through interpretations of statutory and administrative law independent of the Constitution. For example, when a court decides that the attorney general does not have unreviewable discretion to deport aliens, it has made an important policy decision. The issue is not decided on the basis of the Constitution, however, but on interpretation of legislation and administrative practice as well as on prior judicial precedent.[2] Virtually all judicial review of administrative decision making — deciding, for example, whether or not a challenged action went beyond the authority granted to the agency by Congress — is based on statutory interpretation. A related question that frequently arises in judicial review of administrative actions is whether an agency has followed the intent of Congress. Review of state actions is also more often based on statutory rather than on constitutional interpretation.

*The Supreme Court Versus Lower Courts.* Final determinations of constitutional law are made by the Supreme Court (see Figure 9.1). By deciding federal constitutional questions, lower courts may force the Supreme Court to exercise its appellate authority either to ratify or to nullify the action that has been taken. When the Supreme Court refuses to grant review of a lower court decision, it does not necessarily mean that the Court agrees with the reasoning and decision of the lower body. A primary task of the Supreme Court is to foster consistent legal interpretation of the Constitution and federal laws. Conflicting judicial opinions of lower courts are reviewed by the Supreme Court in order to establish uniform legal principles.

One of the most remarkable facts about judicial policymaking in the last several decades is the extent to which it has been innovative, and it has yielded more in this respect than have the other branches of government — Congress, the presidency, and the bureaucracy. Whether the decisions of the Supreme Court are "liberal" or "conservative," one aspect of its operation stands out in stark contrast to most domestic policymaking by coordinate

---

[2]See, for example, *Wong Wing Hang* v. *Immigration and Naturalization Service*, 360 F. 2d 715 (1966).

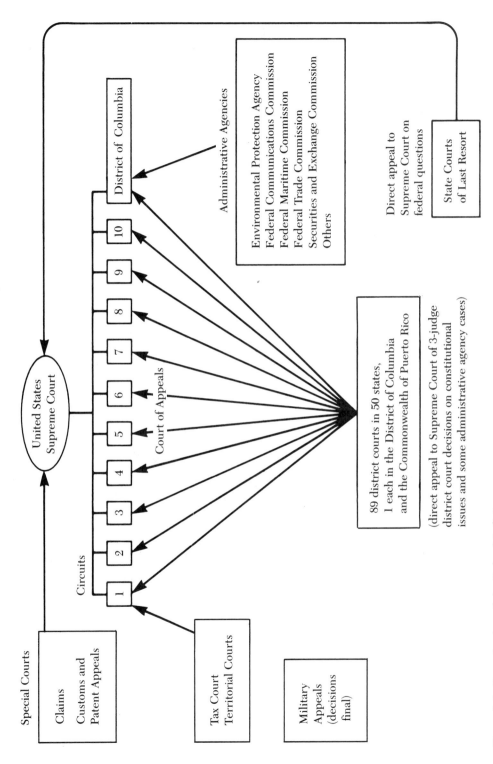

**Figure 9.1.** *Organization of the Federal Judiciary.*

branches — its independence. Of course, no court is an ivory tower, and judges have been accused of everything from "following the election returns" to being the captives of the dominant economic interests of the nation.

## Judicial Procedures and Behavior

The judiciary operates within much more closely defined procedural limits than do the other arms of government. The president can operate secretly, and he need not give reasons for his actions. Congress can obscure its decision-making processes and avoid placing direct responsibility on any one part of the legislature. The bureaucracy too is more flexible procedurally than the courts. Judges, in contrast, must adhere to written standards. Initial decisions must be well reasoned and in writing, available to the parties involved, and subject to appeal.

*Constitutional Courts.* The constitutional courts consist of the Supreme Court and other federal courts created by Congress under the Supreme Court pursuant to Article III. The Stipulations of Article III limit these courts to the consideration of concrete cases and controversies arising under the Constitution, laws, or treaties. Congress cannot delegate "nonjudicial" authority to these courts without violating the Constitution. Historically, judges have been careful to avoid accepting nonjudicial responsibilities when Congress has, from time to time, attempted to lodge such functions in the judicial branch.

The First Congress passed a statute in 1791 that delegated to the circuit courts responsibility for settling the claims of disabled veterans of the Revolutionary War. Circuit judges examined proofs submitted by the veterans regarding the extent of their disabilities, and on the basis of such submissions they determined levels of disability and what benefits veterans would receive. Such judicial determinations under the statute were subject to the supervision of the secretary of war, who could overrule the decisions of the circuit courts. This statute clearly delegated nonjudicial authority to the courts, and in the *Hayburn's* case in 1792 the act was held to be an unconstitutional delegation of authority to the judiciary. Chief Justice Jay declared the statute unconstitutional because

neither the legislative nor the executive branches can constitutionally assign to the judicial [branch] any duties but such as are properly judicial, and to be performed in a judicial manner.

. . . The duties assigned to the circuit courts by this act are not of that description, and . . . the act itself does not appear to contemplate them as such, inasmuch as it subjects the decisions of these courts, made pursuant to those duties, first to the consideration and suspension of the secretary of war, and then to the revision of the legislature; . . . by the Constitution, neither the secretary of war, nor any other executive officer, nor even the legislature, are authorized to sit as a court of errors on the judicial acts or opinions of this court.[3]

The *Hayburn's* case was the first in which the Supreme Court held an act of Congress to be unconstitutional.

A key attribute of judicial power is that it is final, subject to review only within the judicial system itself. Congress cannot confer authority on the judiciary that can subsequently be reviewed by an administrative officer or other outside party. Another important restriction on judicial power is that it can be applied only within the framework of cases and controversies. In *Muskrat v. United States* (1911), the Supreme Court refused to accept jurisdiction that Congress had conferred on it to rule on the constitutionality of certain congressional statutes in an advisory capacity — that is, in the absence of specific cases and controversies. The congressional statute in question clearly violated the case and controversy requirement of Article III.[4]

*Standing, Justiciability, and the Case and Controversy Rule.* The courts can and often have used the provisions of Article III to limit the reach of their authority and thereby to restrict the realm of questions that can be brought before them for consideration. For example, before the Supreme Court ruled the Connecticut birth control law unconstitutional in 1965 (*Griswold v. Connecticut*), it had in other challenges to the law refused to rule on the statute.[5] The Court held that a concrete controversy was not present until Connecticut officials enforced the statute, which, when they finally did, was contested in the *Griswold* case. A law can not be challenged if it is moot. Whether "hypothetical" cases are justiciable, meaning that a controversy does exist and the plaintiff has suffered a legal injury, is for the court involved to decide. For example, in the Connecticut birth control case it would have been possible even before enforcement for the Supreme Court to hold that there was a concrete threat of prosecution for alleged violation of the old Connecticut law banning the use of contraceptives. But the Court's majority, by adhering to the line that such a matter was not ripe for judicial determination, avoided the necessity of ruling on a very delicate case. The Court's opinion was not that such a question was "political" and therefore not properly within the jurisdiction of the Court, but rather that the parties had not presented a real case and controversy.

---

[3]Hayburn's Case, 2 Dallas 409, 410, fn. 2 (1792). *In Re Hayburn's Case* is discussed in *Muskrat v. United States*, 219 U.S. 346 (1911).
[4]*Muskrat v. United States*, 219 U.S. 346 (1911).
[5]*Griswold v. Connecticut*, 381 U.S. 479 (1965).

The concepts of standing (the right to sue), justiciability, and the case and controversy requirement of Article III are linked. A matter is justiciable when there is a case and controversy, which in turn automatically gives the parties standing. In general terms, in order for a court to exercise jurisdiction, opposing interests must present the issues of the case, and a petitioner for court review must be adversely affected in a way that sets him or her apart from the community as a whole. If Congress has provided by statute that the courts are to have jurisdiction over certain matters, then recourse to the judiciary is far easier than where no statute grants the right to judicial review. Courts will not hear cases unless legal interests are at stake — that is, interests protected by statutory or constitutional law. Because these conditions must be met before courts will hear cases, access to the judiciary is extremely limited.

*Changing Standing Doctrine.* In recent years, environmental groups in particular have sought judicial help to stall governmental and private actions that they consider to be detrimental to long-range environmental interests. The courts have responded by developing and expanding the traditional doctrine of standing, generally opening their doors to greater participation by legitimate environmental and other public interest groups. But the courts still demand that groups or individuals seeking judicial review must have personal interests at stake distinguishable from the interests of the public at large. They must show some injury from the government action they are challenging.

The current doctrine of standing is well illustrated by the case of *Sierra Club* v. *Morton* (1972). In this case, the Sierra Club challenged a Forest Service decision that permitted a Disney development in the Mineral King Valley, adjacent to the Sequoia National Park in the Sierra Nevada of California. The Disney Corporation had submitted a plan to the Forest Service to develop a $35 million complex for recreational purposes in the valley, under a thirty-year use permit from the government. Access to the resort was to be gained by a twenty-mile highway, part of which traversed Sequoia National Park. The Forest Service approved the plan and the Sierra Club in June of 1969 filed suit in the District Court for the Northern District of California seeking a judgment that certain aspects of the proposed development were not authorized by federal laws.

Before a court can determine the merits of a case — that is, the issues on which the petitioner is basing the case — standing to sue must be granted. Although the district court granted standing to the Sierra Club in this case, its decision was reversed by the Ninth Circuit Court of Appeals on the grounds that the Sierra Club had not indicated in its complaint that its members would in any way be specifically affected by the Disney development.

The Sierra Club then appealed this decision to the Supreme Court, which granted review and upheld the court of appeals. Like the appellate court, the Supreme Court noted that the Sierra Club had failed in its complaint to indicate how the Disney Development would affect its membership:

The Sierra Club failed to allege that it or its members would be affected in any of their activities or pastime by the Disney Development. Nowhere in the pleadings or affidavits did the Club state that its members used Mineral King for any purpose, much less that they use it in any way that would be significantly affected by the proposed actions of the respondents.

The Club apparently regarded any allegations of individualized injury as superfluous, on the theory that this was a "public" action involving questions as to the use of natural resources, and that the Club's long-standing concern with and expertise in such matters was sufficient to give it standing as a "representative of the public."[6]

The Court held that it was not enough for the Sierra Club merely to assert that the proposed development was contrary to its value preferences without alleging specific injury.

The Court's decision in *Sierra Club* v. *Morton* should not be taken to indicate judicial intention to construct new obstacles in the way of environmental groups seeking to use the courts. But the decision did set some limits, and it required that at least minimum conditions of the case and controversy criteria be met. In reaction to the Supreme Court's decision, the Sierra Club simply rewrote its brief, claiming individualized injury to its membership, which was readily supportable, and refiled its complaint in the case.

A year after the Sierra Club decision the Court granted standing for a group of law students at George Washington University to challenge a decision of the Interstate Commerce Commission that allegedly adversely affected environmental interests. The students claimed that they had used the parks and woodlands in and around the Washington, D.C. area, giving them a personal interest in the ICC's decision. The students' interest was remote, but a majority of the Court nevertheless gave them standing even though their interests were not sharply differentiated from the interests of the general public.[7]

In the mid-1970s the Supreme Court tightened its standing requirements by requiring citizens challenging governmental actions to demonstrate that they had interests in the challenged action that was distinguishable from the general interests of all citizens. To achieve standing, plaintiffs had to show a concrete injury and a personal stake in the outcome of a case.[8] The Court

---

[6]*Sierra Club* v. *Morton*, 405 U.S. 727, 735–36 (1972).
[7]*United States* v. *Students Challenging Regulatory Agency Procedures* (SCRAP), 412 U.S. 669 (1973).
[8]*Schlesinger* v. *Reservists' Committee to Stop the War*, 418 U.S. 208 (1974).

began to require in addition that in order to achieve standing plaintiffs must demonstrate that their alleged injury would very likely be redressed by a favorable judicial decision.[9]

### Judicial Independence

Since the courts interpret both constitutional and statutory law, in a sense they stand above the law. When the courts are determined, even the clearest mandates of Congress can be interpreted out of existence by a clever stroke of the judicial pen. For example, in the late 1960s heated controversy arose over the operation of the Selective Service System, which attempted to punish as "delinquents" under the terms of the Selective Service Act individuals who were involved in demonstrations against the draft and the Vietnam War. The act clearly stated that *preinduction* judicial review of classifications by draft boards was precluded. The only channels of review were within the Selective Service System itself. This was written into law to prevent mass appeals of classifications, which could have had the effect of impeding the operation of the system.

*Overriding Congress.* Regardless of the specific statutory preclusion of judicial review, the courts when presented with cases involving the reclassification of demonstrators and other acts by Selective Service boards that judges considered beyond the boards' authority did not hesitate to step in and exercise judicial review. For example, in the case of *Wolff v. Selective Service Local Board No. 16,* two New York boards, at the request of the New York City Director of Selective Service, reclassified two University of Michigan students for their demonstration protesting the Vietnam War at the offices of the Selective Service local board in Ann Arbor, Michigan in October of 1965.[10] The district court held that it did not have jurisdiction because of the legislative preclusion of judicial review, but on appeal the circuit court held that the action of the Selective Service System endangered constitutional rights. The court declared that "the threat to first amendment rights is of such immediate and irreparable consequence not simply to these students but to others as to require prompt action by the courts to avoid an erosion of these precious constitutional rights."[11]

*The Congressional Reaction to Judicial Override.* Congress's response to the *Wolff* case was swift and straightforward. Congress passed a new law that provided that

[9]*Simon v. Eastern Kentucky Welfare Rights Organization,* 426 U.S. 26 (1976).
[10]*Wolff v. Selective Service Local Board No. 16,* 372 F.2d 817 (1967).
[11]Ibid., p. 820.

No judicial review shall be made of the classification or processing of any registrant by local boards, appeal boards or the president, except as a defense to a criminal prosecution instituted under Section 12 of this Title *after* the registrant has responded either affirmatively or negatively to an order to report for induction, or for civilian work in the case of a registrant determined to be opposed to participation in war in any form.[12]

The explicitness of this language was such that no one could possibly mistake the intent of Congress. Indeed, the Armed Services Committee of the House of Representatives in recommending this change stated that

The Committee was disturbed by the apparent inclination of some courts to review the classification action of local or appeal boards before the registrant had exhausted his administrative remedies. Existing law quite clearly precludes such a judicial review until after a registrant has been ordered to report for induction. . . . In view of this inclination of the courts to prematurely inquire into the classification action of local boards, the Committee has rewritten this provision of the law so as to more clearly enunciate this principle. The Committee was prompted to take this action since continued disregard to this principle of the law by various courts could seriously affect the administration of the selective service system.[13]

Similar expressions of dissatisfaction came from the Senate.

*The Judicial Response.* How would the courts respond to this new law that so clearly precluded judicial review of Selective Service determinations before an order for induction? The issue was immediately raised in *Oestereich v. Selective Service System Local Board No. 11,* involving the reclassification of a theological school student from a status that granted exemption to one that made it almost inevitable that he would be called to serve.[14] Oestereich had returned his registration certificate to the government to express his dissent from U.S. participation in the Vietnam War. In response to this action, his board changed his classification from 4D to 1A. After his administrative appeal failed, he was ordered to report for induction, and at that point he sought to restrain his induction by a suit in district court. Section 10(b)(3) clearly stated that there could be no judicial review of a registrant's classification at this stage unless it were part of his defense in a criminal prosecution (which was not the case here). The Supreme Court, overruling the lower courts, held that judicial review was appropriate because the action of the board exceeded its authority under the law. Speaking for the majority, Justice William Douglas stated in part that

[12]50 U.S.C. §460(b) (3)81, Stat. 100, §10(b) (3) (1967). Emphasis added.
[13]U.S. Congress. House. Committee on Armed Services. 90th Cong. 1st sess. 1967. H. Rept. 267:30–31.
[14]*Oestereich v. Selective Service System Local Board No. 11, 393 U.S. 233 (1968).*

to hold that a person deprived of his statutory exemption in such a blatantly lawless manner must either be inducted and raise his protest through habeas corpus or defy induction and defend his refusal in a criminal prosecution is to construe the act with unnecessary harshness.

These Selective Service cases are examples of how the judiciary can override clearly stated preferences of Congress simply by interpreting statutory language and the "intent of Congress" as something other than what it is. This means that even though Congress has the constitutional authority to control the appellate jurisdiction of the Supreme Court as well as both the original and appellate jurisdiction of lower courts under the terms of Article III, the courts can and have exerted their independence and overridden congressional wishes. This is particularly true when the courts consider that constitutional rights are involved, or that clear *ultra vires* action — that is, action beyond stipulated authority — has been taken by administrative agencies.

### Judicial Activism and Self-Restraint

The Selective Service cases illustrate one aspect of the independence of the judiciary. The courts can be subject to political control and influenced by the demands of Congress. The classic retreat of the New Deal Court in the face of vehement opposition by Roosevelt, who in turn represented a large majority of the people, is a case in point. The fact that courts do not always retreat when confronted with strong political opposition, however, is illustrated by the decisions of the Warren Court. All of the landmark decisions of that Court, from *Brown v. Board of Education* (school desegregation)[15] and *Baker v. Carr* (one man–one vote)[16] through the school prayer decision and the cases that incorporated the Bill of Rights under the due process clause of the Fourteenth Amendment, raised strong opposition from various sections of the country. Nevertheless, the Court did not retreat but rather continued its innovative policymaking.

*The Writ of Certiorari.* The Supreme Court may pick and choose which cases it will hear within its appellate jurisdiction under the provisions of the Judiciary Act of 1925, which was passed to allow the Court discretion in choosing when to grant writs of certiorari (writs to review the record of

[15] *Brown v. Board of Education,* 347 U.S. 483 (1954).
[16] *Baker v. Carr,* 369 U.S. 186 (1962).

lower court decisions). The Court had become overburdened under the old rules, which required the granting of most appeals for writs of certiorari. In practice, then, the Supreme Court may choose to hear a case or not as it wishes. This is not true of lower courts, which must hear cases if jurisdiction is established.

Aside from appellate jurisdiction, the Supreme Court exercises original jurisdiction "in all cases affecting ambassadors, other public ministers and consuls, and those in which a state shall be a party" (Article III). An interesting and generally unknown dimension of judicial self-restraint is that the Court may refuse to hear cases, particularly those involving political questions, that clearly arise within its original jurisdiction. Although Chief Justice Marshall stated in *Cohens* v. *Virginia* (1821) that "we have no more right to decline the exercise of jurisdiction which is given than to usurp that which is not given,"[17] the Supreme Court has not hesitated to dispense with hearing cases that it does not consider appropriate.

## *The Procedural Boundaries of Judicial Decision Making*

The case and controversy requirement of Article III, as well as questions of appellate and original jurisdiction, are all part of the procedural context within which the federal judiciary functions. Beyond formal constitutional requirements and judicial interpretations of them, the courts have established elaborate procedures for the determination of cases that profoundly affect their role. Nowhere is there a more rigid chain of command than in the federal and state judiciaries. Lower courts must operate within the framework of policies set forth by the Supreme Court or face being almost certainly overturned on appeal. The lower the level of court, the less likely it is to establish broad policy principles. Trial courts, in the federal system of the district courts, must base their decisions on the record that is developed by the immediate parties to the proceedings.

In broad terms, judicial decision making takes place within the context of the following procedural boundaries:

1. Cases are initiated by parties outside the judiciary. The courts are helpless to take the initiative to rule and enunciate principles of public policy if an outside agent does not bring a legitimate case and controversy.
2. Assuming that the parties meet the rigid conditions of the case and con-

[17]*Cohens v. Virginia*, 6 Wheaton 264, 404(1821).

troversy rule, once the case is before the court at the trial level the judge (and jury if one is involved) is at least theoretically bound by the factual record developed by the parties themselves and may not take "judicial notice" of matters beyond the record unless they are of common knowledge or involve points of law. Judicial proceedings, unlike many congressional hearings, are not simply rhetorical exercises; rather, they establish records that often determine the outcome of the case. On appeal, judges are limited to the factual record of the trial court, although they may of course overrule points of law that have been established by lower courts.

3. The process of judicial decision making is to be impartial insofar as the interests of judges are not to conflict or to be directly connected with the interests of the parties to the proceeding. Judges may have general policy biases, but they may not have a personal stake in the outcome of a decision.

4. Unless points of law have been improperly applied by lower courts, their decisions are generally upheld if there is substantial factual evidence in the record to support their opinions.

5. When constitutional issues are involved in federal cases, at the trial level three-judge district courts are convened to hear them. Direct appeals may be made from these courts to the Supreme Court.

The case-by-case approach of the judiciary means that policy is established only to the extent that cases set precedents. Since courts do not have to follow the rule of *stare decisis* (adherence to precedent), there is no way to tell how far such precedents will extend, although decisions of the Supreme Court clearly bind all lower courts until the Court itself decides to overrule its prior decision.

## Examples of Judicial Policymaking

Although courts cannot set policy on their own initiative and must operate within the framework of the case and controversy requirement, the number and variety of appeals give judges ample opportunity to shape public policy in many fields. Even a brief glance at American history demonstrates the profound impact that judicial policymaking has had on our society.

### Economic Policy

Sometimes the courts shape policy by negating acts of Congress and state legislatures. In the period from approximately 1890 to 1920, the Supreme Court imposed its own views on state legislators with regard to the scope and content of economic regulations that were permissible under the due process clause of the Fourteenth Amendment. Acting in an entirely subjective manner, the Court defined due process as requiring "reasonable" state action in the regulation of economic interests.

*Determining Reasonable Action.* It was impossible to predict the subjective opinions of the Court regarding what constituted reasonable action, and therefore exactly how it would hold in particular cases. Sometimes the Court upheld state statutes that regulated economic activity and on other occasions it did not. In *Holden* v. *Hardy* (1898), the Court by a seven to two vote held constitutional a Utah statute limiting the hours of workmen in mines, smelters, and ore refineries, to a maximum of eight hours a day.[18] In that case the Court found that the state should have discretion to regulate the hours of workmen. This ruling seemed to negate the right of free contract (part of that of due process) that had previously been established by the Court, which limited the authority of states to interfere in contractual arrangements between employers and employees. In its opinion in the *Holden* case the Court upheld state regulation because of the existence of hazardous working conditions as well as because of the unequal bargaining power of employers and employees.

*Substantive Due Process.* Several years later, in the historic case of *Lochner* v. *New York* (1905), the Court in a five to four decision declared unconstitutional a New York statute that limited the hours of labor in bakery shops to sixty per week, or ten in any one day.[19] The statute, the Court said, violated the right of free contract. Employers should be free to purchase or to sell labor. The contradiction between the *Holden* and *Lochner* decisions illustrates that during this period the Court was not adhering to strict principles of the law. Rather, the Court was going beyond even its own interpretations of the Constitution in previous cases to look at the conditions under which the cases arose, and on this basis trying to make the appropriate decision. This type of substantive decision making extended into all areas of social legislation at that time, with the Court freely imposing its own values on state legislatures and Congress alike. Where economic regulations involved hours of labor, public utility rates, taxation, or other aspects of economic activity, the Court felt itself obliged to act as the final arbiter of the reasonableness of the substantive content of the laws. When the Court acted in this way under the due process clause of the Fourteenth Amendment, it was essentially defining due process in substantive rather

[18] *Holden* v. *Hardy,* 169 U.S. 366 (1898).
[19] *Lochner* v. *New York,* 198 U.S. 45 (1905).

than in procedural terms, and its doctrines became known as "substantive due process" in the economic realm.

*Overseeing the Bureaucracy.* Just as the courts during the later nineteenth and early twentieth centuries were reluctant to grant much leeway to legislatures to make economic policy without careful judicial scrutiny, they were unwilling to allow the infant administrative process to act in an independent fashion. The Interstate Commerce Commission was created in 1887, and Congress delegated to it "quasi-judicial as well as "quasi-legislative" functions. At the beginning, the authority of the ICC was not as great in the exercise of legislative and judicial powers as it was to become in later years. At first the courts carefully supervised the agency and did not hesitate to overrule it when its decisions did not agree with judicial opinion. The initial confusion over whether the agency had the power to fix rates, which seemed to be implied in its enabling statute, was resolved by the Supreme Court in 1896 in a decision holding unequivocally that the ICC could not determine reasonable rates, but only establish facts with regard to rates already in effect.[20] This meant that the ICC was limited to declaring existing rates unreasonable. It had no positive power to set new rates.

In 1897, the Supreme Court again declared emphatically, in *Interstate Commerce Commission v. Cincinnati, New Orleans, and Texas Pacific Railway Co.,* that the ICC could not determine and enforce new rates for a railroad after having first determined that the existing rate structure was unreasonable.[21] Rate making, said the Court, is essentially a legislative function, and the separation of powers requires that if it is to be exercised by government at all it must be carried out within the legislative branch. In another decision the Court held that, although the Interstate Commerce Act of 1887 clearly declared that findings of fact by the ICC were to be taken as conclusive by the courts when they exercised judicial review, the circuit courts of appeals that reviewed the decisions of the ICC were not to be restricted to the agency's factual record, but could accept additional evidence presented by the parties and act on it.[22] Railroads wishing to circumvent the authority of the ICC were thus almost encouraged to withhold information purposely during agency proceedings so that it might later be introduced before a reviewing court in such a way as to make the decision of the commission appear unreasonable.

---

[20] *Cincinnati, New Orleans, and Texas Pacific Railway Co. v. Interstate Commerce Commission,* 162 U.S. 184 (1896).
[21] *Interstate Commerce Commission v. Cincinnati, New Orleans, and Texas Pacific Railway Co.,* 167 U.S. 479 (1897).
[22] *Interstate Commerce Commission v. Alabama Midland Ry. Co.,* 168 U.S. 144 (1897).

Legislatures and administrative agencies became less beholden to subjective judicial opinions as the twentieth century progressed. The judiciary never completely retreated into a doctrine of judicial self-restraint. It tended to become more cautious about involving itself in political disputes with Congress or state legislatures on the one hand, and administrative agencies that were the chosen agents of the legislatures on the other. The invocation of the doctrine of substantive due process in the economic sphere to overrule legislative action was not abandoned by the Supreme Court until after the bitter struggle over the scheme of Franklin Roosevelt to "pack" the Court in an attempt to overcome its opposition to the key legislative proposals of the New Deal.

## The Court in the New Deal Period

The early New Deal period witnessed a conservative and activist Supreme Court holding unconstitutional major legislation designed to curb the economic ills of the country. The Supreme Court, standing alone in the government but reflecting the viewpoints of powerful economic interests on the outside, single-handedly negated presidential and congressional policy proposals.

*The Controversy over the Role of the Supreme Court.* Although some of Roosevelt's advisors — for example, Secretary of the Interior Harold Ickes — thought that the Constitution should be amended to revoke the authority of the Supreme Court to declare acts of Congress unconstitutional, the president took a less drastic course. He recommended to Congress that he be allowed to appoint one new justice for each justice on the Supreme Court over seventy years of age. In 1937 this meant that he would have been able to appoint up to six new Supreme Court justices and thereby have switched the Court from a conservative to a liberal position, assuming his appointees continued to adhere to the policy preferences of the president (which was by no means a certainty).

*A Switch in Time Saves Nine.* Roosevelt's court-packing plan was doomed from the start. Beginning in 1937 the Supreme Court, due to the crossing over of Justice Roberts from the conservative to the liberal side of the bench, changed its position and began to support New Deal programs. The historic case in which the Supreme Court began to shift its position from the conservative to the liberal side was *West Coast Hotel Co. v. Parrish* (1937), upholding a minimum wage statute for women in the state of Washington.[23]

---

[23]*West Coast Hotel Co. v. Parrish*, 300 U.S. 379 (1937).

Taking judicial notice of the Depression, the Court reasoned that states can take into account social problems and legislate accordingly. By implication this applied to the federal government also. Ickes noted in his diary the day after the decision that "Chief Justice Hughes delivered the opinion and he used language, which, if it had been adopted earlier by the Supreme Court and consistently followed, would probably have prevented the strained relationship that now exists between the Supreme Court on the one side and the legislative and executive branches on the other."[24]

The shift in the position of the Supreme Court in the latter 1930s toward judicial self-restraint and a respect for the initiatives of the executive and legislature in public policymaking reflected a recognition that courts cannot stand in the way of legislation that is politically supported and clearly in the public interest. The role of the courts as negators of congressional public policy ended with the New Deal, and no law dealing with economic problems has been declared unconstitutional since 1936.

## The Post–New Deal Period

Between the New Deal Court and the Warren Court there were no significant policy innovations by the federal judiciary.

### From Judicial Restraint to Activism

The doctrine of judicial self-restraint in political questions was at first the rule of the day in the post–New Deal period. In the area of civil liberties and civil rights, the Supreme Court was extremely reluctant to "nationalize" any more provisions of the Bill of Rights than it had during the 1920s and 1930s. It was perfectly willing to overrule state actions on an ad hoc basis when it found that such actions violated fair procedures in criminal proceedings. However, it was unwilling to upset the federal-state balance of power by holding that all of the rights accorded to defendants in federal courts were applied to the states under the due process clause of the Fourteenth Amendment. It also refused to intervene in electoral reapportionment cases.

Another area in which the Court refused to intervene in the late 1940s and early 1950s was that of the loyalty and security policies of federal and state governments, one of the major political issues of the time. Just as Senator Joseph McCarthy embarked on his campaign to ferret out communists in government that was soon to terrorize many elements of the community,

---

[24]Harold L. Ickes, *The Inside Struggle* (New York: Simon & Schuster, 1954), p. 106.

particularly federal employees, the Court was confronted with the question of the validity of the Smith Act in *Dennis* v. *United States* (1951).[25] The law made it a crime to conspire or to teach the duty and necessity to overthrow any government of the United States by force or violence. The Court upheld the 1940 statute on the basis that Congress has the right to proscribe the First Amendment freedoms of expression and association where there is a "clear and present danger" to the security of the nation.

### The Warren Court

A gradual turn to activism began when Earl Warren became chief justice in 1953. The profound impact that the Supreme Court can have on public policy was illustrated during the Warren era. The Court injected a new spirit of innovation throughout the federal judiciary, which had a spillover effect on state courts as well. Of particular importance was the use by the Court of the due process and equal protection clauses of the Fourteenth Amendment to establish federal standards requiring equal educational opportunity by abandoning the "separate but equal" doctrine; the one man–one vote rule that revolutionized electoral apportionment in both congressional and state legislative districts; and the extension of most of the provisions of the Bill of Rights as prohibitions on state action.[26]

## Contemporary Judicial Policymaking

Although President Nixon made a concerted effort to appoint "strict constructionists" or conservatives to the Supreme Court and the lower federal judiciary, the legacy of the Warren Court was too firmly ingrained in our law to be overturned completely.

The Supreme Court under Chief Justice Warren Burger has retreated somewhat the liberal doctrines of the Warren Court — refusing, to cite an instance, to go as far as had the earlier Court in ordering the busing of school children to achieve racial integration — but in general the Burger Court in its first years maintained the policies of its predecessor. In some areas the Court has gone farther than the Warren Court — for example, in extending criminal rights by granting those accused of crimes the right to counsel at preliminary judicial hearings.

Ironically, the conservative Burger Court has infuriated many conservative politicians, such as North Carolina Republican Jesse Helms, because it

[25]*Dennis* v. *United States*, 341 U.S. 494 (1951).
[26]See Chapter 3 for a discussion of the Bill of Rights and Chapter 5 for an examination of equal protection under the laws.

has insisted on continued support for the busing of school children to achieve racial balances in school districts that have a history of past discrimination, or where the weight of evidence suggests that there was an intent to discriminate by drawing school district lines to segregate racial minorities.

### The Abortion Decision

Even more important to conservatives than the busing issue is the stand the Court has taken on the issue of abortion in *Roe* v. *Wade* (1973), in which it upheld the absolute right of a woman to have an abortion during the first trimester of pregnancy.[27] Under the *Roe* decision states can regulate abortions, but only during the last six months of pregnancy and then only when it is demonstrated to be necessary to preserve the health of the mother. The abortion decision spawned a nationwide right-to-life movement that has put pressure on Congress to pass and submit to the states an amendment that would ban abortions.

### Reagan's Impact on the Court

The victory of Ronald Reagan in 1980 and again in 1984 encouraged the antibusing and antiabortion conservatives. The president had not hesitated either during his campaigns or after the elections to affirm his strong views against busing and abortion, announcing at a press conference shortly after his 1980 inauguration his support for a right-to-life amendment as well as congressional legislation to prohibit abortions. Jesse Helms led a group of congressional conservatives in sponsoring legislation that would define the beginning of life at conception, thereby prohibiting abortions because they would constitute taking human life. The passage of such legislation would undoubtedly force a confrontation between Congress and the Supreme Court over what the Court had previously proclaimed as the constitutional right to abortion.

*The Congressional Attack on the Court.* Another tack taken by Court opponents was the introduction of legislation that would withdraw jurisdiction from the Court over cases relating to state laws on prayer in public schools, abortion, or school desegregation plans. The attack on the Court mounted by congressional conservatives was the most serious threat to judicial independence since Roosevelt's court-packing scheme of 1937.

---

[27] *Roe* v. *Wade*, 410 U.S. 113 (1973).

Proponents of legislative restrictions on the jurisdiction of the Court argued that the Constitution clearly states that the appellate authority of the Supreme Court is under congressional control. Congress may thus withdraw jurisdiction from the Court, although it cannot interfere with the Court's original jurisdiction, which is set forth in the Constitution.

*The Court's Defense.* Opponents of the legislation argued that such severe restrictions on the Court's jurisdiction would curb its constitutional role that has evolved over almost two centuries. The Court has assumed the responsibility of maintaining the supremacy of the Constitution from its very first decisions in the first decade of its operation. National supremacy over the states was established in the 1790s and strongly reaffirmed by the Marshall Court. To assert in the 1980s that the Court cannot review state actions involving constitutional questions would render the Court impotent and make the Constitution subject to the inevitably conflicting interpretations of state courts.

The opponents of the efforts to restrict the Supreme Court also argued that the proposed legislation violated the spirit if not the letter of the doctrine of separation of powers. Congress may not, they declared, force its will on the Supreme Court on substantive issues, any more than the legislature may curb the Court's legitimate constitutional powers.

*The Probability of Change.* The Court has in the past weathered many political storms at least as violent as the ones raised by those challenging its jurisdiction during Reagan's presidency. Every controversial decision of the Court — and there have been many — has resulted in vitriolic and scathing attacks on the justices and threats of impeachment. The Supreme Court under John Marshall, Roger B. Taney (*Dred Scott*), Charles Evan Hughes during the New Deal, and Earl Warren was deeply embroiled in political controversy and had to withstand persistent outside attacks. There was nothing new in the efforts of Congress in the early 1980s to limit the Court by reducing its jurisdiction. Congress had made a similar attempt in the most blatant circumstances when in 1869 it repealed the appellate jurisdiction of the Court over habeas corpus cases, which had been granted by an 1867 law, and prohibited appeals that had already been made under the law in order to prevent the Court from ruling on the constitutionality of the Reconstruction Acts. Congress withdrew the Court's jurisdiction just as the justices were about to render their opinion in a case reviewing the denial of a writ of habeas corpus by a federal circuit court.[28]

---

[28] *Ex parte McCardle,* 7 Wallace 506 (1869).

The Court's acquiescence to congressional withdrawal of its jurisdiction over habeas corpus cases after the Civil War, however, involved unusual circumstances and a particularly delicate political situation that the Court thought it best to avoid. Although it has occasionally evaded political controversy through the exercise of judicial self-restraint and acquiescence to Congress, what is remarkable about the Court's history is the extent to which it has exercised independent power to shape the very foundations of the constitutional system in important areas of public policy, ranging from the economic sphere to civil liberties and civil rights. "Conservative" courts, such as that of Chief Justice Hughes during the 1930s, have been as controversial as "liberal" courts, such as that of Chief Justice Warren during the 1950s and 1960s. The nature of political controversy surrounding the Court depends on whose ox is being gored by the decisions of the high tribunal.

The Supreme Court is inevitably thrust into the center of political controversy. It is the responsibility of the Court to hear important constitutional cases, which always involve questions on which there are sharp disagreements among different segments of the population. Sometimes the Court seems to be attacked from all sides, as in its busing decisions, which united liberals and conservatives throughout the nation in strong opposition to the Court.

The Court survived the challenges of the early 1980s as it withstood the numerous attacks made upon it in the past. It may bend a little to meet political opposition by exercising more self-restraint than it has exhibited in many contemporary opinions, which have so strongly buttressed the civil liberties and rights of all citizens. It is unlikely, however, that the Court will relinquish the civil rights policies it has helped to make. If Congress forces a major confrontation with the justices over the fundamental constitutional powers of the Court and its major constitutional decisions, the Court will not back down; in all likelihood it will hold unconstitutional congressional legislation that intrudes on its prerogatives.

## The Courts and Constitutional Democracy

Unique to the American system is the powerful role played by the Supreme Court. The Federalists in the early period of the Republic expected the federal judiciary to be an instrument of national power, upholding against state challenges a nationalist interpretation of the Constitution under the supremacy clause. In *The Federalist* (No. 78) Alexander Hamilton mentioned almost in passing that the Supreme Court would have the authority to review acts of Congress, but it has been the Court's actions in overturning state laws that have raised the most controversy.

Judicial support for expansive national power, although ultimately winning out, is not a constant theme throughout our political history. The federalists recognized that the courts would be deeply involved in politics and would constitute a major political force that they hoped would impose their views of the proper role of the national government. However, after the Marshall era in the early nineteenth century, during which it supported the federalist position favoring a dominant national government, the Court swung far more to the side of the states in interpreting their permissible authority under the Constitution. This judicial tack lasted until the late nineteenth and early twentieth centuries, when the Supreme Court began to apply the concept of substantive due process under the due process clause of the Fourteenth Amendment to overturn state laws regulating economic activity that it considered unfair to business interests. With the end of the early New Deal battles, substantive due process, as well as a narrow interpretation of the commerce clause in the economic sphere, ended in 1937 when the Court reluctantly upheld state regulatory laws and supported an expanded federal role in forming economic policy.

As the ultimate arbiter of constitutional issues, the Supreme Court's power is extraordinary by any measure. Its decisions are often criticized and sometimes attacked as outrageous usurpations of legislative authority, but nevertheless the Court has persevered because of the absence of political majorities capable of agreeing on just how to curb its powers. When such majorities seem to exist, the Court has carefully exercised self-restraint to avoid political combat.

Constitutional democracy is predicated on belief in the rule of law as embodied in the Constitution as well as in a higher law of justice and fairness that may be drawn upon in constitutional interpretation. The Supreme Court is the ultimate guardian of the Constitution and of the precious individual liberties and rights all citizens have under it. Supreme Court justices have not been Platonic guardians, however, but for the most part skilled judges and practical politicians who have done the best that can be expected to balance governmental and private interests while remaining in the political mainstream.

## Suggestions for Further Reading

Abraham, Henry J. *The Judicial Process.* 4th ed. New York: Oxford University Press, 1980. A comparative introductory analysis of the role of the judiciary in the United States, Great Britain, and France.

Jackson, Robert H. *The Struggle for Judicial Supremacy.* New York: Random House, 1941. A firsthand account of the battle between Franklin Roosevelt and the Supreme Court.

Lewis, Anthony. *Gideon's Trumpet*. New York: Random House, 1964. The exciting story of a major Supreme Court case extending the right to counsel is told from beginning to end.

McCloskey, Robert G., ed. *Essays in Constitutional Law*. New York: Random House/Vintage, 1957. Essays by leading scholars on the Supreme Court and the Constitution.

Westin, Alan F., and Barry Mahoney. *The Trial of Martin Luther King*. New York: Thomas Y. Crowell, 1974. An excellent study of a major Supreme Court case involving the right of protest.

Woodward, Bob, and Scott Armstrong. *The Brethren*. New York: Simon & Schuster, 1979. A controversial but fascinating account of Supreme Court decision making.

# The Constitution of the United States of America

*Preamble*

WE THE PEOPLE of the United States, in Order to form a more perfect Union, establish Justice, insure domestic Tranquility, provide for the common defence, promote the general Welfare, and secure the Blessings of Liberty to ourselves and our Posterity, do ordain and establish this Constitution for the United States of America.

## Article I

*Section 1.* All legislative Powers herein granted shall be vested in a Congress of the United States, which shall consist of a Senate and House of Representatives.

*Section 2.* The House of Representatives shall be composed of Members chosen every second Year by the People of the several States, and the Electors in each State shall have the Qualifications requisite for Electors of the most numerous Branch of the State Legislature.

No Person shall be a Representative who shall not have attained to the Age of twenty five Years, and been seven Years a Citizen of the United States, and who shall not, when elected, be an Inhabitant of that State in which he shall be chosen.

Representatives and direct Taxes shall be apportioned among the several States which may be included within this Union, according to their respective Numbers, *which shall be determined by adding to the whole Number of free Persons, including those bound to Service for a Term of Years,* and excluding Indians not taxed, *three fifths of all other Persons.*[1] The actual Enumeration shall be made within three Years after the first Meeting of the Congress of the United States, and within every subsequent Term of ten Years, in such Manner as they shall by Law direct. The Number of Representatives shall not exceed one for every thirty Thousand, but each State shall have at Least one Representative; and until such enumeration shall be made, the State of New Hampshire shall be entitled to chuse three, Massachusetts eight, Rhode-Island and Providence Plantations one, Connecticut five, New-York six, New Jersey four, Pennsylvania eight, Delaware one, Maryland six, Virginia ten, North Carolina five, South Carolina five, and Georgia three.

When vacancies happen in the Representation from any State, the Executive Authority thereof shall issue Writs of Election to fill such Vacancies.

The House of Representatives shall chuse their Speaker and other Officers; and shall have the sole Power of Impeachment.

*Senate Membership*

*Section 3.* The Senate of the United States shall be composed of two Senators from each State, *chosen by the Legislature thereof,*[2] for six Years; and each Senator shall have one Vote.

Immediately after they shall be assembled in Consequence of the first Election, they shall be divided as equally as may be into three Classes. The Seats of the Senators of the first Class shall be vacated at the Expiration of the second Year, of the second Class at the Expiration of the fourth Year, and of the third Class at the Expiration of the sixth Year, so that one third may be chosen every second Year; *and if Vacancies happen by Resignation, or otherwise, during the Recess of the Legislature of any State, the Executive thereof may make temporary Appointments until the next Meeting of the Legislature, which shall then fill such Vacancies.*[3]

No Person shall be a Senator who shall not have attained to the Age of thirty Years, and been nine Years a Citizen of the United States, and who shall not, when elected, be an Inhabitant of that State for which he shall be chosen.

The Vice President of the United States shall be President of the Senate, but shall have no Vote, unless they be equally divided.

The Senate shall chuse their other Officers, and also a President pro tem-

[1] Throughout, italics are used to indicate passages altered by subsequent amendments. In this instance, for example, see the Fourteenth Amendment.
[2] See the Seventeenth Amendment.
[3] See the Seventeenth Amendment.

pore, in the Absence of the Vice President, or when he shall exercise the Office of President of the United States.

## Impeachments

The Senate shall have the sole Power to try all Impeachments. When sitting for that Purpose, they shall be on Oath or Affirmation. When the President of the United States is tried, the Chief Justice shall preside: And no Person shall be convicted without the Concurrence of two thirds of the Members present.

Judgment in Cases of Impeachment shall not extend further than to removal from Office, and disqualification to hold and enjoy any Office of honor, Trust or Profit under the United States: but the Party convicted shall nevertheless be liable and subject to Indictment, Trial, Judgment and Punishment, according to Law.

## Election

*Section 4.* The Times, Places and Manner of holding Elections for Senators and Representatives, shall be prescribed in each State by the Legislature thereof; but the Congress may at any time by Law make or alter such Regulations, except as to the Places of chusing Senators.

*The Congress shall assemble at least once in every Year, and such Meeting shall be on the first Monday in December, unless they shall by Law appoint a different Day.*[4]

## Rules of Congress

*Section 5.* Each House shall be the Judge of the Elections, Returns and Qualifications of its own Members, and a Majority of each shall constitute a Quorum to do Business; but a smaller Number may adjourn from day to day, and may be authorized to compel the Attendance of absent Members, in such Manner, and under such Penalties as each House may provide.

Each House may determine the Rules of its Proceedings, punish its Members for disorderly Behaviour, and, with the Concurrence of two thirds, expel a Member.

Each House shall keep a Journal of its Proceedings, and from time to time publish the same, excepting such Parts as may in their Judgment require Secrecy; and the Yeas and Nays of the Members of either House on any

[4]See the Twentieth Amendment.

question shall, at the Desire of one fifth of those Present, be entered on the Journal.

Neither House, during the Session of Congress, shall, without the Consent of the other, adjourn for more than three days, nor to any other Place than that in which the two Houses shall be sitting.

## Compensation

*Section 6.* The Senators and Representatives shall receive a Compensation for their Services, to be ascertained by Law, and paid out of the Treasury of the United States. They shall in all Cases, except Treason, Felony and Breach of the Peace, be privileged from Arrest during their Attendance at the Session of their respective Houses, and in going to and returning from the same; and for any Speech or Debate in either House, they shall not be questioned in any other Place.

No Senator or Representative shall, during the Time for which he was elected, be appointed to any civil Office under the Authority of the United States, which shall have been created, or the Emoluments whereof shall have been encreased during such time; and no Person holding any Office under the United States, shall be a Member of either House during his Continuance in Office.

## Enacting Bills

*Section 7.* All Bills for raising Revenue shall originate in the House of Representatives; but the Senate may propose or concur with Amendments as on other Bills.

## Veto Power

Every Bill which shall have passed the House of Representatives and the Senate, shall, before it become a Law, be presented to the President of the United States; If he approve he shall sign it, but if not he shall return it, with his Objections to that House in which it shall have originated, who shall enter the Objections at large on their Journal, and proceed to reconsider it. If after such Reconsideration two thirds of that House shall agree to pass the Bill, it shall be sent, together with the Objections, to the other House, by which it shall likewise be reconsidered, and if approved by two thirds of that House, it shall become a Law. But in all such Cases the Votes of both Houses shall be determined by Yeas and Nays, and the Names of the Persons voting for and against the Bill shall be entered on the Journal of each House respectively. If any Bill shall not be returned by the President within ten Days (Sundays excepted) after it shall have been presented to him, the Same shall be a Law, in like Manner as if he had signed it, unless the Congress by their Adjournment prevent its Return, in which Case it shall not be a Law.

Every Order, Resolution, or Vote to which the Concurrence of the Senate and House of Representatives may be necessary (except on a question of Adjournment) shall be presented to the President of the United States; and before the Same shall take Effect, shall be approved by him, or being disapproved by him, shall be repassed by two thirds of the Senate and House of Representatives, according to the Rules and Limitations prescribed in the Case of a Bill.

*Section 8.* The Congress shall have Power To lay and collect Taxes, Duties, Imposts and Excises, to pay the Debts and provide for the common Defence and general Welfare of the United States; but all Duties, Imposts and Excises shall be uniform throughout the United States;

To borrow Money on the credit of the United States;

To regulate Commerce with foreign Nations, and among the several States, and with the Indian Tribes;

To establish a uniform Rule of Naturalization, and uniform Laws on the subject of Bankruptcies throughout the United States;

To coin Money, regulate the Value thereof, and of foreign Coin, and fix the Standard of Weights and Measures;

To provide for the Punishment of counterfeiting the Securities and current Coin of the United States;

To establish Post Offices and post Roads;

To promote the Progress of Science and useful Arts, by securing for limited Times to Authors and Inventors the exclusive Right to their respective Writings and Discoveries;

To constitute Tribunals inferior to the supreme Court;

To define and punish Piracies and Felonies committed on the high Seas, and Offences against the Law of Nations;

To delcare War, grant Letters of Marque and Reprisal, and make Rules concerning Captures on Land and Water;

To raise and support Armies, but no Appropriation of Money to that Use shall be for a longer Term than two Years;

To provide and maintain a Navy;

To make Rules for the Government and Regulation of the land and naval Forces;

To provide for calling forth the Militia to execute the Laws of the Union, suppress Insurrections and repel Invasions;

To provide for organizing, arming, and disciplining, the Militia, and for governing such Part of them as may be employed in the Service of the United States, reserving to the States respectively, the Appointment of the Officers, and the Authority of training the Militia according to the discipline prescribed by Congress;

To exercise exclusive Legislation in all Cases whatsoever, over such District (not exceeding ten Miles square) as may, by Cession of particular States, and the Acceptance of Congress, become the Seat of the Government of the United States, and to exercise like Authority over all Places purchased by the Consent of the Legislature of the State in which the Same shall be, for the Erection of Forts, Magazines, Arsenals, dock-Yards, and other needful Buildings; — And

To make all Laws which shall be necessary and proper for carrying into Execution the foregoing Powers, and all other Powers vested by this Constitution in the Government of the United States, or in any Department or Officer thereof.

*Limits on Congressional Power*

*Section 9.* The Migration or Importation of such Persons as any of the States now existing shall think proper to admit, shall not be prohibited by the Congress prior to the Year one thousand eight hundred and eight, but a Tax or duty may be imposed on such Importation, not exceeding ten dollars for each Person.

The Privilege of the Writ of Habeas Corpus shall not be suspended, unless when in Cases of Rebellion or Invasion the public Safety may require it.

No Bill of Attainder or ex post facto Law shall be passed.

No Capitation, or other direct, Tax shall be laid, unless in Proportion to the Census or Enumeration herein before directed to be taken.

No Tax or Duty shall be laid on Articles exported from any State.

No Preference shall be given by any Regulation of Commerce or Revenue to the Ports of one State over those of another: nor shall Vessels bound to, or from, one State, be obliged to enter, clear, or pay Duties in another.

No Money shall be drawn from the Treasury, but in Consequence of Appropriations made by Law; and a regular Statement and Account of the Receipts and Expenditures of all public Money shall be published from time to time.

No Title of Nobility shall be granted by the United States: And no Person holding any Office of Profit or Trust under them, shall, without the Consent of the Congress, accept of any present, Emolument, Office, or Title, of any kind whatever, from any King, Prince, or foreign State.

*Section 10.* No State shall enter into any Treaty, Alliance, or Confederation; grant Letters of Marque and Reprisal; coin Money; emit Bills of Credit;

make any Thing but gold and silver Coin a Tender in Payment of Debts; pass any Bill of Attainder, ex post facto Law, or Law impairing the Obligation of Contracts, or grant any Title of Nobility.

No State shall, without the Consent of the Congress, lay any Imposts or Duties on Imports or Exports, except what may be absolutely necessary for executing its inspection Laws: and the net Produce of all Duties and Imposts, laid by any State on Imports or Exports shall be for the Use of the Treasury of the United States; and all such Laws shall be subject to the Revision and Controul of the Congress.

No State shall, without the Consent of Congress, lay any Duty of Tonnage, keep Troops, or Ships of War in time of Peace, enter into any Agreement or Compact with another State, or with a foreign Power, or engage in War, unless actually invaded, or in such imminent Danger as will not admit of delay.

## Article II

*Section 1.* The executive Power shall be vested in a President of the United States of America. He shall hold his Office during the Term of four Years, and, together with the Vice President, chosen for the same Term, be elected as follows:

### Presidential Election

Each State shall appoint, in such Manner as the Legislature thereof may direct, a Number of Electors, equal to the whole Number of Senators and Representatives to which the State may be entitled in the Congress: but no Senator or Representative, or Person holding an Office of Trust or Profit under the United States, shall be appointed an Elector.

*The Electors shall meet in their respective States, and vote by Ballot for two Persons, of whom one at least shall not be an Inhabitant of the same State with themselves. And they shall make a List of all the Persons voted for, and of the Number of Votes for each; which List they shall sign and certify, and transmit sealed to the Seat of the Government of the United States, directed to the President of the Senate. The President of the Senate shall, in the Presence of the Senate and House of Representatives, open all the Certificates, and the Votes shall then be counted. The Person having the greatest Number of Votes shall be the President, if such Number be a Majority of the whole Number of Electors appointed; and if there be more than one who have such Majority, and have an equal Number of Votes, then the House of Representatives shall immediately chuse by Ballot one of them for President; and if no Person have a Majority, then from the five highest on the List the said House shall in like Manner chuse the President. But in* chusing the President, the Votes shall be taken by States, the Representation from each State having one Vote; A quorum for this purpose shall consist of a Member or Members from two thirds of the States, and a Majority of all the States shall be necessary to a Choice. In every Case, after the Choice of the President, the Person having the greatest Number of Votes of the Electors shall be the Vice President. But if there should remain two or more who have equal Votes, the Senate shall chuse from them by Ballot the Vice President.[5]

The Congress may determine the Time of chusing the Electors, and the Day on which they shall give their Votes; which Day shall be the same throughout the United States.

### Requirements to Be President

No Person except a natural born Citizen, or a Citizen of the United States, at the time of the Adoption of this Constitution, shall be eligible to the Office of President; neither shall any Person be eligible to that Office who shall not have attained to the Age of thirty five Years, and been fourteen Years a Resident within the United States.

In Case of the Removal of the President from Office, or of his Death, Resignation, or Inability to discharge the Powers and Duties of the said Office, the Same shall devolve on the Vice President, and the Congress may by Law provide for the Case of Removal, Death, Resignation or Inability, both of the President and Vice President, declaring what Officer shall then act as President, and such Officer shall act accordingly, until the Disability be removed, or a President shall be elected.[6]

The President shall, at stated Times, receive for his Services, a Compensation, which shall neither be increased nor diminished during the Period for which he shall have been elected, and he shall not receive within that Period any other Emolument from the United States, or any of them.

Before he enter on the Execution of his Office, he shall take the following Oath or Affirmation: — "I do solemnly swear (or affirm) that I will faithfully execute the Office of President of the United States, and will to the best of my Ability, preserve, protect and defend the Constitution of the United States."

### Powers of the President

Section 2. The President shall be Commander in Chief of the Army and Navy of the United States, and of the Militia of the several States, when

---

[5]Superseded by the Twelfth Amendment.
[6]See the Twenty-fifth Amendment.

called into the actual Service of the United States; he may require the Opinion, in writing, of the principal Officer in each of the executive Departments, upon any Subject relating to the Duties of their respective Offices, and he shall have Power to grant Reprieves and Pardons for Offences against the United States, except in Cases of Impeachment.

He shall have Power, by and with the Advice and Consent of the Senate, to make Treaties, provided two thirds of the Senators present concur; and he shall nominate, and by and with the Advice and Consent of the Senate, shall appoint Ambassadors, other public Ministers and Consuls, Judges of the supreme Court, and all other Officers of the United States, whose Appointments are not herein otherwise provided for, and which shall be established by Law: but the Congress may by Law vest the Appointment of such inferior Officers, as they think proper, in the President alone, in the Courts of Law, or in the Heads of Departments.

The President shall have Power to fill up all Vacancies that may happen during the Recess of the Senate, by granting Commissions which shall expire at the End of their next Session.

### President and Congress

*Section 3.* He shall from time to time give to the Congress Information of the State of the Union, and recommend to their Consideration such Measures as he shall judge necessary and expedient; he may, on extraordinary Occasions, convene both Houses, or either of them, and in Case of Disagreement between them, with Respect to the Time of Adjournment, he may adjourn them to such Time as he shall think proper; he shall receive Ambassadors and other public Ministers; he shall take Care that the Laws be faithfully executed, and shall Commission all the Officers of the United States.

### Impeachment

*Section 4.* The President, Vice President, and all civil Officers of the United States, shall be removed from Office on Impeachment for, and Conviction of, Treason, Bribery, or other high Crimes and Misdemeanors.

## Article III

*Section 1.* The judicial Power of the United States, shall be vested in one supreme Court, and in such inferior Courts as the Congress may from time to time ordain and establish. The Judges, both of the supreme and inferior Courts, shall hold their Offices during good Behaviour, and shall, at stated

Times, receive for their Services, a Compensation, which shall not be diminished during their Continuance in Office.

## Jurisdiction of Federal Courts

*Section 2.* The judicial Power shall extend to all Cases, in Law and Equity, arising under this Constitution, the Laws of the United States, and Treaties made, or which shall be made, under their Authority; — to all Cases affecting Ambassadors, other public Ministers and Consuls; — to all Cases of admiralty and maritime Jurisdiction; — to Controversies to which the United States shall be a Party; — to Controversies between two or more States; — *between a State and Citizens of another State;*[7] — between Citizens of different States; — between Citizens of the same State claiming Lands under Grants of different States, *and between a State or the Citizens thereof, and foreign States, Citizens, or Subjects.*[8]

In all Cases affecting Ambassadors, other public Ministers and Consuls, and those in which a State shall be Party, the supreme Court shall have original Jurisdiction. In all the other Cases before mentioned, the supreme Court shall have appellate jurisdiction, both as to Law and Fact, with such Exceptions, and under such Regulations as the Congress shall make.

The Trial of all Crimes, except in Cases of Impeachment, shall be by Jury; and such Trial shall be held in the State where the said Crimes shall have been committed; but when not committed within any State, the Trial shall be at such Place or Places as the Congress may by Law have directed.

## Treason

*Section 3.* Treason against the United States, shall consist only in levying War against them, or in adhering to their Enemies, giving them Aid and Comfort. No Person shall be convicted of Treason unless on the Testimony of two Witnesses to the same overt Act, or on Confession in open Court.

The Congress shall have Power to declare the Punishment of Treason, but no Attainder of Treason shall work Corruption of Blood, or Forfeiture except during the Life of the Person attainted.

# Article IV

## Full Faith and Credit

*Section 1.* Full Faith and Credit shall be given in each State to the public Acts, Records, and judicial Proceedings of every other State. And the Con-

[7]See the Eleventh Amendment.
[8]See the Eleventh Amendment.

gress may by general Laws prescribe the Manner in which such Acts, Records and Proceedings shall be proved, and the Effect thereof.

### Privileges and Immunities

*Section 2.* The Citizens of each State shall be entitled to all Privileges and Immunities of Citizens in the several States.

### Extradition

A Person charged in any State with Treason, Felony, or other Crime, who shall flee from Justice, and be found in another State, shall on Demand of the executive Authority of the State from which he fled, be delivered up, to be removed to the State having Jurisdiction of the Crime.

*No Person held to Service or Labour in one State, under the Laws thereof, escaping into another, shall, in Consequence of any Law or Regulation therein, be discharged from such Service or Labour, but shall be delivered up on Claim of the Party to whom such Service or Labour may be due.*[9]

### Creation of New States

*Section 3.* New States may be admitted by the Congress into this Union; but no new State shall be formed or erected within the Jurisdiction of any other State; nor any State be formed by the Junction of two or more States, or Parts of States, without the Consent of the Legislatures of the States concerned as well as of the Congress.

The Congress shall have Power to dispose of and make all needful Rules and Regulations respecting the Territory or other Property belonging to the United States; and nothing in this Constitution shall be so construed as to Prejudice any Claims of the United States, or of any particular State.

*Section 4.* The United States shall guarantee to every State in this Union a Republican Form of Government, and shall protect each of them against Invasion; and on Application of the Legislature, or of the Executive (when the Legislature cannot be convened) against domestic Violence.

## Article V

### Amendment Process

The Congress, whenever two thirds of both Houses shall deem it necessary, shall propose Amendments to this Constitution, or, on the Application of

[9]See the Thirteenth Amendment.

the Legislatures of two thirds of the several States, shall call a Convention for proposing Amendments, which, in either Case, shall be valid to all Intents and Purposes, as Part of this Constitution, when ratified by the Legislatures of three fourths of the several States, or by Conventions in three fourths thereof, as the one or the other Mode of Ratification may be proposed by the Congress; Provided that no Amendment which may be made prior to the Year One thousand eight hundred and eight shall in any Manner affect the first and fourth Clauses in the Ninth Section of the first Article; and that no State, without its Consent, shall be deprived of its equal Suffrage in the Senate.

## Article VI

All Debts contracted and Engagements entered into, before the Adoption of this Constitution, shall be as valid against the United States under this Constitution, as under the Confederation.

### Supremacy Clause

This Constitution, and the Laws of the United States which shall be made in Pursuance thereof; and all Treaties made, or which shall be made, under the Authority of the United States, shall be the supreme Law of the Land; and the Judges in every State shall be bound thereby, any Thing in the Constitution or Laws of any State to the Contrary notwithstanding.

### No Religious Test

The Senators and Representatives before mentioned, and the Members of the several State Legislatures, and all executive and judicial Officers, both of the United States and of the several States, shall be bound by Oath or Affirmation, to support this Constitution; but no religious Test shall ever be required as a Qualification to any Office or public Trust under the United States.

## Article VII

### Ratification Process

The Ratification of the Conventions of nine States, shall be sufficient for the Establishment of this Constitution between the States so ratifying the Same.

DONE in Convention by the Unanimous Consent of the States present the

Seventeenth Day of September in the Year of our Lord one thousand seven hundred and Eighty seven and of the Independence of the United States of America the Twelfth. IN WITNESS whereof We have hereunto subscribed our Names.

ARTICLES IN ADDITION TO, AND AMENDMENT OF THE CONSTITUTION OF THE UNITED STATES OF AMERICA, PROPOSED BY CONGRESS, AND RATIFIED BY THE LEGISLATURES OF THE SEVERAL STATES, PURSUANT TO THE FIFTH ARTICLE OF THE ORIGINAL CONSTITUTION.

## Amendment 1

[Ratification of the first ten amendments was completed December 15, 1791.]

*Freedom of Religion, Speech, the Press, and Assembly*

Congress shall make no law respecting an establishment of religion, or prohibiting the free exercise thereof; or abridging the freedom of speech, or of the press; or the right of the people peaceably to assemble, and to petition the Government for a redress of grievances.

## Amendment II

*The Right to Bear Arms*

A well regulated Militia, being necessary to the security of a free State, the right of the people to keep and bear Arms, shall not be infringed.

## Amendment III

*Quartering Soldiers*

No Soldier shall, in time of peace be quartered in any house, without the consent of the Owner, nor in time of war, but in a manner to be prescribed by law.

## Amendment IV

*Search and Seizure*

The right of the people to be secure in their persons, houses, papers, and effects, against unreasonable searches and seizures, shall not be violated, and no Warrants shall issue, but upon probable cause, supported by Oath or affirmation, and particularly describing the place to be searched, and the persons or things to be seized.

## Amendment V

*Due Process of Law*

No person shall be held to answer for a capital, or otherwise infamous crime, unless on a presentment or indictment of a Grand Jury, except in cases arising in the land or naval forces, or in the Militia, when in actual service in time of War or public danger; nor shall any person be subject for the same offence to be twice put in jeopardy of life or limb; nor shall be compelled in any criminal case to be a witness against himself, nor be deprived of life, liberty, or property, without due process of law; nor shall private property be taken for public use, without just compensation.

## Amendment VI

*Trial Rights*

In all criminal prosecutions, the accused shall enjoy the right to a speedy and public trial, by an impartial jury of the State and district wherein the crime shall have been committed, which district shall have been previously ascertained by law, and to be informed of the nature and cause of the accusation; to be confronted with the witnesses against him; to have compulsory process for obtaining witnesses in his favor, and to have the Assistance of Counsel for his defence.

## Amendment VII

*Common Law Suits*

In Suits at common law, where the value in controversy shall exceed twenty dollars, the right of trial by jury shall be preserved, and no fact tried by a jury, shall be otherwise reexamined in any Court of the United States, than according to the rules of the common law.

## Amendment VIII

*Bail, Cruel and Unusual Punishment*

Excessive bail shall not be required, nor excessive fines imposed, nor cruel and unusual punishments inflicted.

## Amendment IX

*Unenumerated Rights*

The enumeration in the Constitution, of certain rights, shall not be construed to deny or disparage others retained by the people.

## Amendment X

*States' Powers*

The powers not delegated to the United States by the Constitution, nor prohibited by it to the States, are reserved to the States respectively, or to the people.

## Amendment XI

[January 8, 1798]

*Suits Against States*

The Judicial power of the United States shall not be construed to extend to any suit in law or equity, commenced or prosecuted against one of the United States by Citizens of another State, or by Citizens or Subjects of any Foreign State.

## Amendment XII

[September 25, 1804]

*Changes in the Electoral College*

The Electors shall meet in their respective states, and vote by ballot for President and Vice-President, one of whom, at least, shall not be an inhabitant of the same state with themselves; they shall name in their ballots the person voted for as President, and in distinct ballots the person voted for as Vice-President, and they shall make distinct lists of all persons voted for as President, and of all persons voted for as Vice-President, and of the number of votes for each, which lists they shall sign and certify, and transmit sealed to the seat of the government of the United States, directed to the President of the Senate; — The President of the Senate shall, in the presence of the Senate and House of Representatives, open all the certificates and the votes shall then be counted; — The person having the greatest number of votes for President, shall be the President, if such number be a majority of the whole number of Electors appointed; and if no person have such majority, then from the persons having the highest numbers not exceeding three on the list of those voted for as President, the House of Representatives shall choose immediately, by ballot, the President. But in choosing the President, the votes shall be taken by states, the representation from each state having one vote; a quorum for this purpose shall consist of a member or members from two-thirds of the states, and a majority of all the states shall be necessary to a choice. And if the House of Representatives shall not choose a President whenever the right of choice shall devolve upon them, *before the fourth day of March next following,*[10] then the Vice-President shall act as President, as in the case of the death or other constitutional disability of the President. — The person having the greatest number of votes as Vice-President shall be the Vice-President, if such number be a majority of the whole number of Electors appointed, and if no person have a majority, then from the two highest numbers on the list, the Senate shall choose the Vice-President; a quorum for the purpose shall consist of two-thirds of the whole number of Senators, and a majority of the whole number shall be necessary to a choice. But no person constitutionally ineligible to the office of President shall be eligible to that of Vice-President of the United States.

## Amendment XIII

[December 18, 1865]

*Slavery Prohibited*

*Section 1.* Neither slavery nor involuntary servitude, except as a punishment for crime whereof the party shall have been duly convicted, shall exist within the United States, or any place subject to their jurisdiction.

*Section 2.* Congress shall have power to enforce this article by appropriate legislation.

## Amendment XIV

[July 28, 1869]

---

[10]Altered by the Twentieth Amendment.

*Citizenship for Slaves; Due Process; Equal Protection*

*Section 1.* All persons born or naturalized in the United States, and subject to the jurisdiction thereof, are citizens of the United States and of the State wherein they reside. No State shall make or enforce any law which shall abridge the privileges or immunities of citizens of the United States; nor shall any State deprive any person of life, liberty, or property, without due process of law; nor deny to any person within its jurisdiction the equal protection of the laws.

*Section 2.* Representatives shall be apportioned among the several States according to their respective numbers, counting the whole number of persons in each State, excluding Indians not taxed. But when the right to vote at any election for the choice of electors for President and Vice President of the United States, Representatives in Congress, the Executive and Judicial officers of a State, or the members of the Legislature thereof, is denied to any of the male inhabitants of such State, being twenty-one years of age, and citizens of the United States, or in any way abridged, except for participation in rebellion, or other crime, the basis of representation therein shall be reduced in the proportion which the number of such male citizens shall bear to the whole number of male citizens twenty-one years of age in such State.

*Section 3.* No person shall be a Senator or Representative in Congress, or elector of President and Vice President, or hold any office, civil or military, under the United States, or under any State, who, having previously taken an oath, as a member of Congress, or as an officer of the United States, or as a member of any State legislature, or as an executive or judicial officer of any State, to support the Constitution of the United States, shall have engaged in insurrection or rebellion against the same, or given aid or comfort to the enemies thereof. But Congress may by a vote of two-thirds of each House, remove such disability.

*Section 4.* The validity of the public debt of the United States, authorized by law, including debts incurred for payment of pensions and bounties for services in suppressing insurrection or rebellion, shall not be questioned. But neither the United States nor any State shall assume or pay any debt or obligation incurred in aid of insurrection or rebellion against the United States, or any claim for the loss or emancipation of any slave; but all such debts, obligations and claims shall be held illegal and void.

*Section 5.* The Congress shall have power to enforce, by appropriate legislation, the provisions of this article.

## Amendment XV

[March 30, 1870]

*The Right to Vote*

*Section 1.* The right of citizens of the United States to vote shall not be denied or abridged by the United States or by any State on account of race, color, or previous condition of servitude.

*Section 2.* The Congress shall have power to enforce this article by appropriate legislation.

## Amendment XVI

[February 25, 1913]

*Income Tax*

The Congress shall have power to lay and collect taxes on incomes, from whatever source derived, without apportionment among the several States, and without regard to any census or enumeration.

## Amendment XVII

[May 31, 1913]

*Popular Election of Senators*

The Senate of the United States shall be composed of two Senators from each State, elected by the people thereof, for six years; and each Senator shall have one vote. The electors in each State shall have the qualifications requisite for electors of the most numerous branch of the State legislatures.

When vacancies happen in the representation of any State in the Senate, the executive authority of such State shall issue writs of election to fill such vacancies: *Provided,* That the legislature of any State may empower the executive thereof to make temporary appointments until the people fill the vacancies by election as the legislature may direct.

This amendment shall not be so construed as to affect the election or term of any Senator chosen before it becomes valid as part of the Constitution.

## Amendment XVIII

[January 29, 1919]

*Prohibition of Liquor*

*Section 1. After one year from the ratification of this article the manufacture, sale, or transportation of intoxicating liquors within, the importation thereof into, or the exportation thereof from the United States and all territory subject to the jurisdiction thereof for beverage purposes is hereby prohibited.*

*Section 2. The Congress and the several States shall have concurrent power to enforce this article by appropriate legislation.*

*Section 3. This article shall be inoperative unless it shall have been ratified as an amendment to the Constitution by the legislatures of the several States, as provided in the Constitution, within seven years from the date of the submission hereof to the States by the Congress.*[11]

## Amendment XIX

[August 26, 1920]

*Women's Right to Vote*

The right of citizens of the United States to vote shall not be denied or abridged by the United States or by any State on account of sex.

Congress shall have power to enforce this article by appropriate legislation.

## Amendment XX

[February 6, 1933]

*Federal Terms to Begin in January*

*Section 1.* The terms of the President and Vice President shall end at noon on the 20th day of January, and the terms of Senators and Representatives at noon on the 3d day of January, of the years in which such terms would have ended if this article had not been ratified; and the terms of their successors shall then begin.

[11]Repealed by the Twenty-first Amendment.

*Section 2.* The Congress shall assemble at least once in every year, and such meeting shall begin at noon on the 3d day of January, unless they shall by law appoint a different day.

*Section 3.* If, at the time fixed for the beginning of the term of the President, the President elect shall have died, the Vice President elect shall become President. If a President shall not have been chosen before the time fixed for the beginning of his term, or if the President elect shall have failed to qualify, then the Vice President elect shall act as President until a President shall have qualified; and the Congress may by law provide for the case wherein neither a President elect nor a Vice President elect shall have qualifed, declaring who shall then act as President, or the manner in which one who is to act shall be selected, and such person shall act accordingly until a President or Vice President shall have qualified.

*Section 4.* The Congress may by law provide for the case of the death of any of the persons from whom the House of Representatives may choose a President whenever the right of choice shall have devolved upon them, and for the case of the death of any of the persons from whom the Senate may choose a Vice President whenever the right of choice shall have devolved upon them.

*Section 5.* Sections 1 and 2 shall take effect on the 15th day of October following the ratification of this article.

*Section 6.* This article shall be inoperative unless it shall have been ratified as an amendment to the Constitution by the legislatures of three-fourths of the several States within seven years from the date of its submission.

## Amendment XXI

[December 5, 1933]

*Repeals Prohibition*

*Section 1.* The eighteenth article of amendment to the Constitution of the United States is hereby repealed.

*Section 2.* The transportation or importation into any State, Territory, or possession of the United States for delivery or use therein of intoxicating liquors, in violation of the laws thereof, is hereby prohibited.

*Section 3.* This article shall be inoperative unless it shall have been ratified as an amendment to the Constitution by conventions in the several States, as provided in the Constitution, within seven years from the date of the submission hereof to the States by the Congress.

## Amendment XXII

[February 26, 1951]

*Two-Term Limit for President*

*Section 1.* No person shall be elected to the office of the President more than twice, and no person who has held the office of President, or acted as President, for more than two years of a term to which some other person was elected President shall be elected to the office of President more than once. But this Article shall not apply to any person holding the office of President when this Article was proposed by the Congress, and shall not prevent any person who may be holding the office of President, or acting as President, during the term within which this Article becomes operative from holding the office of President or acting as President during the remainder of such term.

*Section 2.* This article shall be inoperative unless it shall have been ratified as an amendment to the Constitution by the legislatures of three-fourths of the several States within seven years from the date of its submission to the States by the Congress.

## Amendment XXIII

[March 29, 1961]

*Right to Vote for Residents of the District of Columbia*

*Section 1.* The District constituting the seat of Government of the United States shall appoint in such manner as the Congress may direct:
   A number of electors of President and Vice President equal to the whole number of Senators and Representatives in Congress to which the District would be entitled if it were a State, but in no event more than the least populous State; they shall be in addition to those appointed by the States, but they shall be considered, for the purposes of the election of President and Vice President, to be electors appointed by a State; and they shall meet

in the District and perform such duties as provided by the twelfth article of amendment.

*Section 2.* The Congress shall have power to enforce this article by appropriate legislation.

## Amendment XXIV

[January 23, 1964]

*Prohibition of Poll Taxes*

*Section 1.* The right of citizens of the United States to vote in any primary or other election for President or Vice President, for electors for President or Vice President, or for Senator or representative in Congress, shall not be denied or abridged by the United States or any state by reason of failure to pay any poll tax or other tax.

*Section 2.* The Congress shall have power to enforce this article by appropriate legislation.

## Amendment XXV

[February 19, 1967]

*Presidential Disability and Replacement for Vice President*

*Section 1.* In case of the removal of the President from office or of his death or resignation, the Vice President shall become President.

*Section 2.* Whenever there is a vacancy in the office of the Vice President, the President shall nominate a Vice President who shall take office upon confirmation by a majority vote of both Houses of Congress.

*Section 3.* Whenever the President transmits to the President pro tempore of the Senate and the Speaker of the House of Representatives his written declaration that he is unable to discharge the powers and duties of his office, and until he transmits to them a written declaration to the contrary, such powers and duties shall be discharged by the Vice President as Acting President.

*Section 4.* Whenever the Vice President and a majority of either the principal officers of the executive departments or of such other body as Congress may by law provide, transmit to the President pro tempore of the Senate and the Speaker of the House of Representatives their written declaration that the President is unable to discharge the powers and duties of his office, the Vice President shall immediately assume the powers and duties of the office as Acting President.

Thereafter, when the President transmits to the President pro tempore of the Senate and the Speaker of the House of Representatives his written declaration that no inability exists, he shall resume the powers and duties of his office unless the Vice President and a majority of either the principal officers of the executive department or of such other body as Congress may by law provide, transmit within four days to the President pro tempore of the Senate and the Speaker of the House of Representatives their written declaration that the President is unable to discharge the powers and duties of his office. Thereupon Congress shall decide the issue, assembling within forty-eight hours for that purpose if not in session. If the Congress, within twenty-one days after receipt of the latter written declaration, or, if Congress is not in session, within twenty-one days after Congress is required to assemble, determines by two-thirds vote of both Houses that the President is unable to discharge the powers and duties of his office, the Vice President shall continue to discharge the same as Acting President; otherwise, the President shall resume the powers and duties of his office.

## Amendment XXVI

[June 30, 1971]

*Voting Age Lowered to Eighteen*

*Section 1.* The right of citizens of the United States, who are eighteen years of age or older, to vote shall not be denied or abridged by the United States or by any State on account of age.

*Section 2.* The Congress shall have power to enforce this article by appropriate legislation.

# INDEX

Abortion, 284
Abourezk, James, 221
Abraham, Henry J., 61n, 267n
Adams, John, 184
*Adkins* v. *Children's Hospital,* 40
Administration Committee (House), 216–217
Administrative accountability, 260–264
Administrative agencies. *See* Bureaucracy
Administrative responsibility, 259–260
Advisory Commission on Intergovernmental Relations, 88
Agricultural Adjustment Act of 1933, 209
Agricultural Committee (House), 245
Albert, Carl, 227
Amendments, 16
   1st (freedoms of speech, press, religion and assembly and petition rights), 29–30
   2nd (right to bear arms), 30–31
   3rd (limits on quartering of soldiers), 31–32
   4th (unreasonable searches and seizures), 32–35
   5th (grand juries, double jeopardy, self-incrimination, due process, and eminent domain), 35–42
   6th (rights of accused in federal criminal trials), 42–50
   7th (trial by jury), 50
   8th (prohibition of excessive bail, fines, and cruel and unusual punishments), 50–53
   9th (rights retained by the people), 53–56
   10th (reserved powers of states), 56–58
   12th (election of president), 186
   13th (slavery), 63
   14th (due process), 58–62, 63, 78, 79, 279, 283
   17th (direct election of senators), 205, 246
American Medical Association (AMA), 136–137
Anderson, John, 112–113, 219
Appropriations committees, 215, 216, 217–218, 234, 235
Armed Services committees, 215, 217, 275
Arms, right to bear, 30–31
Articles of Confederation, 70
Ashcroft, John, 149
Assembly right, 29–30
Attainder, bill of, 12, 13, 28n
Authorization committees, 217, 235

Bail, 50–51
Baker, Howard, 238
Baker, James A., III, 193
*Baker* v. *Carr,* 276
*Barenblatt* v. *United States,* 38n
Barker, Ernest, 100n
*Barron* v. *Baltimore,* 77, 78
Beard, Charles, 71
Bentley, Arthur F., 133
*Benton* v. *Maryland,* 37n
Bernstein, Marver, 261
Bicameralism, 10, 205–207
Bill of attainder, 12, 13, 28n
Bill of Rights, 17, 27–67
   assembly and petition rights in, 29–30

on cruel and unusual punishments, 51–53
debate over, 28
drafting of, 29
on double jeopardy, 36
on due process, 38–41
on eminent domain, 41–42
equal protection of the laws and, 62–66
on excessive bails and fines, 50–51
on freedoms of speech, press, and religion, 29–30
on grand juries, 35–36
on limits of quartering of soldiers, 31–32
nationalization of, 58–62
on reserved powers of states, 56–58
on rights of accused in federal criminal trials, 42–50
on rights retained by the people, 53–56
on right to bear arms, 30–31
role of, 66–67
on self-incrimination, 37–38
on trial by jury, 50
on unreasonable searches and seizures, 32–35
Black, Hugo, 35, 51, 55, 62, 142, 179
Black Caucus, 229, 230
Blackmun, Harry, 47–48, 51n, 52, 56
Boland, Edward, 110
*Bolling v. Sharpe*, 40–41, 63
Brandeis, Louis, 34
Brennan, William, 46, 47, 52, 83
Brinkley, David, 122
British–North American Act of 1867, 72
Broder, David S., 123
*Brown v. Board of Education*, 65, 276
Bryce, James, 92, 93
Buckley, James, 143
*Buckley v. Valeo*, 143–144
Budget and Impoundment Control Act of 1974, 232, 233–234, 237
Budget committees, 234–236
Budget-making process, 231–238
Budget resolutions, 234
Bureaucracy, 249–265
accountability of, 260–264
administrative responsibility of, 258–265
Congress and, 239–241, 251–252, 260–261
constitutional context of, 250–255
control of, 249, 251–252
functions of, 252–255
independence of, 264–265
judiciary and, 280–281

political context of, 255–258
president and, 251–252, 255–258, 262–264
Bureau of the Budget, 191, 256
Burger, Warren, 44–45, 47, 48, 51n, 52, 66, 82, 84, 283
Burnham, Walter Dean, 123–124
Burr, Aaron, 185–186
Byrd, Robert, 228

"Calendar Wednesday procedure," 218n
Calhoun, John C., 131–133, 140
Campaign finance laws, 142–144
Cannon, Howard, 257
Capital punishment, 51–53
Cardozo, Benjamin, 36, 60, 61
Carter, Jimmy, 186, 187, 237
foreign policy of, 102, 197
grass-roots support for, 109, 110, 112
as legislator, 183
reorganization by, 256–257
staff of, 193–194
Case and controversy rule, 271–272
Caucuses, 229–230
*Central Hudson Gas and Electric Corporation v. Public Service Commission of New York*, 145n
Certiorari, writ of, 276–277
*Charles River Bridge v. Warren Bridge*, 79n
Checks and balances, 5–6
*Chicago, Milwaukee and St. Paul Ry. Co. v. Minnesota*, 42n
*Chisholm v. Georgia*, 75n
Civil Aeronautics Board (CAB), 158, 159, 257, 258
Civil rights. *See also* Bill of Rights
in Constitution, 27–28
national standards for, 83–84
party positions on, 118–119
Civil Rights Act of 1964, 65, 118, 119, 197
Clark, Thomas, 44–45
Clifford, Clark, 196
Code of Federal Regulations, 252
*Cohens v. Virginia*, 277
Commander in chief, president as, 176–180
Committee on Administrative Management, 240
Committees. *See* Congressional committees; *names of specific committees*
Common Cause, 164, 165

"Concurrent majorities," 132, 133
Congress, 205–246
  budget-making process in, 231–238
  bureaucracy and, 239–241, 251–252,
    260–261
  caucuses in, 229–230
  checks on, 5–6
  constituents and, 242–246
  division of, 5–6, 9, 205–207
  election of, 9, 205, 242–246
  expulsion of members, 10
  interest groups and, 147–150, 241–242
  limitations on, 12
  organization and procedures of, 10–11
  policy-making authority of, 208–212
  political parties in, 105–106, 218–219,
    221–229
  powers of, 5, 12, 207–212
  president and, 238–239
  qualifications of members of, 9–10
  special groups in, 230
  staff members and, 230–231, 232
  support and protection of, 11
  Supreme Court vs., 274–276
  terms of office in, 9
Congressional committees, 212–221. *See
  also names of specific committees*
  appropriations, 217–218
  assignment to, 214
  authorization, 217
  budget, 234–236
  in legislative process, 212
  party, 228–229
  "pork-barrel," 217
  reform of system, 218–221
  role of, 215–217
  select, 214
  types of, 217–218
Congressional Hispanic Caucus, 229
Congressional Record, 11
Congress Watch, 165
Congresswomen's Caucus, 229, 230
*Consolidated Edison Co.* v. *Public Service
  Commission of New York,* 144–145
Constitution, 3–24. *See also* Bill of Rights
  amending of, 16
  civil rights in, 17–23
  on division of power in Congress, 207–
    208
  executive power and, 13–14
  federalism and, 72, 74–84
  framing of, 3–4
  interest groups and, 138–145
  interstate relations and, 15
  judicial power and, 14

  legislative power and, 8–13
  major features of, 4–8
  perspectives on, 17–23
  ratification of, 16–17
  supremacy clause in, 16
Constitutional courts, 270–271
Constitutional review, 268
*Cooley* v. *Board of Wardens,* 78n
Corrupt Practices Act of 1925, 143
Council of Economic Advisors, 187, 192
Council on Environmental Quality, 193
Countervailing power, 138, 139
Courts. *See* Judiciary; Supreme Court
Criminal trials, rights of accused in, 42–50
Cronin, Thomas E., 195
Cuomo, Mario, 121
Curtis, Benjamin R., 39

*Dartmouth College* v. *Woodward,* 76n, 77,
  79n
Dean, John, 194n, 195
Death penalty, 51–53
Deaver, Michael, 194
Declaration of Independence, 53, 69–70
Deficit, 236
Democratic Caucus, 219
Democratic Forum, 230
Democratic party. *See also* Parties
  committees and, 219
  in Congress, 218, 221–229
  early, 85, 86
  federalism and, 92
  policies of, 115, 117–123
Democratic Steering and Policy
  Committee, 214, 219, 228, 229
Democratic Study Group, 218, 230
*Dennis* v. *United States,* 283
Deregulation, 159
Distributive policies, 157
Doggett, Lloyd, 149
Dole, Robert, 103, 207
Domenici, Pete, 236
Dornan, Robert, 149
Double jeopardy, 36–37
Douglas, William O., 52, 54, 56, 142,
  275–276
Drew, Elizabeth, 113n, 114n
Due process of law, 30, 38–41, 58–62,
  279–280, 283
*Duncan* v. *Louisiana,* 42–43
Dutton, Fred, 114

Eccles, Marriner S., 191n
Eckstein, Harry, 139n
Economic Stabilization Act of 1970, 82

Edmisten, Rufus, 149
Ehrlichman, John, 192
Eighth Amendment, 50–53
Eisenhower, Dwight D., 107–108, 118, 182, 183, 197, 256, 263
Electoral College, 73, 184–186
Electoral process, 103–106
Ellsberg, Daniel, 263
Eminent domain, 41–42
*End of Liberalism, The* (Lowi), 261
Environmental Protection Agency (EPA), 156, 253, 256
Environmental Study Conference, 229
Equal protection of the laws, 62–66, 283
*Estelle v. Gamble,* 53n
Executive branch of government. *See* President
*Ex parte McCardle,* 285n
*Ex parte Milligan,* 178
Ex post facto law, 12, 13, 28n
Extradition, 15

Factions, 97–99. *See also* Interest groups
Fair Labor Standards Act, 82
Farrand, Max, 4n, 18n, 63n
FBI, 263
Federal Communications Commission, 255
Federal criminal trials, rights of accused in, 42–50
Federal deficit, 236
Federal Election Campaign Practices Act, 143
Federalism, 4–5, 69–93
    constitutional background of, 71–74
    constitutional standards governing, 78–84
    defined, 71–73
    early constitutional interpretation of, 74–78
    interest groups and, 141
    "New," 90
    politics of, 84–92
*Federalist, The* (Hamilton, Madison, and Jay), 4, 17
    on bureaucracy, 250
    on Congress, 207
    on federalism, 73, 92, 93, 141
    on interest groups, 166, 167
    on parties, 98
    on president, 13, 174, 176, 177
    on right to bear arms, 30
    on separation of powers, 19
    on Supreme Court, 8, 286
Federalist party, 85, 86, 99
Federal Regulation of Lobbying Act of 1946, 141–142, 160, 162

Federal Trade Commission (FTC), 156, 165
Fenno, Richard F., Jr., 216n, 244
Fifth Amendment, 35–42
Finance Committee (Senate), 207–208, 234, 235, 236
Finer, Herman, 259–260
Fines, 50–51
First Amendment, 29–30
*Fletcher v. Peck,* 76n, 77, 79n
Floor leaders, 226–227
Food and Drug Administration (FDA), 165
Ford, Gerald, 91, 109, 112, 120, 122, 183, 194, 257
Foreign Affairs Committee (House), 181
Foreign policy, 118
    Congress and, 208, 210–212
    president and, 180–182, 198–200
Foreign Relations Committee (Senate), 180, 181, 208, 215, 216
Fourteenth Amendment, 58–62, 63, 78, 79, 279, 283
Fourth Amendment, 32–35
Fox, Harrison W., Jr., 231n
Frankfurter, Felix, 55n, 61
Franklin, Benjamin, 3–4
Franklin, Grace A., 156n
Friedrich, Carl, 264
Friendly, Henry J., 261
*Frontiero v. Richardson,* 65n
*Fry v. United States,* 82
Full Employment Act, 187
*Furman v. Georgia,* 51–52

Galbraith, John Kenneth, 138
*Gannett Company v. DePasquale,* 46–47
*Garcia v. San Antonio Metro.,* 82n, 83
Gerry, Elbridge, 31
*Gibbons v. Ogden,* 21, 58, 74, 78n, 79n, 83, 209
*Gideon v. Wainwright,* 49
Gingrich, Newt, 122
*Gitlow v. New York,* 30, 59, 83
Glenn, John, 220
Goldberg, Arthur J., 55
Goldwater, Barry, 103, 119, 120, 122
Governmental Affairs Committee (Senate), 257
Governmental interest groups, 160–162
*Gram v. Richardson,* 65n
Gramm, Phil, 149
Grand juries, 35–36
Grass-roots participation, 109–114
"Great Compromise," 73
Green, Bill, 149
Griswold, Erwin N., 37n

*Griswold* v. *Connecticut,* 54–55, 61, 62, 84, 271
Group theory model of government, 130–140
Gunther, Gerald, 22n

Habeas corpus, 28n
Haldeman, H. R., 192
Hamilton, Alexander, 186
  on Bill of Rights, 53
  on bureaucracy, 250–251
  on Congress, 207
  on militia, 30
  on national bank, 21–22
  on powers of federal government, 17, 19, 21–22, 56–57, 92
  on presidency, 3, 174, 176, 177, 184
  on privileges and immunities, 63
  on separation of powers, 19–20
  on states, 72–73
  on Supreme Court, 8, 286
*Hammer* v. *Dagenhart,* 57
Hammond, Susan Webb, 231n
Harlan, John, 42–43
Hart, Gary, 111, 112
Hatch, Orrin, 103
*Hayburn's* case, 270–271
Hays, Wayne, 217
Helms, Jesse, 149, 283
*Holden* v. *Hardy,* 279
Hollings, Ernest, 231
Hoover, Herbert, 258
Hoover, J. Edgar, 263
Hoover Commission, 262
House Committee on Un-American Activities, 38
House of Representatives. *See also* Congress; Congressional committees
  apportionment of, 9
  decentralization in, 218
  leadership of, 221–227
  party committees in, 228–229
  political parties in, 218–219, 221–229
  powers of, 10, 207–208
  reforms in, 218–220
  Senate vs., 206, 207
  Speaker of, 221, 224–226
Howard, A. F. Dick, 31n
*Hoyt* v. *Florida,* 64n
Hughes, Charles Evans, 80, 81n, 209, 282, 285, 286
Humphrey, Hubert, 108, 109
Hunt, James, 110, 149
Hunt Commission, 110–111
Hyde, Henry, 122

Ickes, Harold L., 210, 281, 282n
*Immigration and Naturalization Service* v. *Chada,* 200
"Implied powers" clause of Constitution, 12, 22
Impoundment, 233
Indictment, 35–36
*Ingraham* v. *Wright,* 51n
*In re Griffiths,* 65n
*In re Oliver,* 44n
Intelligence Oversight Board, 193
Interest groups, 129–168
  Congress and, 241–242
  constitutional checks on, 138–140
  constitutional protection of, 141–145
  control of, 162–165
  countervailing power and, 138, 139
  decision making and, 147–156
  governmental, 160–162
  group theory and, 130–140
  laissez-faire capitalism and, 145–146
  national interest and, 135–136
  policy and, 155–160
  "potential," 134–135
  public, 164–165
Internal Revenue Service, 263
Interstate Commerce Act, 158, 280
Interstate Commerce Commission (ICC), 158, 254, 255, 257, 258, 273, 280
*Interstate Commerce Commission* v. *Alabama Midland Railway Co.,* 280n
*Interstate Commerce Commission* v. *Cincinnati, New Orleans, and Texas Pacific Railway Co.,* 280
Interstate relations, 15
"Iron triangles," 148, 157, 249, 258

Jackson, Andrew, 85, 107
Jackson, Jesse, 111, 112
Jackson, Robert H., 180
Jacobson, Gary, 246
Jay, John, 4, 17, 76n, 270
Jefferson, Thomas, 22, 53–54, 184–186
Johnson, Lyndon B.
  bureaucracy and, 256
  as chief legislator, 182, 183
  on civil rights, 65, 197
  election of, 120
  foreign policy of, 102, 108, 196, 197, 199
  Great Society of, 87, 88, 121, 197
  as strong president, 24, 88, 182, 197
Joint Economic Committee, 187, 192
Jones, Charles O., 245
Jones, James, 111, 149, 236
Jordan, Hamilton, 193

Judicial review, 7–8, 21, 166, 267–268
Judiciary, 267–287. *See also* Supreme
  Court
  activism of, 276–277, 282–283
  decision making of, 277–278
  independence of, 274–276
  interest groups and, 153–155
  organization of, 269
  policymaking by, 278–286
  powers of, 5, 6, 14, 271
  procedures and behavior of, 270–274
  self-restraint of, 277, 282–283
Judiciary Committee (Senate), 215, 216
Jury
  in common law cases, 50
  grand, 35–36
  local, 48–49
  petit, 36

*Kahn* v. *Shevin,* 64n
*Katz* v. *United States,* 35
Kefauver, Estes, 107
Kemp, Jack, 122, 228
Kennedy, Edward M., 109, 110, 112, 186,
  228, 257, 258
Kennedy, John F., 183, 197, 256
*Kinsella* v. *United States ex rel Singleton,*
  36n
Kissinger, Henry, 102, 192, 197
*Klopfer* v. *North Carolina,* 43–44
*Korematsu* v. *United States,* 179

*Labine* v. *Vincent,* 65n
Laissez-faire capitalism, 145–146
Legislative powers, 5, 8–13, 207–212
Legislative process, 213
Legislative Reorganization Acts of 1946
  and 1970, 228, 231, 260
Legislature. *See* Congress
Lincoln, Abraham, 23, 86, 177, 179
Lobbying, 141–142, 160–162
*Lochner* v. *New York,* 79, 80, 279
Long, Russell, 207, 208, 221, 228, 234,
  236
Lott, Trent, 122
*Louisiana ex rel Francis* v. *Resweber, Sherf
  et al.,* 53n
Lowi, Theodore, 156, 165–167, 261

McCarthy, Eugene J., 108–109, 143
McCarthy, Joseph, 38, 282
*McCulloch* v. *Maryland,* 23, 58, 74, 209,
  268
*McGautha* v. *California,* 51n
McGovern, George, 107, 108–109, 110,
  112, 119

McLuhan, Marshall, 113
McNamara, Robert, 195
McReynolds, James C., 31
Madison, James
  Bill of Rights and, 28, 54, 77
  on Congress, 207
  on constitutional limits of government,
    17, 18–19
  on factions, 97–99
  on interest groups, 129, 141, 166, 167
  on presidency, 13
  on separation of powers, 3, 18–19, 20
  on states' rights, 73
Majority, concurrent, 132, 133
Majority leaders, 226–227
Malbin, Michael, 231
*Mallory* v. *Hogan,* 38n
Mansfield, Mike, 228
*Mapp* v. *Ohio,* 33n
*Marbury* v. *Madison,* 267
Marshall, John
  on death penalty, 52
  on national power, 21, 23, 57–58, 74,
    76–78, 209, 268, 285
  on power of Supreme Court, 267, 277
Marshall, Thurgood, 47, 83
Martin, James, 149
Matthews, Donald R., 220n
Maxey, C. C., 243n
Mayhew, David, 242, 243n, 244
Meese, Edwin, III, 193
Michaels, Marguerite, 217n
Michel, Robert, 226, 227
Miller, Warren E., 245
Mills, Wilbur, 207
*Mississippi* v. *Johnson,* 175
*Missouri* v. *Holland,* 211
Model Cities program, 89
Mondale, Walter, 110–111, 112, 113–114,
  150
Monroe, James, 180
Monroe Doctrine, 180
Motor Vehicle Safety Act, 164
Moynihan, Daniel P., 87
*Murphy* v. *Waterfront Commission of New
  York Harbor,* 38n
*Murray's Lessee* v. *Hoboken Land and
  Improvement Company,* 39
Muskie, Edmund, 236
*Muskrat* v. *United States,* 271

Nader, Ralph, 134, 155, 156, 164–165,
  253, 259
National Environmental Policy Act, 193
National Firearms Act, 31

National Industrial Recovery Act of 1933, 80, 209
National interest, 135–136, 167
National Labor Relations Act of 1935, 209–210
National Labor Relations Board (NLRB), 209, 255
*National Labor Relations Board v. Jones and Laughlin Steel Corporation,* 81, 209–210
*National League of Cities v. Usery,* 82, 83
National Security Council, 192
*Near v. Minnesota,* 30, 83–84
*Nebraska Press Association v. Stuart,* 45
"Necessary and proper" clause of Constitution, 12
Neustadt, Richard, 172
New Deal
  Democratic party and, 117, 118, 119, 263
  federalism and, 86, 87–88, 93
  presidency and, 196–197
  Supreme Court and, 21, 57, 79, 81, 209, 281–282
"New Federalism," 90
*New York v. Miln,* 78n
Ninth Amendment, 53–56
Nixon, Richard M.
  bureaucracy and, 256, 263
  economy and, 187
  federalism and, 87, 89, 90, 91
  foreign policy of, 102, 197, 199, 200
  impoundment issue and, 233
  interest groups and, 165
  as legislator, 183, 200
  parties and, 119, 120
  on "silent majority," 135
  staff of, 190, 191–192, 194, 195
  strong presidency of, 24
  Supreme Court and, 283
Nomination, of president, 106–114

Occupational Safety and Health Administration (OSHA), 156, 253
*Oestereich v. Selective Service System Local Board No. 11,* 275–276
Office of Economic Opportunity, 89
Office of Emergency Preparedness, 192
Office of Management and Budget (OMB), 161–162, 188–191, 193, 239, 251, 256
Office of Science and Technology Policy, 193
Office of the Special Representative for Trade Negotiations, 193
*Olmstead v. United States,* 33, 35

O'Neill, Thomas P., 207, 226, 227
OPEC, 187
Opposition party, 101
Orr, Robert, 149
*Orr v. Orr,* 65n
Otis, James, 33

*Palko v. Connecticut,* 36, 60–61
Parris, Stan, 149
Parties, 99–125
  congressional, 105–106, 218–219, 221–229
  constitutional democracy and, 124–125
  early, 85–86, 99
  electoral process and, 103–106
  issue identification and, 115
  liberal–democratic model of, 99–103
  opposition, 101
  policy differences in, 115–123
  as policy instruments, 101–103
  president as leader of, 184–187
  presidential, 105, 111–114
  reform of, 106–114
  role of, 100
  voters and, 123–124
Party committees, 228–229
Party floor leaders, 226–227
Party identification, 115, 116
Party platforms, 121–123
Party whips, 227–228
Petition, right of, 29–30
Petit jury, 36
Pinckney, Charles, 63
*Pointer v. Texas,* 49n
Policy, 155–160
  Congress and, 208–212
  distributive, 157
  interest groups and, 155–160
  parties and, 101–103
  president and, 196–198
  redistributive, 156–157
  regulatory, 158–159
  Supreme Court and, 278–286
Policy committees, 228–229
Political action committees (PACs), 149–150, 151, 168
Political parties. *See* Parties
Politics
  budgetary, 234–238
  of federalism, 84–92
  of interest groups, 165–167
  Washington, 91
Polsby, Nelson W., 107n
"Pork-barrel" legislation, 217, 243
"Potential" interest groups, 134–135
Pound, Roscoe, 258

Powell, Lewis F., Jr., 47, 51n, 52
Powers, separation of, 5–7, 18–19, 20, 172
Presentment, 35
President, 171–202
    bureaucracy and, 251–252, 255–258, 262–264
    checks on, 6
    as chief executive, 175–176
    as chief of state, 174–175
    as commander in chief, 176–180
    Congress and, 238–239
    as diplomat, 180–182
    election of, 184–186
    interest groups and, 150–153
    as legislator, 182
    lobbying by, 160–162
    nomination of, 106–114
    as party leader, 184–187
    policy innovation and, 196–198
    powers of, 5, 13–14, 171, 174–188, 198–200
    responsibilities of, 174–188
Presidential parties, 105, 111–114
Presidential staff agencies, 188–196
    Council of Economic Advisors, 187, 192
    National Security Council, 192
    Office of Management and Budget (OMB), 161–162, 188–191, 193, 239, 251, 256
    White House staff, 191–192, 193–196
President pro tempore of Senate, 226n
President's Committee on Administrative Management, 188, 262, 263
Press, freedom of, 29–30
*Principles of Public Administration* (Willoughby), 262
*Prize* cases, 177, 178
Public advocacy, 144–145
Public Citizen, Inc., 165
Public interest groups, 164–165
Punishment, cruel and unusual, 51–53

Randolph, Edmund, 74
Ray, Elizabeth, 217
Rayburn, Sam, 219
Reagan, Ronald
    affirmative action and, 66
    budget and, 236, 237
    bureaucracy and, 257
    Congress and, 91, 238–239
    distributive policies and, 157
    economic policies of, 117–118, 120, 130–131, 136, 151–152, 187, 192
    foreign policy of, 102, 103, 181

iron triangles and, 148
    nomination of, 109, 112, 124
    policy innovation and, 198
    special interests and, 151–152, 156
    staff of, 193, 194
    success on votes, 183
    Supreme Court and, 284
Reconciliation, 237
Redistributive policies, 156–157
*Reed v. Reed,* 64n
Reedy, George, 194–195
*Regents of the University of California v. Bakke,* 65n, 66
Regulatory policies, 158–159
Rehnquist, William, 47, 51n, 52, 82–83
*Reid v. Covert,* 211–212
Religion, freedom of, 29–30
Reorganization Acts, 188, 256
Representatives, election of, 242–246
Republican Committee on Committees, 214, 219
Republican Conference, 219
Republican party. *See also* Parties
    in Congress, 219, 221–229
    early, 85, 86, 99
    federalism and, 92
    policies of, 115, 117–123
Rhodes, John, 226
Ribicoff, Abraham, 221
Ripley, Randall B., 156n
Rivers, L. Mendel, 217
Roberts, Owen J., 209, 281
*Robinson v. California,* 53n
Roche, John, 4
*Rochin v. California,* 61
Rockefeller, Jay, 149
Rockefeller, Nelson, 119
*Roe v. Wade,* 56, 62, 84, 284
Roosevelt, Franklin D.
    bureaucracy and, 186, 253, 258, 263
    civil rights and, 119
    economic policies of, 192
    foreign policy of, 118, 181, 198
    as party leader, 117, 118, 119, 124
    policy innovation and, 196–197
    special interests and, 150–151
    strong presidency of, 23, 87, 93, 178, 179, 181, 182, 183, 187, 188, 190–191
    Supreme Court and, 21, 57, 79, 80–81, 209, 281–282
    taxation and, 87
    war powers of, 256
Rossiter, Clinton, 175n, 182n, 187n, 262
Rostenkowski, Dan, 207, 227

Rothman, Kenneth, 149
Rules Committee (House), 218–219, 225

Safire, William, 243n
*San Antonio v. Rodriguez,* 65n
Schattschneider, E. E., 136, 137
*Schechter* rule, 261
*Schechter v. United States,* 80, 83
Schlesinger, Arthur M., Jr., 178n, 180n
*Schlesinger v. Reservists' Committee to
    Stop the War,* 273n
Searches, Bill of Rights on, 32–35
Second Amendment, 30–31
Selective Service System, 274–276
Self-incrimination, 37–38
Senate, 9. *See also* Congress;
    Congressional committees
    House of Representatives vs., 206, 207
    leadership of, 224, 225, 226–228
    party committees in, 228–229
    political parties in, 224, 225, 226–229
    powers of, 10, 207–208
    reforms in, 280–281
Senators
    direct election of, 205, 246
    reelection of, 242–246
Separation of powers, 5–7, 18–19, 20
Seventeenth Amendment, 205, 246
Sheppard, Sam, 44–45
*Sheppard v. Maxwell,* 44–45
Sherman Anti-Trust Act of 1890, 21
*Shroeder v. West Virginia,* 48n
*Sierra Club v. Morton,* 272–273
Sixth Amendment, 42–50
*Slaughterhouse* cases, 58–59
Social Security Act of 1935, 87
Soldiers, limits on quartering of, 31–32
Speaker of the House, 221, 224–226
Speech, freedom of, 29–30
"Spoils system," 186
Stanbery, Henry, 175
*Stare decisis,* 278
States
    limitations on, 12–13
    original sovereignty of, 69–71
    relations between, 15
    reserved powers of, 56–58
Steel Caucus, 229
Stein, Andrew, 149
Stenholm, Charles, 230
Stennis, John, 221
Stevens, John P., 46
Stevenson, Adlai, 107
Stewart, Potter, 42, 46–47, 51n, 52
Stockman, David, 117, 130, 152, 187

Stokes, Donald E., 245
Subcommittee(s), 214, 215, 216. *See also*
    Congressional committees
Subcommittee bill of rights, 219
Substantive due process, 279–280
Supply-side economics, 192
Supremacy clause of Constitution, 16
Supreme Court. *See also* Judiciary
    on abortion, 284
    on bail and fines, 50–51
    bureaucracy and, 280–281
    on campaign laws, 143–144
    on capital punishment, 51–53
    checks on, 6–7
    Congress vs., 274–276
    on congressional powers, 209–212
    on due process, 30, 39–41, 58–62, 279–
        280, 283
    on equal protection, 63, 64–66, 283
    on federalism, 74–84
    on free speech and free press, 30
    on grand juries, 36
    interest groups and, 153–155
    judicial review and, 7–8, 21, 267–268
    on lobbying, 142
    lower courts vs., 268–270
    nationalization of Bill of Rights and,
        58–62
    on national power, 23
    policymaking of, 278–286
    powers of, 5, 6, 14
    on presidential powers, 177–178, 179,
        180
    procedures and behavior of, 270–274
    on public advocacy, 144–145
    on reserved powers of states, 57–58
    on rights of accused, 42–49
    on rights retained by the people, 54–56
    on right to bear arms, 31
    on self-incrimination, 37, 38
    self-restraint of, 277
    on unreasonable search and seizure, 33–
        35

Taft, Robert, 107, 178, 199
Taft, William H., 33, 249
Taft-Hartley Act of 1947, 143
Taney, Roger, 79n, 285
*Tate v. Short,* 51n
Taxation, 12, 207
*Taylor v. Louisiana,* 48
Tenth Amendment, 56–58
Textile Caucus, 229
Third Amendment, 31–32
Thirteenth Amendment, 63

Three-fifths Compromise, 9
Ticket splitting, 106
Tobacco interests, 245
Tocqueville, Alexis de, 92, 146
*Toomer v. Witsell,* 63n
Tourism Caucus, 229, 230
Treaties, 210–212
Trials, 42–50
    local juries in, 48–49
    procedural rights in, 49–50
    public, 44–48
    speedy, 42–44
*Trop v. Dulles,* 53n
Truman, David B., 133
Truman, Harry S., 24, 107, 178–179, 181,
    183, 199, 263
Twelfth Amendment, 186
*Twining v. New Jersey,* 60

Ullman, Al, 207
*Ultra vires* action, 276
*United States v. Butler,* 57n
*United States v. Curtiss–Wright
    Corporation,* 102n, 180n, 182n
*United States v. Harriss,* 141, 142n
*United States v. Miller,* 31
*United States v. Students Challenging
    Regulatory Agency Procedures*
    (SCRAP), 273
U.S. Department of Agriculture, 255
U.S. Department of Commerce, 255
U.S. Department of Education, 257
U.S. Department of Energy, 257
U.S. Department of Health and Human
    Services, 253
U.S. Department of Labor, 255
U.S. Department of Urban Affairs, 256

Veterans' Administration (VA), 136–137
Vice-president, 13, 226n
Voluntary associations, 146
Voters, and parties, 123–124
Voting Rights Act of 1965, 65, 66, 118,
    119

Wagner Act, 209–210
War Powers Act of 1973, 179, 199–200
Warren, Charles, 77
Warren, Earl
    activism of, 276, 283, 285, 286
    on due process, 43–44, 62, 84, 283
    on equal protection, 64, 65, 283
    on lobbyists, 142
    on segregation, 65
Washington, George, 21, 22
Washington politics, 91
*Washington v. Texas,* 49n
Watergate scandal, 263, 264
*Watkins v. United States,* 38n
Wattenberg, Martin P., 124, 125n
Ways and Means Committee (House), 207,
    215, 216, 219, 227, 234, 235, 236
*Weber v. Aetna Casualty and Surety Co.,*
    65n
Wednesday Club, 230
*Weinberger v. Weisenfeld,* 64n
*Wesberry v. Sanders,* 63
*West Coast Hotel Company v. Parrish,*
    81n, 210, 281
Whig party, 85, 86
Whips, 227–228
White, Byron, 46, 47, 52, 83
White, Theodore H., 109n
White, William S., 220n
White House staff, 191–192, 193–196
*Williams v. Illinois,* 51n
Willoughby, W. F., 262
Wills, Garry, 69–70
Wilson, Woodrow, 23, 198
Winograd Commission, 110
*Wolff v. Selective Service Local Board No.
    16,* 274–275
Women's Caucus, 229, 230
*Wong Wing Hang v. Immigration and
    Naturalization Services,* 268n
*Wong Yang Sung v. McGrath,* 40n
Workmen's compensation, 254
Wright, James, 226

*Youngstown Sheet and Tube Company v.
    Sawyer,* 179